ECONOMIC ISSUES, PROBLEMS AND PERSPECTIVES

HANDBOOK OF INNOVATION ECONOMICS

ECONOMIC ISSUES, PROBLEMS AND PERSPECTIVES

Additional books in this series can be found on Nova's website under the Series tab.

Additional E-books in this series can be found on Nova's website under the E-books tab.

ECONOMIC ISSUES, PROBLEMS AND PERSPECTIVES

HANDBOOK OF INNOVATION ECONOMICS

GEORGE M. KORRES

University of Newcastle
Centre of Urban and Regional Development Studies
(CURDS)
and
University of the Aegean, Department of Geography

Nova Science Publishers, Inc.
New York

Copyright © 2012 by Nova Science Publishers, Inc.

All rights reserved. No part of this book may be reproduced, stored in a retrieval system or transmitted in any form or by any means: electronic, electrostatic, magnetic, tape, mechanical photocopying, recording or otherwise without the written permission of the Publisher.

For permission to use material from this book please contact us:
Telephone 631-231-7269; Fax 631-231-8175
Web Site: http://www.novapublishers.com

NOTICE TO THE READER

The Publisher has taken reasonable care in the preparation of this book, but makes no expressed or implied warranty of any kind and assumes no responsibility for any errors or omissions. No liability is assumed for incidental or consequential damages in connection with or arising out of information contained in this book. The Publisher shall not be liable for any special, consequential, or exemplary damages resulting, in whole or in part, from the readers' use of, or reliance upon, this material. Any parts of this book based on government reports are so indicated and copyright is claimed for those parts to the extent applicable to compilations of such works.

Independent verification should be sought for any data, advice or recommendations contained in this book. In addition, no responsibility is assumed by the publisher for any injury and/or damage to persons or property arising from any methods, products, instructions, ideas or otherwise contained in this publication.

This publication is designed to provide accurate and authoritative information with regard to the subject matter covered herein. It is sold with the clear understanding that the Publisher is not engaged in rendering legal or any other professional services. If legal or any other expert assistance is required, the services of a competent person should be sought. FROM A DECLARATION OF PARTICIPANTS JOINTLY ADOPTED BY A COMMITTEE OF THE AMERICAN BAR ASSOCIATION AND A COMMITTEE OF PUBLISHERS.

Additional color graphics may be available in the e-book version of this book.

LIBRARY OF CONGRESS CATALOGING-IN-PUBLICATION DATA

Korres, George M.
  Handbook of innovation economics / George M. Korres.
  p. cm.
  Includes bibliographical references and index.
  ISBN 978-1-61209-999-6 (hardcover)
  1. Technological innovations--Economic aspects. I. Title.
  HD45.K674 2011
  338'.064--dc22

2011008466

Published by Nova Science Publishers, Inc. † New York

To my Wife Aikaterini and
In Memory of my Parents Aikaterini and Michael Korres.

CONTENTS

	Page
Preface	ix
1. Measuring Innovation Activities and Technical Change	1
1.1. Introduction	1
1.2. Defining Technical Change and the Innovation Activities	2
1.3. Measurement and Leading Indicators of Innovation Activities	18
1.4. Summary Conclusions	41
2. Modeling Innovation Activities	45
2.1. Introduction	45
2.2. Economic Theory and Technical Change	46
2.3. The Growth-Accounting	52
2.4. New Growth Debate	54
2.5. A Theoretical Approach to Endogenous Theory	55
2.5.1. New Technologies and Product Innovations	56
2.5.2. Existing Technologies and Process Innovations	57
2.5.3. Human Capital	58
2.5.4. Productivity, R and D and Environment	60
2.5.5. Education and Growth	61
2.6. Modeling Innovation Activities and Technical Change	62
2.6.1 Input-Output Analysis and Technological Change	63
2.6.2. Catching up Models	65
2.6.3 An Historical Overview of Functional Forms	68
2.6.4. The Generalised Leontief Function	71
2.7. Modelling Technological Progress in a Production Function	75
2.7.1. The Meta-Production Function	82
2.7.2. The Translog Production Function	84
2.8. Summary Conclusions	91
3. Innovation Activities and the Productivity Puzzle	95
3.1. Introduction	95
3.2. Innovation Activities and the Productivity Growth	96
3.3. Theory and Measurement of Productivity Growth	99
3.4. Measuring the Productivity Growth	101
3.4.1. The Index Number Approach	101
3.4.2. The Parametric Approach	104
3.5. Productivity and Efficiency	106
3.6. Summary Conclusions	109

Contents

4. Technical Change and the Diffusion Models	111
4.1. Introduction	111
4.2. Innovation Activities and the Diffusion Process	112
4.3. Diffusion Models and the New Growth Theory	117
4.4. Inter-Country and International Diffusion Models	125
4.4.1. The International Diffusion Approach	126
4.4.2. Epidemic Model and the Logistic Curve	130
4.4.3. The Probit Models	132
4.4.4. Technological Substitution Models	135
4.5. Summary Conclusions	138
5. National and Regional Systems of Innovation	139
5.1. Introduction	139
5.2. Entrepreneurship, Foreign Direct Investments (FDIs) and Innovation Activities	140
5.3. National and Regional Systems of Innovation	149
5.4. Summary Conclusions	163
6. European Innovation Policy and Regional Convergence	169
6.1. Introduction	169
6.2. Innovation Policy and the Knowledge Based Economy	171
6.3. The European Institutional Framework and the Innovation Activities	174
6.3.1. Human Resources, Education and Training	175
6.3.2. Entrepreneurship and Innovation Activities	175
6.3.3. Innovation, Growth and Employment	176
6.3.4. Innovation and the Convergence Process	177
6.3.5. Innovation and the Public Action	179
6.4. The European Technological Policy	180
6.5. European Innovation Policy and Regional Cohesion in Europe	191
6.6. The European Regional Systems of Innovation	198
6.7. Summary Conclusions	217
7. Policy Perspectives	223
8. Bibliography	229
Index	297

PREFACE

Technology refers to the state of knowledge concerning ways of converting resources into outputs. In other words, technology refers to the state of knowledge concerning ways of converting resources into outputs. Technical change is the shift in the production function (production frontier) over time. Technological progress is at the heart of human progress and development. There are two basic types of technical cooperation:

- Free-standing technical cooperation which is the provision of resources aimed at the transfer of technical and managerial skills or of technology for the purpose of building up general national capacity without reference to the implementation of any specific investment projects; and
- Investment-related technical cooperation which denotes the provision of technical services required for the implementation of specific investment projects.

A technical change is a term used in economics to describe a change in the amount of output produced from the same amount of inputs. A technical change is not necessarily technological as it might be organizational, or due to a change in a constraint such as regulation, input prices, or quantities of inputs. It is also possible to measure technical change as the change in output per unit of factor input. Technological progress can lower costs, improve quality, create new products, and help reach new markets. According to the World Bank, Global Economic Perspectives, 2008:

- Technological progress can spur development by lowering the costs of production and enabling the exploitation of increasing returns to scale.
- Technological progress in one sector can create new economic opportunities in other sectors.
- The benefits of a new technology can extend well beyond the immediate sector or good in which the technology exists.

Technology can yield quality improvements.

Central to understanding the role of technology is the recognition that technology and technological progress are relevant to a wide range of economic activities, not just manufacturing and computers. Finally, in many cases technology is embodied in production and management systems rather than in physical goods or software algorithms. Embodied technical change refers to improvements in the design or quality of new capital goods or intermediate inputs. Disembodied technical change is the shift in the production function (production frontier) over time. Disembodied technical change is not incorporated in a specific factor of production.

Much of the economic and social progress of the past few centuries has been due to technology. Technology has been central to both economic growth and many elements of social welfare that are only partly captured by standard measures of gross domestic product (GDP), including health, education, and gender equality. As measured by total factor productivity, it explains much of the differences in both the level and rate of growth of incomes across countries (Easterly and Levine 2001; Hall and Jones 1999; King and Levine 1994).

Technological capabilities are a key component of competitiveness at national, regional or firm levels. The development of regional innovation capabilities has been of crucial importance for competitiveness building in both developed and developing countries. In the past decade there has been increasing research on the regional innovation system. Active measures to promote technology diffusion and strengthen the linkages between firms and research and development (R&D) agencies are also vital. It is argued that there is something distinctive and systemic about innovation as a localized phenomenon which cannot be predicted by the more familiar national innovation systems frameworks (Braczyk, Cooke, and Meltcalfe, 1997).

Innovation is not a simple linear transformation with basic science and other inputs at one end of a chain and commercialisation at the other (Hughes, 2003). Successful innovation requires more than brilliant scientists. It involves from top management to employees in its R&D, finance, production and marketing divisions. It requires high-quality decision-making, long-range planning, motivation and management techniques, coordination, and efficient R&D, production and marketing.

Only recently technology has been distinguished from science policy. "Science policy" is concerned with education and knowledge. "Technological policy" is concerned with the adoption and use of techniques, innovation and diffusion of techniques. The division between the areas and variables of science policy and technology policy is not so clear. For instance, education and the stock of knowledge play an important role in influencing the rate of innovation and diffusion of technology. Usually, the technological policy should aim to create a favourable "psychological climate" for the development of research and innovations; such as: different financial incentives, support in education and training programmes, provision technical services etc.

Survey on technological innovation has adopted methodologies and definitions from the Oslo and Frascati Manuals on technological innovation. It should be helpful to recall the definition of technological *innovation* suggested to firms surveyed by: "the set of knowledge, professional skills, procedures, capabilities, equipment, technical solutions required to manufacture goods or provide services". Whereas, *innovation in process* is "the adoption of technologically new methods in production or new methods to provide services. Several changes concerning equipment, production organisation or both may be required".

UNESCO, OECD and EUROSTAT divisions organised the systematic collection, analysis publication and standardization of data concerning science and technological activities. The first experimental questionnaires were circulated to member states by UNESCO in 1966 and standardised periodical surveys were established in 1969. The collection of R&D data of regional statistics implied a lot of problems in comparison to data of national statistics. For the collection of regional statistics, we should consideration local differences and difficulties. In addition, we can use either "local-units" or "local-economic-units". R&D and innovation activities are directly related to economic and regional growth. The outcome of international innovation and diffusion process is uncertain; this process may generate either a pattern in which some countries may follow diverging trends or a pattern in which countries converge towards a common trend. Economic development may be analyzed as a disequilibrium process characterized by two conflicting forces:

- innovation which tends to increase economic and technological differences between countries; and
- diffusion (or imitation) which tends to reduce them.

Technological change is a term that is used to describe the overall process of invention, innovation and diffusion of technology or processes. The term of technological change is redundant with technological development, technological achievement, and technological progress. In essence technological change is the invention of a technology (or a process), the continuous process of improving a technology (in which it often becomes cheaper) and its diffusion throughout industry or society. Innovation has been and must continue to be a major driver of rising living standards. Innovation contributes to the creation of new jobs and industries. Invention is the creation of something new, or in other words, it's the breakthrough technology.

A causal reading of recent economic history suggests two important trends in world economy:

- first, technological change and innovations are becoming important contributors to economic growth and to well-being.
- Second, nations in the world economy are becoming increasingly open and interdependent.

These two trends are related. Rapid communication and close contacts among innovations in different countries facilitate the process of invention and the spread of new ideas.

The use of a concept of innovation almost as a synonym to technical change is frequent. In this case, innovation is taken as a process that has linkages and feedbacks and connects all the elements of the Schumpeterian triad: invention, innovation and diffusion, together with the more recent concept of incremental innovation. For Schumpeter, development is understood as the process of economic transformation brought about by innovation. His concept of development could, therefore, be seen, to a certain extension, as a background for the whole conception of the National Innovation Systems' approach, because this is just a tool for the study of a country's ability to generate innovations, and furthermore to "develop".

Scientific and technological innovation may be considered as the transformation of an idea into a new or improved product introduced on the market, into a new or improved operational process used in industry and commerce, or into a new approach to a social service. Chesbrough *et al.* (2006) discussed the broader use of open innovation in practice and analysed whether open innovation concepts were also used in industries other than high technology. Based on a survey (albeit relatively small) he found that:

- Open innovation concepts are increasingly finding application in companies operating outside the "high-technology" industries.
- Open innovation concepts are not employed primarily as a rationale for cost reduction or outsourcing of the R&D function, since internal R&D is maintained or even increased (the importance of absorptive capacity).
- Many of the outbound-oriented concepts have not been adopted yet, mainly some inbound open innovation concepts have been used.

Technological innovations comprise new products and processes and significant technological changes of products and processes. A technological product and process innovating firm is one that has implemented technologically new or significantly technologically improved products or processes during the period under review. OECD Oslo Manual, Second Edition, December 1996. Technological product and process innovation activities are all those scientific, technological, organisational, financial and commercial steps which actually, or are intended to, lead to the implementation of new or improved products or processes. Technological process innovation is the adoption of technologically new or significantly improved production methods, including methods of product delivery. A technologically improved product is an existing product whose performance has been significantly enhanced or upgraded. A technologically new product is a product whose technological characteristics or intended uses differ significantly from those of previously produced products. A technological process innovation is the implementation/adoption of new or significantly improved production or delivery methods. It may involve changes in equipment, human resources, working methods or a combination of these.

This book performs such an empirical analysis. It uses the unique example of the EU to analyze whether convergence or divergence occurred between the EU. Of course, convergence and divergence may occur in numerous ways. Regional conditions are dynamic. Furthermore, there is a wide range of circumstances. Some places may have little difficulty warranting public policy attention. Elsewhere, there are many different regional problems, such as: lagged adjustment to changing economic circumstances, cumulative decline of services, loss of environmental quality, excessive in-migration, community desire for faster economic expansion than currently prevails and temporary shocks.

Several other policy difficulties that policy-makers encounter are competitive federalism, inter and intra-governmental coordination, and the issue of policy instability. Regional development is a difficult policy arena in which all tiers of government have had limited success. Problems also differ according to the scale of analysis: federal, state or local. The factors that contribute to this diversity are themselves numerous and diverse.

The book argues that regional economic development ultimately depends on technical change, social and human capital and civic entrepreneurship, among others. If so, technology in all its facets will be the crucial ingredient in regional improvement, in contrast with the usual regional pleas for better infrastructure, health care and banking facilities.

One important aspect is related to both distributional aspects of innovation and technical change and to some specific characteristics of information and communication technologies which "exclude" all those who are unconnected to information infrastructure. During 1990s, most technology employment analysis focused on the complexity of the many interactions linking the introduction of new technologies, changes in work organisation, skill mismatches and sectoral employment growth and displacement. Thus, to use Schumpeter's expression, the employment impact of technical change was associated with a process of "creative destruction", involving a process of job destruction in some of the older occupations, technologies, firms and industries. It could also involve changes in the international division of labour.

Technological gap models represent two conflicting forces: innovation, which tends to increase productivity differences among countries, and diffusion, which tends to reduce them. According to the Schumpeterian theory, growth differences are seen as the combined results of these forces. Research on *why growth rates differ* has a long history which goes well beyond growth accounting exercises.

Countries that are technologically backward have a potentiality to generate more rapid growth even greater than that of the advanced countries, if they are able to exploit new technologies which have already been employed by the technological leaders. The pace of catching up depends on diffusion of knowledge, rate of structural change, accumulation of capital and expansion of demand. Member states lagging behind in growth rates can succeed in catching up, if they are able to reduce the technological gap. An important aspect of this is that they should not rely only on the combination of technology imports and investment, but they should also increase their innovation activities and improve locally produced technologies, such examples are new industrialised countries like Korea and Singapore.

The book is intended to provide a basic understanding of the current issues and the problems of knowledge economy, technical change, innovation activities; it will also examine many aspects and consequences of regional integration that are obscure or yet to be explored. Most of this research has been presented in variety conferences, seminars, and workshops; some sections have already been published as Departmental papers and in several Journals. After general issues in these fields have been addressed the discussion will turns to empirical and theoretical aspects of technical change, productivity, economic growth, European policy and technology policy. In particular, with its wide range of topics, methodologies and perspectives, the book offers stimulating and wide-ranging analyses that will be of interest to students, economic theorists, empirical social scientists, policy makers and the informed general reader.

The book consists of five main chapters. Chapter 1 is devoted to definitions and measurement of innovation activities and knowledge economy. Three main topics related to such matters will be discussed in this Chapter and are as presented below:

- How the definitions of technological innovation and the knowledge based economy should be applied? Several factors should be actually taken into account, including: the relation between technological and non-technological innovations.
- What are the characteristics of research and development (R&D)?
- How can we apply and estimate the main implications and the effects of these variables?

- What do we want to measure?
- How do we want to measure it?
- Where do we want to measure it?: Technological product & process – TPP – innovations

Chapter 2 investigates the neoclassical growth theory and models of innovation activities and the knowledge based economy. This Chapter attempts to analyse and model the new economy, within the framework of knowledge and innovation activities; It also attempts to estimate socio-economic effects of technical change, using both a theoretical and an empirical approach. Moreover, this Chapter reviews the main statistical measures for research, scientific and technological activities, using various models, through the input-output analysis and the catching-up and production-cost function models, in order to measure the implication on productivity and the growth effects. We would like to tackle upon the following issues in this Chapter:

- Why is innovation important for economic development?
- How can we model innovation activities and knowledge-based economy?
- How can we estimate the effects of innovation activities and the knowledge-based economy?

Chapter 3 deals with the main issues of: technical change, knowledge economy and productivity growth. This Chapter attempts to identify the R&D activities and also to investigate the estimation-methods, the techniques of scientific and technological activities and the measurement problems for productivity growth. Some of the main questions addressed in this Chapter try to answer the questions below:

- How can we model and measure innovation and knowledge for productivity growth?
- What are the main effects of innovation activities and knowledge- based economy on productivity growth?

Chapter 4 investigates the theory and the diffusion models in the context of growth. This Chapter attempts to investigate how the way in which innovation and the "knowledge" can be developed and disseminated and the particular effects on socio-economic effects on modernisation, competitiveness and integration process.

Chapter 5 investigates the role of entrepreneurship, foreign direct investments (FDIs) in the context of national and regional systems of innovation. This Chapter attempts to investigate the strategy and how the way in which "knowledge" can be developed and disseminated and the particular effects on socio-economic effects on modernisation, competitiveness and integration process.

Finally, Chapter 6 deals with the challenges and the institutional matters for the European innovation policy-makes encounter and the effects on regional growth and economic integration, including technology policy, other related policies, the distribution of E.U. funds, regional development and productivity problems. To do this, it examines critically the claims of regional disadvantage and examines the factors that influence regional economic and social conditions. Europe must face up to a number of hard questions which will neither go away nor be resolved for the compelling aim for higher secular growth in the EU:

- How to make the EU member states actually spend more on R&D?
- How to get European business to keep R&D in Europe and spend more on it?
- How to realize genuine, deep reforms of Europe's third-level education (more
- competitive, better geared to the job market, more oriented to technical specializations)?
- How to enhance risk-taking in a prosperous, often risk-averse Europe?
- How to enhance (incentives for) innovation and entrepreneurship in the EU?

Furthermore, we would also like to tackle upon the following four issues in this Chapter:

- Why is innovation important for European regional economic development?
- Why is the regional dimension important for innovation promotion?
- What has our policy response been so far and what lessons have we learnt from it?
- Finally, what are our action lines for the future?

I would also like to thank the anonymous reviewer of the volume, and above all, my publisher for the great encouragement and support.

Associate Prof. Dr. George M. Korres,
Department of Geography
University of the Aegean,
and also Visiting Fellow (Oct.2010/Sept. 2012),
University of Newcastle, Centre of Urban, Regional
and Development Studies (CURDS)
Newcastle, U.K. 2011

Chapter 1

MEASURING INNOVATION ACTIVITIES AND TECHNICAL CHANGE

1.1. INTRODUCTION

Scientific and technological innovation may be considered the transformation of an idea into a new or improved product introduced to the market, into a new or improved operational process used in industry and commerce, or into a new approach to a social service. The word "innovation" can have different meanings in different contexts and the one chosen will depend on the particular objectives of measurement or analysis. So far, international norms for data collection proposed in the Oslo Manual have been developed only for technological innovation.

Technological innovations comprise new products and processes and significant technological changes in products and processes. An innovation has been implemented if it has been introduced to the market (product innovation) or used within a production process (process innovation). Therefore, innovations involve a series of scientific, technological, organisational, financial and commercial activities. R&D is only one of these activities and may be carried out at different phases of the innovation process, acting not only as the original source of inventive ideas but also as a form of problem-solving which can be called at any point up to implementation. The terms "technological change" and "technical change" are used in the literature under review, both being indicators of a shift in the production function. The terms "technological progress" and "technical progress" are synonymous with "technological change" and "technical change" respectively.

This Chapter deals with definition and measurement of innovation activities. Technologically products may indicate the new or improved products and processes. The meaning of the label "technological", as applied to products and processes, and its precise scope in surveys and studies, can be unclear. This is particularly true in an international context. It is not always easy to distinguish between the special meaning attributed here and the dictionary definitions of the word which may differ subtly between countries, as well as the nuances of the word to which respondents may react. For example, it was felt that in the service industries "technological" might be understood as "using high-tech plant and equipment".

Innovation is a complex and multifaceted phenomenon. Technological innovation – even in its broad sense used in the Oslo Manual – is only a part of a set of activities firms carry out to keep or improve their competitiveness. From a statistical point of view, it is not an easy task to identify when technological innovation activities take place or to collect data on activities related to innovation, including scientific research. It is not surprising that several problems have been recorded during the implementation of the survey on innovation. The two most important are the following:

- proposed definitions on technological innovation may not have been fully understood by firms;
- data on technological innovation of firms appear to be substantially different from those referred to manufacturing firms and should be carefully interpreted.

Innovation is about taking risks and managing changes. It is about economics over and above research, science and technology. Some have defined it as "profitable change", others as economic exploitation of new ideas; a more business-related definition could be: "Innovation means harnessing creativity to invent new or improved products, equipment or services which are successful on the market and thus add value to businesses" (Guy de Vaucleroy, European Business Summit, Brussels June 2000).

Moreover, according to Joseph Schumpeter:

«Innovation is at the root of the evolution of the economic system and its main engine for change and "creative destruction".

According to the Oslo Manual, a probable definition of *technological innovation* suggested to firms surveyed by: "the set of knowledge, professional skills, procedures, capabilities, equipment, technical solutions required to manufacture goods or provide services". The *innovation in process* is "the adoption of technologically new methods in production or new methods to provide services. Several changes concerning equipment, production organisation or both may be required".

Three main topics related to such difficulties will be discussed in this Chapter:

- how definitions of technological innovation should be applied; several factors should be actually taken into account, including: the relation between technological and non-technological innovations;
- what the characteristics of Research and Development (R&D) are; and also
- how we can apply and measure the main indexes and estimate the effects through these variables.

1.2. DEFINING TECHNICAL CHANGE AND THE INNOVATION ACTIVITIES

Joseph Schumpeter is often mentioned as the first economist having drawn attention to the importance of innovation and having defined five types of innovation, ranging from introducing a new product to changes in industrial organisation. The Oslo Manual clarifies the definition of the two more technical definitions, but it still appears that "innovation" is not easy to define precisely.

In principle, according to Schumpter's theory, we may consider that innovation can result from technology transfer or the development of new business concepts. It can be therefore technological, organisational or presentational. It is clear there are links between research and innovation, with the research laboratory being the optimal starting point.

Technology transfer is the process by which existing knowledge and capabilities developed with public R&D funding are used to fulfil public and private needs. It is the share of knowledge and facilities among public institutions and private organisations to increase productivity, generate new industry, improve living standards and public services. Technology transfer from public research institutions can occur either through mechanisms - such as scientific publications, training of students, continuing education of engineers already working in industry- or through specific measures taken.

The *Oslo Manual* (OECD, 1997a) defines technological product and process innovations as those implemented in technologically new products and processes and in significant technological improvements in products and processes.

Technological product and process (TPP) innovations comprise implemented technologically new products and processes and significant technological improvements in products and processes. A TPP innovation has been implemented if it has been introduced to the market (product innovation) or used within a production process (process innovation). TPP innovations involve a series of scientific, technological, organisational, financial and commercial activities. The TPP innovating firm is one that has implemented technologically new or significantly technologically improved products or processes during the period under review.

Technological product innovation can take two broad forms:

(a) *Technologically new products*. A technologically new product is a product whose technological characteristics or intended uses differ significantly from those of previously produced products. Such innovations either can involve radically new technologies, or can be based on combined existing technologies in new uses, or can be derived from the use of new knowledge.
(b) *Technologically improved products*. A technologically improved product is an existing product whose performance has been significantly enhanced or upgraded. A simple product may be improved (in terms of better performance or lower cost) by the use of higher-performance components or materials or a complex product consisting of a number of integrated technical sub-systems, which may be improved by partial changes to one of the sub-systems.

The distinction between a technologically new product and a technologically improved product may pose difficulties for some industries, notably in services.

Technological process innovation is the adoption of technologically new or significantly improved production methods, including methods of product delivery. These methods may involve changes in equipment, or production organisation, or a combination of these changes, and may be derived from the use of new knowledge.

The methods may be intended to produce or deliver technologically new or improved products, which cannot be produced or delivered using conventional production methods, or essentially to increase the production or delivery efficiency of existing products.

Table 1.1. Innovation and Non-Innovation Activities

			Innovation		Not Innovation
			New to the World	New to the Firm	Already in the Firm
Innovation	Technologically New	Product			
		Production Process			
		Delivery Process			
	Significantly Technologically Improved	Product			
		Production Process			
		Delivery Process			
		Organisation			
Non Innovation	No Significant Change. Change without novelty or other creative improvements	Product			
		Production Process			
		Delivery Process			
		Organisation			

Source: OECD, (2002a).

A technological product and process innovating firm is one that has implemented technologically new or significantly technologically improved products or processes during the period under review, (OECD Oslo Manual, Second Edition, December 1996). Technological product and process innovation activities are all those scientific, technological, organisational, financial and commercial steps which actually, or are intended to, lead to the implementation of new or improved products or processes. Some may be innovative in their own right, others are not novel but are necessary for implementation. During a given period the innovation activities of a firm may be of three kinds:

- Successful in leading up to the implementation of a new or technologically improved product or process.
- Aborted before the implementation of a new or technologically improved product and process, because the project runs into difficulties or because the idea and know-how is sold or otherwise traded to another firm, or because the market has changed.
- Ongoing, activities which are in progress but have not yet reached implementation.

Technological process innovation is the adoption of technologically new or significantly improved production methods, including methods of product delivery. These methods may involve changes in equipment, or production organization, or a combination of these changes, and may be derived from the use of knew knowledge. The methods may be intended to produce or deliver technologically new or improved products, which cannot be produced or delivered using conventional production methods, or essentially to increase the production or delivery efficiency of existing products.

A technologically improved product is an existing product whose performance has been significantly enhanced or upgraded. A simple product may be improved (in terms of better performance or lower cost) through use of higher-performance components or materials, or a complex product which consists of a number of integrated technical subsystems may be improved by partial changes to one of the subsystems.

A technologically new product is a product whose technological characteristics or intended uses differ significantly from those of previously produced products. Such innovations can involve radically new technologies, can be based on combining existing technologies in new uses, or can be derived from the use of new knowledge. Technological product and process innovation has been implemented if it has been introduced on the market (product innovation) or used within a production process (process innovation). A technological product innovation is the implementation and commercialisation of a product with improved performance characteristics such as to deliver objectively new or improved services to the consumer. A technological process innovation is the implementation/adoption of new or significantly improved production or delivery methods. It may involve changes in equipment, human resources, working methods or a combination of these. (as defined in the OECD Frascati Manual).

Table 1.1 illustrates the innovation and not-innovation activities. Innovation indicators measure aspects of the industrial innovation process and the resources devoted to innovation activities. Furthermore Table 1.2 illustrates the main categories and classifications of innovation activities. They also provide qualitative and quantitative information about the factors that enhance or hinder innovation, the impact of innovation, the performance of the enterprise and about the diffusion of innovation. The variables commonly used for S-R&T activities are:

(a) R&D expenditures;
(b) R&D personnel;
(c) Patents of New Technologies.

UNESCO has developed a broad concept of STA (Scientific and Technological Activities) and included in its "Recommendation concerning the International Standardisation of Statistics on Science and Technology" (UNESCO, 1978). In addition to R&D, scientific and technological activities comprise scientific and technical education and training (STET) and scientific and technological services (STS). The latter include, for example, S&T activities of libraries and museums, translation and editing of S&T literature, surveying and prospecting, data collection of socio-economic phenomena, testing, standardisation and quality control, client counselling and advisory services, patent and licensing activities by public bodies. R&D (defined similarly by UNESCO and OECD) is thus to be distinguished from both STET (Scientific and Technical Education and Training) and STS (Scientific and Technological Services).

The concept of Scientific and Technological Activities has been developed by OECD and UNESCO and EUROSTAT. According to 'International Standardization of Statistics on Science and Technology', we can consider as scientific and technological activities as: "The systematic activities which are closely concerned with the generation, advancement, dissemination and application of scientific and technical knowledge in all fields of scientific and technology. These include activities on R&D, scientific and technical education and training and scientific and technological services".

Furthermore, we can distinguish R&D activities from Scientific and Technical Education and Training and Scientific and Technological Services.

"Scientific and Technical Education and Training activities comprising specialised non-university higher education and training, higher education and training leading to a university degree, post-graduate and further training, and organised lifelong training for scientists and engineers", while Scientific and Technological Services consider as comprisisng: "scientific and technological activities of libraries, museums, data collection on socio-economic phenomena, testing, standardization and quality control and patent and license activities by public bodies".

According to the definition provided by UNCTAD, technology can be considered as: "the essential input to production which can embodied either in capital and in intermediate goods or in the human labour and in manpower or finally in information which is provided through markets" (United Nations, 1983).

Nevertheless, we can distinguish between *technology transfer* and *technology capacity* (that is the flow of *knowledge* as against the *stock of knowledge*), and *technology of innovation* (which indicates the type of technology that enables the country's recipients to establish a new infrastructure or upgrade obsolete technologies).

Technological innovation activities are the scientific, technological, organisational, financial and commercial steps, including investments in new knowledge, which actually, or are intended to, lead to the implementation of technologically new or improved products and processes. R&D is only one of these activities and may be carried out different phases of the innovation process. It may act not only as the original source of inventive ideas but also as a means of problem solving which can be called upon at any point of implementation.

Besides R&D, other forms of innovative activities may be distinguished in the innovation process. According to the *Oslo Manual* (OECD, 1997a), these are "acquisition of disembodied technology and know-how, acquisition of embodied technology, tooling up and industrial engineering, industrial design, other capital acquisition, production start-up and marketing for new or improved products".

The most widely used definitions of research and innovation activities are provided by the *Frascati-Manual*. In an effort to standardise definitions and data collection on research expenditures, the Organisation of Economic Cooperation and Development (OECD) has proposed in the so-called *Frascati Manual* (1981, and 1989) that: "Research and Experimental Development comprise creative work undertaken on a systematic basis in order to increase the stock of knowledge.... and the use of this stock of knowledge to devise new applications".

Within this general definition, *pure research* broadly corresponds to activities aimed at enhancing knowledge growth, whereas *applied research* involves the search for applications. *Development* concerns the activities of design, implementation, and prototype manufacturing of the new applications themselves.

From a statistical point of view, while when measuring research and innovation activities there are two inputs:

(a) The people who work in research activities and
(b) The expenditures related to research and technological activities.

Table 1.2. Main Categories and Classifications of Innovation Activities

Main Categories and Classifications
R&D
R&D is 'classic' innovation investment: scientific research and development that produces new knowledge in the form of ideas or products that can be marketed by firms.
Design
Investment in design has been described by some macroeconomists as 'non-scientific R&D'. These designs may be critical in the innovation process, as they play an important role in new product and service development. This category is also assumed to include those investments aimed at developing new services and financial products.
Organisational improvement
Organisational innovation drives the efficiency and effectiveness of organisations. Investing in this type of knowledge is critical to stay competitive and be able to leverage innovative ideas and commercially exploit them.
Training & skills development
Investment in workforce skills turns out to be one of the most important sources of investment. Therefore the investment in training and skills development is critical to the innovative capacity of firms; it is particularly important for service innovations: the most significant investment to realise these may be in human capital.
Software development
Resources invested in developing software and databases creates a valuable asset.
Market research & advertising
Market research is at the front end of innovation aiming to identify the market potential for new products companies must at the outset anticipate future demand. This category captures other investments made to develop brands in order to take products to market. Both are strategic elements of the innovation process.
Other (Copyright development and mineral exploration)
Investment in new knowledge of exploitable mineral sources and copyrighted ideas both lead to assets that firms can commercially exploit and which are frequently capitalized in firms' financial accounts. These two apparently dissimilar types of asset are grouped together to reflect the way they are treated in the national accounts, but represent the smallest category of investment measured.

Source: NESTA (2009), The Innovation Index Measuring the UK's investment in innovation and its effects, Index report: November 2009, United Kingdom.

Research data usually refer to research expenditures (such as gross research expenditures) or innovation criteria (such as the number of external patent applications and the national patent applications) and to the scientific criteria (such as research and scientific personnel).

R&D covers both formal R&D in R&D units and informal or occasional R&D in other units. However, interest in R&D depends more on the new knowledge and innovations and their economic and social effects than on the activity itself. Unfortunately, while indicators of R&D output are clearly needed to complement input statistics, they are very difficult to define and produce.

The output of R&D or science and technology (S&T) in general can be measured in several ways. Innovation surveys are an attempt to measure outputs and the effects of innovation process in which R&D plays an important role. A manual of innovation surveys has been issued and revised by OECD.

Expenditure on technological product and process innovation includes all expenditure related to those scientific, technological, commercial, financial and organisational steps which are intended to lead, or actually lead, to the implementation of technologically new or improved products and processes. Research and development is a term covering three activities: basic research, applied research, and experimental development. Research and development by a market producer is an activity undertaken for the purpose of discovering or developing new products, including improved versions or qualities of existing products, or discovering or developing new or more efficient processes of production. Research and development services in natural sciences and engineering; social sciences and humanities and interdisciplinary. Any creative systematic activity undertaken in order to increase the stock of knowledge, including knowledge of man, culture and society, and the use of this knowledge to devise new applications. Includes fundamental research, applied research in such fields as agriculture, medicine, industrial chemistry, and experimental development work leading to new devices, products or processes. Research and development expenditure is the money spent on creative work undertaken on a systematic basis to increase the stock of knowledge and the use of this knowledge to devise new applications. Expenditure on Research and Development (R&D) refers to all expenditure on research performed at universities and at other institutions of tertiary education, regardless of whether the research is funded from general institutional funds or through separate grants or contracts from public or private sponsors. This includes all research institutes and experimental stations operating under the direct control of, or administered by, or associated with, higher education institutions. (Education at a Glance, OECD, Paris, 2002, Glossary).

Research and experimental development (R&D) comprises creative work undertaken on a systematic basis in order to increase the stock of knowledge, including knowledge of man, culture and society, and the use of this stock of knowledge to devise new applications (as defined in the OECD Frascati Manual).

Gross domestic expenditure on research and development (GERD) is total intramural expenditure on research and development performed on the national territory during a given period. (as defined in the OECD Frascati and Oslo Manuals).

Expenditures for research and development are current and capital expenditures (both public and private) on creative work undertaken systematically to increase knowledge, including knowledge of humanity, culture, and society, and the use of knowledge for new applications. R&D covers basic research, applied research, and experimental development. (United Nations Educational, Scientific, and Cultural Organization (UNESCO) Institute for Statistics).

Expenditure on research activities may be spent within the statistical unit (*intramural*) or outside (*extamural*). According to the OECD, *intramural expenditures* are defined as: "All expenditure on research activities performed within a statistical unit or sector of the economy, whatever the source of funds. Expenditures made outside the statistical-unit or sector but in support of intramural R&D (such as, purchase of supplies of R&D) are included. In addition, for R&D purposes, both current and capital expenditures are measured, while depreciation payments are excluded".

The main disadvantage of R&D input series expressed in monetary terms is that they are affected by differences in price levels over time and across countries. Compared to the output measures, the input measures do not offer qualitative or other efficiency indicators for current innovation activities and scientific manpower inputs. Scientific and technological indicators may also be used to measure the effects of a given technology on the welfare of a specific target group of people.

R&D is an activity during which there are significant transfers among units, organizations and sectors. R&D activities are usually classified under the following three headings:

(a) *Basic research*, which can be defined as: "Experimental or theoretical work undertaken primarily to acquire new knowledge of the underlying foundations of phenomena and observable facts, without any particular application or use in view".
(b) *Applied research,* which is: "Original investigation undertaken in order to acquire new knowledge, which however is directed primarily towards a specific practical aim or objective".
(c) *Experimental development,* which can be defined as: "Systematic word, drawing on existing knowledge gained from research and practical experience, that is directed to producing new materials, products and devices, to installing new processes, systems and services and also to improve substantially those already produced or installed".

The European Commission uses slightly different variation of these definitions and makes the following classification:

(a) *Fundamental research* which is similar to the Basic Research as defined by OECD (in Frascati Manual, (1981) and (1989));
(b) *Basic industrial R & D* which is concerned with the development of industrial technology;
(c) *Applied R&D* which refers to the application of technologies to the new products.

The figures of GERD (*Gross Expenditures of Research and Development*) include those research and technological activities which are performed within a country, but they exclude payments for research and technological activities which are made abroad.

The figures of *Gross National Expenditure on R&D* (GNERD) comprises the aggregate total expenditure on research and innovation activities financed by the institutions of a country during a given period and include the research activities performed abroad but financed by the national institutions; R&D performed within a country but funded from abroad should be excluded. In addition, according to Frascatti Manual, OECD, the *Gross Domestic Expenditure on R&D* (GERD) can be defined as the total expenditures *on R&D* performed on the national territory during a given period.

Beside R&D, six fields of innovative activities may often be distinguished in the innovation process:

(a) *Tooling-up and industrial engineering* cover acquisition of and changes in production machinery and tools and in production and quality control procedures, methods, and standards required to manufacture the new product or to use the new process.
(b) *Manufacturing start-up and preproduction development* may include product or process modifications, retraining personnel in the new techniques or in the use of new machinery, and trial production if it implies further design and engineering.
(c) *Marketing for new products* covers activities in connection with launching of a new product. These may include market tests, adaptation of the product to different markets and launch of advertising, but will exclude the building of distribution networks for market innovations.
(d) *Acquisition of disembodied technology* includes acquisition of external technology in the form of patents, non-patented inventions, licenses, disclosure of know-how, trademarks, designs, patterns, and services with a technological content.
(e) *Acquisition of embodied technology* covers acquisition of machinery and equipment with a technological content connected with either product or process innovations introduced by the firm.
(f) *Design* is an essential part of the innovation process. It covers plans and drawings aimed at defining procedures, technical specifications, and operational features necessary to the conception, development, manufacturing and marketing of new products and processes. It may be a part of the initial conception of the product or process, as for instance, research and experimental development, but it may also be associated with tooling-up, industrial engineering, manufacturing start-up, and marketing of new products.

Measurement of the *personnel employed on research activities* involves, firstly, the identification of what types of personnel should be initially included, and, secondly, the measurement of research activities in the full time equivalent. Personnel is a more concrete measure and, since labour costs normally account for 50-70 per cent of total R&D expenditures, it is also a reasonable short-term indicator of efforts devoted to R&D. Personnel can be defined as: "All the persons directly on R&D, as well as those providing direct services such as R&D, managers, administrators and clerical staff. In particular, *Research personnel* can be considered either as the number of *researchers, scientists and engineers*, or the *technicians and equivalent staff*".

According to OECD (Oslo and Frascati Manuals):

(a) *Researchers, scientists and engineers* are usually those who are: "Engaged in the conception or creation of new knowledge, products, processes, methods and systems".
(b) *Technicians and equivalent staff* include those: "Who participate in R & D projects by performing S&T tasks normally under the supervision of scientific and engineers".

The measurement of personnel employed in R&D involves three exercises:

- identifying which types of personnel should be initially included;
- measuring their number;
- measuring their R&D activities in full-time equivalent (person-years).

All persons employed directly in R&D should be counted, as well as those providing direct services such as R&D managers, administrators and clerical staff. For statistical purposes, two inputs are measured: R&D expenditures and R&D personnel. Both inputs are normally measured on an annual basis, how much spent during a year, how many person-years used during a year. Both series have their strengths and weaknesses, and, in consequence, both are necessary to secure an adequate representation of the effort devoted to R&D. Data on the utilisation of scientific and technical personnel provide concrete measurements for international comparisons of resources devoted to R&D. It is recognised, however, that R&D inputs are only one part of the input of a nation's human resources to the public welfare; scientific and technical personnel contribute much more to industrial, agricultural and medical progress with their involvement in production, operations, quality control, management, education and other functions. The measurement of these stocks of scientific and technical manpower is the subject of the *Canberra Manual* (OECD, 1995). The focus in this Manual is the measurement and classification of R&D resources instead. For R&D personnel data, the problem lies in reducing such data to full-time equivalent (FTE) or person-years spent on R&D. The national R&D effort requires a wide variety of personnel. Because of the range of skills and education required, it is essential to classify R&D personnel into categories. R&D personnel data are not affected by differences in currency values. However, there are some problems with the classification of full-time with the equivalent and person-years-on-R&D. Researchers in R&D are professionals engaged in the conception or creation of new knowledge, products, processes, methods, or systems and in the management of the projects concerned. Postgraduate PhD students (ISCED97 level 6) engaged in R&D are included. (United Nations Educational, Scientific, and Cultural Organization (UNESCO) Institute for Statistics). Research and development personnel includes all persons employed directly on research and development activities, as well as those providing direct services such as research and development managers, administrators and clerical staff. Those providing an indirect service, such as canteen and security staff, should be excluded, even though their wages and salaries are included as an overhead cost when measuring expenditure. (as defined in the OECD Frascati Manual). Technicians and equivalent staff are persons whose main tasks require technical knowledge and experience in one or more fields of engineering, physical and life sciences, or social sciences and humanities. They participate in research and development (R&D) by performing scientific and technical tasks involving the application of concepts and operational methods, normally under the supervision of researchers. Equivalent staff perform the corresponding R&D tasks under the supervision of researchers in the social sciences and humanities. Technicians and equivalent staff are persons in ISCO-88 Major Group 3 "Technicians and Associate Professionals", notably in Sub-major 31 "Physical and Engineering Science Associate Professionals" and 32 "Life Science and Health Associate Professionals" plus "Statistical, Mathematical and Related Associate Professionals" (ISCO-88, 3434). Any members of the

Armed Forces working on similar tasks should be included in this category. Full-time equivalent employment is the number of full-time equivalent jobs, defined as total hours worked divided by average annual hours worked in full-time jobs. Researchers are professionals engaged in the conception or creation of new knowledge, products processes, methods, and systems, and in the management of the projects concerned. Researchers are all persons in the International Standard Classification of Occupations-88 (ISCO-88) Major Group 2 "Professional Occupations" plus "Research and Development Department Managers" (ISCO- 88 1237). By convention, any members of the Armed Forces with similar skills performing R&D should also be included in this category. (as defined in the OECD Frascati Manual).

Technicians in R&D and equivalent staff are people whose main tasks require technical knowledge and experience in engineering, physical and life sciences (technicians), or social sciences and humanities (equivalent staff). They participate in R&D by performing scientific and technical tasks involving the application of concepts and operational methods, normally under the supervision of researchers. (United Nations Educational, Scientific, and Cultural Organization (UNESCO) Institute for Statistics.

Human capital is productive wealth embodied in labour, skills and knowledge, Human development is the process of enlarging people's choices. Their three essential choices are to lead a long and healthy life, to acquire knowledge and to have access to the resources needed for a decent standard of living. Additional choices, highly valued by many people, range from political, economic and social freedom to opportunities for being creative and productive and enjoying personal self—respect and guaranteed human rights. (defined in the OECD Frascati Manual)

A patent is an intellectual property related to inventions in the technical field. A patent may be granted to a firm, an individual or a public body by a patent office. An application for a patent has to meet certain requirements: the invention has to be novel, involve a (non-obvious) inventive step and be applied to industry. A patent is valid in a given country for a limited period (20 years). For purposes of international comparison, statistics on patent applications are preferable to statistics on patents granted because of the lag between application date and grant date, which may be up to ten years in certain countries. Patent indicators based on simple counts of patents filed at an intellectual property office are influenced by various sources of bias, such as weaknesses in international comparability (home advantage for patent applications) or high heterogeneity in patent values within a single office.

Patent data applications can be considered as partial proxy measures of the output of R&D in the form of inventions. Information about the country concerned is completed with data for *external patent applications (EPA)* by the residents of the country for patents in other countries. The data usual cover applications processed through national and international patent offices. We can define as *patents*: "The right which is granted by a government to an inventor in exchange for the publication of the invention and entitles the inventor for an agreed period to prevent any third party from using the invention in any way". Patent applications are worldwide patent applications filed through the Patent Cooperation Treaty procedure or with a national patent office for exclusive rights for an invention--a product or process that provides a new way of doing something or offers a new technical solution to a problem. A patent provides protection for the invention to the owner of the patent for a limited period, generally 20 years. (World Intellectual Property Organization (WIPO), WIPO Patent Report: Statistics on Worldwide Patent Activity).

Trademark applications filed are applications to register a trademark with a national or regional Intellectual Property (IP) office. A trademark is a distinctive sign which identifies certain goods or services as those produced or provided by a specific person or enterprise. A trademark provides protection to the owner of the mark by ensuring the exclusive right to use it to identify goods or services, or to authorize another to use it in return for payment. The period of protection varies, but a trademark can be renewed indefinitely beyond the time limit on payment of additional fees. Direct nonresident trademark applications are those filed by applicants from abroad directly at a given national IP office, (World Intellectual Property Organization (WIPO), WIPO Patent Report: Statistics on Worldwide Patent Activity). Royalty and license fees are payments and receipts between residents and nonresidents for the authorized use of intangible, non-produced, nonfinancial assets and proprietary rights (such as patents, copyrights, trademarks, industrial processes, and franchises) and for the use, through licensing agreements, of produced originals of prototypes (such as films and manuscripts). (International Monetary Fund, Balance of Payments Statistics Yearbook and data files). High-technology exports are products with high R&D intensity, such as in aerospace, computers, pharmaceuticals, scientific instruments, and electrical machinery.

Technological balance can be considered as what measures a country's balance of payments and receipts concerning the sale and purchase of knowledge and technological information. The technology balance of payments (TBP) registers the commercial transactions related to international technology and know-how transfers. It consists of money paid or received for the use of patents, licences, know-how, trademarks, patterns, designs, technical services (including technical assistance) and for industrial research and development (R&D) carried out abroad, etc. The coverage may vary from country to country and the TBP data should be considered as only partial measures of international technology flows. (OECD: Frascati and Oslo Manuals). Technology Balance of Payments (TBP) registers the international flow of industrial property and know-how. The following operations are included in the TBP: patents (purchases, sales); licences for patents; know-how (not patented); models and designs; trademarks (including franchising); technical services; finance of industrial R&D outside national territory.

The "contribution to the trade balance" makes it possible to identify an economy's structural strengths and weaknesses via the composition of international trade flows. It takes into account not only, but also imports, and tries to eliminate business cycle variations by comparing an industry's trade balance with the overall trade balance. It can be interpreted as an indicator of "revealed comparative advantage", as it indicates whether an industry performs relatively better or worse than the manufacturing total, whether the manufacturing total itself is in deficit or surplus.

If there were no comparative advantage or disadvantage for any industry *i*, a country's total trade balance (surplus or deficit) should be distributed across industries according to their share in total trade. The "contribution to the trade balance" is the difference between the actual and the theoretical balance, as expressed in the following equations:

$$(X_i - M_i) - (X - M)\frac{(X_i + M_i)}{(X + M)}$$

where $(X_i - M_i)$ = observed industry trade balance

and $(X - M)\dfrac{(X_i + M_i)}{(X + M)}$ = theoretical trade balance

Table 1.3. Classification of R & D intensive products

(SITC) Product Group	(SITC) Product Group
Leading-edge technology	High-level technology
(516) Advanced organic chemicals	(266) Synthetic fibres
(525) Radioactive materials	(277) Advanced industrial abrasives
(541) Pharmaceutical products	(515) Heterocyclic chemistry
(575) Advanced plastics	(522) Rare inorganic chemicals
(591) Agricultural chemicals	(524) Other precious chemicals
(714) Turbines and reaction engines	(531) Synthetic colouring matter
(718) Nuclear, water, wind power generators	(533) Pigments, paints, varnishes
(752) Automatic data processing machines	(542) Medicaments
(764) Telecommunications equipment	(551) Essential oils, perfume, flavour
(774) Medical electronics	(574) Polyethers and resins
(776) Semi-conductor devices	(598) Advanced chemical products
(778) Advanced electrical machinery	(663) Mineral manufacturers, fine ceramics
(792) Aircraft and spacecraft	(689) Precious non-ferrous base metals
(871) Advanced optical instruments	(724) Textile and leather machinery
(874) Advanced measuring instruments	(725) Chapter and pulp machinery
(891) Arms and ammunition	(726) Printing and bookbinding machinery
	(727) Industrial food processing machines
	(728) Advanced machine-tools
	(731) Machine tools working by removing
	(733) Machine tools without removing
	(735) Parts for machine tools
	(737) Advanced metalworking equipment
	(741) Industrial handling equipment
	(744) Other non-electrical machinery
	(746) Boll and roller bearings
	(751) Office machines, word-processing
	(759) Advanced parts for computers
	(761) Television and video equipment
	(762) Radiobroadcast, radio telephony goods
	(763) Sound and video recorders
	(772) Traditional electronics
	(773) Optical fibre and other cables
	(781) Motor vehicles for persons
	(782) Motor vehicles for goods transport
	(791) Railway vehicles
	(872) Medical instruments and appliances
	(873) Traditional measuring equipment
	(881) Photographic apparatus and equipment
	(882) Photo and cinematographic supplies
	(884) Optical fibres, contact, other lenses

Source: Hariolf Grupp: (1995) "Science, high technology and the competitiveness of EU countries", Cambridge Journal of Economics Note.

A positive value for an industry indicates a structural surplus and a negative one a structural deficit. The indicator is additive and individual industries can be grouped together by summing their respective values: by construction, the sum over all industries is zero.

The *international technological competitiveness* has been becoming an increasingly important issue. However, *high technology* is not a well- defined issue in economics. For some authors *high technology* is defined by R&D intensity and R&D activities. OECD, U.N and U.S. Department of Commerce use the classification of high technology industries which is based on the criterion of R&D expenditures. The International Trade Classification, the Lower Saxony Institute for Economic Research and the Fraunhofer Institute for Systems and Innovation Research have designed a new list of R&D intensive products.

Table 1.3 presents the product groups considered to have been fall into high technology categories; this list divides the R&D intensive sector into two parts: *the leading edge products* and *the high level technology products*. *Leading edge technology* includes the products that are subject to protectionism, such as aeronautics, and nuclear energy, whereas, the *high level products* include the mass consumption products. Patent statistics measure innovation activities, while R&D data measures both innovation and imitating activities. From *the patent index*, it seems that the (absolute) technological difference is bigger than that indicated by research expenditures.

Furthermore, diffusion is defined as the way in which innovations spread, through market or non-market channels, from their first implementation anywhere in the world, to other countries and regions and to other industries/markets and firms. In order to map innovation activities and draw a picture both of some of the links involved and of the level of diffusion of advanced technologies.

Expenditure on R&D may be made within the statistical unit (intramural) or outside it (extramural) R&D expenditure data should be compiled on the basis of performers' reports of intramural expenditures. Intramural expenditures are all expenditures for R&D performed within a statistical unit or sector of the economy, whatever the source of funds. Expenditures made outside the statistical unit or sector but supporting intramural R&D (as for instance, purchase of supplies for R&D) are included; both current and capital expenditures are included. Research and experimental development (R&D) comprise creative work undertaken on a systematic basis in order to increase the stock of knowledge, including knowledge of man, culture and society, and the use of this stock of knowledge to devise new applications. R&D is a term covering three activities: basic research, applied research, and experimental development.

Business enterprise R&D (BERD) covers R&D activities carried out in the business sector by performing firms and institutes, regardless of the origin of funding. While the government and higher education sectors also carry out R&D, industrial R&D is most closely linked to the creation of new products and production techniques, as well as with a country's innovation efforts. The business enterprise sector includes: all firms, organisations and institutions whose primary activity is production of goods and services for sale to the general public at an economically significant price.

Government Appropriations or Outlays for R&D (GBAORD) measures the funds committed by the federal/central government for R&D (including those by international organisations) to be carried out in one of the four sectors of performance –business enterprise, government, higher education, private non-profit sector – at home or abroad. These data are usually based on budgetary sources and reflect the views of funding agencies. They are generally considered less internationally comparable than the performer-reported data used in other tables and figures; yet they have the advantage of being more time and reflecting current government priorities, as expressed in the breakdown of socio-economic objectives. A first distinction can be made between defence programs, which are concentrated in a small number of countries, and civil programs, which can be broken down as follows:

- Economic development: agricultural production and technology; industrial production and technology; infrastructure and general planning of land use; production, distribution and rational utilisation of energy.
- Health and environment: protection and improvement of human health, social structures and relationships, control and care of the environment, exploration and exploitation of the Earth.
- Exploration and exploitation of space.
- Non-oriented research.
- Research financed by General University Funds (GUF). The estimated R&D content of block grants to universities.

The basic measure is *"intramural expenditures"*; that is expenditures for R&D performed within a statistical unit or sector of the economy. Another measure, "extramural expenditures", covers payments for R&D performed outside the statistical unit or sector of the economy. For R&D purposes, both current costs and capital expenditures are measured. In the case of government sector, expenditures refer to direct rather than indirect expenditures; depreciation costs are excluded.

R&D is an activity involving significant transfers of resources among units, organisations and sectors and especially between government and other performers. It is important for science policy advisors and analysts to know who finances R&D and who performs it. The main disadvantage of expressing R&D input series in monetary terms is that they are affected by differences in price levels between countries and over time. It can be shown that current exchange rates often do not reflect the balance of R&D prices between countries and that in times of high inflation general price indexes do not accurately reflect trends in the cost of performing R&D.

Labour costs. These comprise annual wages and salaries and all associated costs or fringe benefits -such as bonus payments, holiday pay, contributions to pension funds and other social security payments, payroll taxes, etc. Labour costs of persons providing indirect services and which are not included in the personnel data (such as security and maintenance personnel or the staff of central libraries, computer departments, or head offices) should be excluded and included in other current costs. Only the actual "salaries"/stipends and similar expenditures associated with postgraduate students should be reported.

Other current costs. These comprise non-capital purchases of materials, supplies and equipment to support R&D performed by the statistical unit in a given year. Examples are: water and fuel (including gas and electricity); books, journals, reference materials, subscriptions to libraries, scientific societies and so on; imputed or actual cost of small prototypes or models made outside the research organisation; materials for laboratories (chemicals, animals, etc.). Administrative and other overhead costs (such as interest charges and office, post and telecommunications, and insurance costs) should also be included, if necessary, prorated to allow for non-R&D activities within the same statistical unit. All expenditures on indirect services should be included here, whether carried out within the organisation concerned or hired or purchased from outside suppliers.

Table 1.4. Classification of R&D Activities in Social Sciences and Humanities

Basic Research	Applied Research	Experimental Development
Study of causal relations between economic conditions and social development	Study of the economic and social causal of agricultural workers rural districts to towns, for the purpose	Development and testing of a program of financial assistance to prevent rural immigrants to large cities.
Study of the social structure and the socio-occupational mobility of a society.	Development of a model using the data obtained in order to foresee future consequences of recent trends in social mobility	Development and testing of a program to stimulate spread mobility among certain social and ethic groups
Study of the role of the family in different civilizations past and present	Study of the role and position of the family in a specific country or a specific region at the present time for the purpose of preparing relevant social measures	Development and testing of a program to maintain family structure in low income working groups
Study of the reading process in adults and children.	Study of the reading process for the purpose of developing new method of teaching children and adults to read	Development and testing of a special reading program among immigrant children
Ding Study of the international factors influencing national economic development.	Study of the national factors determining the economic development of a country in a given period with a view to formulating an operational model for modifying government foreign trade policy.	—
Study of specific aspects of a particular language.	Study of the of the children aspects of a language for the purpose of devising a new method of teaching that language or of translating from or into that language.	—
Study of the historical development of a language.	—	—
Study of sources of all kinds (i.e. manuscripts, documents, buildings, etc), in order to better comprehend historical phenomena (for instance, political, social, cultural development of a country, biography of an individual etc).	—	—

Source: UNESCO (1984) "Manual for Statistics on Scientific and Technological Activities".

Gross domestic expenditure on R&D (GERD) is total intramural expenditure on R&D performed on the national territory. GERD includes R&D performed within a country and funded from abroad but excludes payments made abroad for R&D. Research and experimental development (R&D) comprise creative work undertaken on a systematic basis in order to increase the stock of knowledge, including knowledge of human beings, culture and society, and the use of this stock of knowledge to devise new applications.

- *Basic research* is "experimental or theoretical work undertaken primarily to acquire new knowledge of the underlying foundation of phenomena and observable facts, without any particular application or use in view". Basic research analyses properties, structures, and relationships to formulate and test hypotheses, theories or laws. The results of basic research are not sold; they are rather published in scientific journals or circulated to interested colleagues. Occasionally, basic research may be "classified" for security reasons.
- *Applied research* is also "original investigation undertaken in order to acquire new knowledge". It is, however, directed primarily towards a specific practical aim or objective. The results of applied research are intended primarily to be valid for a single or limited number of products, operations, methods, or systems. Applied research develops ideas into operational form. The knowledge or information derived from it is often patented but may also be kept secret.
- *Experimental development* is "systematic work, drawing on existing knowledge gained from research and/or practical experience, which is directed to producing new materials, products or devices, to installing new processes, systems and services, or to improving substantially those already produced or installed". R&D covers both formal R&D in R&D units and informal or occasional R&D in other units".

Table 1.4 illustrates the three main types of research namely basic research, applied research and experimental research in the Social Sciences and Humanities.

1.3. MEASUREMENT AND LEADING INDICATORS OF INNOVATION ACTIVITIES

Measurement of innovation and technological change have played a major role in the analysis and understanding of the links between entrepreneurship and innovation. Measures of technological change have typically involved one of the three major aspects of the innovative process:

(a) A measure of the inputs into the innovative process, such as R&D expenditures, or else the share of the labor force accounted for by employees involved in R&D activities;
(b) An intermediate output, such as the number of inventions which have been patented; or
(c) A direct measure of innovative output.

There is growing recognition that innovation encompasses a wide range of activities in addition to R&D, such as organisational changes, training, testing, marketing and design. By definition, all innovation must contain a degree of novelty. The Oslo Manual distinguishes three types of novelty: an innovation can be new to the firm, new to the market or new to the world. The first concept covers the diffusion of an existing innovation to a firm – the innovation may have already been implemented by other firms, but it is new to the firm. Innovations are new to the market when the firm is the first to introduce the innovation on its market. An innovation is new to the world when the firm is the first to introduce the innovation for all markets and industries. Innovation, thus defined, is clearly a much broader notion than R&D and is therefore influenced by a wide range of factors, some of which can be influenced by policy. Innovation can occur in any sector of the economy, including government services such as health or education. However, the current measurement framework applies to business innovation, even though innovation is also important for the public sector. Consideration is being given to extending the methodology to public sector innovation and innovation for social goals. (*Source*: OECD and Eurostat (2005), *Oslo Manual – Guidelines for Collecting and Interpreting Innovation Data,* OECD, Paris).

The summary indexes, the overall index of technological achievement, and the technological adaptive capacity index were calculated by aggregating some 34 separate variables, with the weights used in the aggregation calculated by principal components analysis. This approach distinguishes these indexes, which even though they are based on similar underlying base data, use arbitrary weighting schemes with limited theoretical or empirical bases (see Archibugi and Coco 2005). A number of existing measures of technological achievement or technological progress emphasize inputs into technological advancement (numbers of scientists and engineers, R&D expenditure, or levels of R&D personnel), including, in some cases, even more indirect inputs, such as the general level of education of the population and governance factors that facilitate the absorption of technology (UNCTAD 2005). Other measures focus on outputs, that is, on indicators of technological performance, such as the shares of high-tech industries in exports and in manufacturing value added (UNIDO 2002).

- The index of competitive industrial performance is published by the United Nations Industrial Development Organization (UNIDO 2002) and is calculated as a simple average of four basic indicators: manufacturing value added per capita, manufactured exports per capita, share of medium- and high-tech activities in manufacturing value added, and share of medium- and high-tech products in manufactured exports.
- Investment in knowledge is defined and calculated as the sum of expenditure on R&D, on total higher education from both public and private sources and on software. Simple summation of the three components would lead to overestimation of the investment in knowledge owing to overlaps (R&D and software, R&D and education, software and education). Therefore, before calculating total investment in knowledge, the data must be reworked to derive figures that meet the definition. The R&D component of higher education, which overlaps R&D expenditure, has been estimated and subtracted from total expenditure on higher education (both public and private sources). Not all expenditure on software can be considered investment. Some should be considered as intermediate consumption. Purchases of packaged software by households and operational services in firms are estimated. The software

component of R&D, which overlaps R&D expenditure, is estimated when information from national studies and subtracted from software expenditure is used. Due to a lack of information, it was not possible to separate the overlap between expenditure on education and on software; however, the available information indicates that this overlap is quite small. A more complete picture of investment in knowledge would also include parts of expenditure on innovation (expenditure on the design of new goods), expenditure by enterprises on job-related training programs, investment in organisation (spending on organisational change, etc.), among others. However, due to the lack of available data, such elements could not be included. Knowledge-economy is closely related to the Information Technology (IT) and Information Communication Technology (ICT). *IT* covers both hardware and software. Their development and diffusion is believed to have had a major impact on the pattern of production and employment in a wide range of industries. In the case of hardware, it may be interesting not only to know when a company innovates by first introducing a technologically new or improved piece of IT equipment but also the IT proportion of its total stock of equipment including subsequent purchases of further machines of the same model.

- The amount of tax subsidy to R&D is calculated as 1 minus the B index. The B index is defined as the present value of before-tax income necessary to cover the initial cost of R&D investment and to pay corporate income tax, so that it becomes profitable to perform research activities. Algebraically, the B index is equal to the after-tax cost of an expenditure of USD 1 on R&D divided by one minus the corporate income tax rate. The B index is a unique tool for comparing the generosity of the tax treatment of R&D in different countries. However, its computation requires some simplifying assumptions. It should therefore be examined together with a set of other relevant policy indicators. Finally, these calculations are based on reported tax regulations and do not take into account country-specific exemptions and other practices. B indexes have been calculated with the assumption that the "representative firm" is taxable, so that it may enjoy the full benefit of the tax allowance or credit. For incremental tax credits, calculation of the B index implicitly assumes that R&D investment is fully eligible for the credit and does not exceed the ceiling if there is one. Some detailed features of R&D tax schemes (for instance, refunding, carry-back and carry-forward of unused tax credit, or flow through mechanisms) are therefore not taken into account. The effective impact of the R&D tax allowance or credit on the after-tax cost of R&D is influenced by the level of the CITR. An increase in the CITR reduces the B index only in those countries with the most generous R&D tax treatment. If tax credits are taxable (as in Canada and the United States), the effect of the CITR on the B index depends only on the level of the depreciation allowance. If the latter is over 100% for the total R&D expenditure, an increase in the CITR will reduce the B index. For countries with less generous R&D tax treatment, the B index is positively related to the CITR. The after-tax cost is the net cost of investing in R&D, taking into account all the available tax incentives. $B_{index} = \frac{(1-A)}{(1-\tau)}$, where $A =$ the net present discounted value of depreciation allowances, tax credits and special allowances on R&D assets; and t = the statutory corporate income tax rate (CITR). In a country with full write-off of current R&D expenditure and no R&D tax incentive

scheme, $A = t$, and consequently $B = 1$. The more favourable a country's tax treatment of R&D, the lower its B index.
- The index of innovation capability is published by the United Nations Conference on Trade and Development (UNCTAD 2005) and consists of an unweighted average of an index of human capital (calculated as a weighted average of tertiary and secondary school enrollment rates and the literacy rate) and a technological activity index (calculated as an unweighted average of three indicators: R&D personnel, U.S. patents granted, and scientific publications, all per million population).
- The technology achievement index is published by the United Nations Development Programme (UNDP 2001) and combines (a) the indicators of human skills (mean years of schooling in the population age 15 and older and enrollment ratio for tertiary-level science programs); (b) the diffusion of old innovations (electricity consumption per capita and telephones per capita) and of recent innovations (Internet hosts per capita and high- and medium-tech exports as a share of all exports); and (c) the creation of technology (patents granted to residents per capita and receipts of royalties and license fees from abroad). The index is constructed as simple averages of these indicators within subgroups and then across groups.
- The national innovative capacity index (Porter and Stern 2003) focuses on government-and firm-level policies associated with successful innovation. It is composed of four subindexes: proportion of scientists and engineers in the population, innovation policy, innovation linkages and what they call the cluster innovation environment. The overall index is calculated as an unweighted sum of the four subindexes, but the weights assigned to each indicator in the subindexes are determined by the coefficients obtained from a regression of the number of U.S. Patent and Trademark Office patents on the relevant indicators controlling for total population, the proportion of scientists and engineers employed, and the stock of international patents generated by the country between 1985 and 1994.
- The Knowledge Innovation Index using around 109 structural and qualitative variables for 146 countries to measure their performance on four Knowledge Economy pillars: Economic Incentive and Institutional Regime, Education, Innovation, and Information and Communications Technologies.
- The Technological Achievement Index (TAI), a composite index of technological achievement, reflects the level of technological progress and thus the capacity of a country to participate in the network age. A composite index helps a country situate itself relative to others, especially those farther ahead. Many elements make up a country's technological achievement, but an overall assessment is more easily made based on a single composite measure than on dozens of different measures. Like other composite indices in *Human Development Reports* such as the Human Development Index (HDI), the TAI is intended to be used as a starting point to make an overall assessment, to be followed by examining different indicators in greater detail. The index aims to capture technological achievements of a country in four dimensions:

- creating new technology;
- diffusing recent innovations;
- diffusing existing technologies that are still basic inputs to the industrial and the network age; and
- building a human skill base for technological creation and adoption.

The technological achievement index focuses on outcomes and achievements rather than on effort or inputs such as numbers of scientists, R&D expenditures, or policy environments. The TAI is not a measure of which country is leading in global technology development, but focuses on how well the country as a whole is participating in creating and using technology. The methodology used to calculate the TAI is similar to the HDI: a simple average of the dimensions of the index, which in turn is calculated based on the selected indicators. The TAI has eight indicators, two in each of the four dimensions.

- Technology creation, measured by the number of patents granted to residents per capita and by receipts of royalties and license fees from abroad per capita.
- Diffusion of recent innovations, measured by the number of Internet hosts per capita and the share of high-technology and medium-technology exports in total goods exports.
- Diffusion of old innovations, measured by telephones (mainline and cellular) per capita and electricity consumption per capita.
- Human skills, measured by the mean years of schooling in the population aged 15 and older, and the gross tertiary science enrolment ratio.
- Another Index is the Social Science Citation Index (SSCI). This database was used to find scientific papers that give insights into the processes of innovation, technological change and growth in regions.
- The innovation system can be defined as a network of actors and institutions that develop, diffuse and use innovations (Malerba, 2002). On the other hand, there is a clear correlation between the share of enterprises receiving public funding and the business R&D expenditure (% of the GDP) at geographic and firm level, (Toivanen, Niininen, 1998; Busom, 2000; Walsten, 2000; Czarnitzki, Fier, 2001; Almus, Czarnitzki, 2003). In order to measure the progress in that policy area, we proposed to use the following indicators: "Share of enterprises that received any public funding" (Source: CIS). The indicator shows a breakdown by source of funding making a distinction between the "share of enterprises that received funding from local or regional authorities" and the "share of enterprises that received funding from central government" (including central government agencies or ministries).
- The indicators for creation of technology are patents granted per capita and royalty and license fees received from abroad per capita. Diffusion of recent innovations is calculated from the number of Internet hosts per capita and the share of high- and medium-technology exports as a percentage of all exports. Indicators for diffusion of old technology are telephones (land line and cellular) per capita and electricity consumption per capita. Human skills are calculated based on the average number of years of schooling and the gross enrolment ratio at the tertiary level in science, mathematics and engineering.

- The Technology Index (TI) published in the Harvard Competitiveness Reports focuses on the enabling policy environment for technological innovation and diffusion.
- The Index of Technological Progress (ITP) developed by Rodriguez and Wilson focuses only on information telecommunications technologies.
- The index of Research intensity (RI) in high technology industries is the ratio of Manufacturing R&D expenditures over the manufacturing production.
- The index of Export specialisation in high technology industries is the ratio of high-technology exports over the manufacturing exports.
- RCA (Revealed Comparative Advantage Index) for the Information Communication Technologies (ICT) manufacturing industry in an individual country k relative to the total world is calculated as follows:

$$\text{RCA}_{ICT}^{k} = \frac{\frac{X_{ICT}^{k}}{X_{manufacturing}^{k}}}{\frac{X_{ICT}^{World}}{X_{manufacturing}^{World}}}$$

where X denotes exports.

- RTB (Revealed Technological Advantage Index) for the ICT services industry in an individual country k is calculated as follows:

$$\text{RTB}_{ICT}^{k} = \frac{(X_{ICT}^{k} - M_{ICT}^{k})}{(X_{ICT}^{k} + M_{ICT}^{k})}$$

where X and M denotes exports and imports respectively.

- RTB (Revealed Technological Advantage Index) is a country's share of patenting in a particular sector relative to its share of all patents and it's calculated as follows:

$$\text{RTB} = \frac{\frac{P_i^X}{P_i^{TOT}}}{\frac{\sum_i P_i^X}{\sum_i P_i^{TOT}}}$$

where P_i^X is the total number of patents in sector X in country i and P_i^{TOT} is the total number of patents in all sectors in country i. The Standardized Revealed Technological Advantage Index is equal to: $\frac{(RTA-1)}{(RTA+1)}$.

- The most widely used method of measuring intra-industry trade is the Grubel-Lloyd Index (GLI). Using disaggregated trade data, the extent of intra-industry trade in product class I in country j can be expressed as:

$$\text{GL}_i = 1 - \frac{|X_{ij} - M_{ij}|}{X_{ij} + M_{ij}}$$

where X_{ij} represents exports of product class i by country j and M_{ij} represents imports of product class i by country j. The Grubel-Lloyd Index is zero when trade is entirely inter-industry, (for instance either imports or exports of a product is equal zero), and is 1 when trade is entirely intra-industry, (for instance either imports or exports of a product is equal to each other).

- The European Regional Innovation Scoreboard (ERIS) used a composite indicator - the Revealed Regional Summary Innovation Index (RSII) which is calculated as the weighted average of the re-scaled values for Regional National Summary Innovation Index and the Regional European Summary Innovation Index. It locates *local* leaders by taking into account both the region's relative performance within the EU and the region's relative performance within the country (Danciu Aniela, Goschin Zizi, 2010). The Innovation Index was designed to measure a broad range of innovative activity, from the R&D that lies behind innovative technologies to the service design and organisational innovations and by linking investment in innovation clearly to productivity improvement, it underscores the central importance of innovation to economic growth, (NESTA, 2009)

The variables related to technological achievement and those related to technological absorptive capacity are reported in the following Table 1.5-1.12.

Table 1.5. Indicators for the Summary Index and the Overall Index of Technological Achievement (TAI)

Scientific innovation and invention
• Scientific and technical journal articles by population • Patents granted by the United States Patent and Trademark Office by population • Patents granted by the European Patent Office by population
Penetration of older technologies
• Electrical Power Consumption kilowatt-hours/capita • International outgoing telephone traffic percent of GDP per 1,000 people • Main lines per 100 inhabitants • Air transport, registered carrier departures worldwide percent of GDP per 1,000 people • Agricultural machinery: tractors per 100 hectares of arable land • Exports of manufactures percent of merchandise exports • Medium-tech exports percent of total exports
Penetration of recent technologies
• Internet users per 1,000 people • Personal computers per 1,000 people • Cellular subscribers per 100 inhabitants • Percentage of digital mainlines • High-tech exports percent of total exports
Exposure to external technology
• FDI net inflows percentage of GDP • Royalties and license fee payments percent of GDP • Imports of high-tech goods percent of GDP • Imports of capital goods percent of GDP • Imports of intermediary goods percent of GDP

Source: World Bank.

Note: BACI _ Banque analytique de commerce internationale, CEPII _ Centre d'Etudes Prospectives et d'Informations Internationales.

EPO _ European Patent Office, FDI _ foreign direct investment, GDP _ gross domestic product, USPTO _ United States Patent and Trademark Office.

Table 1.6. Indicators for the Summary Index and the Overall Index of Technological Absorptive Capacity (ITAC)

Macroeconomic environment
• General government balance as percentage of GDP
• Annual CPI inflation rate
• Real exchange rate volatilty
Financial structure and intermediation
• Liquid liabilities percent of GDP
• Private credit percent of GDP
• Financial system deposits percent of GDP
Human capital
• Primary educational attainment percent of population aged 15 and over
• Secondary educational attainment percent of population aged 15 and over
• Tertiary educational attainment percent of population aged 15 and over
Governance
• Voice and accountability
• Political stability
• Government effectiveness
• Regulatory quality
• Rule of law
• Control of corruption

Source: World Bank.

Following the build-up of the EIS composite innovation index, the regional innovation indexes have been calculated as a weighted average of the average performance for Enablers, Firm activities and Outputs (INNOMETRICS, 2009):

- CI Enablers = Average of normalized transformed scores for the indicators Tertiary education, Life-long learning, Public R&D expenditures and Broadband access.
- CI Firm activities = 8/11 * average of normalized transformed scores for the indicators Business R&D expenditures EPO patents
    + (plus)
    3/11 * average of normalized transformed scores for the indicators Non-R&D innovation expenditures, SMEs innovating in-house and Innovative SMEs collaborating with others, (where the weights of 8/11 and 3/11 represent the share of non-CIS and CIS indicators in the EIS).
- CI Outputs = 4/9 * average of normalized transformed scores for the indicators
    Employment in medium-high & high-tech manufacturing and Employment in knowledge-intensive services
    + (plus)
    5/9 * average of normalized transformed scores for the indicators Product and/or process innovators, Marketing and/or organizational innovators, Resource efficiency innovators, New-to-market sales and New-to-firm sales, (where the weights of 4/9 and 5/9 represent the share of non-CIS and CIS indicators in the EIS).
- CI RIS (RII) = 9/29 * CI Enablers + 11/29 * CI Firm activities + 9/29 * CI Outputs, (where the weights represent the share of the indicators captures in Enablers).

Table 1.7. Indicators for the European Innovation Scoreboard(EIS) 2008-2010

Enablers
Human resources & Input Innovation drivers
• S&E and SSH graduates per 1000 population aged 20-29 (first stage of tertiary education)   • S&E and SSH doctorate graduates per 1000 population aged 25-34 (second stage of tertiary education)   • Population with tertiary education per 100 population aged 25-64   • Participation in life-long learning per 100 population aged 25-64   • Broadband penetration rate (number of broadband lines per 100 population)   • Youth education attainment level (% of population aged 20-24 having completed at least upper secondary education)
Finance and support & Knowledge Creation
• Public R&D expenditures (% of GDP)   • Venture capital (% of GDP) EVCA /   • Private credit (relative to GDP) IMF (2007)   • Broadband access by firms (% of firms)   • Business R&D expenditures (% of GDP)   • Share of medium-high-tech and high-tech R&D (% of manufacturing R&D expenditures)   • Share of enterprises receiving public funding for innovation   • Share of university R&D expenditures financed by business sector
Firm Activities
Firm investments
• Business R&D expenditures (% of GDP)   • IT expenditures (% of GDP)   • Non-R&D innovation expenditures (% of turnover)
Linkages, Innovation & Entrepreneurship
• SMEs innovating in-house (% of SMEs)   • Innovative SMEs collaborating with others (% of SMEs)   • Firm renewal (SME entries plus exits) (% of SMEs)   • Public-private co-publications per million population   • Innovation expenditures (% of total turnover)   • Early-stage venture capital (% of GDP)   • ICT expenditures (% of GDP)   • SMEs using non-technological change (% of all SMEs)
Throughputs
• EPO patents per million population   • Community trademarks per million population   • Community designs per million population   • Technology Balance of Payments flows (% of GDP)

Outputs
Innovators & Intellectual Property
• SMEs introducing product or process innovations (% of SMEs   • SMEs introducing marketing or organisational innovations (% of SMEs)   • Resource efficiency innovators, unweighted average of: • Share of innovators where innovation has significantly reduced labour costs (% of firms)   • Share of innovators where innovation has significantly reduced the use of materials and energy (% of firms)   • EPO patents per million population   • USPTO patents per million population   • Triadic patent families per million population   • New community trademarks per million population   • New community designs per million population
Economic effects & Applications
• Employment in medium-high & high-tech manufacturing (% of workforce)   • Employment in knowledge-intensive services (% of workforce)   • Medium and high-tech manufacturing exports (% of total exports)   • Knowledge-intensive services exports (% of total services exports)   • New-to-market sales (% of turnover)   • New-to-firm sales (% of turnover)   • Exports of high technology products as a share of total exports   • Sales of new-to-market products (% of total turnover)   • Sales of new-to-firm not new-to-market products (% of total turnover)   • Employment in medium-high and high-tech manufacturing (% total workforce)

Source: European Innovation Scoreboard, (2006, 2009, & 2010).

Note: Enablers capture the main drivers for innovation that are external to the firm as (European Innovation Scoreboard, 2009 & 2010):
- Human resources the availability of high skilled and educated people.
- Finance and support the availability of finance for innovation projects and the support of governments for innovation activities.

Firm activities capture innovation efforts that firms undertake recognizing the fundamental importance of firms' activities in the innovation process (European Innovation Scoreboard, 2009 & 2010):
- Firm investments cover a range of different investments firms make in order to generate innovations.
- Linkages and entrepreneurship captures entrepreneurial efforts and collaboration efforts among innovating firms and also with public sector.
- Throughputs capture the Intellectual Property Rights (IPR) generated as a throughput in the innovation process and Technology Balance of Payments flows.

Outputs capture the outputs of firm activities as (European Innovation Scoreboard, 2009 & 2010):
- Innovators capture the number of firms that have introduced innovations into the market, or, within their organizations covering technological and non-technological innovations.
- Economic activities capture the economic success of innovation in employment, exports and sales due to innovation activities.

Table 1.8. EU27–US-Japan Indicators

Enablers
• S&E graduates per 1000 population aged 20-29 • Population with tertiary education per 100 population aged 25-64 • Researchers per 1000 population • Public R&D expenditures (% of GDP) • Venture capital (% of GDP) • Broadband subscribers per 1000 population
Firm Activities

• Business R&D expenditures (% of GDP)
• IT expenditures (% of GDP)
• Public-private co-publications per million population
• EPO patents per million population
• PCT patents per million population
• Trademarks per million population, average of:
   – Community trademarks per million population
   – Trademark applications (residents) per million population
• World Develop ment Indicators
• Technology Balance of Payments flows (% of GDP)

Outputs
• Employment in medium-high & high-tech manufacturing (% of workforce) • Employment in knowledge-intensive services (% of workforce) • Medium and high-tech manufacturing exports (% of total exports) • Knowledge-intensive services exports (% of total services exports)

Source: European Innovation Scoreboard, 2009.

Table 1.9. A Proposal for Innovation Policy Framework

1.	Research & Innovation governance and strategic intelligence for policy-making. • Development of long term vision, studies and strategies in the field of R&D and Innovation policies • Definition of regional targets priorities for public and private investments in R&D and Innovation • Implementation of R&D and innovation governance structures (including specific regulation) • Encouraging transnational cooperation in R&D and innovation.
2.	Research & innovation friendly environment, including regulatory framework, taxes and regional aid. • Grants to public sector R&D and Innovation Institutions • Grants supporting business R&D and Innovation including aid for researchers • Increase access to sources of finance for R&D and Innovation including tax incentives • Improving regulatory environment, administrative simplification and public procurement
3.	Technology and knowledge transfer to enterprises and development of innovation poles and clusters and cooperation between public research and industry • Developing public private partnerships for R&D and Innovation (Research Centres, Universities Business)

	• Promoting centres & networks of excellence, regional research driven clusters and innovation poles • Improving R&D cooperation and technology transfer • Strengthen innovation intermediaries
4.	Creation and growth of innovative enterprises • Funding facilities for innovative enterprises and start-ups including leveraging private funding • Supporting the promotion of innovation skills and the recruitment (identification) of innovators • Specific monitoring and R&D programmes aimed to innovative enterprises • Disseminating the importance of business innovation culture
5.	Intellectual property. • Improvement of Intellectual Property Right regimes • Supporting the Intellectual Property protection at public and private level • Commercialization and transfer of IPR • Promote the use of IPR for Start -ups
6.	Regional infrastructures for research and innovation. • Encouraging the R&D and Innovation system. • Promotion of R&D services for enterprises • Infrastructures for start -ups and innovative enterprises • Supporting infrastructures for R&D and Innovation (ICT, training…)
7.	Human resources in research and innovation. • Enhancing the mobility of researchers both at national and international level • Developing suitable conditions to attract researchers • Raising young people's interest in science, research and innovation • Cooperation between University and Enterprise (teaching and research)

Source: Juan Vicente Garcva Manjon (2010).

Regarding the collection of innovation data, there are two main approaches to collecting data about innovations:

(a) The "subject approach" survey starts from the innovative behaviour and activities of the firm as a whole. The idea is to explore the factors influencing the innovative behaviour of the firm (strategies, incentives and barriers to innovation) and the scope of various innovation activities, and above all to get some idea of the outputs and effects of innovation. These surveys are designed to be representative of each industry as a whole, so the results can be grossed up and comparisons can be made between industries.

(b) The other survey approach involves the collection of data about specific innovations (usually a "significant innovation" of some kind, or the main innovation of a firm) – the "object approach". This starts by identifying a list of successful innovations, often on the basis of experts' evaluations or new product announcements in trade journals. The suggested approach is to collect some descriptive, quantitative and qualitative data about the particular innovation at the same time as data is sought about the firm.

Table 1.10. Technology Achievement Index

Countries	Technology Achievement Index
Finland	0.93 % of GDP
Sweden	0.93 % of GDP
France	0.81 % of GDP
Germany	0.81 % of GDP
United States	0.77 % of GDP
Netherlands	0.74 % of GDP
Switzerland	0.73 % of GDP
Norway	0.72 % of GDP
Austria	0.71 % of GDP
Australia	0.71 % of GDP
Denmark	0.71 % of GDP
Japan	0.59 % of GDP
New Zealand	0.59 % of GDP
Italy	0.53 % of GDP
Canada	0.52 % of GDP
United Kingdom	0.52 % of GDP
Belgium	0.46 % of GDP
Ireland	0.31 % of GDP
Weighted average	0.7 % of GDP

Table 1.11. The Knowledge Economy Index (KEI)

Rank	Country	KEI	KI	Economic Incentive Regime	Innovation	Education	ICT
1	Denmark	9.52	9.49	9.61	9.49	9.78	9.21
2	Sweden	9.51	9.57	9.33	9.76	9.29	9.66
3	Finland	9.37	9.39	9.31	9.67	9.77	8.73
4	Netherlands	9.35	9.39	9.22	9.45	9.21	9.52
5	Norway	9.31	9.25	9.47	9.06	9.60	9.10
6	Canada	9.17	9.08	9.45	9.44	9.26	8.54
7	United Kingdom	9.10	9.06	9.24	9.24	8.49	9.45
8	Ireland	9.05	8.98	9.26	9.08	9.14	8.71
9	United States	9.02	9.02	9.04	9.47	8.74	8.83
10	Switzerland	9.01	9.09	8.79	9.90	7.68	9.68
11	Australia	8.97	9.08	8.66	8.88	9.69	8.67
12	Germany	8.96	8.92	9.06	8.94	8.36	9.47
13	Iceland	8.95	8.76	9.54	8.07	9.41	8.80
14	New Zealand	8.92	8.97	8.79	8.66	9.78	8.46
15	Austria	8.91	8.78	9.31	9.00	8.48	8.85
16	Belgium	8.80	8.77	8.87	8.93	9.14	8.25
17	Luxembourg	8.64	8.37	9.45	9.00	6.61	9.51

Rank	Country	KEI	KI	Economic Incentive Regime	Innovation	Education	ICT
18	Taiwan, China	8.45	8.79	7.42	9.27	7.97	9.13
19	Singapore	8.44	8.03	9.68	9.58	5.29	9.22
20	Japan	8.42	8.63	7.81	9.22	8.67	8.00
21	Estonia	8.42	8.31	8.76	7.56	8.32	9.05
22	France	8.40	8.64	7.67	8.66	9.02	8.26
23	Hong Kong, China	8.32	7.92	9.54	9.04	5.37	9.33
24	Spain	8.28	8.18	8.60	8.14	8.33	8.07
25	Slovenia	8.15	8.17	8.10	8.31	8.31	7.88
26	Israel	8.01	7.93	8.24	9.40	6.86	7.54
27	Hungary	8.00	7.88	8.35	8.21	7.73	7.70
28	Czech Republic	7.97	7.90	8.17	7.78	8.23	7.70
29	Korea, Rep.	7.82	8.43	6.00	8.60	8.09	8.60
30	Italy	7.79	8.18	6.62	8.00	7.96	8.59
31	Lithuania	7.77	7.70	7.98	6.70	8.40	7.99
32	Latvia	7.65	7.52	8.03	6.63	8.35	7.58
33	Portugal	7.61	7.34	8.42	7.41	6.95	7.66
34	Malta	7.58	7.18	8.78	7.95	5.86	7.74
35	Cyprus	7.50	7.47	7.60	7.81	6.65	7.95
36	Slovak Republic	7.47	7.37	7.78	6.89	7.26	7.95
37	Poland	7.41	7.38	7.48	7.03	8.02	7.09
38	Greece	7.39	7.58	6.82	7.57	8.21	6.94
39	Aruba	7.38	7.26	7.74	7.73	7.03	7.01
40	Croatia	7.28	7.28	7.26	7.67	6.56	7.62
41	Barbados	7.16	7.58	5.92	7.63	8.09	7.00
42	Chile	7.09	6.53	8.76	6.85	6.48	6.27
43	Bulgaria	6.99	6.94	7.14	6.43	7.65	6.74
44	Qatar	6.73	6.63	7.05	6.45	5.37	8.06
45	United Arab Emirates	6.73	6.72	6.75	6.69	4.90	8.59
46	Uruguay	6.49	6.54	6.35	5.37	7.79	6.45
47	Romania	6.43	6.25	6.98	5.74	6.47	6.55
48	Malaysia	6.07	6.06	6.11	6.82	4.21	7.14
49	Bahrain	6.04	5.80	6.75	4.29	5.82	7.30
50	Costa Rica	6.03	5.84	6.60	6.25	5.19	6.07
51	Ukraine	6.00	6.58	4.27	5.83	8.15	5.77
52	Kuwait	5.85	5.63	6.50	4.98	4.93	6.96
53	Serbia	5.74	6.32	4.01	6.15	5.83	6.99
54	Brazil	5.66	6.11	4.31	6.19	6.02	6.13
55	Dominica	5.65	5.47	6.19	3.67	6.40	6.34

Table 1.11. Continued

Rank	Country	KEI	KI	Economic Incentive Regime	Innovation	Education	ICT
56	Armenia	5.65	5.37	6.48	6.25	6.36	3.52
57	Trinidad and Tobago	5.59	5.49	5.88	6.10	4.43	5.95
58	Macedonia, FYR	5.58	5.66	5.34	4.67	5.42	6.88
59	Argentina	5.57	6.50	2.78	6.89	6.64	5.96
60	Russian Federation	5.55	6.82	1.76	6.88	7.19	6.38
61	Turkey	5.55	5.07	6.98	5.83	4.46	4.92
62	Jordan	5.54	5.39	5.99	5.59	5.62	4.95
63	Thailand	5.52	5.66	5.12	5.76	5.58	5.64
64	Mauritius	5.48	4.63	8.01	3.63	4.03	6.23
65	South Africa	5.38	5.33	5.55	6.85	4.68	4.45
66	Oman	5.36	4.77	7.15	4.94	4.47	4.90
67	Mexico	5.33	5.42	5.06	5.82	4.88	5.56
68	Saudi Arabia	5.31	5.10	5.94	3.97	4.89	6.43
69	Georgia	5.21	5.15	5.36	5.22	6.46	3.78
70	Panama	5.16	5.10	5.35	5.35	4.90	5.06
71	Moldova	5.07	5.30	4.38	4.79	6.05	5.08
72	Kazakhstan	5.05	5.17	4.70	3.68	7.07	4.76
73	Belarus	4.93	6.19	1.15	5.79	8.02	4.74
74	Jamaica	4.90	5.19	4.01	5.03	4.13	6.41
75	Colombia	4.84	5.02	4.27	4.48	5.09	5.50
76	Lebanon	4.81	4.93	4.42	4.53	4.92	5.35
77	Peru	4.79	4.88	4.49	3.87	5.61	5.16
78	Mongolia	4.72	4.67	4.86	3.21	6.43	4.37
79	Bosnia and Herzegovina	4.58	4.68	4.26	3.11	5.70	5.24
80	Guyana	4.57	4.97	3.34	4.78	5.94	4.21
81	China	4.47	4.66	3.90	5.44	4.20	4.33
82	Tunisia	4.42	4.54	4.04	4.65	4.08	4.88
83	Cuba	4.36	5.37	1.31	5.14	8.36	2.61
84	Kyrgyz Rep.	4.29	4.23	4.49	2.93	6.35	3.40
85	Namibia	4.28	3.37	7.01	3.14	2.65	4.34
86	Fiji	4.20	4.47	3.40	5.03	4.25	4.12
87	Venezuela, RB	4.18	5.41	0.48	5.46	5.33	5.46
88	Sri Lanka	4.17	4.04	4.56	4.13	5.00	2.98
89	Philippines	4.12	4.03	4.37	3.80	4.69	3.60
90	Egypt, Arab Rep.	4.08	4.24	3.59	4.44	4.35	3.92
91	El Salvador	4.06	3.74	5.02	3.29	3.37	4.56

92	Paraguay	4.00	4.15	3.56	3.90	4.25	4.29
93	Albania	3.96	3.92	4.09	2.82	4.97	3.96
94	Ecuador	3.90	4.55	1.94	4.00	4.52	5.12
95	Botswana	3.88	3.37	5.38	4.06	2.65	3.41
96	Dominican Republic	3.85	3.77	4.09	2.91	4.39	4.03
97	Azerbaijan	3.83	4.05	3.18	3.64	5.01	3.49
98	Iran, Islamic Rep.	3.75	4.67	0.99	4.56	3.80	5.65
99	Morocco	3.54	3.35	4.12	3.72	1.95	4.37
100	Vietnam	3.51	3.74	2.79	2.72	3.66	4.85
101	Bolivia	3.46	3.61	3.01	2.95	4.81	3.08
102	Cape Verde	3.35	3.01	4.37	2.16	3.03	3.85
103	Indonesia	3.29	3.17	3.66	3.19	3.59	2.72
104	Uzbekistan	3.25	3.95	1.13	3.35	6.15	2.35
105	Algeria	3.22	3.57	2.18	3.59	3.66	3.46
106	Tajikistan	3.22	3.33	2.88	2.01	5.53	2.46
107	Honduras	3.21	3.09	3.59	3.16	2.97	3.13
108	Syrian Arab Republic	3.09	3.57	1.65	3.17	3.10	4.43
109	India	3.09	2.95	3.50	4.15	2.21	2.49
110	Guatemala	2.89	2.69	3.50	2.01	2.75	3.31
111	Nicaragua	2.81	2.60	3.46	2.09	3.09	2.61
112	Swaziland	2.78	2.87	2.51	4.17	1.97	2.45
113	Kenya	2.77	2.69	2.99	3.83	1.83	2.41
114	Senegal	2.57	2.16	3.79	2.85	1.00	2.63
115	Ghana	2.46	1.97	3.93	2.02	1.78	2.12
116	Mauritania	2.36	1.94	3.64	2.24	0.89	2.68
117	Uganda	2.36	1.76	4.18	2.33	1.18	1.76
118	Pakistan	2.34	2.48	1.91	2.88	1.17	3.39
119	Zimbabwe	2.25	2.96	0.12	3.55	2.38	2.94
120	Madagascar	2.21	1.47	4.45	2.11	1.11	1.18
121	Yemen, Rep.	2.20	2.04	2.66	2.67	1.79	1.67
122	Tanzania	2.17	1.54	4.05	2.10	1.17	1.36
123	Zambia	2.12	1.85	2.92	2.02	1.69	1.84
124	Mali	2.06	1.37	4.16	1.79	0.83	1.48
125	Lesotho	2.05	1.89	2.54	2.76	1.76	1.15
126	Benin	2.05	1.78	2.87	2.73	1.01	1.59
127	Angola	2.00	2.11	1.69	3.62	0.79	1.91
128	Lao PDR	1.94	2.09	1.47	2.00	2.25	2.03
129	Nigeria	1.84	2.12	0.99	2.29	1.83	2.23
130	Sudan	1.78	2.22	0.48	1.86	1.28	3.52
131	Nepal	1.74	1.62	2.11	2.27	1.79	0.80
132	Burkina Faso	1.71	1.09	3.58	1.78	0.31	1.18
133	Cameroon	1.71	1.91	1.12	2.65	1.38	1.68

Table 1.11. Continued

Rank	Country	KEI	KI	Economic Incentive Regime	Innovation	Education	ICT
134	Malawi	1.69	1.19	3.17	2.00	0.92	0.67
135	Cote d'Ivoire	1.65	1.75	1.37	2.28	1.09	1.87
136	Mozambique	1.58	1.08	3.06	1.67	0.30	1.27
137	Cambodia	1.56	1.54	1.63	2.07	1.93	0.62
138	Bangladesh	1.48	1.55	1.28	1.60	1.53	1.53
139	Djibouti	1.47	1.30	1.99	1.68	0.88	1.32
140	Myanmar	1.34	1.69	0.31	1.30	3.06	0.70
141	Ethiopia	1.30	0.91	2.48	1.39	0.59	0.75
142	Eritrea	1.27	1.29	1.18	2.03	0.71	1.13
143	Rwanda	1.14	0.85	2.02	1.22	0.67	0.64
144	Guinea	1.07	1.22	0.62	1.51	1.09	1.05
145	Sierra Leone	0.96	0.87	1.22	1.47	0.58	0.55
146	Haiti	n/a	n/a	2.41	1.54	n/a	3.16
1	Western Europe	8.76	8.78	8.71	9.27	8.29	8.78
2	G7	8.72	8.91	8.15	9.19	8.75	8.80
3	Europe and Central Asia	6.45	6.69	5.71	6.99	6.62	6.46
4	East Asia and the Pacific	6.41	6.71	5.52	8.49	5.00	6.64
5	All Countries	5.95	6.19	5.21	8.11	4.24	6.22
6	Middle East and North Africa	5.47	5.68	4.86	7.57	3.75	5.71
7	Latin America	5.21	5.37	4.71	5.80	5.05	5.27
8	Africa	2.71	2.72	2.68	4.31	1.38	2.45
9	South Asia	2.58	2.55	2.65	3.29	1.92	2.45
1	High Income	8.23	8.30	8.02	9.02	7.47	8.42
2	Upper Middle Income	5.66	5.85	5.08	6.03	5.63	5.89
3	Lower Middle Income	3.78	4.04	3.01	4.96	3.32	3.85
4	Low Income	2.00	1.98	2.05	2.52	1.61	1.82

Note: By default, the table is sorted by the Knowledge Economy index (KEI) index. Countries may miss certain key variables - a pillar index is not calculated if more than one variable from the pillar is missing. Correspondingly, KEI/KI indexes are not calculated if any of the pillar indexes are missing.

Table 1.12. Indicators for the Regional Innovation Scoreboard

	Numerator	Denominator	Interpretation
Human Resources in Science and Technology – Core (% of population)	Number of persons who have successfully completed education at the third level in a S&T field of study and who are employed in S&T	Total population as defined in the European System of Accounts (ESA 1995)	Data on Human Resources in Science and Technology (HRST) can improve our understanding of both the demand for, and supply of, science and technology personnel
Participation in life-long learning per 100 population aged	Number of persons involved in life-long learning	Reference population is all age classes between 25 and 64 years inclusive	Individuals need to continually learn new ideas and skills or to participate in life-long learning.
Public R&D expenditures (% of GDP)	Difference between GERD (Gross domestic expenditure on R&D) and BERD (Business enterprise expenditure on R&D)	Gross domestic product as defined in the European System of Accounts	Trends in the R&D expenditure indicator provide key indications of the future competitiveness and wealth of the EU. Research and development spending is essential for improving production technologies and stimulating growth.
Business R&D expenditures (% of GDP)	All R&D expenditures in the business sector (BERD)	Gross domestic product as defined in the European System of Accounts (ESA 1995)	The indicator captures the formal creation of new knowledge within firms. It is particularly important in the science-based sector (pharmaceuticals, chemicals and some areas of electronics) where most new knowledge is created in or near R&D laboratories.
Employment in medium-high and high-tech manufacturing (% of total workforce)	Number of employed persons in the medium-high and high-tech manufacturing sectors	Total workforce includes all manufacturing and service sectors	An indicator of the manufacturing economy that is based on continual innovation through creative, inventive activity. A better indicator than using the share of manufacturing employment alone, since the latter will be affected by the hollowing out of manufacturing
Employment in high-tech services (% of total workforce)	Number of employed persons in the high-tech services sectors. (post and telecommunication, information technology including software development and R&D services	Total workforce includes all manufacturing and service sectors.	The high technology services provide services directly to consumers, such as telecommunications, and inputs to the innovative activities of other firms in all economy. It can increase productivity throughout the economy and support the diffusion of a range of innovations.
EPO patents per million population	Number of patents applied for at the European Patent Office (EPO), by year of filing.	Total population as defined in the European System of Accounts	The capacity of firms to develop new products will determine their competitive advantage. One indicator of the rate of new product innovation is the number of patents.

Source: 2006 European Regional Innovation Scoreboard, p.4.

The main expenditure aggregate used for international comparison is gross domestic expenditure on R&D (GERD), covering all expenditures for R&D performed on national territory in a given year. It thus includes domestically performed R&D, which is financed from abroad, but excludes R&D funds paid abroad, notably to international agencies. The corresponding personnel measure does not have a special name; it covers total personnel working on R&D (in FTE), on national territory, during a given year. International comparisons are sometimes restricted to researchers (or university graduates), because they are considered to be the true core of the R&D system.

There is a huge literature studying the effects of innovation activities. However, only a small part of it studies the effects of innovation activities to a regional level. One of the major problems with the measurement of innovation activities is the availability of dissaggregate data and the lack of information at a regional level (in particular, for the less advanced technological countries). OECD publishes data on ICT skills according to three categories of ICT competencies; ICT specialists, advanced users and basic users. Based on these three categories, OECD has developed two definitions of ICT skilled workers. ICT skilled workers according to the *narrow definition*, comprises the first category, ICT specialists, while the sum of all three categories make up the *broad definition*. ICT skilled workers according to the narrow definition are "ICT specialists, who have the ability to develop, operate and maintain ICT systems. ICTs constitute the main part of their job." (OECD (2004). *OECD Information Technology Outlook*. OECD, Paris).

The use of research and technological data imply a lot of problems with the collection and measurement. The problems of data quality and comparability are characteristic for the whole range of data on dynamic socio-economic activities. However, most of the research and technological indicators capture technological investment in small industries and in small firms only imperfectly. Usually, only manufacturing firms with more than 10,000 employees have established some research and technological laboratories, while industrial units with less than 1,000 employees usually do not have any particular research activities. Finally, the research and technological statistics concentrate mostly on the manufacturing sectors, while neglecting some service activities.

Table 1.13. Data Sources

	R&D	
Micro-level	**Public**	**Private**
Meso-level	• RD&D • Eurostat • NSF	• OECD –Eurostat • NSF • EU KLEMS
Macro-level	• NSF • OECD • Eurostat	• NSF • OECD • Eurostat • EU KLEMS

The collection of R&D data of regional statistics implies a lot of problems in comparison to data of national statistics. For the collection of regional statistics, we should take into account the local differences and difficulties. R&D units can operate in more than one regions and we should allocate these activities between regions. Usually, regional statistics focus on the three first levels of NUTS (Nomenclature of Territorial Units for Statistics). The reliability of R&D and innovation regional statistics is directly connected with and depends on estimation-methods and application of statistical techniques.

An additional promising database is currently established by the EU KLEMS project. This database intends to provide measures on various economic indicators, as for instance, growth, productivity, capital formation and technological change, to name just a few. These data aim at capturing productivity contributions of capital, labour, energy, materials and services for all member countries of the EU-25 for the time period since 1970. Table 1.13 summarizes the data availability for the coverage of R&D investments. Data availability differs between EU countries. Data availability is good for some countries and very poor for others, mostly for former Eastern bloc countries. This limits cross-country analyses. Europe also lacks a common standard of data gathering. This refers to the different methods of data collection in the countries and to the temporal as well as sectoral coverage of the relevant database.

Another important question about R&D and innovation regional statistics is the confidentiality and the collection-method of data-set that may be cover the whole or the majority of local-units. For statistical methods focused on a regional level, we can use either "local-units" (as for instance, enterprises, office, manufacturing etc.) or "local-economic-units" (NACE codes, which is a division of national codes of European member states).

Therefore, we can use the first method "top-to-the-bottom method" for the collection of aggregate R&D data (corresponds to the whole country) and, after that, for the distribution of these figures into a regional-level. The disadvantage of this method is that there is not a direct collection of data from the regions.

The second method "bottom-to-the-top method" for the collection of dissaggregate R&D data (for the whole regions) is based on the direct-collection at a regional-level and, after that, on the summation of these figures in order to obtain the aggregate-total R&D data (for the whole country). The advantage of this method is that there is a consistency in the summary of figures between regional and national level.

Data about European Patent Applications refers to those fields designated to European Patent Office (EPO); the data presented are based on a special extraction from the European Patent Office and, therefore, the figures of total national patent applications are somewhat different from the national totals presented by European Patent Office itself.

Major sources of these data come from the OECD, the United Nations and the E.U. and local authorities. Since 1965, the statistics divisions of the OECD and UNESCO have organised the systematic collection, publication and standardisation of research and technological data. We can collect and present data both for Business, Government and Private non-profit sectors. Table 1.14 illustrates some of the main type of variables in relation to the measurement of scientific and technological activities and the Titles and Sources from which they derived. However, R&D statistics is not enough. Within the context of the knowledge-based economy, it has become increasingly clear that such data need to be examined within a conceptual framework that relates them both to other types of resources and to the desired outcomes of given R&D activities. Similarly, R&D personnel data need to be viewed as part of a model for the training and use of scientific and technical personnel. R&D covers three activities:

- basic research,
- applied research and
- experimental development.

As OECD documents mentioned, the national surveys providing R&D data that are reasonably accurate and relevant to national users' needs may not be internationally comparable. This may simply be because national definitions or classifications deviate from international norms. The situation is more complex when the national situation does not correspond to the international norms.

Table 1.14. Type of Variables and Titles for the Measurement of Scientific and Technological Activities

Type of Main Variables	Titles and Sources
Research and Development (R&D)	Frascati Manual: "Standard Practice of Research and Experimental Development" and Frascati Manual Supplement: "Research and Development Statistics and Output Measurement in the Higher Education Sector".
Technology Balance of Payments	OECD: "Manual for the Measurement and Interpretation of Technology Balance of Payments Data"
Innovation	Oslo Manual: OECD Proposed Guidelines for Collecting and Interpreting Technological Innovation Data
Patents	OECD-Patent Manual: "Using Patent Data as Science and Technology Indicators"
Scientific and Technical Personnel	OECD-Canberrra Manual: "The Measurement of Human Resources Devoted to Science and Technology"
High Technology	OECD: "Revision of High Technology Sector and Product Classification"
Bibliometrics	OECD: "Bibliometric Indicators and Analysis of Research Systems, Methods and Examples" (Working Chapter – Yoshika Okibo).
Globalisation	OECD: "Manual of Economic Clobalisation Indicators"
Education Statistics	OECD: "OECD Manual for Comparative Education Statistics"
Education Classification	OECD: "Classifying Educational Programmes: Manual for Implementation in OECD countries"
Training Statistics	OECD: "Manual for Better Training Statistics: Conceptual Measurement and Survey Issues"

Source: OECD (2001c).

We can use these measures, in order to estimate to evaluate the effects on capacity, efficiency and growth. To measure *technological capacity*, *efficiency of the research and scientific structure*, and their effects on economic and regional growth it is necessary to use some of the above international indicators related to research, scientific and technological data. These indicators aim to evaluate innovation activities and technological infrastructure at a national level. In particular, the use of these indicators gives an overall view of *technological capabilities* and facilitates comparison between and within countries.

The *Business Enterprise Sector* includes all firms, organisations and institutions whose primary activity is the market production of goods or services (other than higher education) for sale to the general public at an economically significant price, and the private non-profit institutes mainly serving them. The core of the sector is made up of private enterprises (corporations or quasi-corporations) whether or they do not make profit. Among these enterprises these may be found some firms for which R&D is the main activity (commercial R&D institutes and laboratories). Any private enterprises producing higher education services should be included in the higher education sector. In addition, this sector includes public enterprises (public corporations and quasi-corporations owned by government units) mainly engaged in market production and sale of the kind of goods and services which are often produced by private enterprises, although, as a matter of policy, the price set for goods and services may be less than the full cost of production. This sector also includes non-profit institutions (NPIs) who are market producers of goods and services other than higher education.

The *Government Sector* consists of all departments, offices and other bodies furnished but normally do not sell to the community those common services, other than higher education, which cannot otherwise be conveniently and economically provided and administer the state and the economic and social policy of the community.

Public enterprises are included in the business enterprise sector, and NPIs controlled and mainly financed by government. Private non-profit sector includes both private or semi-public organisations and individuals and households. However, all enterprises serving government, those being financed and controlled by government, those offering higher education services or controlled by institutes of higher education should be excluded. Higher education comprises of all universities, colleges of technology and other institutes of post-secondary education. Finally, data from abroad includes all institutions and individuals located outside the political frontiers of a country, and all international organisations (except business enterprise) including facilities and operations within the frontiers of a country. Apart form the OECD and the U.N. research departments, there is another committee (the *Scientific and Technical Research Committee*) dealing with research and innovation statistics. The research and scientific indicators not only provide a view of the innovation and research structure of a given country but also indicate its *technological strength and capacity*.

Various research and technological indicators attempt to explain *technological relationships* at a specific point of time or for a whole period. The aim is to measure the nature, the capacity and the efficiency of scientific and technological activities both at a national level and at a sectoral level. High Technology products are defined as the sum of the following products: Aerospace, computers, office machinery, electronics, instruments, pharmaceuticals, electrical machinery and armament. The total exports for the EU do not include the intra-EU trade.

Technological indicators related to *output measures* are more meaningful than those related to *input measures* (such as the number of scientists and engineers which are involved in research activities or the number of research institutions), since the later say little about the achieved research.

Furthermore, we can classify four-groups using four different scientific criteria of UNESCO so to be able to measure and to evaluate the *technological efficiency and capabilities strength*. Table 1.15 illustrates the classification according to scientific and research criteria. The first criterion refers to *scientists and engineers engaged in research activities per million inhabitants (full-time equivalents)*. For instance, according to this criterion, we can classify Greece in the third group of the new industrialised countries (those which had established a research and scientific apparatus).

Table 1.15. Classification of Scientific and Research Capabilities

Groups of S&T capabilities	Countries
Group A:	Most underdeveloped countries (without S&T capabilities)
Group B:	Most developing countries (with some fundamental elements of S&T base)
Group C:	New & semi-industrialised countries (for instance, Greece, Israel Finland, Singapore, New Zealand and so on (with S&T base established)
Group D:	Industrialized countries: (advanced EEC states) with effective S&T base.

Source: UNESCO, "Science & technology in developing countries-strategies.

Using the second criterion of research and development personnel in higher education per thousand inhabitants (full-time equivalent), Greece belongs to the second group of the developing countries (the countries which had established some initial elements of innovation activities). The third criterion refers to the *third level students per 100,000 inhabitants*. According to this criterion, Greece belongs to the fourth group of industrialised countries (that is, the countries with an effective scientific and technological apparatus).

According to the fourth measure of the *percentage of manufacturing in GDP and the growth of manufacturing in the value added,* Greece is classified in the third group of the new industrialised countries (that is, those countries which had established a scientific apparatus). Finally, using the measure of *scientific and capabilities strength,* Greece belongs to the second group of developing countries (that is, those countries which have established some initial elements of research and technological apparatus).

Finally, with regard to *non-technological innovation,* it covers all those innovation activities which are excluded from technological innovation; that is it includes all innovation activities of firms which do not relate to the introduction of a technologically new or substantially changed good or service or to the use of a technologically new or substantially changed process. Major types of non-technological innovation are likely to be organisational and managerial innovations. Purely organisational aned managerial innovations are excluded from technological innovation surveys. These types of innovation will only be included in innovation surveys if they occur as part of some technological innovation project. The minimum set of data that need to be collected in an innovation survey is:

- the type of non-technological innovation;
- economic benefits flowing from a non-technological innovation activity;
- expenditures on non-technological innovation activity;
- the purpose of the non-technological innovation activity; and
- the source of ideas/information for the non-technological innovation activity.

1.4. SUMMARY CONCLUSIONS

As a driving force, innovation points firms towards ambitious long-term objectives. Innovation also leads to the renewal of industrial structures and is behind the emergence of new sectors of economic activity. In brief, innovation is:

- the renewal and enlargement of the range of products and services and the associated markets;
- establishment of new methods of production, supply and distribution;
- introduction of changes to management, work organisation, and working conditions and skills of the workforce.

To understand R&D activity and its role, one must examine it in terms of the organisations performing and funding R&D (institutional classification) and in terms of the nature of the R&D programs themselves (functional distribution). Various studies have shown that R&D activities are more and more a worldwide activity and that a bigger share of R&D is performed in co-operation with individual researchers, research teams and research units. Multinational enterprises play an increasing role as does R&D co-operation between university and other research units and enterprises, both formally, via organisations such as the European Union (EU) or the European Organisation for Nuclear Research (CERN), or informally, via multilateral and bilateral agreements. There is a clear need for more information on these trends.

Research, development and the use of new technologies - in a word, the technological factor - are key elements in innovation, but they are not the only ones. Incorporating them means that the firm must make an organisational effort by adapting its methods of production, management and distribution. Human resources are thus the essential factor. In this respect, initial and ongoing training plays a fundamental role in providing the basic skills required and in constantly adapting them. Many studies and analyses show that a better-educated, better-trained and better-informed workforce helps to strengthen innovation. The ability to involve the workforce to an increased extent, and from the outset, in technological changes and their implications for the organisation of production and work must be considered a deciding factor.

Innovation in work organisation and the exploitation of human resources, together with the capacity to anticipate techniques and trends in demand and the market, are frequently necessary preconditions for the success of the other forms of innovation. Innovation in processes increases the productivity of the factors of production by increasing production and/or lowering costs. It provides room for flexible pricing and increased product quality and reliability. Competition makes this quest for productivity an ongoing activity: successive improvements are a guarantee of not falling behind. Replacement of equipment is increasingly accompanied by changes to and improvements in methods, such as in organisation. Radical changes, which are rarer, completely transform the methods of production and sometimes pave the way for new products.

Innovation in terms of products (or services) makes for differentiation vis-à-vis competing products, thus reducing sensitivity to competition on costs or price. Improved quality and performance, better service, shorter response times, more suitable functionality and ergonomics, safety, reliability, etc., are all elements which can be strengthened by innovation and which make all the difference for demanding customers. Here again, progressive innovation is predominant. Radical innovation in products, for its part, opens up new markets. Properly protected and rapidly exploited, it confers for a certain time a decisive advantage for the innovator. In association with business start-ups (and the subsequent development of the businesses), it gives a country or a supranational group temporary domination of the growth markets, thereby ensuring a renewal of the economic fabric

Innovation is at the heart of the spirit of enterprise: practically all new firms are born from a development which is innovative, at least in comparison to its existing competitors on the market. If it is subsequently to survive and develop, however, firms must constantly innovate - even if only gradually. In this respect, technical advances are not themselves sufficient to ensure success. Innovation also means anticipating the needs of the market, offering additional quality or services, organising efficiently, mastering details and keeping costs under control.

Innovation and technology management techniques -such as the quality approach, participative management, value analysis, design, economic intelligence, just-in-time production, re-engineering, performance ratings etc.- give the firms concerned an undeniable competitive advantage.

This Chapter has attempted to identify the R&D activities and investigate estimation-methods, techniques of scientific and technological activities and measurement problems. According to 'International Standardization of Statistics on Science and Technology', we can estimate the most important inputs and outputs of scientific and technological activities and also the Scientific and Technical Education and Training and Scientific and Technological Services. The term of "Research and Development Statistics" covers a wide range of statistical series measuring the resources devoted to R&D stages, R&D activities and R&D results. It is important for science policy advisors to know who finances R&D and who performs it.

Series of R&D statistics are only a summary of quantitative reflection of very complex patterns of activities and institutions. In the case of international comparisons, the size aspirations and institutional arrangements of the countries concerned should be taken into consideration. One way of constructing reliable indicators for international comparisons is to compare R&D inputs with a corresponding economic series, for example, by taking GERD as a percentage of the Gross Domestic Product. However, its quite difficult to make detailed comparisons between R&D data and those of non-R&D series both because of the residual differences in methodology and because of defects in the non-R&D data.

UNESCO, OECD and EUROSTAT divisions organised the systematic collection, analysis publication and standardization of data concerning science and technological activities. The first experimental questionnaires were circulated to member states by UNESCO in 1966 and standardized periodical surveys were establised in 1969.

The collection of R&D data of regional statistics implied a lot of problems in comparison to data of national statistics. For the collection of regional statistics, we should take into the local differences and the difficulties. In addition, we can use either the "local-units" or the "local-economic-units". The first method "top-to-the-bottom method" focused on the collection of aggregate R&D data (for the whole country) and after that on the distribution of these figures into a regional-level; the disadvantage of this method is that there is not a direct collection of data from the regions or the second method "bottom-to-the-top method" for the collection dissaggregate R&D data (for the whole regions) based on the direct-collection at a regional-level and after that on the summation of these figures in order to obtain the aggregate-total R&D data (for the whole country).

Technological progress has become virtually synonymous with long- run economic growth. It raises a basic question about the capacity of both industrial and newly industrialized countries to translate their seemingly greater technological capacity into productivity and economic growth. Usually, there are difficulties with the estimation the relation between technical change and productivity. Technological change may have accelerated but, in some cases, there is a failure to capture the effects of recent technological advances in productivity growth or a failure to account for the quality changes of previously introduced technologies.

In literature, there are various explanations for the slow-down in productivity growth for OECD countries. One source of the slow-down may be substantial changes in the industrial composition of output, employment, capital accumulation and resource utilization. The second source of the slow-down in productivity growth may be that technological opportunities have declined; otherwise, new technologies have been developed but the application of new technologies to production has been less successful. Technological factors act in a long run way and should not be expected to explain medium run variations in the growth of GDP and productivity.

Chapter 2

MODELING INNOVATION ACTIVITIES

2.1. INTRODUCTION

Innovation activities contribute essentially to the regional dimension and growth. The technological infrastructure and innovation capabilities affect not only the regional growth but also the whole periphery and economy. In the last decades, OECD introduced some measures and indexes, concerning the Research and Development Expenditures, patents research personnel and technological balance flows, that measure mainly the innovation activities. However, there are a lot of problems and questions regarding the measurement of innovation activities at a regional level. This chapter attempts to analyze the whole framework of innovation statistics and in particular to examine the measurement and the statistical estimation of innovation activities. Within this context, it is also aiming to emphasize and review appropriate techniques, the most common methods and particular problems.

Technical change and innovation activities have an important role for growth and sustainable development. There is a huge literature for the role and economic impact of invention and innovation activities; many studies investigate the relationship between productivity, technical change, welfare, growth and regional development. Technology has two aspects, called "embodied" or "disembodied". The former is identified with "hardware" and consists of tools, machinery, equipment and vehicles, which together make up the category of capital goods. The other is identified with "software" and encompasses the knowledge and skills required for the use, maintenance, repairs, production, adaptation and innovation of capital goods. Local produced technologies may affect and determine the rate of regional growth. It is important to estimate the effects of technical change and innovation activities. However, how we can determine and measure innovation activities and technical change? This chapter attempts to analyze the framework of innovation statistics, to examine the major indexes and measures for innovation activities. The notion of a production function has been used for a long time. In the theoretical literature, in the first edition of his 1980 famous text *Principles of Economy*, Alfred Marshall emphasized theoretical relationships between production function and factor demands. However, empirical analysis has lagged considerably behind theoretical developments.

We can classify two categories of the concept of technology; first, there is the *neoclassical conception of technology* in the form of a production function and, secondly, there is what might be called as the *pythagorean concept of technology*, in terms of patent statistics, etc. The *pythagorean conception of technology* is based on contributions from fields as diverse as economics, history of science, sociology and theoretical physics (Merton 1935, May 1996, Moravcsik 1973, Schmookler 1966). Both the *neoclassical* and *pythagorean* viewpoints have been the subject of a huge literature. Technological knowledge indicates the manner in which resources can be combined to yield outputs of goods and services. Most countries have relied either on the *disembodied innovative capacity* (measured as a proxy of R&D intensity) or as the *technology embodied in investment* (measured as a proxy of capital formation per employee). Technological knowledge can be embedded in the designs of equipment and machinery, the skills or even in technical literature. Technical change can be considered as a change that affecting a set of existing techniques where the new knowledge affects the output (*disembodied technical change*) or a change that affect through the introduction of new techniques where the new techniques replace the old ones. On the other hand, in *disembodied technical change* the output that can be produced by any technical feasible factor combination is greater than before; thus given the input levels, the output is *augmented* and can be represented by an upward shift in the output surface. On the other hand, the *embodied technical change* implies an incremental improvements in the output yield; we can consider that the *embodied technical change* is a kind of *biased technical change*. The adoption of the new techniques may depend on the elasticities of factor supplies. If new inventions and techniques are embodied in new machinery, that implies new capital should be more productive than the older one.

This chapter attempts to review the theory to analyze the framework of more contemporary functional forms for innovation activities and technical change. We will begin with an historical overview of literature, notably with the famous Cobb-Douglas model and the constant elasticity of substitution (CES); we will them move to the more flexible forms of Generalised Leontief and translog function.

2.2. Economic Theory and Technical Change

Werner Sombart (1863-1941) deserves credit for being the first economist who analyzed the role of technology and technological change in long term economic development. For Sombart, both sources, for instance, the writings of Karl Marx and the literature on the history of technology were indispensable elements for his investigations into the role of technological change for the evolution of capitalism. Sombart (1916-Vol. I, pp 200ff) characterizes the technology of the crafts system as "empirical-organic". According to Sombart, technical skills are based on personal knowledge of the craftsman, of the artisan, who has been taught his art by an other master. Improvements are only made possible through practical experience. Knowledge is transferred from person to person through the apprenticeship system. Rules of secrecy prevent knowledge which is specific of a certain trade from becoming disclosed to wider circles of the population. Karl Marx assigned an important role to the development of new technologies as principal means of capitalist entrepreneurs to achieve extra profits, especially in the chapter on machinery and big industry in Das Kapital, Vol. 1.

Economic theory is relatively clear about the positive long-term consequences of the introduction of new technologies which lead to increased factor productivity. Despite this fairly straightforward neo-classical view, there are nonetheless concerns, especially for the short and medium term, that increased labour productivity associated with new technologies may reduce the demand for labour and thereby aggravate the already serious unemployment problem in the European area. It is argued, for instance, that the introduction of new technologies may lead to job destruction for some industries and some skill categories without creating sufficiently offsetting new job opportunities in others. There has been a considerable debate about the economic consequences of technological progress over the last decades. At the macro-economic level however, the expected positive impact of new technologies on trend factor productivity has not been easy to identify. On the contrary, as underlined by the often-quoted "Solow paradox", most economies experienced a slowdown in productivity growth in the aftermath of the first oil shock and the subsequent pick-up in the 1980s, 1990 and early 2000s is, at best, modest despite significant changes in information technologies. A trade-off between technical change and technological change emerges whether to change just the technique, in the existing map of isoquant or changing the technology and hence the shape of the isoquants. The trade-off will be tilted towards the introduction of technological changes when the access to knowledge is easy and conversely switching costs. Following the literature of economic theory the main forces of economic growth are:

- Capital accumulation including all new investment in physical equipment and human resources.
- Technological progress and
- Growth in human capital and labor force.

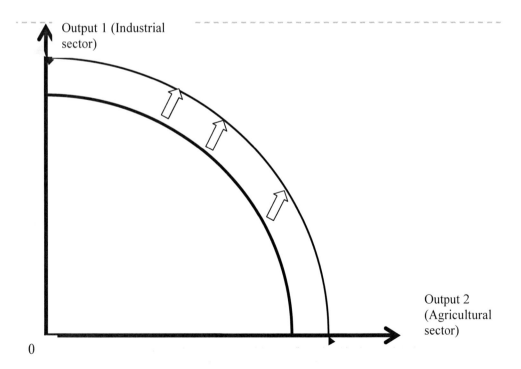

Figure 2.1. The Effect of Increases in Physical and Human Resources on the Production Possibility Frontier.

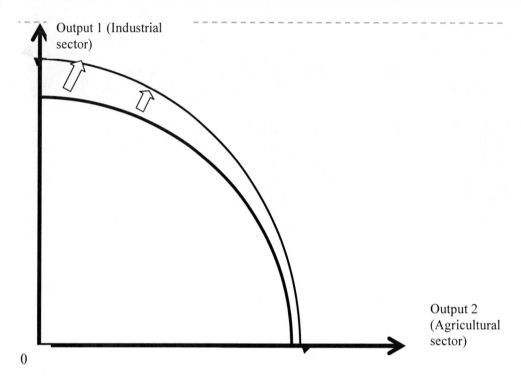

Figure 2.2. The Effect of Growth of Capital Stock on the Production Possibility Frontier.

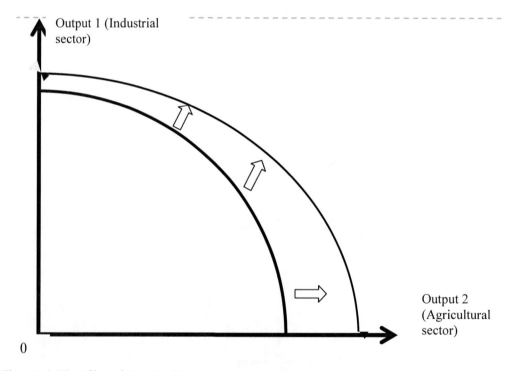

Figure 2.3. The Effect of Growth of Labor on the Production Possibility Frontier.

Let us assume the proportionate of all factors of production, and lets say, that only capital and land is increased in quality and quantity. Since normal conditions, both products will require the use of both factors as productive inputs, in different combinations, in order to shift the production possibility frontier. Figures 2.1-2.5 illustrate the effects of technological change on the production possibility frontier. Technological progress results to increase applications of new scientific knowledge in form of inventions and innovations with regard to capital, both physical and human. Such progress has been a major factor in stimulating the long-term economic growth of advanced countries. There are three basic classifications of technological progress (Todaro):

- The world's scientific Neutral technological progress shifts outwards the production possibility curve, where the double of total output is conceptually equivalent to a double of all productive inputs.
- Labor saving technological progress where the higher level of output can be achieved with the same quantity of labour inputs. . In other words, technological progress may be capital augmenting (or capital intensive) occurs when the quality of labor force or skills are upgraded.
- Capital saving (or labour intensive) technological progress where the higher level of output can be achieved with the same quantity of capital inputs Capital saving technological progress. is much rarer phenomenon. In other words, technological progress may be labor augmenting (or labour intensive) occurs when the capital and technological research aiming to save capital and not labor. In labor abundant countries, capital saving technological progress is what most needed.

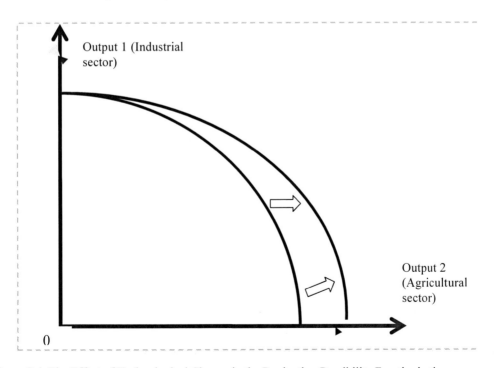

Figure 2.4. The Effect of Technological Change in the Production Possibility Frontier in the Agricultural Sector.

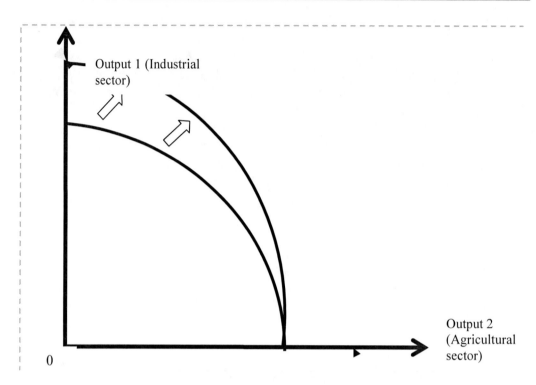

Figure 2.5. The Effect of Technological Change in the Production Possibility Frontier in the Industrial Sector.

Technology is generally represented graphically with the help of level curves or isoquants. Technological progress in this simple framework is a shift upwards of the production function, or shift downwards of the representative isoquant. An alternative way is to look at cost functions which relate levels of cost of production to level of output and to factor prices. In many cases, cost functions are easier to characterise production functions. Given input prices, we can view technological improvement as a downward shift of cost function. Technological change does not affect all factors equally. When it does, it is considered neutral technical change. Otherwise, it may have a specific factor using or factor saving bias.

Developed countries invested extensively in education and in the accumulation of substantial physical capital. The ratio of investment from relatively low levels to more than 30 percent in the 1980s. Figure 2.6 below illustrates the interaction of knowledge acquisition, investment and human capital. Initially, the economy is at the point A on production function f_0. As physical and human capital accumulation proceed, it moves to point E on the production function f_1. The shift to the higher production function is realised because of the growing utilisation of international best practice. However, the benefit from this accumulation of knowledge would have been less AB < DE, if capital per worker had not grown. Thus the size of the benefit from the growing import of knowledge and from local efforts to increase productivity depends on the stock of physical investment and skills complementing local unskilled labor (Nelson, 1973).

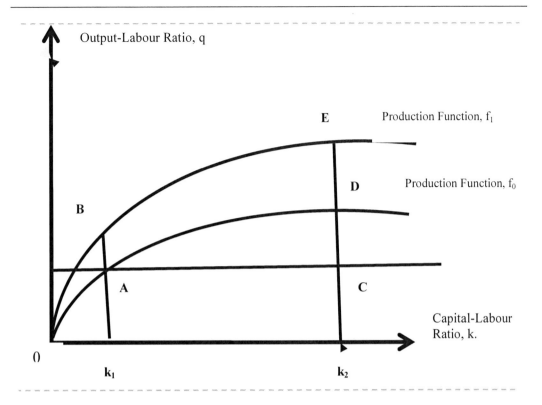

Figure 2.6. The Interaction of Knowledge Acquisition, Investment and Human Capital.

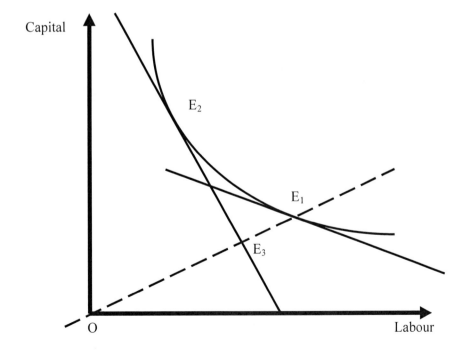

Figure 2.7. Trade-off Between Technical Change and Technological Change.

Because learning is the main source of new knowledge and learning is mainly local, and because of the irreversibility of production factors and lay-out, technological change is localized: for instance, induced by changes in factor and product markets that cannot be accommodated by technical changes in a given map of isoquants and the related price and quantity adjustments and based upon the local opportunities for learning and generating new knowledge (Antonelli 1999, 2001).

In Figure 2.7 we can see that a change in relative factor price affects the viability of previous equilibrium E_1. The firm can either change the technique and move to E_2 or change the technology by means of the introduction of technological innovations, so as to find a new equilibrium in the proximity of the isocline O E_1, in E_3 or (possibly) beyond. The outcome will depend upon the levels of switching costs, that is the amount of resources that are necessary to perform all the activities to move from E_1 to E_2, compared to the amount of resources that are necessary to innovate and move towards and beyond E_3. Typically new firms with lower levels of irreversible factors, that are able to produce in the new equilibrium point E_2.

2.3. THE GROWTH-ACCOUNTING

Growth accounting tries to explain changes in real product and total factor productivity based mainly on a comparison between the growth of inputs (capital and labour) and the growth of output. One part of actual growth cannot be explained and has been classified as 'unexplained total factor productivity growth' (or the so called residual). In particular, following the decomposition analysis by Solow (1957), many alternative factors can explain the path of economic growth. According to Solow's findings, technology has been responsible for 90 per cent of the increase in labour productivity in the twentieth century United States. The unexplained decline in productivity growth can thus be regarded as resulting from a collapse in technological activities. This may have happened because the availability of technological opportunities has been temporarily or permanently reduced.

The growth regressions approach (Bosworth and Collins, 2003) originates from the empirical literature on growth and convergence staring with the resurgence of the endogenous growth literature. This debate is related with the question of whether TFP convergence is taking place and under what conditions. One of the main controversies in the empirical growth literature is to identify how much of the convergence that we observe is due to convergence in technology versus convergence in capital – labour ratios, since convergence may be the result of three different mechanisms:

- Convergence due to capital accumulation;
- due to technology transfer and
- due to both.

Growth accounting methodology was theoretically motivated by Jorgenson and Griliches (1967) and put in a more general input-output framework by Jorgenson, Gollop and Fraumeni (1987) and Jorgenson, Ho and Stiroh (2003). Growth accounting allows one to assess the relative importance of labour, capital and intermediate inputs to growth, and to derive measures of multi-factor productivity (MFP) growth. MFP indicates the efficiency with which inputs are being used in the production process and is an important indicator of technological change. Under the assumptions of competitive factor markets, full input utilization and constant returns to scale, the growth of output in industry j can be expressed as the (compensation share) weighted growth of inputs and multifactor productivity (denoted by AY):

$$\Delta \ln Y_{jt} = \bar{v}_{jt}^{X} \Delta \ln X_{jt} + \bar{v}_{jt}^{K} \Delta \ln K_{jt} + \bar{v}_{jt}^{L} \Delta \ln L_{jt} + \Delta \ln A_{jt}^{Y},$$

where v_i denotes the two-period average share of input i in nominal output and $vL + vK + vX = 1$. Each element on the right-hand side indicates the proportion of output growth accounted for by growth in intermediate inputs, capital services, labour services and MFP, respectively.

Growth accounting is looking at the same equation growth in output is attributed to labour, capital, intermediate inputs and residual changes in MFP. The theoretical framework for the growth-accounting approach is rooted in the economic theory of production. The standard model is based on the seminal work by Tinbergen (1942) and Solow (1957) and its development, in particular by Zvi Griliches, Dale Jorgenson, and Erwin Diewert. The standard growth-accounting model is based on the microeconomic theory of production and relies on a number of the followings assumptions.

- Production processes can be represented by production or transformation functions at various levels of the economy. Production functions relate maximum producible output to sets of available inputs.
- Producers behave efficiently, *i.e.* they minimise costs and/or maximise revenues.
- Markets are competitive, and market participants are price-takers who can only adjust quantities but not individually act on market prices.
- There exists a production technology that can be represented by a production function, relating gross output, Q, to primary inputs labour L and capital services K as well as intermediate inputs such as material, services or energy (M).
- The production function exhibits constant returns to scale.
- Neither labor nor capital inputs are necessarily homogenous. There are N different types (qualities) of labor, $L_1, L_2, \ldots L_N$, M different types of capital services, $K_1, K_2, \ldots K_M$, and R different types of intermediate inputs $M_1, M_2, \ldots M_R$:
  $Q = f(L_1, L_2, \ldots L_N, K_1, K_2, \ldots K_M, M_1, M_2, \ldots M_R, t)$
- Productivity changes are of a Hicks-neutral type, *i.e.* they correspond to an outward shift of the production function, captured by a parameter A:
  $Q = A f(L_1, L_2, \ldots L_N, K_1, K_2, \ldots K_M, M_1, M_2, \ldots M_R)$
- Factor input markets are competitive and for any desired level of output, the firm minimises the costs of inputs, subject to the production technology.
- Labour and intermediate inputs can be hired at any moment at the market rates $w_i =$ for labour and p_m for intermediate inputs.
- Provision of capital services requires investment in the different types of capital and there are no adjustment costs associated with investment.

Growth accounting and most other approaches to measuring productivity are firmly rooted in a standard neo-classical equilibrium concept. Equilibrium conditions are very important because they help to guide measurement of parameters that would otherwise be difficult to identify. Although its usefulness is generally recognised, it has been argued that an equilibrium approach sits uneasily with the notion of innovation and productivity growth. Evolutionary economists (*e.g.* Dosi, 1988; Nelson and Winter, 1982; Nelson, 1981), in the tradition of Schumpeter, argue that innovation and technical change occur as a consequence of information asymmetries and market imperfections. Indeed, such asymmetries can scarcely be termed market imperfections when they are necessary conditions for any technical change to occur in a market economy (Metcalfe, 1996). The point made by evolutionary economists is that equilibrium concepts may be the wrong tools to approach the measurement of productivity change, because if there truly was equilibrium, there would be no incentive to search, research and innovate, and there would be no productivity growth

2.4. New Growth Debate

Solow (1994) writes "I think that the real value of endogenous growth theory will emerge from its attempt to model the endogenous component of technological progress as in integral part of the theory of economic growth. Here the pioneer was Romer (1990). Many others have followed his lead: my short list includes Grossman and Helpman (1991), Aghion and Howitt (1992), Stokey (1992) and Young (1991), (1993), but there are others."

Solow (1956) expanded the work by John Stuart Mill and developed *neoclassical growth models*. *Neoclassical growth theory* as developed by Solow and his followers dominated over the literature of *long term or trend movements* in per capita income for more than three decades. The starting *neoclassical growth models* of Solow are important studies for economic growth and convergence. In these models, the rate of exogenous technical progress is the key parameter determining the steady state growth rate of per capita income. Since Solow 1956, technological change is regarded as one of the main sources of economic growth. According to the neoclassical models based on the assumptions of marginal productivity, technological change (or labour growth) is needed to compensate for the negative productivity effects of capital accumulation.

The recent debate about the determinants of output growth has concentrated mainly on the role of knowledge, typically produced by a specific sector of the economy. This approach considers the economy in a three sector framework (Romer 1990a, 1990b), where the R & D sector produces knowledge to be used as an input by firms producing capital goods. Output growth rate is indigenously determined by the allocation of human capital in research and manufacturing sectors and is not affected by other crucial variable such as the unit cost of production of new capital goods.

Schumpeter and Schmooker supported that productivity growth is related to an economy's structure and policies; from one hand, they tried to explain the links between industrial innovation and economic growth, while from the other hand, they also tried to explain the market conditions and innovation rates. Many of the early models treated technological progress as an exogenous process driven by time.

Technological progress has often been treated as an exogenous process in the long-run economic analysis. This treatment would be appropriate for studying the growth of industrial economies, if advances in industrial know-how are followed automatically by fundamental scientific discoveries and if basic research is guided mostly by non-market forces. This would seem an appropriate assumption if advanced technical knowledge stems largely from activities that take place outside of the economic sector. The view that innovation is driven by basic research, which is implicit in the models with exogenous technology, was made explicit by Shell (1967). He introduced a public research sector that contributes technical knowledge to profit-entities in the Solow economy. Arrow viewed technological progress as an outgrowth of activities in the economic realm. Romer (1986) discussed the possibility that learning-by-doing might be a source of sustained growth, maintained this treatment of technological progress as wholly the outgrowth of an external economy. Romer (1987b) has described a competitive equilibrium where ongoing growth in per capita income is sustained by endogenous technological progress. Many others have followed his lead, such as, Grossman and Helpman (1991a), Aghion and Howitt (1992), Stokey (1995) and Young (1993), (1998).

However, recent work by Harrigan (1995) shows that there are systematic differences across countries in industry outputs that cannot be explained by differences in factor endowments. While there are many possible explanations for this result, such an explanation is that technology is not the same across countries. This is a hypothesis which has gained greater attention from international economists recently, including Trefler (1993, 1995), Dollar and Wolff (1993) and Harrigan (1997a). If technology is not the same across countries, then much of the theoretical work in neoclassical trade theory is irrelevant to applied research on cross-country comparisons, and much applied research that assumes identical technology (for example, many applied general equilibrium models and factor endowment regressions) is misspecified.

In general, this Chapter is a brief overview of theoretical foundations of models with endogenous technical change. In particular, in this Chapter we attempt to analyse two types of technological change: the first type *generates new technologies,* while the second type *generates quality improvements.*

2.5. A THEORETICAL APPROACH TO ENDOGENOUS THEORY

The concept of endogenous technological change has resulted in the so-called "new growth theory". Embodies technical change refers to the improvements in the design or quality of new capital goods or intermediate inputs. Disembodied technical change is not incorporated in a specific factor of production. (Rennings Klaus and Sebastian Voigt 2008). The literature of endogenous growth provide us with better insights in the causes and effects of technological change as a determinant of economic growth. We can distinguish two different types of technological change. On the other hand, an increase in the number of technologies (the embodied technological change or, otherwise, the product-innovation); and on the other hand a quality improvement of existing technologies (the disembodied technological change or otherwise the process-innovation). In order to present the different approaches of endogenous technical change which can be found in the literature, we will essentially follow the exposition scheme proposed by Barro and Sala-i-Martin (1995) in distinguishing three main models of endogenous growth motivated by endogenous technological change: models based on expanding product variety; Shumpeterian models based on improvements in the quality of products;, and models based on human capital accumulation. Taking an exogenous rate of technological change and keeping it constant over a long-period of time might neglects the fact that new technologies depend on R&D expenditures, investment decisions and economic policy.

Schumpeter and Schmooker supported that productivity growth is related to an economy's structure and policies. On the other hand, they tried to explain the links between industrial innovation and economic growth, while, on the other hand, they tried to explain the market conditions and innovation rates too.

2.5.1. New Technologies and Product Innovations

The seminal works on endogenous growth theory of Romer (1990a), Grossman and Helpman (1991a), Young (1993) consider innovations as means of expanding the variety of available goods. These models treat R&D activity like other production activities, which converts primary inputs, as capital and labour, into knowledge. Young (1993) adds another dimension to the research process: she stressed the importance of learning-by-doing before the adoption of any innovation.

Let us adopt the presentation of the encompassing model by Romer (1996), or by Aghion & Howitt (1998), in order to emphasise the main features of such theoretical explanations of growth through an endogenous technological change. Two sectors are considered: the first one produces the "final good", and the second is the "Research and Development" sector whose activity aims to increase the level of technology.

For instance, the speed of elevation of the technological level depends on both the aggregate amount of research the number of researchers involved, and the current level of technology. The total amount of knowledge in the economy, an indicator of human capital or, in Romer's model, as the number of new intermediate products or designs.

In the simplest case where there is no accumulation of capital (and no capital in the production functions), one shows that the growth rate of economy is equal to the growth rate of the level of technology A_t, denoted g_A, which satisfies the following equation: $g_A^* = (\gamma n + (\theta - 1) g_A) g_A$

- if $\theta \leq 1$ that is if the technological progress is less than proportional to the existent level of technology, the economy grows increasingly then decreasingly until a steady state when its growth rate is reached: the output per capita can't grow without population growth, and, surprisingly, this rate of technological progress is independent from the quantity of labour involved in R&D activities.
- if $\theta \geq 1$, the growth rate of knowledge and, subsequently the growth rate of the output per capita always increases.

Assuming that H represents the human capital, K is physical capital and A is the existing level of technology. Human capital can be used both for the production of the final goods Y and the generation of new technologies, which use the human capital and the stock of knowledge. Therefore, the equation for the generation of technology can be written as follows:

$$\frac{dA}{dt} = \delta v H A,$$

where: v is the fraction of total-stock of human capital devoted to R&D and δ is a productivity-parameter.

Research sector is human-capital intensive and technology- intensive, while physical capital K does not enter the technology-equation; it is used in the production of final goods only: $Y = [(1-v)H]^\alpha \sum_{i=1}^{A}(x_i)^{1-\alpha}$, where x_i represents the amount of capital of type i.

In this context, growth is driven by technological change that results from the research and development activities of profit-maximising firms. An important implication of this mechanism is that the government policies and, especially, subsidies to R&D may influence the long-run rate of economic growth. However, Jones emphasises the growth rate of the economy should be proportional to the number of researchers - which is not confirmed by statistical observation. He assumes that the absolute productivity of innovators remains constant, unsensitive to past innovation, and this assumption results in the fact that, as technology advances, an increasing quantity of resources have to be devoted to innovative activity to sustain a given growth rate. The growth rate in this model depends only on parameters which are usually taken as exogenous and is independent of policy changes like subsidies to R&D or to capital accumulation; growth is only "semi-endogenous".

At the same direction, Young (1998) proposes a model of endogenous innovation in which a rise in the profitability of innovative activities could lead to an increased variety of technologies which consequently will increase the level of utility of the representative consumer and a rise in the scale of the market could raise the equilibrium quantity of R&D without increasing the economy's growth rate.

2.5.2. Existing Technologies and Process Innovations

Aghion & Howitt (1992) built an endogenous growth model involving creative destruction, in the Schumpeterian tradition (Schumpeter (1934)), very close to the model by Grossman & Helpman (1991a). There are three sectors in the economy: producing respectively the intermediate good, the final good and research. Technical progress appears as a rise of the productivity of the intermediate good in the production of the final good, because each innovation produced by the research sector improves the quality of the intermediate good.

This model can easily be presented in a simple way. Let the current level of aggregate productivity be denoted by A, the amount of intermediate product by x, the production function of the final good y is given by:

$$y = AF(x) \quad \text{where} \quad F' \geq 0, F'' \leq 0$$

The productivity in the final good sector is increased by each innovation, by a factor y, so that after t innovations:

$$A_t = A_0 y^t$$

This model takes into consideration the inherent uncertainties associated with scientific and industrial research: technological advances are essentially stochastic. The arrival of an innovation is here uncertain, its probability of arrival being characterized by a Poisson process depending positively on the number of researchers: the time interval between two innovations is a random variable. The endogenous number of researchers depends negatively on interest rate, positively on the size of the innovation and the size of the qualified labour population. This kind of endogenous growth model embodies two kinds of externalities: a positive intertemporal externality, because a given innovation raises productivity not only in the present period, but also in the following periods, and a negative externalilty, because each new innovation makes the previous one obsolete.

Technological change can be modelled as an increase in the quality of a fixed number of already existing technologies. We can rewrite the production function, according to the lines used by Barro and Sala-i-Martin (1995) as follows: $Y = [(1-v)H]^\alpha \sum_{i=1}^{A}(qx_i)^{1-\alpha}$, where the number of technologies A is regarded as fixed. The increase in the quality q increases the total efficiency of capital-goods x_i and therefore increases the total output Y. The engine of growth is no-longer the increase in the number of technologies, but the increase in the quality of existing technologies. The relevant technology generation equation is now:

$$\frac{dq}{dt} = \delta v H q,$$

We are assuming that only human-capital is needed to improve the quality of existing technologies. Human capital is a scale-variable in the sense that an exogenous increase in the stock of human capital increases the growth rate of quality improvements.

2.5.3. Human Capital

By "human-capital" we mean a set of specialised skills that agents can acquire by devoting time to an activity which called "schooling": the more time that an individual spends in school, the greater is the measure of human capital that the individual acquires. A variety of approaches to training and education process could be combined with the underlying models of technological change.

The accumulation of human capital h by an individual is specified by a "production function of human capital" (which embodies an intertemporal externality, but not an interindividual one), where u is the fraction of time spent by him on the production of final good, and thus (1-u) is the fraction of time spent on the acquisition of knowledge or skills:

$$h' = \delta(1-u)h$$

The production function of the final good combines physical capital K, specific human capital h and average level of human capital h_a (representing here an interindividual positive externality: the higher is the average level of knowledge, the more efficient is any individual); all agents being assumed identical, $h_a = h$:

$$Q = AK^\beta(uh)^{1-b}h = AK^\beta(uh)^{1-\beta}h^\gamma$$

The optimal rates of growth of human capital (g_h^*) and production (g^*) are respectively:

Cross-country regressions enlight the special role that human capital plays in growth process (Mankiw *et al.* (1992), for example). Human capital is defined as the sum of the abilities specific to individuals; it is often seen as the accumulation of effort devoted to schooling and training that is, as an accumulable factor in some models, the engine of growth. Lucas (1988) proposed the first endogenous growth model based on human capital, which will be here quickly presented (following Amable, 1994). In Romer's model (1990), the steady state growth rates of A, K and Y were equal. This means that since $Y = \alpha A + (1-\alpha)K$, the marginal rate of productivity (MGP) of human capital equals:

Table 2.1. Some Insights and Characteristics of Endogenous Growth Rate

References-Models:	Type of Innovation Process	Factors influencing positively the growth rate	Factors influencing negatively the growth rate
Romer (1986)	Process Innovation through knowledge accumulation	Accumulation of knowledge	Discount-rate
Lucas (1988)	Process Innovation through capital accumulation	Effectiveness of investment in human capital	Elasticity of substitution: discount-rate
Romer (1990)	Process Innovation through addition of new intermediate-goods	Efficiency in the research sector	Elasticity of substitution: discount-rate
Grossman and Helpman (1991)	Process Innovation Through improvements in quality of consumer-good	Size of innovation and efficiency of research	Discount-rate
Aghion and Howitt (1992)	Process Innovation through stochastic improvements for intermediate-goods.	Size of innovation and efficiency of research	Interest-rate

Source: Korres (2003).

$$MGP = \frac{\partial Y}{\partial (vH)} = \frac{\partial A}{\partial (vH)} = \delta,$$

where vH corresponds to the amount of human-capital allocated to the production of new technologies.

Following the framework in which technological change is generated by improving existing technologies, it follows that: Y=(1-α)q+(1-α)K, the marginal rate of productivity of human capital equals:

$$MGP = \frac{\partial Y}{\partial (vH)} = \left(\frac{1-\alpha}{\alpha}\right)\frac{\partial q}{\partial (vH)} = \left(\frac{1-\alpha}{\alpha}\right)\delta = \delta',$$

where vH corresponds to the amount of human-capital allocated to the generation of better-quality. The factor of $\left(\frac{1-\alpha}{\alpha}\right)$ appears because of the different way of quality improvement and the amount of new technologies influence the production-process.

Table 2.1 illustrates the characteristics of the main previously reviewed models, in a way which emphasise the main features to keep in any future empirical modelling work.

R&D expenditures are often used as an indicator of the technological change, but most studies are limited to the link between productivity and R&D engaged in the sector itself, but they are not R&D used by the sector, while being engaged by other productive sectors. The efforts of research and development is often only caught by the amount of expenditures involved, but patents data would be more appropriate to capture the efficiency of R&D process. The productive potential of the research process has thus decreased ratio patents / R&D become lower, but the link between innovation and factor productivity remains strong.

In most empirical works, an accumulated stock of R&D is included in the production function as an additional input. This R&D stock stands for a measure of the current level of knowledge: it ought to proxy for the number of varieties of intermediate products in Romer's model or for the aggregate quality index of goods in Aghion & Howitt's model (Barro & Sala-i-Martin (1995)). It should be considered that technological externalities between different productive sectors: empirical studies stress the importance of inter-industrial externalities for explaining the growth of productivity growth.

2.5.4. Productivity, R and D and Environment

Most literature on environmental policy and economic growth (Jorgenson & Wilcoxen (1990), for example) assumes that technological progress is exogenous and, thus, is not affected by environmental policy. Hence, Bovenberg & Smulders (1996) argue that the experience of industrial countries shows that active environmental policies -such as taxes or introduction of pollution permits- induce major technological advances in new technologies, and that environmental quality enhances the productivity of inputs into production by providing non-extractive services. In the computable general equilibrium model by Jorgenson and Wilcoxen (1990), the technical progress is not exactly endogenous; it is rather modelled in an interesting way which we should mention here: introducing standard exponential temporal biases of technical progress in a macroeconomic model would necessarily lead in the long term the saved inputs to "vanish", which can be avoided by modelling the temporal bias with a logistic trend.

2.5.5. Education and Growth

It is well known that human capital is important for development and for individual earnings in particular. In a recent extensive robustness analysis by Sala-i-Martin et al. (2004), primary schooling turns out to be the second most robust factor influencing growth in GDP per capita out of sixty-seven explanatory variables in growth regressions on a sample of eighty-eight countries 1960–96. Macro studies indicate that the rate of return to schooling across countries is on average about ten percent. Returns appear higher for low income countries, at lower levels of schooling and for women (Psacharopoulos and Patrinos 2004).

Similarly, human capital influences occupational choice and performance patterns within occupations. There is a huge literature with respect to the relationship between education on entry into and performance in entrepreneurship in developed countries. However, the relationship between schooling and performance is unambiguously positive. In developing countries an additional year of schooling raises enterprise profits by 5.5% which is lower than the impact of an additional year of education on wage income and lower than the effect in developed countries, estimated to 6.1%. Universities and research institutes have a large impact on technological performance. It is well known that the quality of labour force is enhanced by investment in human capital (training and education). For many future employees the educational institutes can provide a first contact with the new techniques that they will employ in the workplace. In addition, educational bodies and research institutions can often play an important role in building up a core of expertise for a new industry before the industry becomes commercially viable. An important question is to examine not only the availability of human resources, but also the way in which these resources are used.

The importance of educational policy and human capital for economic growth has been emphasized by economic literature. Much of the recent work on economic growth can be viewed as refining the basic economic insights of classical economists. The recent debate on the determinants of output growth has concentrated mainly on the role of knowledge typically produced by a specific sector of the economy, and furthermore in the role of human capital and the implications on economic growth. Investment in education largely depends on three elements:

- The institutional framework of the education system;
- The expected private rate of return on investing in education; and
- Financing options available to education.

The growing importance of human capital for innovation at the frontier is illustrated by the results of the following regression:

- 80 countries, 1960-2000
  - Output, investment data: Penn World Tables 6.1 (2002)
  - Human capital data: Barro-Lee (2000)

$$g_t = a_0 + a_1 d_{t-1} + a_2 u_t + a_3 s_t + a_4 u_t d_{t-1} + a_5 s_t d_{t-1} + \varepsilon_t$$

where g: productivity, either total factor productivity (TFP) or labour productivity, growth over 5 years
  d: distance to productivity frontier
  u: share of population primary/secondary education
  s: share of population with higher education

	TFP	TFP Labour Productivity
d_{t-1}	0.140 (0.55)	0.372 (1.24)
u_t	0.306 (3.89)*	0.634 (4.34)*
s_t	-0.0592 (-1.53)	-0.251 (-2.58)
$s_t^* d_{t-1}$	0.143 (2.1)*	0.404 (3.02)*
$u_t^* d_{t-1}$	-0.15 (-0.89)	-0.432 (-2.0)
Constant	0.638 (6.31)*	0.33 (1.93)

(t statistic in parentheses); *indicates the coefficient is significant at 5%

For both total factor productivity and labour productivity, the regression of the interaction between distance to the technological frontier and skilled labour is positive and significant. This demonstrates the importance of higher education for growth (Aghion et al., 2003)

According to the UNESCO study for education determinant factors, Table 2.2 summaries and illustrates the main determinant demand and supply factors. The various factors which affect education can be grouped in the following main categories:

- On the *demand side* socio-economic and cultural factors which affect the behaviour and the choices of parents and students;
- On the *supply side* political and institutional factors and factors linked to the school.

2.6. MODELING INNOVATION ACTIVITIES AND TECHNICAL CHANGE

There is a huge literature suggesting and demonstrating that research and scientific indicators make an important contribution to the growth at the firm, industry and national levels. Most studies have investigated the relation between productivity, employment, growth and R&D.

Table 2.2. Demand and Supply Factors

Socio-Economic Factors	Political and Institutional factors	Cultural Factors	Factors linked to education
• Poverty • Direct costs (fees, uniforms, transportation) • High opportunity costs and lower rate of return • Limited employment opportunities or graduates • Lower remuneration for graduates	• Budget constraints • Insufficient public support for education • Political instability • Inconsistent educational policies • Poor quality of education programmes • Lack of clear strategy for education. • Lack of public support for education activities.	• Parents' low level of education • Lower priority for education • Sceptical attitudes towards the benefits and outcomes from educating persons	• Low proportion of teachers • Teachers untrained • Stereotypes at school (curricula, textbooks) • School curricula in conflict with traditional culture • Lack of accommodations • Distance from school • Poor quality of hygienic facilities

Source: Unesco

2.6.1. Input-Output Analysis and Technological Change

The structural decomposition analysis can be defined as a method of characterizing major shifts within an economy by means of comparative static changes. The basic methodology has introduced by Leontief (1953) for the structure of the US economy and has been extended in several ways. Carter (1960) has incorporated some dynamic elements with a formal consideration of the role of investment in embodied technical change. Chenery, Syrquin and others (1963) has added elements of trade into this framework.

Growth decomposition analysis uses input-output techniques, because they capture the flows of goods and services between different industries. Input-output methods exploit the inter-linkages effects and search for the components of growth. In addition, input-output techniques allow us to calculate the contribution of *technical change* to output growth. The principal argument of the method of inter-industry analysis is to show explicitly the interdependence of growth rates in different sectors of the economy. Usually, two different compositional indicators are used to analyse the extent of structural change, the annual growth rate of real output in each industry and the share of national real output accounted for each industry.

Input-output tables are available both in current and constant prices. Following Kubo et al. (1986), we can consider the *basic material balance condition* for the gross output of a sector as given by:

$$X_i = W_i + F_i + E_i - M_i \text{ (material balance equation)},$$

where X_i=the gross output,
  W_i=the intermediate demand for the output of sector i by sector j,
  F_i=the domestic final demand for the output of sector i,
  E_i=the export demand, and
  M_i=the total imports classified in sector i.

The gross output of sector i is the sum of output to intermediate demand plus the domestic final demand plus the exports less the imports. In the matrix notation the *material balance condition* becomes:

$$X=AX+F+E-M=(I-A)^{-1}(F+E-M),$$

where $(I-A)^{-1}$, the inverse of the coefficients matrix, captures the indirect as well as the direct flows of intermediate goods.

Holding one part of the material balance equation constant and varying the other components over time, the change in an industry's output can be decomposed into the following factors:

- technical change (corresponding to changes in the inverted I-A matrix);
- changes in final demand;
- changes in the structure of exports; and
- changes in the structure of imports.

At an aggregate level, this equation provides a comprehensive picture of structural change for each country. It does not explain why the structure of an economy changes, but it describes how it comes about and measures the relative importance each factor in each industry's growth. Growth effects are analyzed in order to reveal how much output in each industry would have changed with the same growth rate for each element in the final demand category. When growth rates differ between the final demand categories, the resulting growth rates for the industrial output will also vary.

Positive or negative effects of structural change affect final demand categories. Technological change plays an important role for the expansion and decline of sectors. Technology intensity and real growth rates of output can be used to classify individual industries into different performance groups. These groups can then be used to describe the patterns of structural change and to make comparisons among various countries.

The effects of technical change are analysed in order to find out how much the use of primary inputs has changed, due to changes in the endogenous factors of the model. Furthermore, the effects of technical change on industrial output are analysed in order to reveal how much output in each industry has changed, because input-output coefficients have altered.

A way of measuring changes in input-output coefficients is to compute the weighted average changes in input-output coefficients of various sectors and to compare matrices at two different points of time. For instance, we can use the following formula to compute the weighted indexes:

$$T_j = \frac{1}{\frac{1}{2}\Sigma(X_{ij}^2 + X_{ij}^1)} \Sigma\left[\frac{(A_{ij}^2 - A_{ij}^1)}{(A_{ij}^2 + A_{ij}^1)}(X_{ij}^2 + X_{ij}^1)\right]$$

here A^2_{ij} is the elements of matrix of input-output coefficients for the second period,
A^1_{ij} is the elements of matrix of input-output coefficients for the first period,
X^2_{ij} is the matrix of interindustry transactions for second period at constant 1975 prices,
X^1_{ij} is the matrix of interindustry transactions for first period at constant 1975 prices.

This index measures the overall input changes in each of the n production sectors due to technological changes, changes in the prices, and product mix (the so called *Rasmussen index of structural change*). The total change in sectoral output can be decomposed into sources by category of demand. The total change in output equals the sum of the changes in each sector and can also be decomposed either by sector or by category of demand. The relations, (with the two intermediate terms combined), can be shown as following:

$$DD_1 + EE_1 + IS_1 + IO_1 = \Delta X_1$$
$$DD_2 + EE_2 + IS_2 + IO_2 = \Delta X_2$$
$$\cdots\cdots$$
$$\cdots\cdots$$
$$\cdots\cdots$$
$$\cdots\cdots$$
$$DD_n + EE_n + IS_n + IO_n = \Delta X_n$$
$$\Sigma DD_i + \Sigma EE_i + \Sigma IS_i + \Sigma IO_i = \Sigma \Delta X_i = \Delta X$$

where DD_i = domestic demand expansion in sector i,
EE_i = export expansion in sector i,
IS_i = import substitution of final and intermediate goods in sector i,
IO_i = input-output coefficients in sector i,
ΔX_i = change in the output of sector i.

Reading down the columns gives the sectoral composition of each demand category, while reading across the rows gives the decomposition of changes in sectoral demand by different demand categories. When comparisons across countries and time periods are made, it is convenient to divide the entire table by $\Sigma \Delta X_i$, so that all components across sectors and demand categories sum to 100. Alternatively, it is sometimes convenient to divide the rows by ΔX_i and then to look at the percentage contribution of each demand category to the change in sectoral output. Table 2.3 illustrates the basic decomposition formulas.

At this stage, we can give an *alternative model*, which is known as the *deviation model* and measures changes in the relative shares of output. The deviation model starts from balanced growth, where it is assumed that all sectors grow at the same rate equal to the growth rate of total output.

2.6.2. Catching up Models

Technological gap theories (Abramovitz, 1986; Fagerberg, 1987, 1988, 1994) relate the technological level and innovation activities to the level of economic growth. According to these theories, countries where more innovation activities take place tend to have a higher level of value added per worker (or a higher per capita GDP). The size of the productivity factor differs substantially across countries with Japan and France having the highest rates for their respective time periods and the US and the UK having the lowest.

Catching-up theory (Abramovitz, 1986; Fagerberg, 1987) starts with the investigation of growth performance. The main idea is that large differences in productivity among countries tend to be due to unexpected events (for instance wars). According to these studies, the only possible way for technologically weak countries to converge or catch up with advanced countries is to copy their more productive technologies. The outcome of international innovation and diffusion process is uncertain; the process may generate a pattern where some countries follow diverging trends or one where countries converge towards a common trend. In this literature, economic development is analysed as a disequilibrium process characterised by two conflicting forces:

- innovation, which tends to increase economic and technological differences between countries, and
- diffusion (or imitation), which tends to reduce them. Technological gap theories are an application of Schumpeter's dynamic theory.

A higher level of innovation activities tend to have a higher level of value added per worker (or a higher GDP per head) and a higher level of innovation activities than others. Following technological-gap arguments, it would be expected that the more technologically advanced countries would be the most economically advanced (in terms of a high level of innovation activities and in terms of GDP per capita). The level of technology in a country cannot be measured directly. A proxy measure can be used to give an overall picture of the set of techniques invented or diffused by the country of the international economic environment. For productivity measure, we can use the real GDP per capita as an approximate measure. The most representative measures for *technological inputs and outputs* are indicators of patent activities and research expenditures.

For the level of productivity, we can use as a proxy real GDP per capita (GDPCP). For the measurement of *national technological level*, we can also use some approximate measures. For instance, we can again use the traditional variables of *technological input* and *technological output* measures, (GERD and EXPA). The majority of empirical studies in estimations between productivity growth and R&D follow a standard linear model. In the present context we use a similar approach. The reason is that even though there is a dynamic relationship, data limitations (lackness of time series annual data on R&D activities for most countries) prevent the application of some complex models.

We can test the basic technological gap model (with and without these variables) reflecting the structural change in order to decide to what degree these variables add something to the other explanatory variable of the model. We can use the external patent applications (EXPA) and gross expenditures on research and development (GERD) as proxies for the growth of the national technological activities, GDP per capita (GDPCP) (in absolute values at constant prices) as a proxy for the total level of knowledge appropriated in the country (or *productivity*). Investment share (INV) can be chosen as an indicator of growth in the capacity for economic exploitation of innovation and diffusion; the share of investment may also be seen as the outcome of a process in which institutional factors take part (since differences in the size of investment share may reflect differences in institutional system as well). For the structural change we used approximation changes in the shares of exports and agriculture in GDP.

We can test the following version of the models:

GDP (or PROD)=f[GDPCP, EXPA (or GERD), INV] basic model
GDP (or PROD)= f[GDPCP, EXPA (or GERD), INV, EXP]
GDP = f[GDPCP, EXPA (or GERD), INV, TRD]

The first model may be regarded as a pure *supply model*, where economic growth is supposed to be a function of the level of economic development GDPCP (GDP per capita with a negative expected sign), the growth of patenting activity (EXPA with a positive sign) and the investment share (INV with a positive sign). However, it can be argued that this model overlooks differences in overall growth rates between periods due to other factors and especially differences in economic policies.

Following the model by Fagerberg (1987, 1988, 1994), we can test the basic technological gap model (with and without these variables), reflecting structural change in order to determine the degree to which these variables have added something to the other explanatory variable of the model. We shall use external patent applications (EXPA) and gross expenditure on research and development (GERD) as proxies for the growth of national technological activities, and GDP per capita (GDPPC) (in absolute values at constant prices) as a proxy for the total level of knowledge appropriated in the country (or productivity).

Table 2.3. Decomposition Formulas[*]

Sources of growth:	Variable	being	decomposed	
Domestic-final-demand expansion (F.E.)	Output ΔX	Val.Add. ΔV	Imports ΔM	Empl. ΔL
Export expansion (E.E.)	$B_0\hat{u}^f_0\Delta F$	$v_0B_0\hat{u}^f_0\Delta F$	$(m_{11}f_0+m^w_0A_0B_0\hat{u}^f_0)\Delta F$	$l_0B_0\hat{u}^f_0\Delta F$
Import-substitution of final goods (I.S.F.)	$B_0\Delta E$	$v_0B_0\Delta E$	$m^w_0A_0B_0\Delta E$	$l_0B_0\Delta E$
Import- substitution of intermediate goods (I.S.W.)	$B_0\Delta\hat{u}^fF_1$	$v_0B_0\Delta\hat{u}^fF_1$	$(I-m^w_0A_0B_0)\Delta m^wW_1$	$l_0B_0\Delta\hat{u}^fF_1$
Technical change (I.O.A.)	$B_0\Delta\hat{u}^wW_1$	$v_0B_0\Delta\hat{u}^wW_1$	$(I-m^w_0A_0B_0)\Delta m^wW_1$	$l_0B_0\Delta\hat{u}^wW_1$
Change in value-added-ratio (I.O.V.)	$B_0\hat{u}^w_0\Delta AX_1$	$v_0B_0\hat{u}^w_0\Delta AX_1$	$(m^w_0+m^w_0A_0B_0\hat{u}^w_0)\Delta AX_1$	$l_0B_0\hat{u}^w_0\Delta AX_1$
Labour-productivity-growth (I.O.L.)	—	ΔvX_1	—	—
Labour-productivity-growth (I.O.L.)	—	—	—	Δ_lX_1

[*] The previous analysis can be extended to value added, employment, and imports.
Source: *OECD Document: "Structural change and Industrial performance", 1992.*

Investment share (INV) has been chosen as an indicator of an improvement in the capacity for economic exploitation of innovation and diffusion; the share of investment may also be seen as the outcome of a process in which institutional factors take part (since differences in the size of investment share may reflect differences in the institutional system).

2.6.3. An Historical Overview of Functional Forms

Paul Douglas was very devoted paid much attention to explain the movements of labour productivity and real wages over time, (Cobb Charles and Paul H. Douglas (1928), "A Theory of Production", American Economic Review, Supplement Vol. 18, pp. 139-165). Douglas wanted to test the marginal productivity theory. The important issue for him was if labour was in fact paid the value of its marginal product. Furthermore Cobb and Douglas assumed that production was characterized by constant returns to scale. They related empirically in a logarithmic form the value added output to the inputs of capital and labour for the U.S. manufacturing based on annual data for the period 1899-1922.

$$\ln Y = \ln A + \alpha_K \ln K + \alpha_L \ln L$$

where: Y are the output (value added), and K, L is capital and labour respectively.

The assumption of constant returns to scale (or otherwise the homogeneity of degree one) imply the restriction for the parameters $\alpha_K + \alpha_L = 1$. The non-logarithmic form is $Y = A K^\alpha L^\beta$, and multiplying by $\lambda > 1$, we have: $\lambda^\mu Y = A(\lambda K^\alpha)(\lambda L^\beta) = A K^\alpha L^\beta \lambda^{\alpha+\beta}$. This function is homogeneous of degree $\mu = \alpha + \beta$ and when $\mu = 1$ then $\alpha + \beta = 1$. Rearranging the above logarithmic equation of labour productivity to the capital/labour ratio:

$$\ln(Y/L) = \ln A + \alpha_K \ln(K/L)$$

The corresponding non-logarithmic form with constant returns to scale using for the empirical implementation has the following form:

$$Y = A K^\alpha L^{1-\alpha}$$

Rearranging the above non-logarithmic equation, taking the partial derivatives of Y with respect to K and L and equating the marginal products with the real input prices and solving, we can obtain:

$$\alpha_K = \frac{P_K K}{PY} \text{ and}$$

$$\alpha_L = 1 - \alpha_K = \frac{P_L L}{PY}$$

Cobb and Douglas argued that if markets were competitive, if marginal products equated to the real prices and if production technology following the constant returns to scale, then the least squares estimates of the parameters α_K and α_L should be equal approximately to the value shares of capital and labour.

Nevertheless, other economists were more interested in measuring substitution elasticities among inputs. They defined the substitution elasticity between capital and labour as following:

$$\sigma = \frac{\partial \ln(K/L)}{\partial \ln(F_L/F_K)} = \frac{\partial \ln(K/L)}{\partial \ln(P_L/P_K)}$$

where: F_K and F_L are the marginal products of capital and labour respectively.

For the Cobb-Douglas function the substitution of elasticity (σ) always equals to unity. Using the theory of cost and production Ragnar Frisch was attempted to measure the substitution elasticities between the inputs and estimated a substitution coefficient (the ratio of marginal productivities) between the inputs, (Frisch Ragnar (1935) "The principle of substitution: an example of its application in the chocolate industry", *Nordisk Tidsskrift for Teknisk Okonomi*, 1:1, pp: 12-27.).

Later, an extension of the Cobb-Douglas function was introduced by Kenneth Arrow, Hollis Chenery, Bagicha Minhas, and Robert Solow. In their model, Arrow, Chenery, Minhas, and Solow tried to search in which functional form the substitution of elasticity (σ) will be constant but not constrained to unity. They concluded in the following equation:

$$\ln(K/L) = \text{constant} + \sigma \ln(F_K/F_L)$$

where the second term (F_K/F_L) indicates the marginal rate of substitution.

The above function indicates the well-known Constant Elasticity of Substitution (CES) production function with constant returns to scale, which can be expressed as follows:

$$Y = A[\delta K^{-\rho} + (1-\delta)L^{-\rho}]^{-1/\rho}$$

where the substitution of elasticity σ = 1/(1+ρ)

There is a limiting case in which $\rho \to 0$, $\sigma \to 0$, the Cobb-Douglas function is a limiting form of the CES function. In fact, the Constant Elasticity of Substitution, CES, production function has appeared in the literature a quarter century earlier than Cobb-Douglas production function. The CES production function has been derived from consumer demand analysis. Abraham Bergson used the following function, (Bergson (Burk) Abraham (1936) "Real Income, Expenditure proportionality, and Frisch's New Method of Measuring utility", Review of Economic Studies, vol. 4:1, October, pp: 33-52.):

$$Y^{-\rho} = A\left(\sum_{i=1}^{n}\delta_i X_i^{-\rho}\right)$$

Nerlove estimated a three input Cobb-Douglas cost function (namely, capital, labour and fuels) with returns to scale to be other than constant; his empirical analysis indicated that the returns to scale were increasing rather than being constant, (Bergson (Burk) Abraham (1936) "Real Income, Expenditure proportionality, and Frisch's New Method of Measuring utility",

Review of Economic Studies, vol. 4:1, October, pp: 33-52.). However, Nerlove was unsatisfied with the restricted assumptions of Cobb-Douglas function according to which the substitution of elasticities required to be equal to unity and by CES which implied some other restrictions for the substitution of elasticities; that is, it required to be constant and equal to each other.

Lucas et al. have attempted to reconcile the seemingly disparate cross-sectional and time-series estimates of substitution of elasticity (σ), (Lucas Robert (1969) "Labour-Capital Substitution in U.S. Manufacturing" in Arnold C. Harberger and Martin J. Bailey eds. *The Taxation of Income from Capital*, Washington, D.C.: Ther brooking Institution, pp: 223-274).

In 1961 in their book *Agricultural Production Function*, Earl Heady and John Dillon experimented with Taylor's series expansion introduced the second-degree polynomial in logarithms that added quadratic and cross-terms to the Cobb-Douglas function, (Heady Earl and John L. Dillon (1961) Agricultural Production Functions, Ames, Iowa: Iowa State University Press). They estimated the production function directly using least square methods and called this procedure production function contour fitting. They reported the least squares estimates of a square root transformation that included the generalized linear production function introduced by Erwin Diewert in 1971, (Diewert Erwin (1971) "An Application of the Shepard Duality Theorem: A Generalized Linear Production Function", *Journal of Political Economy*, vol. 79:3, May/June, pp: 482-507). Diwert's Generalized Leontief Functional Form was the first in the theory of dual cost and production.

Daniel McFadden focused on the theory and its applications of duality in production, (McFadden Daniel (1978) *Production Economics: A Dual Approach to Theory and Applications*, volume 1, Amsterdam: North-Holland). He examined both the use of duality theory and the problem of generating more flexible functional forms with more than two or three inputs and less restrictive forms than the Cobb-Douglas and CES specifications.

Moreover, several other empirical results have been reported in literature in 1971. Nervlove surveyed empirical findings, (Nerlove Marc (1967) "Recent empirical studies of the CES and Related Production Functions" in Murray brown ed., *The Theory and Empirical Analysis of Production*, Studies in Income and Wealth, vol. 32, New York, Columbia University Press for the National Bureau of Economic Research, pp: 55-122), and, in 1973, Berndt summarized additional empirical findings, (Berndt Ernst (1976) "Reconciling Alternative Estimates of the Elasticity of Substitution", *Review of Economics and Statistics*, vol. 58:1, February, pp: 59-68).

A decade later, (1970), Laurits Christensen, Dale W. Jorgenson, and Lawrence J. Lau introduced a flexible functional form, the "translog production function", a form that placed no restrictions on the substitution of elasticities, (Christensen Laurits, Dale W. Jorgenson and Lawrence J. Lau (1971) "Conjugate Duality and the Transcendental Logarithmic Production Function", *Econometrica*, vol. 39:4, July, pp: 255-256, and Christensen Laurits, Dale W. Jorgenson and Lawrence J. Lau (1973) "Conjugate Duality and the Transcendental Logarithmic Production Function", *Review of Economics and Statistics*, vol. 55:1, February, pp: 28-45). The translog function was a second order Taylor's series in logarithms and was identical to the production function considered by Heady some decades earlier. It should be mentioned however that Heady emphasized only the primal production function; he did not consider the dual cost or even the specifications of the profit function.

Lastly, Boskin and Lau introduced another flexible functional form "the meta-production function", that is an extension of translog production function and can be employed with the panel or pool data, (Boskin M.J. and Lau L.J.: (1992) "Capital, technology and Economic growth", chapter 2 in Rosenberg, Landau and Mowery (ed.) *Technology and the wealth of nations*, Stanford University press). This function form places no *a priori* restrictions on the substitution possibilities among the inputs of production. It also allows scale economies to vary with the level of output. This feature is essential because it enables the unit cost curve to attain the classical shape.

Econometric applications of cost and production functions differ in their assumptions. In the regression of the production function, output is endogenous and input quantities are exogenous. In the dual cost function, the production costs and the input quantities are endogenous. When output and input prices can be considered as exogenous, then it is better to apply a cost function that has input prices as regressors, rather than a production function in which input quantities are the right-hand variables, (Zellner Arnold, Jan Kmenta and Jaques Dreze (1966) "Specification and estimation of Cobb-Douglas Production Function Models", *Econometrica*, vol.34:3, October, pp: 784-795).

Empirical research on estimating cost and production function relationships has a long history, trying to explain the average labour productivity, and the interrelationship between inputs and outputs, to estimate the substitution elasticities among inputs and, finally, to estimate the returns to scale. The production function parameters can be uniquely recovered from estimation of the demand equations derived from the dual cost function, (A cost function is dual in the sense that it embodies all the paraneters of the underlying production function; see Berbdt Ernst (1991) The Practice of Econometrics: Class and Contemporary, Addison-Wesley Publishing Company).

The empirical analysis of input demands and input substitution patterns provides an example of the strong links between economic theory and econometric implementation. The econometric techniques that we employ deal with estimation of parameters in systems of equations.

In addition, the implementation of a multiproduct cost functions can permit a richer analysis of the effects on costs and factor demands of various changes in the composition and levels of output; some recent examples of empirical implementation of multiproduct cost functions can be found among others in Douglas Caves and Lauritis Christensen.

2.6.4. The Generalised Leontief Function

There is a number of ways to approach the estimation of production function and technical progress. The aim of this section is to examine the theory of *Generalised Leontief production function* and the translog cost function. The *Generalised Leontief functional form* which proposed by Diewert has been established as a useful alternative for the long-run production studies. We can consider the following *Generalised Leontief functional form* for a cost function. Using the following equation:

$$C(w_K, w_L, Y, T) = \alpha_0 + \alpha_Y Y + \alpha_{YY} Y^2 + \sum_{i=1}^{n} \alpha_i w_i + \sum_{i=1}^{n} \sum_{j=1}^{n} \gamma_{ij} w_i^{1/2} w_j^{1/2} +$$

$$\sum_{i=1}^{n} \gamma_{it} w_i^{1/2} T + \gamma_t \sum_{i=1}^{n} w_i^{1/2} T + \gamma_{YY} \sum_{i=1}^{n} w_i^{1/2} Y^2 + \gamma_{iT} \sum_{i=1}^{n} w_i^{1/2} T^2 Y + \gamma_{TT} T^2 + \gamma_{YT} T$$

where C is the total cost, Y is the output, w_{ij} the prices of n inputs (i, j = 1,.........,n), Q_{ij} the n input quantities, and T is the time trend, with the constant returns to scale that can be written as:

$$C = Y\left[\sum_{i=1}^{n}\sum_{j=1}^{n}\gamma_{ij}(w_i w_j)^{1/2}\right]$$

where C is the total cost, Y is the output, w_{ij} the prices of n inputs (i, j = 1,.........,n), and Q_{ij} the n input quantities, with $\gamma_{ij}=\gamma_{ji}$ (i,j=1,2,...., n). The parameters γ_{ij} are such that (a) $\gamma_{ij} = \gamma_{ji}$ and (b) $\gamma_{ij} \geq 0$ (for i, j=1,2,...,n).

Let us assume that we have n inputs, as w_i, (i=1,...,n), with the n input quantities Q_i, and the total cost indicating by C and the output by Y.

We assume that the output and the input prices Y and w_{ij} are exogenous, while the input quantities Q_{ij} are endogenous.

The cost C defined by equation (2.1) is linearly homogeneous in input-prices w and has N(N=1)/2+2N+3 independent d parameters, just the right number to be flexible functional form, (Diwert and Wales, 1987 and Diewert Erwin and Terence J. Wales (1987) "Flexible Functional Forms and Global Curvature Conditions", *Econometrica*, vol.55:1, January, pp:43-68).

The first set of N(N+1)/2 independent terms on the right had side of equation (2.1) correspond to the "*Generalised Leontief cost function*" for a constant returns to scale technology with no technological progress, (Diewert), (Diewert Erwin (1971) "An Application of the Shepard Duality Theorem: A Generalized Linear Production Function", *Journal of Political Economy*, vol. 79:3, May/June, pp: 482-507 and also, Diewert Erwin (1974) "Applications of Duality Theory" in Michael D. Intriligator and David A. Kendrick eds., *Frontiers of Quantitative Economics*, vol. II, Amsterdam: North-Holland, pp: 106-171).

The ith input demand function which correspond to equation (1) can be obtained by differentiating C with respect to w_i (using the "*Shephard's lemma*").

$$X_i(w,Y,T) = \sum_{i=1}^{n}\gamma_{ij}w_i^{1/2}w_j^{1/2}Y + \gamma_i + \gamma_{it}TY + \gamma_t T + \gamma_{YY}Y^2 + \gamma_{TT}T^2 Y$$

with (i=1,2,,...n).

The *Generlaised Leotief linear function* can also be written as: Y=H(A11K+A12K1/2L1/2+A22L), where, Aii's are parameters and H is a single value increasing function. We also assume the *homotheticity hypothesis* for H, (Yasushi Toda).

The function $w_i^{1/2}w_j^{1/2}$ is concave in w and as a nonnegative sum of concave functions is concave. That function is a nondecreasing in γ follows from the nonnegativity of the parameters γ_{ij}. If all $\gamma_{ij}=0$ (for i, j) then the above equation reduces to a linear production function.

The production function given by equation exhibits constant returns to scale; we can generalize equation to any degree of returns to scale by:

$$c = f\left(\sum_{i=1}^{n}\sum_{i=j}^{n}\gamma_{ij}w_i^{1/2}w_j^{1/2}\right)$$

where, $\gamma_{ij} = \gamma_{ji} \geq 0$ and f is a continuous monotonically increasing function which tends to plus infinity and has f(0)=0.

The "*Generalized Leontief cost function*" and the "*Generalized linear production function*" are very useful by providing a second-order approximations to an arbitrary twice differentiable cost function (or production function) at a given vector of factor prices or at a given vector of inputs using minimal number of parameters.

In order to be able to obtain equations that are responsible to estimation, it is convenient to employ the shephard's lemma which states that the optimal cost-minimising demand for input i can simply be derived from differentiating the cost function with respect to w_i.

Therefore, if we differentiate the first equation with respect to w_i yielding the second equation and dividing the equation by Y, then yielding the optimal input-output equation denoted by α_i:

$$\alpha_i = \frac{X_i}{Y} = \sum_{j=1}^{n} \gamma_{ij} (w_j / w_i)^{1/2}$$

$$\frac{\partial C}{\partial w_i} = X_i = Y \left[\sum_{j=1}^{n} \gamma_{ij} (w_i w_j)^{1/2} \right]$$

when, i = j then $(w_j/w_i)^{1/2}$ is equal to 1 and the γ_{ij} is a constant term in the input-output equation.

Assuming two inputs, such as K = the capital and L = the labour and also Y = the output. The "*Generalised Leontief cost-minimising*" equations are the followings:

$$\alpha_K = \frac{K}{Y} = \gamma_{KK} + \gamma_{KL} (w_L / w_K)^{1/2}$$

$$\alpha_L = \frac{L}{Y} = \gamma_{LL} + \gamma_{KL} (w_K / w_L)^{1/2}$$

The estimates of all parameters in the "*Generalised Leontief cost-function*" can be obtained by estimating only the input-output demand equations (3) and (4); this occurs because there is no intercept term in the "*Generalised Leontief cost-function*" owing to the assumption of the constant returns to scale. Finally, if $\gamma_{ij}=0$ for all i and j, then the input-output demand equations are independent of the relative input prices and all the cross-price elasticities are equal to zero.

Although equation by equation OLS estimation might appear attractive since the input demand functions are linear in the parameters, these demand equations have cross-equation symmetry constraints. Even these constraints hold in the population, for any given sample equation-by-equation OLS estimates will not reveal such restrictions; for example, γ_{KL} in the K/Y equation estimated by OLS will not necessarily equal γ_{LK} estimated in the L/Y equation, (for a more detailed analysis see Berbdt Ernst (1991) The Practice of Econometrics: Class and Contemporary, Addison-Wesley publishing company).Constant returns to scale restrictions imply the symmetry restrictions (the cost shares sum to one).

To implement the "*Generalised Leontief model*" empirically, a stochastic framework must be specified. An additive disturbance term is appended to each of the input-output equations and is typically assumed that the resulting disturbance vector is independently and identically normally distributed with mean vector zero and constant, nonsingular covariance matrix Ω.

An attractive feature of the "*Generalised Leontief cost-function*" is that they place no a-priory restrictions on the substitution elasticities. The elasticity of factor substitution measures the responsiveness of the ratio of factor inputs to changes in the ratio of the marginal product of the inputs.

The Hicks-Allen partial elasticities of substitution for a "*general dual cost-function*" (between inputs i and j in a general functional form with n inputs) can be expressed as:

$$\sigma_{ij} = (C^* C_{ij}) / (C_i^* C_j),$$

where the subscripts i and j refer to the first and the second partial derivatives of the cost function with respect to the input prices w_i and w_j.

In particular, for "*Generalised Leontief cost-function*" the cross-substitution elasticities are given:

$$\sigma_{ij} = \frac{1}{2} \frac{C \gamma_{ij}(w_i w_j)^{-1/2}}{Y \alpha_i \alpha_j}$$

where i, j = 1,........, n (with $i \neq j$).
while the own-substitution elasticities are given as following:

$$\sigma_{ii} = \frac{-\frac{1}{2} C \sum_{\substack{j=1 \\ j \neq 1}}^{n} \gamma_{ij}(w_j^{1/2} w_i^{-3/2})}{Y \alpha_i^2}$$

where i, j = 1,........, n.

We will be able to estimate the price elasticities with the output quantity, while assuming that all the other input prices are fixed. The familiar price elasticities are given by:

$$\varepsilon_{ij} = \frac{\partial \ln X_i}{\partial \ln w_j} = \left(\frac{\partial X_i}{\partial w_j}\right)\left(\frac{w_j}{X_i}\right)$$

(see Berbdt Erns, 1991 The Practice of Econometrics: Class and Contemporary, Addison-Wesley Publishing Company).

We can also use the calculation of the following formula:

$$\varepsilon_{ij} = S_i^* \sigma_{ij},$$

where S_i is the cost share of the jth input in the total production costs.

For the "*Generalised Leontief cost-function*" the cross-prices elasticities are computed as following:

$$\varepsilon_{ij} = \frac{1}{2} \frac{\gamma_{ij}(w_i/w_j)^{-1/2}}{\alpha_i}$$

where i, j = 1,........, n (with $i \neq j$).

while the own-prices elasticities are computed as follows:

$$\varepsilon_{ij} = \frac{-\frac{1}{2} \sum_{\substack{j=1 \\ j \neq 1}}^{n} \gamma_{ij}(w_i/w_j)^{-1/2}}{\alpha_i}$$

where i, j = 1,........, n. In order the own-prices elasticity to be negative it is necessary the summation portion of last equation to be positive.

Because the equations last two equations of elasticity computations are based on the estimated parameters, and the predicted or fitted values of C and α_i, α_j, it is necessary to check the elasticity calculations which always must be hold:

$$\sum_{j=1}^{n} \varepsilon_{ij} = 0, \text{ (with i = 1,...,n)}$$

(see Berbdt Ernst (1991) The Practice of Econometrics: Class and Contemporary, Addison-Wesley Publishing Company).

Since the input prices and α_i vary between observations, then the estimators of σ_{ij} and ε_{ij} will also differ between observations. The price elasticities are not symmetric that means $\varepsilon_{ij} \neq \varepsilon_{ji}$ unlike the Hicks-Allen elasticities and our assumption of $\sigma_{ij} = \sigma_{ji}$. According to the above equations the input i and j are substitutes, independent or complement inputs depending on whether the estrimated γ_{ij} is positive, zero, or negative values. To ensure as its required by theory that the estimated cost function is monotonically increasing and strictly quasi-concave in input prices, we must verify that the fitted values for all the input-output equations are positive and that the n x n matrix of the σ_{ij} substitution elasticities is negative semi-definite at each observation. Because the computed elasticites depend on the estimated parameters and therefore are stochastic, the estimated elasticities have also variances and covariances, we should calculate these variances.

2.7. Modelling Technological Progress in a Production Function

The cost function approach does not dominate the production function approach; the choice depends on the parameters to be estimated. For example, for reasons much the same as the ones given above, the production function approach is preferable when estimates of factor productivity is sought. A production function is by definition a relationship between outputs and inputs. For a single country, say ith, the production function may be written as:

$$y_{it}=F_i(X_{i1t}, X_{i2t},........,X_{imt},t),$$

where: y_{it} is the quantity of output produced per producer unit and X_{ijt} is the quantity of the jth input employed per producer unit (j=1,2,....m) in the ith country for the period.

This model contributes substantially and upgrade the methodologies adopted therein. It is possible to distinguish several different aspects of this procedure. For instance:

The model was first proposed by Jorgenson D.W. and Fraumeni B.M. (1983). Their main innovation was that they estimated the rate of technical change along with income share equations as functions of relative input prices. The shares and the rate of technical change are derived from a translog production function.

The procedure is decomposed i the estimated technical change of three components: *pure technology*, which is only the time element times a coefficient; *non-neutral* component, which shows how time trend influences the usage of inputs; *scale augmenting* component, which suggests how time affects the economies of scale. The sum of these three components give the growth of *multifactor productivity*.

In addition, we can relax the assumption of constant returns to scale by estimating the initial cost function along with factor shares and the rate of technological change, and so provides the evidence for the existence of *scale economies*.

In a cross section study, technology can be regarded as given in each country, but this is clearly not in the case when we consider a single country over a period of time. The country's production function will shift as new and more efficient techniques are adopted. A major problem with time series data is to distinguish between increases in output resulting from movements along the production function (for instance, from increased inputs) and increases in output which occur because of shifts in the production function resulting from the technical progress. The problem of simultaneous equation bias is present with time-series data as with cross sectional data. However, there is a more serious problem with time series data that of the technical progress or innovation over time. With cross sectional data, the identification problem can arise if product and factor prices show any marked tendency to change at similar rates over time, as this may leave price ratios constant; see also Thomas R.L., 1993.

The concept of a production function plays an important role in both micro-and macro-economics. At the macro level, it has been combined with the marginal productivity theory to explain the prices of the various factors of production and the extent to which these factors are utilised. The production function has been used as a tool for assessing what proportion of any increase in the output over time can be attributed first to increase in the inputs of factors in the production, second to the increasing returns to scale and third to *technical progress*.

Most studies of the production function (Solow 1957, Griliches 1967) have been handled under one or more traditionally maintained hypothesis of *constant returns of scale*, *neutrality of technical progress* and *profit maximisation* with competitive output and input markets. Therefore, the validity or otherwise of each of these hypotheses affects the measurement of technical progress and the decomposition of economic growth into its sources.

Following Landau's analysis, we can assume that there is a production function that relates output to capital per unit of labour and that the economy is at the point A, where labour force growth is static and investment is at an average level. When a new technology is introduced, there is an upward shift of the production function. Of course, the shift of the production function will be different across different countries. This shift of the production function implies additional output per person, and this most likely can lead to extra savings and consequently to more capital per worker, which means that economy will move along the production function. Figure 2.8 shows that the economy reaches the point E for less advanced countries and point D for more advanced countries. The real effects of innovation can now be measured by the distances AE and AD respectively.

The methodology of a translog function is based on a two-input (capital and labour) case dual translog cost function (Christensen, Jorgenson and Lau 1971, 1973), the derived factor shares and on the rate of technical change for all twenty industrial sectors. All these variables are functions of relative prices and time. Implicitly, it is assumed that total cost and input shares are translog functions of their corresponding prices and time. Technology is in fact endogenous in our sectoral models and is parametrically rather than residually estimated.

Implementing Jorgenson and Fraumeni's methodology, we fitted the models so that they embrace all of these theoretical requirements. Since perfect competition is assumed, the input prices are exogenously determined.

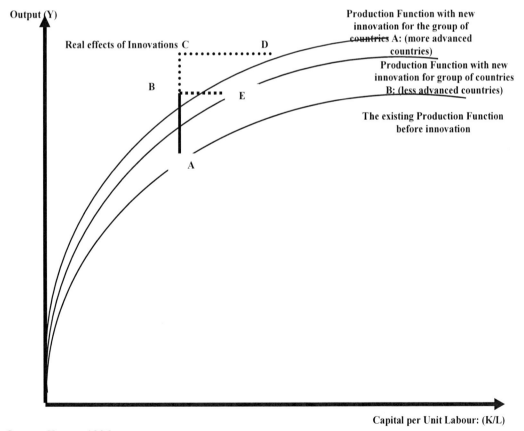

Source: Korres, 1996.

Figure 2.8. Technical Change and Innovation in a Production Function.

The translog cost function can be written

$$\ln c^v(w_K, w_L, Y, T) = \alpha_0^v + \alpha_y^v \ln y^v + \frac{1}{2}\alpha_{yy}^v(\ln y^v)^2 + \sum_{i=1}^{n}\alpha_i^v \ln w_i^v + \frac{1}{2}\sum_{i=1}^{n}\sum_{j=1}^{n}\gamma_{ij}^v \ln w_i^v \ln w_j^v + \sum_{i=1}^{n}\gamma_{iy}^v \ln w_i^v \ln y^v$$

$$\gamma_T^v T + \frac{1}{2}\gamma_{TT}^v T^2 + \sum_{i=1}^{n}\gamma_{iT}^v \ln w_i^v T + \gamma_{yT}^v \ln y^v T$$

where C = total cost, W_i (i = K,L) = input prices (price of capital and labour), Y = value-added, and T = technical change index.

Since we use the averages, we have to transform the cost function, the share equations and the rate of technical change as, (for simplicity purposes, we can drop the superlative index which declares the number of sectors):

$$\overline{\ln c}^v(\overline{w_K}, \overline{w_L}, \overline{Y}, T) = \alpha_0^v + \alpha_y^v \overline{\ln y}^v + \frac{1}{2}\alpha_{yy}^v (\overline{\ln y}^v)^2 + \sum_{i=1}^{n}\alpha_i^v \overline{\ln w_i}^v + \frac{1}{2}\sum_{i=1}^{n}\sum_{j=1}^{n}\gamma_{ij}^v \overline{\ln w_i}^v \overline{\ln w_j}^v$$

$$+ \sum_{i=1}^{n}\gamma_{iy}^v \overline{\ln w_i}^v \overline{\ln y}^v + \gamma_T^v T + \frac{1}{2}\gamma_{TT}^v T^2 + \sum_{i=1}^{n}\gamma_{iT}^v \overline{\ln w_i}^v T + \gamma_{yT}^v \overline{\ln y}^v T + \overline{e}_c^{-v}$$

where the share equation and the rate of technical change take the form:

$$\overline{S}_i^v(w_K, w_L, Y, T) = \alpha_i^v + \sum_{j=1}^{n}\gamma_{ij}^v \overline{\ln w_j}^v + \gamma_{iy}^v \overline{\ln Y}^v + \gamma_{iT}^v T + \overline{e}_i^{-v}$$

$$-\overline{S}_T^v(w_k, w_L, Y, T) = \gamma_T^v + \gamma_{TT}^v T + \sum_{i=1}^{n}\gamma_{iT}^v \overline{\ln w_i}^v + \gamma_{yT}^v \overline{\ln Y} + \overline{e}_T^{-v}$$

where v = 1,...,20 and i = K, L, are the average error terms. The share equations have the following form: S_K (share of capital) = $(P_K^* Q_K)/TC$ and S_L (share of labour) = $(P_L^* Q_L)/TC$, where $P_{K,L}$ is the price of capital and the price of labour, $Q_{K,L}$ is the capital and labour and TC is the total cost.

The Allen-Uzava partial elasticities of substitution, σ_{ij}, and price elasticities of input demands, P_{ij} are given by following equations:

$$\sigma_{ij} = (\gamma_{ii} + S_i^2 - S_i)/(S_i^2), \ i = K, L \ i = j \text{ and}$$

$$\sigma_{ij} = (\gamma_{ij} + S_i S_j)/(S_i S_j), \ i,j = K, L \ i \neq j$$

where the own-partial elasticities of substitution, σ_{ii}, are expected to be negative. The cross-partial elasticities of substitution can be either positive, suggesting substitutability between inputs, or negative, suggesting input complementarity.

$$P_{ij} = \sigma_{ij} S_j, \ i = K, L \ i \neq j \text{ and}$$

$$P_{ii} = \sigma_{ii} S_i, \ i = K, L \ i = j$$

Several comments should be made on these substitution elasticity estimates. First, parameter estimates and fitted shares should replace the γ's and S's, when computing estimates of the σ_{ij} and P_{ij}. This implies that, in general, the estimated elasticities will vary across observations. Second, since the parameter estimates and fitted shares have variances and covariances, the estimated substitution elasticities also have stochastic distributions. Third, the estimated translog cost function should be checked to ensure that it is monotonically increasing and strictly quasi-concave in input prices, as required by theory. For monotonicity, it is required that the fitted shares all be positive, and for strict quasi-concavity the (n x n) matrix of substitution elasticities must be negative semidefinite at each observation. Moreover, we may calculate the scale elasticities, (which is the percentages change of the total cost after the change one percentage in the output). As Giora Hanoch (1975) has shown that scale elasticities are computed as the inverse of costs with respect to output. More specifically, *scale*=1/e_{cy} where e_{cy}= ∂lnc/∂lny, that is, for the translog function:

$$\overline{e_{cy}^{-v}} = a_y + a_{yy}\overline{lnY}^v + \Sigma_i^n \gamma_{ij}\overline{lnP_i}^v + \gamma_{YT}\overline{T}$$

A number of additional parameter restrictions can be imposed on the translog cost function, corresponding to further restrictions on the underlying technology model. For the translog cost function to be homothetic, it is necessary and sufficient that $\gamma_{iy}=0 \ \forall \ i= 1,...,n$. Homogeneity of a constant degree in output occurs if, besides these homotheticity restrictions, we have $\gamma_{yy}= 0$. In this case, the degree of homogeneity equals $1/\alpha_y$. Constant returns to scale of the dual production function occurs when, in addition to the above homotheticity and homogeneity restrictions, $\alpha_y=1$.

The specification of the cost-function does not impose any restriction on technological change and returns to scale. Invoking Shephard's lemma obtains the familiar cost shares, which together with the above equations, provide the basis for the estimation:

$$\frac{\partial \ln C^v}{\partial T} = -S_T^v(w_k, w_L, Y, T)$$

where

$$S_i^v(w_K, w_L, Y, T) = \alpha_i^v + \sum_{i=1}^{n} \gamma_{ij}^v \ln w_j^v + \gamma_{iy}^v \ln Y^v + \gamma_{iT}^v T$$

The rate of technical change in each sector is given as the negative of the rate of growth of sectoral cost with respect to time, holding input prices constant. Doing this, we can get:

$$\frac{\partial \ln C^v}{\partial T} = -S_T^v(w_k, w_L, Y, T)$$

$$-S_T^v(w_k, w_L, Y, T) = \gamma_T^v + \gamma_{TT}^v T + \sum_{i=1}^{n} \gamma_{iT}^v \ln w_i^v + \gamma_{yT}^v \ln Y$$

or s.t.: $\gamma_{ij} = \gamma_{ji}$, $i \neq j$, $i,j = K,L$, $v = 1,...,20$ is the number of sectors.

$$\Sigma \alpha_i = 1 \; ; \; \Sigma \gamma_{ij} = \Sigma \gamma_{ji} = 0$$
$$\Sigma \gamma_{it} = 0; \text{ and } \Sigma \gamma_{yi} = 0$$

The restrictions (equations e) imposed on the cost function, the cost-shares and on the rate of technological change imply that the share equations satisfy:

$$\Sigma \alpha_i = 1 \; ; \; \Sigma \gamma_{ij} = \Sigma \gamma_{ji} = \Sigma \gamma_{iy} = \Sigma \gamma_{it} = 0$$

The second order parameters, for instance γ_{KK}, γ_{LL} and γ_{KL} are defined as the constant share elasticities which are derived from the differentiation of the factor shares with respect to logarithmic prices. The coefficients γ_{KT} and γ_{LT} are the biases of technical change and they are given by differentiating the rate of technical change with respect to input prices. If we differentiate again the rate of technical change equation (c) with respect the time then we get γ_{TT}, which shows the rate of change of the negative of the rate of technical change.

The function C has to be non-decreasing in input prices so the factor shares have to be non-negative throughout the sample period. If we denote as (S) the matrix of shares and (H) the Hessian matrix of the second order terms, then we may represent the matrix of share elasticities, say Q, in the form:

$$Q = (1/C) \, P^* H^* P - ss' + S$$

where

$$P = \begin{bmatrix} w_K & 0 \\ 0 & w_L \end{bmatrix} \quad S = \begin{bmatrix} S_K & 0 \\ 0 & S_L \end{bmatrix} \quad s = \begin{bmatrix} S_K \\ S_L \end{bmatrix}$$

Now, concavity implies that the cost function has to have a negative semi-definite H matrix. If we rewrite equation (Q), we can get:

$$(1/C) \, P^* H^* P = Q + ss' - S$$

which is negative semidefinite, if and only if, H matrix is negative semidefinite. This is very useful outcome because it gives right to represent the unknown parameters using the Cholesky factorization:

$$Q + ss' - S = L^* D^* L'$$

where L is a unit lower triangular matrix and D is a diagonal matrix with non-positive terms. Implementing the above transformation permits to the share elasticities matrix and to guarantee concavity in the sample period.

The idea here is to estimate the rate of technical change along with the share equations but what is the quantity of S_T? Although it is unobserved, we may circumvent this problem by considering the *translog price index* for the rate of technical change. We may say that the technical change between any two points of time, T and T-1 is given by the subtraction from the growth of total cost the growth of each input price weighted by their corresponding average shares:

$$-\bar{S}_T^v = [(lnc\text{-}(T)^v - lnc\text{-}(T-1)^v) - \sum_{i=1}^{n} \bar{S}_i^v (lnw_{i(T)}^v - lnw_{i(T-1)}^v)]$$

where T = time, (i = K, L and v = 1,...,20 the number of sectors).

Within the same context we may derive the average shares as:

$$\bar{S}_i^v = \frac{1}{2}[S_{i(T)}^v + S_{i(T-1)}^v]$$

T = time, (i = K, L and v = 1,...,20 the number of sectors).

The above restrictions also imply an adding up condition of the share equation system, such as:

$$\sum_i \bar{S}_i^v = 1$$

This adding up feature of the share equation has several important econometric implications, to which we now turn our attention.

$$\bar{e}_c^v = \frac{1}{2}(e_{c(T)}^v + e_{c(T-1)}^v)$$

$$\bar{e}_i^v = \frac{1}{2}(e_{i(T)}^v + e_{i(T-1)}^v)$$

$$\bar{e}_T^v = \frac{1}{2}(e_{T(T)}^v + e_{T(T-1)}^v)$$

First, since the shares always sum to unity and only n-1 of the share equations are linearly independent, for each observation the sum of the disturbances across equations must always equal zero. Second, because the shares sum to unity at each observation, when the symmetry restrictions are not imposed, the residuals across equations will sum to zero at each observation; that is,

$$\bar{e}_K^v + \bar{e}_L^v = 0$$

Finally, from the translog function reduces to the constant returns into scale Cobb-Douglas function when, in addition to all the above restrictions, each of the $\gamma_{ji}=0$ i, j=1,...,n.

2.7.1. The Meta-Production Function

This approach enables us to identify not only the returns to scale and the rate of technical progress in each economy but also their biases, if any. The estimated aggregate *meta-production function* can be used as the basis for a new measurement of technical progress as well as a new measurement of the relative contributions of capital, labour and technical progress to economic growth. The concept of a *meta-production function* is theoretically attractive because it is based on the simple hypothesis that all countries (producers) have potential access to the same technology. The production function applies to standardised (or efficiency equivalent) quantities of outputs and inputs; that is,

$$Y^*_{it} = F(K^*_{it}, L^*_{it}) \quad i=1,2,....,n$$

where: Y^*_{it}, K^*_{it}, L^*_{it} are the quantities of output, capital and labour respectively of the ith country at the time t, and n is the number of countries. Furthermore,

$$Y'_{it} = A_{i0}(t)Y_{it}, \quad K'_{it} = A_{i0}(t)K_{it}, \quad L'_{it} = A_{i0}(t)L_{it}, \quad (i=1,2,...,n)$$

In terms of the measured quantities of outputs, the production function may be rewritten as:

$$Y_{it} = A_{i0}(t)^{-1} F(K'_{it}, L'_{it}) \quad (i=1,2,....,n)$$

so that the complementary factor of output-augmentation $A_{i0}(t)$ has the interpretation of the possibly time varying level of technical efficiency of the production, in the ith country at time t. These augmentation factors are not likely to be identical across the countries and this can be a result of different factors, (such as differences in the composition of outputs, in the quality and in infrastructure). The commodity augmentation factors are assumed to have the constant exponential form with respect to time:

$$Y'_{it} = A_{i0} exp(B_{i0}t)Y_{it}, \quad K'_{it} = A_{i0} exp(B_{iK}t)K_{it}, \quad L'_{it} = A_{i0}(B_{iL}t)L_{it}, \quad (i=1,..,n)$$

where: A_{i0}'s, A_{ij}'s, B_{i0}'s, B_{ij}'s, are constants.

The used inputs are the capital K and labour L and the translog function in terms of *efficiency-equivalent* output and inputs takes the following form:

$$nY^*_{it} = lnY_0 + \alpha_K lnK^*_{it} + \alpha_L lnL^*_{it} + \gamma_{KK}(lnK^*_{it})^2/2 + \gamma_{LL}(lnL^*_{it})^2/2 + \gamma_{KL}(lnK^*_{it})(lnK^*_{it})$$

substituting in the last equation the terms of Y^*_{it}, K^*_{it}, L^*_{it} of second equation, we can get:

$$lnY_{it} = lnY_0 + lnA^*_{it} + \alpha^*_{iK} lnK_{it} + \alpha^*_{iL} lnL_{it} + \gamma_{KK}(lnK_{it})^2/2 + \gamma_{LL}(lnL_{it})^2/2 + \gamma_{KL}(lnK_{it})(lnL_{it}) + \beta^*_{i0}t + (\gamma_{KK}\beta_{iK} + \gamma_{KL}\beta_{iL})(lnK_{it})t + (\gamma_{KL}\beta_{iK} + \gamma_{LL}\beta_{iL})(lnL_{it})t + (\gamma_{KK}\beta^2_{iK} + \gamma_{LL}\beta^2_{iL} + 2\gamma_{KL}\beta_{iK}\beta_{iL})t_2/2$$

where A^*_{i0}, α^*_{iK}, α^*_{iL}, β^*_{i0} are the country specific constants;
the parameters γ_{KK}, γ_{KL} and γ_{LL} are independent of i of the particular country.

The parameters γ_{KK}, γ_{KL}, γ_{LL} are independent of i that is, of the particular individual country and they must be identical across the countries. This is the *common link* between the aggregate functions of different countries, and this tests the hypothesis that there is a single aggregate meta-production function for all countries. The parameter corresponding to the $t^2/2$ term for each country is not independent; it is rather determined given the γ_{KK}, γ_{KL}, γ_{LL}, β_{iK}, and β_{iL} and this test the second hypothesis that technical progress may be represented in the constant exponential commodity-augmentation form. Consequently, the above equation can test the maintained hypotheses of constant returns to scale, the neutrality of technical progress and the profit maximization with competitive output and input markets. In addition to the aggregate *meta-production function*, we can also consider the behavior of the share of labour costs in the value of output:

$$w_{it}L_{it}/p_{it}Y_{it}$$

where: w_{it} is the wage rate and p_{it} is the nominal price of output at time t.

Under profit maximization with competitive output and input markets, the assumption of profit maximisation with respect to labour implies that the elasticity of output with respect to labour which is equal to the share of labour cost in the value of output. We can also test the hypothesis of profit maximisation with respect to labour and, if this hypothesis does not hold, then the parameters of third equation will not be the same as those in the aggregate meta-production function. A similar analysis can be derived for the capital:

$$r_{it}K_{it}/p_{it}Y_{it}$$

where r_{it} is the interest rate and p_{it} is the price of output at time, in order to test the hypothesis of profit maximisation with respect to capital. Finally, the following equation gives the same approach to the time: for a more detailed analysis, see Boskin and Lau, 1993.

$$w_{it}L_{it}/p_{it}Y_{it}=\partial \ln Y_{it}/\partial \ln L_{it}=\alpha^*_{iL}+\gamma_{KL}\ln K_{it}+\gamma_{LL}\ln L_{it}+(\gamma_{KL}\beta_{iK}+\gamma_{LL}\beta_{iL})t$$

$$r_{it}K_{it}/p_{it}Y_{it}=\partial \ln Y_{it}/\partial \ln K_{it}=\alpha^*_{iK}+\gamma_{KK}\ln K_{it}+\gamma_{KL}\ln L_{it}+(\gamma_{KK}\beta_{iK}+\gamma_{KL}\beta_{iL})t$$

The restrictions imposed on the inputs' shares imply that the parameters must satisfy the following properties:

(a) Meta-production function is *homogeneous* of degree one in input quantities; that is:
$\Sigma\alpha_i = 1$; $\Sigma\alpha_{ij} = \Sigma\alpha_{j\,i} = \Sigma\gamma_{iT} = 0$
The above restrictions are necessary, if we want the function to be well defined.

(b) Another crucial property for the twice-differentiable function to content is the *concavity principle*.
Apart from the above restrictions there is also an adding up condition of the share equation system, such as, see also Jorgenson:
$\Sigma S_i = 1$

Regarding the Allen-Uzava partial elasticities of substitution, σ_{ij}, and price elasticities of input demands, they are expressed by the following equations:

$$\sigma_{ij} = (\gamma_{ii} + S_i^2 - S_i)/(S_i^2), \ i = K, L \ i = j \quad \text{and}$$

$$\sigma_{ij} = (\gamma_{ij} + S_i S_j)/(S_i S_j), \ i,j = K, L \ i \neq j$$

The choice of a particular algebraic form of the production function is associated with the question of substitution between different inputs. The elasticity of technical substitution can be defined as the division of the percentage change in k by the percentage change in α or, otherwise:

$$\sigma = d(K/L)/(K/L)/d(MP_K/MP_L)/(MP_K/MP_L)$$

where k = K/L (capital / labour ratio) and $\alpha = MP_K/MP_L$ (ratio of the marginal products of capital and labour respectively). If the elasticity of factor substitution is high, then this implies that the marginal rate of substitution does not change relative to changes in the capital / labour ratio. In case that $\sigma = +\infty$, then the isoquant will be a straight line, and when $\sigma = 0$ then the isoquant curve would be right-angled; for a more detailed analysis see Sato and Suzawa (1983).

The own-partial elasticities of substitution, σ_{ii}, are expected to be negative. The cross-partial elasticities of substitution can be either positive, suggesting substitutability between inputs, or negative, suggesting input complementarity.

$$P_{ij} = \sigma_{ij} S_i, \ (i = K, L \ i \neq j) \text{ and}$$
$$P_{ii} = \sigma_{ii} S_i, \ (i = K, L \ i = j)$$

Whereas using productivity growth capital is associated with a positive bias of productivity growth for the capital input, implementing that an increase in the price of capital input diminishes the rate of productivity growth, capital saving productivity growth implies that productivity growth increases with the price of capital input.

2.7.2. The Translog Production Function

The aggregate cost (or production) function is based on a cost function (or a production function), which is characterised by constant returns to scale:

$$C = F(P_K, P_L, Y, T)$$

where: P_K, P_L, Y, T indicate the price of capital input, labour input, the value added and time. The translog cost function can be written, (where ij=K,L):

$$\ln C(P_K, P_L, Y, T) = \alpha_0 + \alpha_y \ln y + \frac{1}{2}\alpha_{yy}(\ln y)^2 + \sum_{i=1}^{n}\alpha_i \ln P_i + \frac{1}{2}\sum_{i=1}^{n}\sum_{j=1}^{n}\gamma_{ij}\ln P_i \ln P_j$$
$$+ \sum_{i=1}^{n}\gamma_{ij}\ln P_i \ln y + \gamma_T T + \frac{1}{2}\gamma_{TT}T^2 + \sum_{i=1}^{n}\gamma_{iT}\ln P_i T + \sum_{i=1}^{n}\gamma_{yT}\ln y T,$$

We can use aggregate data assuming that input prices are endogenous in order to estimate the *translog share equation system* and avoid the simultaneous equation problems; we employ three stage least squares with an instrumental variable estimator provided that appropriate instruments are available. Output measured as value added. Labour is measured as the number of employees and capital is measured as the capital stock. As price of capital we use the long-term interest rate and as price of labour wages and salaries. To estimate the above model of the average cost functions along with the share of one input and the rate of technical change, we adopt the three stage least squares, using instrumental variables with endogenous lag variables, such as lag shares, lag prices of capital, labour and output and some exogenous variables, such as export and import prices and consumer prices.

Parameters α_K and α_L can be interpreted as the average value shares of capital and labour inputs. Parameters γ_T and α_Y indicate the average (negative) rate of technical change and the average share of output in total cost and parameter γ_T can also be interpreted as the average rate of productivity growth.

Parameters γ_{KK}, γ_{KL}, γ_{LL} can be interpreted as constant share elasticities. These parameters describe the implications of patterns of substitution for the relative distribution of output between capital and labour. A positive share elasticity implies that the corresponding value share increases with an increase in quantity. A share elasticity equal to zero implies that the corresponding value share is independent of quantity. The bias estimates γ_{KT} and γ_{LT} describe the implications of patterns of productivity growth for the distribution of output. A positive bias implies that the corresponding value increases with time, while a negative bias implies that the value share decreases with time. Finally, a zero bias implies that the value share is independent of time. An alternative and equivalent interpretation of the biases is that they represent changes in the rate of productivity growth with respect to proportional changes in input quantities.

The parameter γ_T can be interpreted as the average rate of productivity growth, while parameters γ_K and γ_L can be interpreted as the average value shares of capital and labour inputs. The elasticity of substitution (σ_{KL}) for the production function is equal to:

$$\sigma_{ij} = (\gamma_{ij} + S_i S_j)/S_i S_j.$$

If σ_{KL} is greater than zero then inputs are substitutes for this country; otherwise if σ_{KL} is less than zero then they are complements. The price elasticities can be defined as:

$$P_{ij} = (\gamma_{ij} + S_i S_j)/S_i.$$

Multifactor productivity MFP (or the rate of technical change) is decomposed into three parts, pure technology, non- neutral technology and scale augmenting technology.

Table 2.4. Results from Growth-Regression Studies

Topic	Author	Data period(s) and coverage	Dependent variables	Comments
a-general	Cellini, 1997	Annual time series, 1960-1985. Regressions for the G7 and Europe are run alongside broader regressions.	Labour productivity	The specification is derived from a basic model with error-correction terms used to deal with short-run variation.
a- general	Cellini et al 1999	Annual panel data, varying time periods. Regressions for OECD countries are run alongside other country groupings.	Labour productivity and change in investment share.	Augments the annual time-series panel approach taken in Cellini (1997) (see above) with variables indicating social and political stability.
a-general	De la Fuente (1995)	21 OECD countries, 5-year panel data 1963-1988.	Labour productivity	Regressions are based on the model used by Mankiw, Romer and Weil (1992) with additional variables indicating R&D intensity and labour utilisation. Stresses the significance of R&D in the regressions and of rapid technological catch-up in the first half of the sample period
a-general	Englander and Gurney (1994)	19 OECD countries over 4 time periods between 1960s and 1990s.	Labour productivity growth. TFP growth.	growth. TFP growth. Concludes that: -capital, schooling and labour force growth have robust links with growth. (positive); -some role played by catch-up, R&D spending and inflation; -no evidence from indicators of financial deepening or trade intensity; -regressions explaining TFP growth suggest no externalities through capital accumulation.
a-general	Englander and Gurney (1994)	25 "high productivity" countries (including 16 OECD countries) over 3 time periods between 1960 and 1985.	Labour productivity growth.	Essentially a replication of De Long and Summers (1992) work on the role of different forms of investment. The equipment investment share produces a robust result whilst transport and investment is insignificant. However, it is pointed out that regressions explaining output per worker in the business sector show the equipment investment share to also be insignificant.

a-general	Englander and Gurney (1994)	24 OECD countries.	Growth rate of real per capita GDP, 1960-1985.	This regression replicates the Barro (1991) regression for OECD countries. Notable in that the statistical performance is poor.
a-general	Lee (1995)	16 OECD countries, panel data.	Growth rates in GDP per capita	Regressions suggest several important factors: private investment (positive), government consumption and debt (negative) and inflation (negative).
a-general	Mankiw, Romer and Weil (1992)	22 OECD countries.	GDP per person of working-age, 1985.	OECD regressions are run as part of their test of the augmented Solow model. The OECD regressions perform poorly in relation to wider samples of countries but show signs of stronger convergence compared to other samples of countries. It is hypothesised that this is due to the Second World War generating greater departures from steady states.
a-general	Vasudeva Murthy and Chien (1997)	OECD countries, crosssection data.	GDP per person of working age.	The paper tackles a similar issue that of Mankiw, Romer and Weil (1992), further confirming the importance of human capital in an augmented Solow model context
b-public capital	Ford and Poret (1991)	12 OECD countries, annual data from 1960s to 1980s.	TFP growth.	The paper questions the validity of the "Aschauer hypothesis" which argues the productivity returns to public infrastructure are high. The results of separate time-series regressions for each country fail to show infrastructure capital to important in explaining TFP growth.
b-public capital	Nourzad and Vrieze (1995)	7 OECD countries, panel data.	Labour productivity growth.	Finds public capital formation to have a positive influence on labour productivity growth. Conditioning variables include private-sector employment, private-sector investment and an indicator for the stock of natural resources.
b-public capital	Fowler and Richards (1995)	Annual panel data for 16 countries.	Growth rate in real GDP.	Finds little support for the view that the size of the public enterprise sector affects growth in growth regressions controlling for investment and human capital.

Table 2.4. (Continued)

Topic	Author	Data period(s) and coverage	Dependent variables	Comments
c-R&D	Fagerberg (1987)	25 countries, all OECD except 2. Panel data.	Growth rate in real GDP.	A patent index equal to the growth of patent applications made in other countries proves significant, alongside a catch-up and investment.
c-R&D	Park (1995)	10 OECD countries, panel data.	Growth rates in real GDP	Main result is that private sector R&D appears more important than public sector R&D. It is suggested, however, that public-sector R&D acts to stimulate private-sector research. Conditioning variables cover catch-up, non-R&D investment and an indicator of capacity utilisation.
d-human capital	Domenech and de al Fuente, 2000	21 OECD countries.	Labour productivity.	The results are based on a revised version of the 'Barro-Lee' data on human capital and show that this adjusted data set appears to produce significant results not only where the level of human capital is used but also changes in human capital.
d-human capital	Wolff and Gittleman (1993)	19 industrial market economies.	Growth rates in real GDP per capita.	Runs regressions for a number of samples of countries and time periods, investigating the differences between education as measured by enrolment rates compared with attainment rates. For OECD countries only tertiary enrolment rates are significant, whilst attainment is always more significant for primary education. It is noted that inclusion of investment strongly affects the significance of the attainment variables.
e-inflation	Alexander (1997)	Small number of OECD countries, panel data.	Growth rate in real GDP.	Both levels of inflation and changes in inflation are significant.
e-inflation	Andres and Hernando (1997)	OECD countries, panel data.	Growth rates in GDP per capita.	In an analysis based on several econometric approaches, consistently finds inflation to be negatively correlated with growth. Conditioning variables include catch-up, investment, human capital and population growth.

e-inflation	De Gregorio (1996)	21 OECD countries.	Growth rate in real GDP per capita.	Runs regressions for a number of groups of countries and concludes a significant negative impact of inflation on growth. OECD regressions include catch-up, initial education levels and government consumption.
f-fiscal	Agell et al. (1998)	23 OECD countries, panel data.	Growth rate in real GDP per capita.	A critique of Folster and Henrekson (1998) with replication of results and additional analysis to support their claim of there being no evidence to support a fiscal effect on growth.
f-fiscal	Agell et al. (1997)	23 OECD countries.	Growth rate in real GDP per capita.	Finds no support for significant influence of either the tax or expenditure share on growth. Conditioning variables include catch-up and shares of young and older cohorts in the population.
f-fiscal	Hansson and Henrekson (1994)	Industry-level data for 14 OECD countries.	Industry-level rate of growth.	The regressions examine the link between industry-level rates of growth and various components of government expenditure. The results find that government transfers, consumption and total outlays have a negative impact on growth whilst education expenditure has a positive impact and government investment is not significant.
f-fiscal	Folster and Henrekson (1999)	23 OECD countries, panel data.	Growth rate in real GDP per capita.	In response to the conclusion of Agell *at al.* (1997), claims that their conclusion is based on poor regression results. Perform some panel regressions and find a robust (negative) link between tax or expenditure shares and growth.
f-fiscal	Folster and Henrekson (2000)	23 OECD countries, cross country and panel regressions, 1960-75.	Growth rate in real GDP per capita.	Builds on Folster and Henrekson (1999), and claims that the more econometric problems are address, the more clearly the data show a negative relationship between the 'size' of government and growth.

Table 2.4. (Continued)

Topic	Author	Data period(s) and coverage	Dependent variables	Comments
f-fiscal	Kneller et al. (1999)	22 OECD countries, panel data.	Growth rate in real GDP per capita.	Classifies tax revenue into 'distortionary' and 'non-distortionary' and classifies expenditure into "productive" and "non-productive". Conditioning variables include catch-up, investment and labour force growth. Concludes from results that non-distortionary revenue and productive expenditure are a zero impact on growth. Furthermore suggests results imply an increase in productive expenditure, if financed from non-distortionary tax and non-productive expenditure has a positive impact on growth. Acknowledges that results are weakened by the finding that coefficients vary significantly depending on time period chosen.
f-fiscal	Medoza at al. (1997)	18 OECD countries, panel data.	Growth rate in real GDP per capita.	Introduces data on tax rates on consumption, labour, capital and personal taxation to growth regressions and finds that they are not statistically significant determinants of growth. Concludes that the evidence supports the Harberger hypothesis that in practice tax policy is an ineffective instrument to influence growth.
f-fiscal	Miller and Russek (1997)	16 countries, panel data.	Growth rate in real GDP per capita.	Disaggregates revenue and expenditure into different components and runs regressions for both OECD and developing countries. Conditioning variables include catch-up, population growth, investment, openness and inflation. For developed countries, concludes that debt-financing increases in expenditure have no effect on growth but that tax-financed increases do. In terms of expenditure, education expenditure is positively linked with growth whilst other forms of expenditure have no significant impact.

Source: OECD, "Economic Growth: the Role of Policies and Institutions. Panel Data Evidence from OECD Countries" by Andrea Bassanini, Stefano Scarpetta and Philip Hemmings, Economics Department, Working paper, No: 283, Paris, OECD, 2001.

An initial investigation of the aggregate function allows for the possibility that the growth of conventional inputs may be *non-neutral* in the sense that the marginal productivity of those inputs does not increase at the same rate through time. An interesting question is to see whether technical progress is *capital or labour augmenting* and if it is *capital (or labour) saving* in the sense that the demand for capital (labour) relative to the labour (capital) at a given quantity of output is reduced as a result of the technical progress. *Neutrality of technical change* implies that the *rate of technical progress* is independent of capital and labour. *Non-neutrality of technical progress* implies that the *rate of technical progress* at time t will vary depending on the quantities of capital and labour inputs at time t and to that extent may be regarded as endogenous.

To explore the link to productivity measurement, it is useful to state the growth-accounting approach: the rate of change of output, $dlnQ/dt$ that is a weighted average of the rate of growth of labor input $dlnL/dt$, the rate of growth of capital input $dlnK/dt$ intermediate inputs, $dlnM/dt$, and technical change designated $dlnA/dt$. Empirically estimations from econometric studies state that MFP growth is not necessarily caused by technological change. The residual reflects all technology shifts, such as non-technology factors adjustment costs, economies of scale, cyclical effects, some changes in efficiency and measurement errors that will bear on measured MFP (OECD, Manual for Measuring Productivity, 2001).

MFP is commonly defined as the portion of output growth left after accounting for growth in capital and labour, where both capital and labour are expressed in quality-adjusted terms. Arguably, this measure captures disembodied technological and organisational improvements that increase output for given amount of inputs. Dale Jorgenson, in particular, argues that this is the only identifiable component of technological progress. The other procedures to calculate MFP that use different measures for the capital aggregate (*e.g.* capital stock at acquisition prices) are likely also to pick up changes in the composition and quality of the capital stock due to other reasons than technological change. Table 2.4 illustrates some of the main growth regression studies for productivity growth and innovation activities.

2.8. SUMMARY CONCLUSIONS

Neoclassical theory suggests that convergence will be taken across countries in either growth rates or income levels. Poor countries will perform lower capital-labour ratios, implying a higher marginal product of capital. Given equal rates of labour force growth, technical progress and domestic savings, their capital stock will exceed and they will tend to converge with richer countries; as convergence will occur, growth rates of poorer countries should be greater. However, convergence in *neoclassical theory* will not occur if differences exist across countries in the production function. *Endogenous growth theory* suggests that it is possible that there would be sustained differences in both rates and levels of growth of national income.

Both diffusion and neoclassical models suggest the convergence to a unique equilibria. However, neither considers the possibility of multiple convergent equilibria; this has come out of new endogenous growth models. Romer provide important insights for the relation between growth and R&D and place them with a general equilibrium growth model.

The so-called *new growth theories* argue that greater investment (both in physical and human capital) creates externalities and economies of scale effects. These theories emphasize the role of economy returns for scale, expenditure on R&D, human capital formation and the role of investment on diffusion and technical change. Higher rates of gross investment could raise the rate of growth of productivity by increasing the rate of substitution of the old by new capital. Solow focused his attention on the process of capital formation.

On the other hand, *new growth theories* examine the way in which some countries been able to grow with no apparent tendency to slow down and try to explain why some countries exhibited medium or long term accelerations or decelerations in their growth. Romer makes technological change endogenous by assuming that technology is a public good and private investment in capital increases the level of technology available to entrepreneurs; higher investment rate will accelerate the economic growth.

Technological change drives long-term economic growth and improved standards of living (OECD, 1998, 2000). Technological change does not necessarily translate into MFP growth. Economic theory and empirical work pay particular emphasis to the distinction between embodied and disembodied technology. Embodied technological changes are advances in the design and quality of new vintages of capital and intermediate products: machinery and equipment embody the fruits of research performed by the capital goods-producing industry, and other sectors obtain access to the outcome of this research through the purchase of new capital equipment or intermediate goods, (OECD, Manual for Measuring Productivity, 2001). Disembodied technical change relates to the advances in science, to blueprints and formulae and to the diffusion of knowledge of how things are done, including better management and organizational change (OECD, Manual for Measuring Productivity, 2001).

Other researchers have recently focused on the identification of the "embodied" part of technological progress. In particular, Greenwood *et al.* (1997) and Hercowitz (1998) have suggested a way to tackle the "embodiment" controversy by adding an additional source of information (and in fact mixing the primal and dual approach). On the one hand they suggest the estimation of the disembodied component as the residual of a production function where the aggregate flow of capital services is obtained through the user costs aggregation procedure and hedonic prices. On the other hand they suggest computing the growth rate of the embodied component as the growth rate of the inverse of the hedonic deflator of equipment multiplied by its share in value-added. The rationale behind this procedure is that, in a general equilibrium vintage model, *ceteris paribus,* the fall in the price of existing vintages as they age (mirrored by the hedonic deflator) reflects technological change.

Two measures of the effectiveness of R&D are commonly used: the output elasticity of the R&D stock, and the rate of return to R&D investment. Both measures are usually based on a Cobb-Douglas production function that includes the R&D capital stock (or, more often, R&D intensity) as a separable factor of production. This is equivalent to saying that R&D can be used as an explanatory variable of MFP. See, amongst many others, Romer (1990), Aghion and Howitt (1998), Barro (1998) and, *ante litteram*, Nelson and Winter (1982).

As summarised by Nadiri (1993), the output elasticities of R&D at the firm level tend to be around 0.1 to 0.3 and the rates of return around 20 per cent to 30 per cent. At the industry level, elasticities have roughly the same range, while the rates of return are estimated to be between 20 per cent to 40 per cent. Evidence also suggests that basic research has higher returns than applied R&D (Griliches, 1986) and that process R&D has higher returns than product R&D. There is also evidence that the role of R&D may differ between small and large economies. In large countries, R&D mainly helps to increase the rate of innovation, while in smaller countries, R&D primarily serves to facilitate the transfer of technology from abroad. (Bassanini Andrea, Stefano Scarpetta and Ignazio Visco, 2000)

Theoretical and empirical models of *endogenous growth* emerged in the 2000s. The approach of *endogenous growth* suggests that growth rates are not exogenous rather depend on internal allocation processes; this arises rather because of non-decreasing returns to scale or because of the production externalities. *Endogenous growth* differs from *neoclassical growth models* because it assumes that economic growth is an endogenous outcome of an economic system and not the result of forces that infringe from outside. *Endogenous growth theory* has the advantage of explaining the forces that give rise to technological change rather than following the assumption of *neoclassical theory* that such change is exogenous. *Endogenous growth models* emphasize the role of international trade; they suggest that high productivity growth is possible in poor countries as a result of the diffusion of knowledge already available in industrial countries. Since Solow (1956), technological change has been regarded as one of the main sources of economic growth. Neoclassical models are assuming marginal productivity, technological change (or labour growth) are needed to compensate for the negative productivity effects of capital accumulation.

In this chapter, we have attempted to analyse the determinant factors of technological change. In the steady state of technological change, we can present both types of technological change: the actual amounts of basic research and quality improvement depend on the different marginal growth productivity of human capital between basic research and quality improvements.

In literature, there are various explanations for the slow-down in productivity growth. One source of the slow-down may be substantial changes in the industrial composition of output, employment, capital accumulation and resource utilisation. The second source may be that technological opportunities have declined and furthermore the application of new technologies to production has been less successful. Technological factors act in long run and should not be expected to explain medium-run variations in the growth of GDP and productivity.

Technological gap models represent two conflicting forces: innovation, which tends to increase the productivity differences between countries, and diffusion, which tends to reduce them. In the Schumpeterian theory, growth differences are seen as the combined results of these forces. Research on *why growth rates differ* has a long history which goes well beyond growth accounting exercises.

Following the technological-gap argument, it would be expected that the more technologically advanced countries would also be the most economically advanced (in terms of innovation activities and per capita GDP). Technology-intensive industries play an increasingly important role in the international manufacturing trade of EU countries. In the 1990s, OECD exports of high- and medium-high-technology industries grew at an annual rate of around 7%, and their shares in manufacturing exports reached 25% and 40% respectively, in 1999. Substantial differences in the shares of high- and medium-high-technology industries in manufacturing exports are observed across the OECD area, ranging from over 75% in Japan, Ireland, and the United States, to less than 20% in Greece, New Zealand and Iceland.

Between 1990 and 1999, the annual growth rate of exports in technology-intensive industries was highest in Mexico (29%), followed by Ireland (18%). A catch-up effect can also be seen in Iceland and Turkey which still have a relatively low share of high- and medium-high-technology industries in manufacturing exports; they experienced annual growth of trade in technology-intensive industries of 17% and 15%, respectively.

The catching-up hypothesis is related to economic and technological relations among countries. There are different opportunities for countries to pursue a development strategy that depends on resource and scale factors. In summary, we can say that the introduction of new technologies has influenced industrialisation and economic growth. Of course, for countries with poor technological apparatus the impact of new technologies is much smaller. Finally, it seems that the technological gap between the less and more advanced countries is still widening.

Chapter 3

INNOVATION ACTIVITIES AND THE PRODUCTIVITY PUZZLE

3.1. INTRODUCTION

This Chapter investigates the relationship between productivity and technological change. The question that we shall address in this Chapter is whether the recent slow down in productivity can be explained by the slow-down of innovation activities. This Chapter attempts to measure technical change in order to measure the effects of economic growth for European member states. It introduces the reader, first, to some basic elements and concepts central to the understanding of this approach. The characteristics of the innovation process such as its nature and sources as well as some factors shaping its development are examined. Particular emphasis is laid on the role of technical change and dissemination based on the fundamental distinction between codified and tacit forms. These concepts recur throughout the Chapter and particularly in discussions about the nature and specifications of systems approach. The Chapter concludes summarizing some major findings of the discussion and pointing to some directions for future research activities.

Many studies have suggested that there is a interrelation between technological development and productivity (see, for example, Abramovitz, 1986; Fagerberg, 1987, 1988, 1994), and economists have analysed different possible views of why productivity growth has declined. These alternative explanations can be grouped into the following categories:

- the capital factor; for instance, investment may have been insufficient to sustain the level of productivity growth;
- the technology factor; for instance, a decline in innovation might have affected productivity growth;
- the increased price of raw materials and energy;
- government regulations and demand policies that affect the productivity level;
- skills and experience of the labour force may have deteriorated or workers may not work as hard as they used to;
- products and services produced by the economy may have become more diverse; and
- productivity levels may differ greatly across industries.

In summary, this Chapter attempts to measure the relationship between technology and productivity or, more precisely, to investigate the correlation between technological development and the decline in productivity growth. We shall empirically test technological and catching-up models, using data mainly for the EU member states.

3.2. INNOVATION ACTIVITIES AND THE PRODUCTIVITY GROWTH

Productivity growth is the basis of efficient economic growth. Economic growth has been defined as the process of a sustained increase in the production of goods and services with the aim of making available a progressively diversified basket of consumption goods to population Scarcity of resources, which includes physical, financial and human resources, has been recognized as a limiting factor on the process of economic growth. While output expansion based on increased use of resources is feasible, it is not sustainable.

Therefore, efficiency or productivity of resources becomes a critical factor in economic growth. These terms, which will be defined more precisely in the following section, indicate ability to obtain a given amount of good or service by using a lesser amount of input. Productivity growth, therefore, is critical for ensuring sustained increase in the production of goods and services. Economic growth is traditionally been associated with industrialisation. At least that is what makes the diversity in the basket of consumption goods and services possible, when trading possibilities are limited. But industrialisation at the initial stages has the effect of making resource scarcities more acute, making it all the more necessary that available resources are utilised more productively.

Role of productivity growth in the process of economic growth became clear when it was found that accumulation of productive factors (capital and labour) could explain only a fraction of actual expansion of output in the 1950s. Empirical work on the American economy by Tinbergen (1992), Schmookler (1966), Fabricant (1954), Abramovitz (1956), Kendrick (1961), Solow (1957) and Denison (1962) showed that between 80 to 90 percent of observed increase in output per head could not be explained by increase in capital per head and was attributed to productivity growth. Further, Terleckyi (1974), Scherer (1982a, 1982b) and Griliches (1980) showed that technological advancement was a major source of productivity improvement for the American industry.

While productivity growth and technological change affect the use of all factors, it is important to single out energy for a separate treatment. Energy is essential for economic growth and rapid increases in economic activity associated with accelerating economic growth lead to large increases in demand. As economic growth progresses and the economy moves away from agricultural to industrial modes of production, energy intensity, that is, energy use per unit of GDP, first increases and then declines.

Productivity growth in the manufacturing sector in general and in the energy intensive industries in particular has the effect of moderating the growth of energy demand. The degree of this moderation of course depends on magnitude and the nature of technological change. If technological change is neutral, in the sense that it affects all inputs equally, the degree of moderation will depend on the overall growth of technological progress. On the one hand, if it has an energy saving bias, there will be significant degree of moderation. On the other hand, if technological change has an energy using bias, the economy is likely to experience a rapid increase in energy demand, requiring explicit policy initiatives. Table 3.1 presents a macro and micro approach for the measurement of productivity.

Table 3.1. Macro and Micro-Approaches to Measuring Productivity

Question	Measure (Agency)	Information Needs	Methodology	Current Status	Gaps and Challenges
Micro Approach: (establishment, enterprise (firm), or enterprise segment)					
Impact	Productivity	Output Inputs: Labour (for instance, payroll hours) Other Inputs (for instance, capital services, materials, energy) E-commerce, e-Business	Model-based estimates of labour and multi-factor productivity at the business using: Economic Annual, quarterly, and monthly	Several completed for manufacturing. New studies for selected other sectors just started. Subject to gaps and measurement challenges	Gaps: Limited information (for instance, detail on inputs) in sectors outside manufacturing. None on use of e-business processes. Challenges: Capturing changes to the structure of firms, such as vertical integration and contracting-out.
Macro Approach: (industry, sector, nation)					
Impact	Productivity	Output Inputs: Labour (for instance, hours) Other Inputs (for instance, capital services, materials, energy) E-commerce, e-Business	Model-based estimates of labour and multi-factor productivity at the industry and national level. Economic Annual, quarterly, and monthly Other non-Census Data	Labour productivity estimated for all sectors. MFP not estimated for services	Gaps: Lack of detailed information on inputs calculate MFP for industries outside manufacturing. Challenges: Measures of inputs, Outputs, prices.

Source: Atrostic, B.K., A. Colecchia and B. Pattinson (2000b).

Table 3.2. Share of Value Added in Total Gross Value Added, (current prices, as a percentage) for Technology-Based Industries

	High technology manufactures	Medium-high technology manufactures	Post and telecommunications services	Finance and insurance services	Business activities (excluding real estate activities)	Total with 'market' sevices	Education and health	Total
	2423, 30, 32, 33, 353	24less2423, 29, 31, 34, 352, 359	64	65-67	71-74		80, 85	
Canada	2.1	5.8	2.8	6.9	6.9	24.4	11.1	35.5
Mexico	2.4	5.6	1.7	2.3	6.5	18.4	8.9	27.3
United States	3.7	4.2	3.5	8.8	10.3	30.4	11.5	41.9
Australia	3.3	→	3.1	7.1	11.5	25.0	10.9	35.9
Japan	3.9	6.0	1.6	6.4	7.8	25.7	..	..
Korea	7.0	7.0	2.1	6.6	4.0	26.8	7.6	34.4
Austria	2.1	5.4	2.0	6.8	7.9	24.2	9.8	34.0
Belgium	2.2	5.9	1.6	5.9	..	..	12.9	..
Czech Republic	1.7	8.3	4.3	4.5	6.9	25.7	7.1	32.8
Denmark	2.3	3.9	2.4	5.0	8.1	21.7	15.2	36.9
Finland	6.1	5.0	3.2	3.8	6.1	24.3	12.2	36.5
France	2.4	5.1	2.2	5.0	13.4	28.0	11.4	39.4
Germany	2.4	9.3	2.3	4.5	13.2	31.7	10.2	41.9
Greece	0.5	→	3.3	5.0	7.0	17.1	10.1	27.2
Hungary	11.8	→	3.8	3.9	8.6	28.1	9.2	37.3
Iceland	2.3		..	6.5	..	..	13.3	..
Ireland	8.6	10.4	..	4.5	..	..	8.3	..
Italy	1.9	5.6	2.3	6.2	9.1	25.0	9.7	34.7
Luxembourg	2.1	→	..	25.6	8.6	36.3	7.2	43.5
Netherlands	6.0	→	2.4	6.4	12.0	26.8	11.5	38.3
Norway	1.0	2.4	2.2	3.9	9.4	19.0	13.6	32.6
Poland	6.4	→	2.1	2.2	..	..	8.4	..
Portugal	1.1	2.8	2.9	6.4	..	..	12.7	..
Slovak	7.7	→	2.7	3.6	6.0	20.0	7.4	27.5
Spain	1.2	4.8	2.6	5.2	5.9	19.8	10.2	29.9
Sweden	3.7	7.1	2.8	3.8	10.0	27.4	14.8	42.2
Switzerland	9.3	→	3.0	16.1	8.5	37.0	5.8	42.8
United Kingdom	3.0	4.3	2.9	5.2	12.7	28.2	12.1	40.2
E. U.	2.3	6.0	2.4	5.3	11.0	27.0	11.0	38.0
Total OECD	3.2	5.2	2.7	6.7	9.6	27.4	..	..

Source: OECD, STAN.

In particular, following the decomposition analysis by Solow (1957), many alternative factors can explain the path of economic growth. According to Solow's findings, technology has been responsible for 90 per cent of the increase in labour productivity in the United States in the twentieth century. The unexplained decline in productivity growth can thus be regarded as resulting from a collapse in technological activities. This may have happened because the availability of technological opportunities has been temporarily or permanently reduced.

Table 3.2 indicates for technology based industries, the share of value added in total gross value added as a percentage. The level of technology in a country cannot be measured directly, but an approximation measure can be used to obtain an overall picture of the set of techniques invented or diffused by that country. We shall use real per capita GDP as an approximate productivity measure. The most representative measures for technological inputs and outputs are patent activities and research expenditures.

3.3. THEORY AND MEASUREMENT OF PRODUCTIVITY GROWTH

Productivity is a relationship between production and the means of production, or, more formally, a relation of proportionality between the output of a good or service and inputs used to generate that output. This relationship is articulated through the given technology of production. There are two general types of studies that have calculated international TFP differentials:

(a) Studies of value added and
(b) Studies of gross output.

Among the studies which calculate TFP using a value added output measure are Dollar and Wolff (1993), Dollar, Wolff and Baumol (1988), Maskus (1991), van Ark (1993), and van Ark and Pilat (1993). The first three of these researchers use overall GDP price levels to deflate sectoral outputs. The second class of studies of TFP uses data on gross output, and deflates all inputs (capital, labour, materials, energy, etc) in a symmetric way. This procedure was pioneered by Jorgenson and various co-authors, and is undoubtedly the most theoretically appealing and least restrictive method of making productivity comparisons.

Productivity growth is crucially affected by technological change. Their relationship is so close that the two terms are often used interchangeably. Productivity is a wider concept. Even though a crucial one, technological change is only one of the many factors which affect productivity growth; Other being social, cultural, educational, organisational and managerial factors. Better management of workers and machinery and appropriate incentive structures can increase production and/or reduce costs. But these are different from technological change.

It is not easy or straightforward to disentangle the effects of technological change from social and cultural factors. One simple way to conceptualise the differences is the way suggested by Spence (1984). On the other hand, if changes concern primarily people, then they may reasonably be considered as being *social* in nature. On the other hand, if they appear to be fundamentally about material products and related processes, then they can be more easily viewed as *technological*.

The notion of a production function is central for the meaning of technology. It is consequently crucial for the measurement of productivity. A production function is a technological relationship which specifies the maximum level of output of a good which can be obtained from a given level of one or several inputs. In its general form, two-input production function can be written as

$$V_t = f(K_t, L_t)$$

where V_t = level of net output (value added).
K_t = capital input (or service of factor capital)
L_t = labour input
t = time

Partial or single factor productivity (PP) of labour or capital is indicated by the ratio V/L, or V/K for instance, output per unit, or the average product of the factor concerned. Productivity defined this way is merely the inverse of factor intensity. An increase in this ratio, while assuming that other things remaining the same, implies an increased efficiency of input use, whereby the same level of output can be produced by a smaller quantity of given input. However, when other things cannot be assumed to be the same, the interpretation of these output factor ratios as indicators of productivity becomes problematic. For example, an increase in labour productivity may only reflect capital deepening - a rise in the K/L ratio. In such cases it becomes necessary to compute total factor productivity.

Total factor productivity (TFP) extends the concept of single factor productivity such as output per unit labour or capital to more than one factor. Thus, TFP is the ratio of gross output to a weighted combination of inputs. For the case of production function shown above, TFP at time t would be given by:

$$A_t = \frac{V_t}{g(K_t, L_t)}$$

where A_t: Index of TFP at time t.
  g the aggregation procedure is implicit in the specific production function adopted.
  Different functional forms of production functions imply different aggregation procedures or weighting schemes for combining factor inputs.
  Moreover, a general functional form (which has recently come to be known as KLEM type production function) can be used:

$$Y_t = g(K_t, L_t, E_t, M_t, t)$$

where: Y_t = level of gross output per unit of time,
  K_t = capital input (or service of factor capital)
  L_t = labour input
  E_t = input of energy
  M_t = material inputs
  t = time

The choice between the two alternative forms depends on what one believes to be the correct measure of output. It also depends on whether one thinks the production function to be separable in factor and material inputs or not. One can define the productivity measure associated with the value added (V) production function as total factor productivity (TFP) and that associated with gross output (Y) production function as total productivity (TP).

3.4. MEASURING THE PRODUCTIVITY GROWTH

There are three principal approaches to measurement of productivity growth. These are:

(i) The index number approach and
(ii) The parametric approach.

3.4.1. The Index Number Approach

In the index number approach the observed growth in output is sought to be explained in terms of growth in factor inputs. The unexplained part or the residual is attributed to growth in productivity of factors. It consists in assuming a certain functional form for the producers' production function and then deriving an index number formula that is consistent (exact) with the assumed functional form. Preferred functional forms are the flexible ones. These indexes differ from each other on the basis of underlying production function or the aggregation scheme assumed. Following are some of the most commonly used indexes.

Kendrick's index of total factor productivity for the case of value added as output, and two inputs can be written as

$$A_t = \frac{V_t}{(r_0 K_t + w_0 L_t)}$$

where:
A_t is the value of index in a given year,
V_t is the value of gross output,
w_0 and r_0 denote the factor rewards of labour and capital respectively in the base year.

The index measures average productivity of an arithmetic combination of labour and capital with base year period factor prices. It assumes a linear and a homogeneous production function of degree one. Besides constant returns to scale and neutral technical progress, it assumes an infinite elasticity of substitutability between labour and capital. The index can be generalised to allow for more than two factors. If a sufficiently long time series for this index can be constructed, then a trend rate of growth can be estimated econometrically. From the time series of Kendrick index, yearly series (gt) can be formed by writing growth between successive years as

$$g_{t+1}^K = (A_{t+1} - A_t)/A_t$$

The growth rates thus obtained can be appropriately averaged for sub-periods.

Another index measure for productivity growth has been introduced by Solow. Solow's measure of productivity growth for two input case is given by the following equation:

$$g_{t+1}^S = \left[\frac{V_{t+1} - V_t}{V_t}\right] - \left[\frac{L_{t+1} - L_t}{L_t} + \frac{K_{t+1} - K_t}{K_t}\right]$$

where V_j = measure of output.

This measure is based on general neo-classical production function. It assumes constant returns to scale, Hicks-neutral technical change, competitive equilibrium and factor rewards being determined by marginal products. Under these conditions, the growth of total factor productivity is the difference between the growth of value added and the rate of growth of total factor inputs. The latter is in the form of a Divisia index number for instance, a weighted combination of the growth rates, the weights being the respective shares. If we assumed specific Cobb-Douglas production function, with unit elasticity of output (unlike in the general functional form above) and took base year factor shares as weights, we would get Domar's geometric index of TFPG.

Assuming $A_1 = 1$, a time series of Solow index of productivity (A_t) can be formed from the formula:

$$A_{t+1} = A_t * (1 + g_{t+1}^S)$$

Furthermore, over twenty-five years ago, Malmquist (1983) proposed a quantity index for use in consumption analysis. The index scales consumption bundles up or down, in a radial fashion, to some arbitrarily selected indifference surface. In this context Malmquist's scaling factor turns out to be Shephard's (1953) input distance function, and Malmquist quantity indexes for pairs of consumption bundles can be constructed from ratios of corresponding pairs of input distance functions.1 Although it was developed in a consumer context, the Malmquist quantity index recently has enjoyed widespread use in a production context, in which multiple but cardinally measurable outputs replace scalar-valued but ordinally measurable utility. In producer analysis, Malmquist indexes can be used to construct indexes of input, output or productivity, as ratios of input or output distance functions. The period t output-oriented Malmquist productivity index is

$$M_0^t(x^t, y^t, x^{t+1}, y^{t+1}) = D_0^t(x^{t+1}, y^{t+1})/D_0^t(x^t, y^t).$$

$M_0^t(x^t, y^t, x^{t+1}, y^{t+1})$ compares (x^{t+1}, y^{t+1}) to (x^t, y^t) by scaling y^{t+1} to Isoquant $P^t(x^{t+1})$, that is, by using period t technology as a reference. Although $D_0^t(x^t, y^t) \leq 1$, it is possible that $D_0^t(x^t, y^t) > 1$, since period t+1 data may not be feasible with period t technology. Thus $M_0^t(x^t, y^t, x^{t+1}, y^{t+1}) \gtreqless 1$ according as productivity change is positive, zero or negative between periods t and t+1, from the perspective of period t technology. The period t output-oriented Malmquist productivity index decomposes as:

$$M_0^t(x^t, y^t, x^{t+1}, y^{t+1}) = \Delta TE(x^t, y^t, x^{t+1}, y^{t+1}) * \Delta T^t(x^t, y^t, x^{t+1}, y^{t+1}) =$$

$$= \frac{D_0^{t+1}(x^{t+1}, y^{t+1})}{D_0^t(x^t, y^t)} \bullet \frac{D_0^t(x^{t+1}, y^{t+1})}{D_0^{t+1}(x^{t+1}, y^{t+1})},$$

where, $\Delta TE(^*)$ refers to technical efficiency change and $\Delta T^t(^*)$ refers to technical change.

Finally, another interesting index for productivity growth is the translog measure index. Translog measure of TFPG is given by:

$$g_{t+1}^T = \ln\left[\frac{Y_{t+1}}{Y_t}\right] - \left[\left[\frac{s_{t+1}^L + s_t^L}{2}\right] * \ln\left[\frac{L_{t+1}}{L_t}\right] + \left[\frac{s_{t+1}^K + s_t^K}{2}\right] * \ln\left[\frac{K_{t+1}}{K_t}\right]\right]$$

This expresses TFP as the difference between growth rate of output and weighted average of growth rates of labour and capital input. This is equivalent to Tornquist's discrete approximation to continuous Divisia index. The index is based on the translog function which describes the relationship both between outputs and inputs and between the aggregate and its components. The homogeneous translog functional form is flexible in the sense that it can provide a second order approximation to an arbitrary twice continuously differentiable linear homogeneous function. This functional form helps overcome the problem which arises with the Solow index where discrete set of data on prices and quantities need to be used in a continuous function. This index also imposes fewer a priori restrictions on the underlying production technology. The index can be generalised for more than two inputs.

Like in the previous case, from year to year changes in productivity growth one can construct a time series of the translog index as follows:

$$A_{t+1} = A_t * (1 + g_{t+1}^T)$$

An alternative approach is to use economic aggregators based directly on technology and input and output quantities. Generalizing to the case in which we have also multiple outputs and inputs requires a close relative of production function, namely, the distance function, denoting the distance from some observed input – output combination to the frontier of technology. Distance functions constitute the building blocks for a measure of productivity change (Fried et al, 2008). Malmquist (1953) introduced the input distance function in the context of consumption analysis. His objective was to compare alternative consumption bundles. He did so by developing a standard of living (or consumption quantity) index as the ratio of a pair of input distance functions. In the context of production analysis, Malmquist's standard of living index becomes an input quantity index. An analogous output quantity index is expressed as the ratio of a pair of output distance functions.

3.4.2. The Parametric Approach

Parametric approach consists in econometric estimation of production functions to infer contributions of different factors and of an autonomous increase in production over time, independent of inputs. This latter increase, which is a shift over time in the production function, can be more properly identified as technological progress. It is one of the factors underlying productivity growth. An alternative to estimation of production functions is estimation of cost functions using results from the duality theory. Below we give some commonly used specifications of production functions.

In the parametric approach, we can first consider the general form of Cobb-Douglas Function has the following form:

$$V = A_0 e^t LK$$

where, V, L, K and t refer to value added, labour, capital and time. a and b give factor shares respectively for labour and capital. A_0 describes initial conditions. Technological change takes place at a constant rate l. It is assumed to be disembodied and Hicks-neutral, so that when there is a shift in the production function, K/L ratio remains unchanged at constant prices. In log-linear form this function can be written as:

$$\log V = a + \alpha \log L + \beta \log K + \lambda_t$$

The estimated value of l provides a measure of technological progress, which is often identified with total factor productivity growth.

In addition, for the parametric analysis we can consider the general form of Constant-Elasticity of Substitution Function has the following form:

$$V = A_0 e^t \left(L^{-\delta} + (1-\lambda)K^{-\rho}\right)^{-v}$$

where l is the efficiency parameter, δ the distribution parameter, ρ the substitution parameter and u is the scale parameter. The elasticity of substitution $\sigma = 1/(1 + \rho)$ varies between 0 and μ. Technical change is Hicks neutral and disembodied. The value of λ (a measure of technical progress) can be estimated using a non-linear estimation procedure, or by using the following Taylor-series linear approximation to the CES function:

$$\ln V = \ln A_0 + \lambda t + v\delta \ln L + v(1-\delta)\ln K - (1/2)\rho v\delta(1-\delta)(\ln L - \ln K)^2$$

This function can be estimated by OLS.

Furthermore, for the parametric analysis, the general form of Transcendental Function can be estimated in the following form:

$$\log V = \alpha_0 + \beta_L (\log L) + \beta_K (\log K) + \frac{1}{2}\beta_{LL}(\log L)^2 + \frac{1}{2}\beta_{KK}(\log K)^{2^2}$$

$$+ \beta_{LK}(\log L)(\log K) + \beta_{Lt}(\log L)t + \beta_{Kt}(\log K)t + \frac{1}{2}\beta_{tt}t$$

where α's and β's are the parameters of the production function.
The rate of technical progress or total factor productivity growth is given by:

$$\frac{\log V}{t} = \alpha_t + \beta_{tt}t + \beta_{Lt}(\log L) + \beta_{Kt}(\log K)$$

where: α_t is the rate of autonomous total factor productivity growth.

β_{tt} is the rate of change of TFPG, and
β_{Lt}, β_{Kt} define the bias in TFPG.

If both β_{Lt} and β_{Kt} are zero, then the TFPG is Hicks-neutral type. If β_{Lt} is positive then the share of labour increases with time and there is labour using bias. Similarly, a positive β_{Kt} will show a capital using bias.

We can also use a cost function for the parametric analysis. Due to results of duality theory, one may estimate a cost function instead of production function to calculate technical progress. In its general form, a four-factor cost function can be written as:

$$C = C(P_L, P_K, P_E, P_M, Q, t)$$

Specific forms of cost functions corresponding to each of the above functional forms can be derived. We give below the translog cost function which has many desirable properties sought out by researchers and which has been used most commonly in recent years.

An extension of this is the translog function. The general form of Translog Function has the following form:

$$\log C = \beta_i + \sum_i \beta_i \log p_i + \frac{1}{2}\sum_i \sum_j \log p_i \log p_j + \beta_Q \log Q +$$

$$+ \frac{1}{2}\beta_{QQ}(\log Q)^2 + \beta_{Qt}\log Q \log t + \beta_t \log t + \frac{1}{2}\beta_{tt}(\log t)^2 +$$

$$+ \sum_i \beta_{Qi}\log Q \log p_j + \sum_i \beta_{ti}\log t \log p_i$$

Using Shepherd's lemma one can estimate demands for individual factors and shares in total cost of individual factors as follows:

$$\frac{\log C}{\log p_i} = \frac{x_i p_i}{C} = S_i = \beta_i + \sum_j \beta_{ij}\log p_j + \beta_{Qi}\log Q + \beta_{ti}\log t$$

Rate of technical progress (λ_t) is given by

$$(t) = \frac{\log C}{t} = \frac{1}{t}\left(\beta_t + \beta_{tt}\log t + \beta_{Qt}\log Q + \sum_j \beta_{ti}\log p_i\right)$$

Technical progress has a factor i using bias if $\beta_{ti} > 0$. It is neutral with respect to factor i if $\beta_{ti} = 0$ and it is factor i saving if β_{ti} is < 0.

Schmookler (1966), Kendrick (1991), and Abramovitz (1986) have studied the interaction between technological change and productivity. In these studies, factor prices were used to weight the various inputs in order to obtain a measure of total input growth. The approach developed by Abramovitz (1986), Solow (1957) and Denison (1962) involves the decomposition of output growth into its various sources, which can be defined as the growth accounting and residual method. Growth accounting tries to explain changes in real product and total factor productivity based mainly on a comparison between the growth of inputs (capital and labour) and the growth of output. One part of actual growth cannot be explained and has been classified as 'unexplained total factor productivity growth' (or the so called residual).

3.5. PRODUCTIVITY AND EFFICIENCY

According to the growth accounting literature, output growth is decomposed into two parts: one explained by input changes and the other the unexplained residual, or 'technical change'. However, the interpretation of the unexplained residual as technical change is unreasonable unless it is assumed that all sectors in all countries are producing on their frontiers, namely as producing on total efficiency level (Koop, 2001). However, at a given moment of time, when the technology and the production environment are essentially the same, producers may exhibit different productivity levels due to differences in their production efficiency (Kokkinou, 2010a).

Within economic growth process, therefore, efficiency of productivity of resources becomes a critical element in economic growth, through utilising available resources more productively. More precisely, interest in measuring efficiency and productivity may be attributed to three reasons (Kokkinou, 2010b):

- First, only by measuring efficiency and productivity, and by separating their effects from those of the operating environment, can we explore hypotheses concerning the sources of efficiency or productivity differentials, which are essential to improve performance.
- Second, macro performance depends on micro performance and so the same reasoning applies to the study of growth in aggregate level.
- Third, efficiency and productivity measures are success indicators by which producers are evaluated. It follows that productivity growth leads to improved financial performance, provided it is not offset by declining price recovery attributable to falling product prices and / or rising input prices.

- Finally, the ability to quantify efficiency and productivity provides management with a control mechanism with which to monitor the performance of a production unit.

Efficiency of a production unit represents a comparison between observed and optimal values of its output and input. This comparison comes in two forms. The first is the ratio of observed to maximum potential output obtainable from a given level of input. The second is defined by considering first the given level of input, and is measured as the ratio of minimum potential to observed input required producing the given output. The difference can be explained in terms of technical and allocative inefficiencies, as well as a range of unforeseen exogenous shocks. As stated above, even though in the real economic life, it is unlikely that all (or possibly any) producers, firms or, even, economies operate at the full efficiency frontier, however, in research, failure to attain the frontier implies the existence of technical or allocative inefficiency (Reifschneider and Stevenson, 1991).

Although the importance of efficient use of resources has long been recognized, neoclassical economics assume that producers in an economy always operate efficiently. In reality, however, the producers are not always efficient. Two otherwise identical firms never produce the same output, and costs and profit are not the same. This difference in output, cost, and profit can be explained in terms of efficiency and some unforeseen exogenous shocks over time and / or space.

During the recent years, there is a rapid increase in the volume of research on analysis of efficiency in production, both in theoretical and empirical foundations, focusing on the nature, magnitude, and influences of productive efficiency. Economists are primarily concerned about the efficient use of scarce resources. The main goal of the relevant studies has been to search for evidence of inefficiency. A question of interest is whether inefficiency occurs randomly across firms, or whether some firms have predictably higher levels of inefficiency than others. If the occurrence of inefficiency is not totally random, than it should be possible to identify factors that contribute to the existence of inefficiency (Reifschneider and Stevenson, 1991).

By the efficiency of a producer, we have in mind a comparison between observed and optimal values of its output and input. The optimum is defined in terms of production possibilities, and efficiency is technical. It is also possible to define the optimum in terms of the behavioral goal of the producer. In this event, efficiency is measured by comparing observed and optimum cost, revenue, profit, or any other goal, subject to any appropriate constraints on quantities and process. In these comparisons, the optimum is expressed in value terms and efficiency is economic. In what follows, producers are characterized as efficient if they have produced as much as possible with the inputs they have actually employed or if they have produced that output at minimum cost.

- First, 'productive efficiency' refers to the use of productive resources in the most technologically efficient manner. Put differently, technical efficiency implies the maximum possible output from a given set of inputs. Technical efficiency may then refer to the physical relationship between the resources used (say, capital, labour and equipment) and some outcome. These outcomes may either be defined in terms of intermediate outputs or a final outcome. As rigorously described in Kumbhakar and Lovell (2000), productive efficiency represents the degree of success producers achieve in allocating the inputs at their disposal and the outputs they produce, in an effort to meet specific set productive objectives. Thus, in order to measure productive efficiency it is first necessary to specify producers' objectives and then to quantify their degrees of success. At an elementary level, the objective of producers can be as simple as seeking to avoid waste of resources, by obtaining maximum outputs from given inputs or by minimizing input use in the production of given outputs. In this case, the notion of productive efficiency corresponds to technical efficiency. At a higher level, the objective of producers might entail the production of given outputs at minimum cost or the utilization of given inputs in order to maximize revenues or the allocation of inputs and outputs in order to maximize profit. In this case, productive efficiency corresponds to economic efficiency, and the objective of producers becomes attaining a higher degree of economic (cost, revenue, or profit) efficiency. Where perfect technical efficiency exists, it is impossible to reduce any input without reducing at least one output or to increase any output without increasing at least one input. In order to measure the relative efficiency of a producer, it is defined as either the ratio of its actual output, or some weighted average of them to its expected output, given its input(s), namely output efficiency, or the ratio of its expected input, or some weighed combination of them to its actual input, namely input efficiency.

- Second, 'allocative efficiency' reflects the ability of an organization to use these inputs in optimal proportions, given their respective prices and the production technology. In other words, allocative efficiency is concerned with choosing between the different technically efficient combinations of inputs used to produce the maximum possible outputs. Since different combinations of inputs are being used, the choice is based on the relative costs of these different inputs (assuming outputs are held constant).
- Finally, when taken together, allocative efficiency and technical efficiency determine the degree of 'economic efficiency' (also known as total economic efficiency). Thus, if an organization uses its resources completely allocatively and technically efficiently, then it can be said to have achieved total economic efficiency. Alternatively, to the extent that either allocative or technical inefficiency is present, then the organization will be operating at less than total economic efficiency.

The measurement of productive efficiency through the estimation of production or cost frontiers has received an increasing amount of attention from both academics and practitioners over the last twenty years. Until 1950s, efforts were made to measure efficiency by interpreting the average productivity of inputs. However, in the 1950s, economists found that this method of measuring efficiency was unsatisfactory as it ignored other inputs used in the process of production. This method suffered from main drawbacks, such as:

- data aggregation;
- an a priori assumption that all firms produce efficiently;
- no allowance for random noise in measurement; and
- little or no knowledge about the functional form of production and the values of the parameters of the underlying technology.

The efficiency literature was started by Farrell's seminal paper in 1957, which built upon Debreu (1951) and Koopmans (1951). Farrell proposed to measure the efficiency of a productive unit in terms of the realized deviations from an idealized frontier isoquant (Farrell, 1957). The empirical identification of such a benchmark is the main issue of the literature on efficiency measurement. Farrell (1957) extended the work initiated by Koopmans and Debreu by noting that production efficiency has a second component reflecting the ability of producers to select the right technically efficient input- output vector in light of prevailing input and output prices. This led Farrell to define overall productive efficiency as the product of technical and allocative, or price, efficiency. Implicit is the notion of allocative efficiency is a specific behavioural assumption about the goal of the producer. Farrell considered cost minimisation in competitive input markets, although other behavioural assumptions can be considered (A detailed treatment on efficiency measurement and the related concepts is provided by Färe, Grosskopf and Lovell, 1985, 1994 and Lovell, 1993). When a firm is technically efficient, the *maximum output* is generated from a given level of inputs. An allocatively efficient firm would produce that output using the lowest cost combination of inputs. Therefore, technical efficiency illustrates a comparison of actual output and the maximum output, while allocative efficiency deals with the relationship between the minimum cost and actual cost bundles of inputs. The combination of the two measures provides the measure of productive or economic efficiency. Thus, if an organization uses its resources completely allocatively and technically efficiently, then it can be said to have method for measuring efficiency, known as stochastic frontier analysis. In this case, a stochastic frontier is defined as the locus of best performing agents within a data set. The other data points of the other firms are located "below" this estimated frontier. The relative distance measured between this best performance and the other data points is interpreted as inefficiency, which is the main approach followed today in productive efficiency estimation [Coelli et al. (1988, 2005), Fried et al. (1993, 2008)].

3.6. SUMMARY CONCLUSIONS

In this chapter, we have also attempted to analyse the theoretical background of innovation activities and productivity growth. Technological progress has become virtually synonymous with long-term economic growth. This raises a basic question about the capacity of both industrial and newly industrialised countries to translate their seemingly greater technological capacity into productivity and economic growth. Usually, there are difficulties in estimating the relation between technology change and productivity. Technological change may have accelerated, but in some cases there is a failure to capture the effects of recent technological advances in productivity growth or a failure to account for quality changes in previously introduced technologies. The countries of Europe have a long cultural and scientific tradition and major scientific discoveries and developments in technology are products of European civilisation. There is a close relationship between innovation and productivity levels. However there are large technological disparities between the European member states affecting productivity performance, increases economic disparities and hinders economic integration.

There are various explanations in literature for the slow-down in productivity growth in the E.U. countries. One source of the slow-down may be substantial changes in the industrial composition of output, employment, capital accumulation and resource utilisation. Another may be that technological opportunities have declined; or else new technologies have been developed but their application to production has been less successful. Technological factors act in a long-term way and should not be expected to explain medium-term variations in the growth of GDP and productivity.

Research on why growth rates differ has a long history that goes well beyond growth accounting exercises. The idea that poorer countries eventually catch up with richer ones was advanced as early as in the nineteenth century to explain continental Europe's convergence with Britain. In the 1960s, one of the most basic model, was the Marx~Lewis model of abundant labour supplies, which explained the divergent growth experience of the Western European countries.

To achieve safe results it is necessary to conduct a cross-country, multi-sectoral analysis of how technological activities affect different sectors. The pace of the catching up depends on diffusion of knowledge, the rate of structural change, accumulation of capital and the expansion of demand. Those member states whose growth rates are lagging behind could catch up if they reduce the technological gap. An important aspect of this is that they should not rely only on technology imports and investment, but should also increase their innovation activities and improve their locally produced technologies (as happened in Korea and Singapore). However, our results confirm that some of the small and medium-sized EU member states have attained high levels of per capita GDP without a large innovation capacity. To explain the differences in growth between these countries in the postwar period a much more detailed analysis of economic, social and institutional structures should be conducted. When we compare the technologically advanced and less advanced member states, it is not difficult to see that the less advanced countries lack experience of large-scale production, technical education and resources.

Chapter 4

TECHNICAL CHANGE AND THE DIFFUSION MODELS

4.1. INTRODUCTION

Technological creativity and advancement are key components of not only innovation and growth but also of their sustainability in the long term. Most economy consists of users of a given technology and is concerned chiefly with the breadth of the application of technology outside the sector that invented it. Therefore, R&D is an incomplete indicator for innovative capacity. Liberalisation and macroeconomic adjustment are increasingly motivated by the movement toward globalisation rather than the balance of payments crises of the 1980s, at least in middle-income developing countries and are central for the transmission of the effects of globalisation to the household level.

The improvement of technological infrastructure and human resources may improve the quality of life, and have more impact on production and development of a nation. R&D and technical change are directly related to industrial infrastructure, productivity effects and regional development. The term "technological policy" indicates both the national technological capabilities and the structure as well as planning of research and development. This chapter attempts to examine the role of "technological policy" and its effects on sustainable development; in particular, the implications on growth and social change. The growing importance of technological change in world production and employment is one of the characteristics of the last four decades. Technological change is not only a determinant of growth but also affects the international competition and the modernisation of a country.

It is difficult to record and analyse the results from a research and technological policy. It is well known that the adoption and diffusion of new technologies affect the structure and the competitiveness level of economy as well as. The choice of technology depends upon a large number of factors. It depends upon the availability of technologies, the availability of information to the decision makers, the availability of resources, the availability of technology itself and its capacity for successful adoption to suit the particular needs and objectives.

The advanced countries, which are among the leaders in technological change and which rely on well-functioning large economies, have tended to put more emphasis on policies aiming to encourage the development of research and technological activities. Technological policy only recently has been distinguished from the science policy. Whereas the "science policy" is concerned with education and the stock of knowledge, "technology policy" is concerned with the adoption and use of techniques, innovation, diffusion of techniques. The borderline between the areas and variables of science policy and technology policy is blurred. Education and stock of knowledge, for instance, play an important role in influencing the rate of innovation and diffusion of technology. Usually, technological policy should aim to create a favourable "psychological climate" for the development of research and innovations.

New technologies imply some micro effects (that is on firms, and organisations) and some macro effects (that is on industrial sectors) for the whole economy. In addition, new technologies play an important role to productivity and to competitiveness of a country. For instance, the faster the technological progress is, the faster should the factor productivity should rise and the less "cost-push" exert upward pressure on the price level. The principal effects for technological policy can be distinguished in demand and supply sides.

Diffusion is the way in which technological product and process (TPP) innovations spread, through market or non-market channels, from their first worldwide implementation to different countries and regions and to different industries, markets and firms.

Technological change is the result of both research and imitation activities. As soon as the information about the advantages provided by the innovation becomes available to the potential adopter, the adoption will take place. Adoption is the result of a complex process of decision-making. Absorption is just the process of diffusion perceived from the perspective of the recipient of the technique. The adoption of a new technology is in fact part of a broader process of technological change.

The distinction between innovation and imitation has been first introduced by Joseph Schumpeter and eventually has become a landmark in the economics of innovation and new technology. A new technology, either a new product or a new process is first introduced by an innovator and eventually imitated by competitors. Imitators copy the innovation and in so doing enter the market and reduce the excess profits of the innovator. Imitation restores perfect competition. The economics of diffusion addresses relevant questions about the characteristics and the determinants, and the effects of the diffusion process. The most controversial is why imitation is not instantaneous and all firms adopt at the same time the innovation (Stoneman, 1976, 1983, 1987).

This Chapter attempts to examine the diffusion process and to review the diffusion models. In addition, it attempts to investigate the correlation between technical change, innovation activities, diffusion process and productivity growth.

4.2. INNOVATION ACTIVITIES AND THE DIFFUSION PROCESS

Recognition of the interactive nature of innovation process has resulted in the breakdown of the earlier distinction between innovation and diffusion. Innovation activities and diffusion usually emerge as a result of an interactive and collective process within a web of personal and institutional connections which evolve over time. Knowledge transfer may occur through disembodied or equipment-embodied diffusion. The latter is the process by which innovations spread in the economy through the purchase of technology-intensive machinery, such as computer-assisted equipment, components and other equipment. Disembodied technology diffusion refers to the process during which technology and knowledge spread through other channels not embodied in machinery (OECD 1992).

Knowledge spillovers, for instance, knowledge created by one firm can be used by another without compensation or with compensation less than the value of the knowledge, arise because knowledge and innovation are partially excludable and non-rivalrous goods (Romer 1990). Lack of exclusivity implies that knowledge producers have difficulty in fully appropriating the returns or benefits and thereby preventing other firms from utilising the knowledge without compensation (Teece 1986). Patents and other devices, such as lead times and secrecy, are a way for knowledge producers to partially capture the benefits related to their knowledge generation. It is important to recognise that even a completely codified piece of knowledge cannot be utilised at zero cost by everyone. Only those economic agents who know the code are able to do so (Saviotti 1998).

A *system of innovation* can be thought of as consisting of a set of actors or entities such as firms, other organisations and institutions that interact in the generation, use and diffusion of new - and economically useful - knowledge in the production process. At the current stage of development, there is no general agreement as to which elements and relations are essential to the conceptual core of the framework and what is their precise content (Edquist 1997b).

A coherent system of innovation has necessarily to include a series of more or less coordinated network-like relations such as (Fischer 1999):

- *Customer-producer relations,* for instance,, forward linkages of manufacturing firms with distributors, value-added resellers and end users,
- *Producer-manufacturing supplier relations* which include subcontracting arrangements between a client and its manufacturing suppliers of intermediate production units,
- *Producer-service supplier relations* which include arrangements between a client and its producer service partners (especially computer and related service firms, technical consultants, business and management consultants),
- *Producer network relations* which include all co-production arrangements (bearing on some degree or another on technology) that enable competing producers to pool their production capacities, financial and human resources in order to broaden their product portfolios and geographic coverage,
- *Science-industry collaboration* between universities and industrial firms at various levels pursued to gain rapid access to new scientific and technological knowledge and to benefit from economies of scale in joint R&D, such as direct interactions between particular firms and particular faculty members, or joint research projects, as through consulting arrangements, or mechanisms that tie university or research programs to groups of firms.

Diffusion, defined as a sequence of adoption lags, is fully explained by the characteristics of the spreading of the information. Much attention has been paid to the identification of the determinants of the diffusion of the demand side and the determinants of the supply side. In the first case diffusion, that is the process of delayed adoptions and imitations of a given innovation, with fixed economic characteristics, including the performances and the price, takes place because of dynamics on the demand side. The main engine is the well know epidemic contagion in a population of heterogeneous agents, characterized by information asymmetries, and the eventual decay of information costs for potential adopters, driven by the dissemination of information carried out by all those who have already adopted (Griliches, 1957).

Rank models are focused on the idea that heterogeneity among firms explains observed diffusion patterns. Heterogeneity differs with regard to some critical variable that affects the expected present discounted profitability of the new technology relative to the old one -- the "net return on adoption" for short. Seven different critical variables have been identified.

- Capital vintage ;
- Firm size;
- Beliefs about the return on the new technology;
- Search costs;
- Input prices;
- Factor productivity;
- Regulatory costs.

Order models are based on the idea that the order in which firms adopt the new technology determines the net return that they obtain from it, with earlier adopters obtaining higher net returns. The order effect arises from the existence of a fixed critical input into production such skilled labor for software developers or access to prime drilling sites for petroleum explorers. However, over time, the net return on adoption increases (for the same reasons as in rank models) so that eventually more and more firms can adopt.

Stock models are emphasized on the idea that the net return on adoption for any firm depends on the total stock of firms that have adopted, with the net return on adoption declining as the stock increases. Stock effects are hypothesized to arise when the adoption of a new technology by a subset of firms in the industry lowers their average production costs to such an extent that output prices fall. Lower output prices in turn, reduce the net return on adoption. This effect does not depend on heterogeneity among firms or on the order in which firms adopt. Stock models hypothesize that firms adopt at different times because the net return on adoption falls as the stock of adopters grows. However, the net return on adoption rises so that more and more firms adopt. Successful absorption of foreign technology depends on the technological absorptive capacity of the economy. Absorptive capacity depends on the overall macroeconomic and governance environment, which influences the willingness of entrepreneurs to take risks on new and new-to-the-market technologies; and the level of basic technological literacy and advanced skills in the population, which determines a country's capacity to undertake the research necessary to understand, implement, and adapt them.

We can explain briefly why the importance of innovation as opposed to imitation should depend on a country's distance to the technological frontier.

Let A_t denote a country's productivity at date t. Let A_t^{max} denote frontier productivity at date t. Then the convergence process of the country towards the frontier can be described by an equation of the form: $A_t = n A_{t-1}^{max} + \gamma A_t$, where A_{t-1}^{max} is the imitation of frontier technology, γA_t is the innovation upon previous local technology, $\eta < 1, \gamma > 1$. Suppose the frontier grows at rate g, i.e. $A_t^{max} = A_{t-1}^{max}(1 + g)$, Combining the above, one obtains: $\frac{A_t}{A_t^{max}} = a^t = \frac{1}{(1+g)}(\eta + \gamma a_{t-1})$, where at measures the country's distance to the technological frontier. In particular when the country is far from the frontier, such as when at is close to zero, then imitation (such as the term η) is the main source of productivity growth as measured by a_t/a_{t-1}. But as the country moves closer to the frontier, such as at becomes closer to one, innovation (such as the term γa_{t-1}) becomes important for growth. The occurrence of a new technological wave (like the ICT revolution) will further increase the importance of innovation by increasing γ. In other words, the closer the country is to the world frontier, that is the closer a_{t-1} is to one, the more innovation matters for growth relative to imitation, and therefore the more important it is to establish innovation enhancing institutions and policies, (Acemoglu et al., 2002).

The balance between imitation and innovation has thus shifted decisively in favor of the second. In addition, a greater proportion of that innovation is radical rather than elemental. Growth becomes driven by innovation at the frontier and fast adaptation to technical progress. Now, as new growth theories suggest, most innovations result from entrepreneurial activities or investments - typically, investments in R&D - which involve risky experimentation and learning. In particular research investment is encouraged by:

- a good system to protect intellectual property rights on innovations;
- a high productivity of R&D, which itself requires a good education and research subsidy system;
- low interest rates as R&D investments are forward-looking; this in turn calls for a stable macroeconomy;
- product market competition, low entry costs, and market openness to stimulate innovation by incumbents;
- good access to risk capital by new start-up firms;
- more flexible labor market institutions, so that new innovators can quickly find workers that match their new technologies.

In the supply side approach, heterogeneity of potential adopters consists in their cost conditions (David, 1969; Metcalfe, 1981). Diffusion, is now defined now by the structure and the sequence of delays in the adoptions of a family of closely related technologies with changing economic and technical characteristics, rather a single and given technology with static features. Potential adopters can be ranked in terms of cost characteristics. Diffusion here is driven by the dynamics on the supply side and specifically by the introduction of an array of events including:

- incremental changes in the prototype introduced by the innovator and or by imitators
- the decline of the market price due to the entry of new competitors and the decline of market power and hence mark-up for early innovators, or due to the positive effects of increasing returns either associated to sheer economies of scale and density, or to the dynamics of learning by doing.

Many efforts have been made to combine the supply and the demand side approaches into a single more comprehensive model. Much progress has been made possible by the insight of Metcalfe (1981) where the epidemic, demand side mechanism is implemented by the shifting conditions on the supply side so as to define the traditional S-shaped process as the envelope of a double shift. Beyond the capacity to use or adopt new techniques, developing countries also need capacity to invent and adapt new technologies.

The identification of the role of adoption costs paves the way to the distinction between gross profitability of adoption and net profitability of adoption. Adoption costs are defined by the broad range of activities that are necessary to identify an innovation and adapt it to the existing production process. Adoption costs include the costs of search and adaptive research, the costs of scrapping the existing fixed production factors, the restructuring of the production and marketing organizations, the re-skilling of personnel, the actual purchase of the capital good and intermediary input embodying the new knowledge, the purchase of patents and licenses, the costs of technical assistance. Net profitability of adoption is the result of the algebraic sum of the gross profitability engendered by the adoption of an innovation and the costs that it is necessary to carry out in order to identify select and finally adapt the new technology to the existing production conditions.

Recent empirical evidence shows that the adoption of an innovation requires the active participation of the firm and as such it is the result of an activity. The characteristics of adoption activity in turn are much closer to the traditional views about original research and development activities, than it is currently assumed (Antonelli, 1991; Antonelli, Petit and Tahar, 1992; Stoneman and Toivanen, 1997; Arvanitis and Holenstein, 2001; Faria, Fenn and Bruce, 2002).

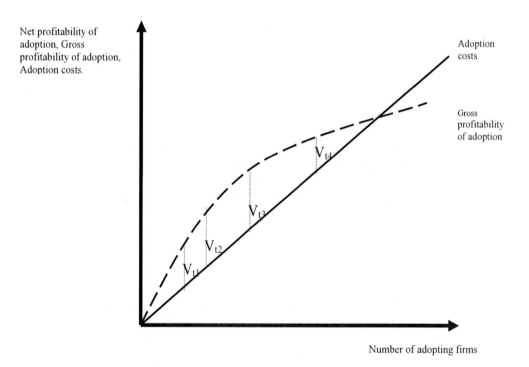

Figure 4.1. Adoption Costs, Gross and Net Profitability of Adoption and the Diffusion Process.

Figure 4.1 illustrates that because the positive and constant slope of adoption costs is associated with the number of adopters and the positive, but decreasing slope of the gross profitability of adoption is also associated with the number of adopters, the net profitability. The rate of the diffusion will be influenced by the adoption costs and gross profitability of adoption, but also, and also by the dynamics of technological change.

Adoption and innovation are two complementary aspects of a broader process of reaction to the mismatch between expectations and facts and eventual introduction of technological changes that build upon the creative adoption and recombination of internal and external technological knowledge.

The distinction between diffusion within final consumers and diffusion within firms makes it possible to stress the related distinction between gross and net profitability of adoption and the identification of the costs of adoption. The distinction between net and gross profitability together with the grasping of their dynamics, including the effects of the stocks of adoption on the evolution of the net profitability of adoption, provides an analytical probe that combines the demand and supply tradition of analysis of diffusion and shows the complementarity between innovation and adoption within the context of the economics of technological change.

4.3. DIFFUSION MODELS AND THE NEW GROWTH THEORY

The importance of diffusion of technology for economic growth has been emphasized by several authors. Specifically, the term *dissemination of technology* is used to include both voluntary and involuntary spread of technology. The term of *technology transfer* is defined as voluntary dissemination, while involuntary dissemination is labelled *imitation*. In literature on the diffusion process, there is considerable agreement on the time pattern of diffusion which may be expected to follow the first introduction of a new technique (or innovation).

The first important point is to distinguish between diffusion and adoption of technology. In the analysis of adoption one considers the decisions taken by agents to incorporate a new technology in their activities. A typical measure of adoption would be the proportion of eligible firms in an industry using a given technology.

By contrast, in the analysis of diffusion one is concerned with measuring the change of economic significance of a technology with the passage of time. In a sense, the analysis of diffusion is closely related to the analysis of *technological substitution* in which the displacement of one technology by another is the focus of attention. The spread of new technology occurs in a number of dimensions. The potential buyers of a technology can be public institutions, firms and households. The notion of technology diffusion must be taken today to include "the adoption by other users as well as more extensive use by the original innovator. More generally, it encompasses all those actions at the level of a firm or an organisation taken to exploit the economic benefits of the innovation", (OECD, 1989). Thus diffusion cannot be reduced in the introduction of new machinery to the factory floor or the office or the adoption by firms of new intermediate goods.

The formal model is based on Roomer specification (Romer 1990a, 1990b, and River Batiz-Rimer 1991). Let us consider a closed economy with three sectors:

(a) a final good sector;
(b) an intermediate good sector and
(c) the research sector.

In the first sector, final output is produced by means of physical labour (L). human capital (H) and physical capital (x). The physical capital is assumed to be the sum of an infinite number of distinct types of producer durables.

Final output can be represented by the following production function:

$$Y = g(H,L) \sum_{i=1}^{\infty} x_i$$

As in Romer specification, this production function is homogeneous of degree one, as g(H, L) is homogeneous of degree 1 and x of degree 0.

The research sector produces knowledge which is incorporated in designs. Each design is then sold to a single firm in the producer durables sector. Each firm in this sector produces a single capital good which is acquired by the final goods sector. The production function of the Research sector is given, as in Romer, by equation b:

$$\dot{A} = \delta H_\alpha A$$

where $\dot{A}$ is the number of designs produced at time t, being proportional to the existent stock of knowledge A. H_α is the amount of human capital employed in the research sector and δ is a positive parameter.

Treating it as a continuous variable, the sum on the right hand side of equation (a) can be substituted by an integral. At any time (t) a firm will use only the durables that have already been invented. The range of integration varies between 0 and A, where A is the number of capital goods invented and produced. As it will be clear later, it is assumed that A(t) is a linear function of time, this imply a constant number of invented capital goods at any time (t). Therefore, equation (a) becomes:

$$Y = g(H,L) \int_0^A x(i)^0 \, di$$

Integration by parts. Recall that: $\int_0^\infty f'(t)g(t)dt = f(t)g(t) - \int_0^\infty f(t)g'(t)dt$ and $x = z$

The final output sector can be thought of in terms of a representative firm, whereas in the intermediate goods sector each capital good is produced by a single monopolistic firm. We can now consider the way in which the model behaves. To simplify and to link our discussion with the problem of diffusion, we can think of a demand and supply sector is described in terms of decisions taken by a single aggregate price taking firm. This firm represents, therefore, the demand side of the technology that is incorporated in capital good (i) produced by the supplying sector. The production function of the representative firm determines the demand size.

Therefore the only way to think of diffusion is to consider intra-firm diffusion. One can think of the representative firm as a repeating buyer of capital good (i) produced by the supplying sector. F(x) is now defined as the increase in revenues of the representative firm, determined by the additional purchase of capital good (i) in time t. Recall that the representative firm is a repeating buyer. It continues to buy until x(i)=x*; for instance, the capital stock is at its post diffusion or equilibrium level. Moreover, assume that the increase in revenue is perpetual; the implies a present value gain of f(x)/r. The cost of acquisition of capital good (i) in time t is p(t). We can now more formally represent the problem facing the representative firm. It will buy a certain level of capital good (I) in time t if two conditions hold:

$$f(x) \geq rp(t)$$

$$-\hat{p}(t) + rp(t) - f(x) \leq 0$$

Condition (1) is a simple profitability. For profit maximization it will hold with equality. Condition (2), states that the representative firm will acquire in time t if it is not profitable to wait until time $t + dt$.

We assume that the buyer is taking into account the expectation about the future price of capital good (i). P represents buyer's expectation of the change in price, equivalent to the discrete time form:

We can now define different expectations regimes. We specify two models:

- Myopic expectations. Under this assumption $p_t = p^e_{t+1}$ or, in continious time, $\hat{p}(t) = 0$. In other words, the price $p(t)$ is expected to hold forever. In this case condition 2 collapses into 1,

- Perfect foresight. Under this assumption $\hat{p}(t) = p(t)$ (for insatnce, $p_t = p^e_{t+1}$ Furthermore, if condition (2) holds as an equality condition (1) holds as well (but not vice versa). Following Ireland-Stoneman (1986), we can therefore write a generalised dynamic demand function, which incorporates both these two different expectation regimes.

$$-p + rp = \alpha_0 f_x z + \alpha_1 f(x)$$

where z=x represents the current acquired level of capital good (i). In other words, it represents the difference in the used level of capital good (i) at time t and $t + dt$.

Under myopia $\alpha_0 = -1/r$ and $\alpha_0 = 0$, , whereas an $\alpha_0 = 1$, under perfect foresight. Given the production function of first equation (c), the above two conditions become:

$$\phi g(H, L) x^{\phi-1} \geq p$$

$$-p+rp \leq \phi g(H,L)x^{\phi-1}$$

The dynamic demand function under myopia becomes: these conditions hold for each capital good (i).

$$-p+rp = -\frac{1}{r}\phi(\phi-1)g(H.L)^{\phi-2}z + \phi g(H,L)x^{\phi-1}$$

Under perfect foresight this equation becomes:

$$-p+rp = \phi g(H,L)x^{\phi-1}$$

Consider again the second sector, for instance, the sector which produces capital goods, used by the final good sector. The basic assumption here is that each capital good (i) is produced by identical monopolistic firms, which have bought the design of the capital good from the research sector. There costs for a design are sunk costs. The objective of each firm can be represented by the usual inter temporal maximization problem. Furthermore, one must take into account that the production of each capital good takes place as soon as the capital good is invented. The profit function for the monopolistic supplier of capital good of vintage (v) is given by:

$$\Pi = \int_{v}^{\infty}(p(t)-\mu(t))z(t)e^{-r(t-v)}dt$$

where $p(t)$ and $u(t)$ are unit price and unit of capital good i and $z(t)$ is the current production level of capital good i. The problem can be solved by integrating by parts the integral in the above equation and then using the dynamic demand functions. From this problem it is possible to determine the diffusion path (for instance, the supply trajectory). Furthermore, we need to specify that p(t) is derived from the production function (on the demand side) as an input price and $\mu(t,v)$ is such that $\mu < 0$; for instance, function decreases with time. This assumption is justified by considering the effect of learning economies on $\mu(t,v)$ (Stoneman-Ireland 1983; Ireland-Stoneman 1986), Integrating by parts yields:

$$\Pi = \int_{v}^{\infty}(-p+rp-\mu-r\mu)xe^{-r(t-v)}dt$$

Consider now the simple case of myopic expectations. Substituting two equations yields:

$$\Pi = \int_{v}^{\infty}\left[\left(-\frac{1}{r}\phi(\phi-11)g(H,L)x^{\phi-2}z + \phi g(H,L)x^{\phi-1}\right) + \mu - r\mu\right]xe^{-r(t-v)}dt$$

The problem is to maximise (9) under these constraints:

$$x = z \quad z \geq 0$$

Hamiltonian conditions. From the maximization of the last equation under the above conditions we can get the following Hamiltonian conditions:

$$H = \left[-\frac{1}{r}\phi(\phi-1)g(H,L)x^{\phi-2}z + \phi g(H,L)x^{\phi-1} + \mu - r\mu \right] xe^{-r(t-v)} dt$$

$$H_x = -\lambda$$

$$H_z = 0$$

Differentiating with respect to time (c) and substituting yields the following equation. The optimal trajectory of capital good i is given by the following equation.

$$\phi g(H,L)x^{\phi-1} = r\mu - \mu$$

As $t \to \infty$ the diffusion of capital good i terminates and $x(i)=x^*$. Therefore, it must be:

$$\phi g(H,L)x(t_v)^{\phi-1} = r\mu(t_v)$$

In order to fully characterise the diffusion path, we must define $\mu(t,v)$. Recall that we have assumed that this function is affected by learning economies; for instance, $\mu < 0$. Furthermore, we assume that:

$$\mu(t,v) = \Omega e^{-\theta(t-v)} + c$$

where Ω and θ are positive parameters and c is a positive constant which determines the production cost when $t \to \infty$.

Figure 4.2 shows different costs function for capital goods of different vintage.
From the above equation we can get:

$$\phi g(H,L)x^{\phi-1} = (r+\theta)\Omega e^{-\theta(t-v)} + c$$

The diffusion path is then given by:

$$x(t,v) = \left(\frac{\phi g(H,L)}{(r+\theta)\Omega e^{-\theta 9 t-v)} + c} \right)^{\frac{1}{1-\phi}}$$

the diffusion path for capital good of vintage v is also shown in Figure 4.3.

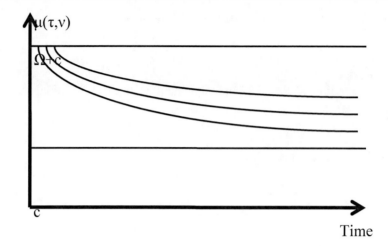

Figure 4.2. The Cost Functions.

Given the supple trajectory we can modify the production function on the demand side, yielding

$$Y = g(H,L)\delta H_a e^{\delta H_a t} \int_0^t e^{-\delta H_a t} \left(\frac{\phi g(H,L)}{(r+\theta)\Omega e^{-\theta r} + c} \right)^{\frac{\phi}{1-\phi}} dt$$

Derivation of equation.
Let us consider equation.

$$Y = g(H,L) \int_0^A x(i)^\phi \, di$$

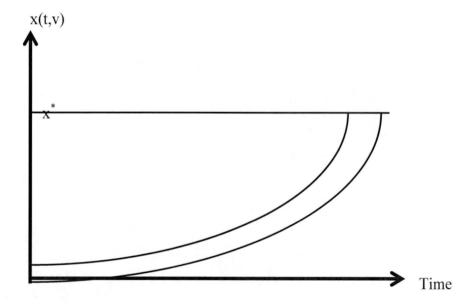

Figure 4.3. The Diffusion Path.

From product name i. consider its vistage v.

$$Y = g(H,L)\delta H_a \int_{-\infty}^{t} e^{\delta H_a v} x(t-v)^\phi dv$$

Given that: $i = e^{\delta H_a v}$

This equation can be expressed in terms of a new variable, for instance, the age of capital. We define this variable as $\tau = t - v$, ($v = [0,1]$).
Therefore, it will be:

$$Y = g(H,L)\delta H_a \int_{-\infty}^{t} e^{\delta H_a v} x(t-v)^\phi dv$$

This transformation is also used by Jovanovic and Lach (1993).

Equation (n'') suggests that there are ($\delta H_a e^{\delta H_a(1-t)}$) capital goods of age t, each of them used according to the supply trajectory given by equation (n').

Given this specification, we consider the growth rate of the economy in the long run; for instance, we consider the asymptotic property of the growth rate calculated from the last equation. It is possible to show that:

$$\frac{\dot{Y}}{Y} = \delta H_a + \frac{\left(\frac{\phi g(H,L)}{(r+\theta)\Omega e^{-\theta r}+c}\right)^{\frac{\phi}{1-\phi}}}{e^{\delta H_a t}\int_0^t e^{-\delta H_a t}\left(\frac{\phi g(H,L)}{(r+\theta)\Omega e^{-\theta r}+c}\right)^{\frac{\phi}{1-\phi}} dt}$$

Output growth in this case depends on time and on all the parameters that define the diffusion path. For instance, in the long run, as $t \to \infty$ output growth rate approaches δH_a, that is, the balanced growth rate. The second term on the right hand side of equation (n'') goes to zero as $t \to \infty$. Indeed, the integral at the denominator converges as $e^{-\delta H_a t} > e - \delta H_a t \left(\frac{\phi g(H,L)}{(r+\theta)\Omega e^{-\theta r}+c}\right)^{\frac{\phi}{1-\phi}} dt$. We also need to show that the growth rate of capital is equal to δH_a as $t \to \infty$. Following Romer (1990) the accounting measure of capital is given by:

$$K(t) = \int_0^t \mu(t)x(t)dt \quad \text{(n''')}$$

Substituting the functional forms adopted into equation (n''') yields:

$$K(t) = \delta H_a e^{\delta H_a t} \int_0^t (\Omega e^{-\theta t} + c)\left(\frac{\phi g(H,L)}{(r+\theta)\Omega e^{-\theta(r)} + c}\right)^{\frac{\phi}{1-\phi}} e^{-\delta H_a t} dt$$

The growth rate of capital is given by:

$$\frac{\dot{K}}{K} = \delta H_a + \frac{(\Omega e^{-\theta t} + c)\left(\dfrac{\phi g(H,L)}{(r+\theta)\Omega e^{-\theta r} + c}\right)^{\frac{\phi}{1-\phi}}}{e^{\delta H_a t}\int_0^t (\Omega e^{-\theta t} + c)\left(\dfrac{\phi g(H,L)}{(r+\theta)\Omega e^{-\theta(r)} + c}\right)^{\frac{\phi}{1-\phi}} e^{-\delta H_a t} dt}$$

As $t \to \infty$ the growth rate of capital approaches δH_a.

It is worth emphasising the conclusion about the determinants of output growth rate. In Romer specification, growth rate of economy is determined either by the allocation of human capital in the research sector (Roomer 1990a, 1990b) or by the parameters that define the production function (River Batiz-Romer 1991). In the specification adopted here, growth rate is determined in the short run by the diffusion path of capital goods produced by the producer durable sector. The definition of growth rate allows to takes into account the difference between the long and the short run determinants of output growth rate.

In long run, output growth is just determined by the allocation of human capital to the research sector. In short run, together with this latter effect, there is the impact of diffusion. Indeed, output growth rate is given by the sum of the parameter δH_a and the ratio of newly diffused

capital $\left[\left(\dfrac{\phi g(H,L)}{(r+\theta)\Omega e^{-\theta r} + c}\right)^{\frac{\phi}{1-\phi}}\right]$ to the already diffused capital

stock $\left[e^{\delta H_a t}\int_0^t e^{-\delta H_a t}\left(\dfrac{\phi g(H,L)}{(r+\theta)\Omega e^{-\theta r} + c}\right)^{\frac{\phi}{1-\phi}} dt\right]$. The definition of output growth

allows to take into account policy intervention, as the speed of diffusion and the unit cost of investment in new capital goods (respectively parameters è and Ù) enter the short run definition of output growth.

4.4. INTER-COUNTRY AND INTERNATIONAL DIFFUSION MODELS

Inter-country differences tend to be explained in terms of three groups of variables:

(a) the most popular is the measurement of proxies for *profitability of innovation* in different countries;
(b) *technological and institutional differences*, which are mentioned in a number of cases;
(c) *economic industrial characteristics*, such as growth and size of market, size of firms and age of existing equipment.

Literature on diffusion of technology incorporates three different approaches. The most well-known is the *inter-industry innovation approach* pioneered by Mansfield (1969). They studied diffusion in one or more innovations in a number of industries, and they attempted to explain empirically the variance of the speed of diffusion in terms of differences in the attributes of the industries and innovations concerned.

Mansfield (1969) suggested that if other things were equal, then length of time that a firm waits before using a new technique will be inversely related to its size. Large firms are more likely to have more units to replace, and conditions are usually more favourable and better for a large firm, such as financial resources, engineering and research departments. For these reasons, large firms would be expected in general to use a new technique more quickly than the small ones.

In the *inter-firm model*, at any point of diffusion process, the number of users acquiring technology is related to risk attached to acquisition, the expected profitability of acquisition and the number of potential adopters. According to the inter-firm decision theories, the most important elements that contribute to determine the actual cost of entry can be considered to be:

- fixed investment costs;
- the cost of scientific and technical knowledge required to assimilate the innovation;
- the cost of acquiring the experience required to handle it and successfully bring it to the market;
- the cost of overcoming any locational disadvantages related to the general infrastructure and other economic and institutional conditions.

For any innovation, the costs of entry for the innovator can be represented as the sum of the following components: the fixed investment cost in plant and equipments, the cost incurred by the innovator in acquiring scientific and technical knowledge which was not possessed by the firm at the beginning of innovation process; the cost incurred by the innovator in acquiring the relevant experience (know-how in organisation, management, marketing or other areas) required to carry the innovation through; and the cost borne by the innovator to compensate for whatever relevant externalites are not provided by the environment in which the firm operates. Imitators will compare the cost of buying the technology with the cost of developing it themselves, if they can.

However, the imitators' knowledge related to the entry costs will depend crucially on the own initial scientific and technical knowledge base in the relevant areas. Consequently, the entry costs may be much higher or much lower than the innovators', depending on their relative starting positions in the knowledge level of the firm.

Moreover, government regulations, taxes, tariffs and other relevant policies will affect strongly *environment* and actual cost for an innovator. Specifically, the difficulty of *catching-up* for industries/firms in the developing countries is because scientific and technical knowledge, practical experience and locational advantages may be lower than in the more advanced countries, while of technology may be higher.

In the diffusion context, two factors are critical but each works to an opposite direction; if early adopters are large, medium or small firms will depend upon the importance of cost/risk considerations relative to innovativeness considerations and upon the way in which qualities vary with the firm size. This approach can be applied so as to investigate the diffusion of the same innovation in a number of different countries and to explain the observed differentials in the diffusion performance in the terms of the characteristics of the countries and industries concerned.

4.4.1. The International Diffusion Approach

International diffusion of technology has been a major factor behind most industrial nations economic growth. Information and particular characteristics of each country are key points for international diffusion of technologies through different countries. Moreover, the *international approach* attempts to explain international differences in the speed of diffusion of innovations in terms of the characteristics of the countries and industries concerned. An overall assessment of international differences in the rate of diffusion of new innovation technologies is extremely difficult to make for a variety of technical applications and for innovations that are continuously are introduced. *International diffusion* can be considered in connection with *international technology transfer* (through multinationals and licensing); including various variables (such as profitability and transfer cost). An important factor affecting the level of diffusion is the nature of competition in the user's industry. It has also been argued that firms are more likely to experiment with new products and methods during a phase of increasing competition.

The framework of international diffusion can be considered through the following approaches:

(a) the *Schumpeterian approach* that tried to investigate and to explain long-waves in economic activity (*the Kondratieff cycle*). The Schumpeterian hypothesis is concerned with the implications of new technology in economy. In Schumpeterian theory, the entrepreneur introduces innovations and the resulting profits derived from new innovations give the signal and attribute to be imitated by other entrepreneurs. The introduction of new technologies would result in the reduction of factor and product prices. The change of prices will induce non-adopters to use the new technology.

(b) The *vintage approach*; the great strength of the vintage model is that it is perfectly rational for entrepreneurs to use old technologies even when new best-practice techniques exist. Introduction of new technologies under perfect competition will depend on the age structure of the capital stock, improvements in new technologies over time and movements in relative prices. *Old machines* can still yield a contribution to profits if price covers operating costs. One disadvantage of the vintage models is for instance that all investment in machines involves the latest type. Moreover, these models give us no guarantee that the diffusion will be sigmoid. The length of time between an initial innovation and an imitation in another country defines the *innovation lag*.

The Figure 4.4 illustrates the process of technological change. According to the classification analysis of Posner and Soete (1988), *innovation-lag* can be viewed as a sum of the following components:

(a) *Foreign reaction lag*, as the product innovations are usually introduced into foreign markets through exports from the country in which the innovation initially occurred. The length of foreign reaction lag depends on the magnitude of the threat to the foreign industry's market resulting from imports of the new innovated product, the greater the competitiveness between domestic and foreign producers for the share of the market, the shorter will be *foreign reaction-lag*.

(b) *Domestic reaction lag* can be considered as the time elapsing between a positive *foreign reaction* to an innovation and the actual decision to imitate. The length of time that an industry waits before imitating tends to be inversely related to its size. Generally, large industries produce a wide range of products and usually have better facilities and technical skills for the improvement or introduction of products.

(c) Finally, *learning period*, where international communications channels tend to accelerate the diffusion of innovations.

The most important determinants in diffusion lag can be considered the following:

(a) The *size of the country*. According to Mansfield (1969) and Metcalfe (1981), size plays a positive role in the reduction of diffusion-lags. Small countries seem to have better opportunities than large ones to adopt earlier innovations that originate abroad, and they are more receptive to innovation that originates elsewhere.

(b) *Technological capability* of the country. Many studies (i.e. Antonelli, 1986) have suggested that the R&D influence reduces diffusion-lags.

(c) The *origin of technology* seems important in explaining diffusion lags. According to Metcalfe (1981), diffusion process of an innovation is affected by the characteristics of supply and demand of technology. Firms are more able to capitalise on technological opportunities when the origin of the technology is internal. Moreover, as Benvignati (1982) has shown, domestic technologies diffuse much quicker than foreign ones.

(d) *Multinational firms*. According to Antonelli (1986), multinational firms have played an important role in diffusion of technology. However, it seems that multinational firms can help spread product innovations rather than process innovations. In fact, product innovations are introduced to imitating countries by multinational firms that have already benefited from capitalised know-how and research spending in the innovating country.

An economic analysis of international diffusion patterns of technological innovations distinguishes four different aspects:

(a) the *speed* with which a country initially tries a new product or the demand-lag;
(b) how quickly the use of the product *spreads* among consumers after introduction into the domestic market, as indicated by the growth in the country's consumption;
(c) the *speed* with which the country acquires the production technology from abroad or *imitation lag rate*;
(d) how quickly the domestic producers *adopt* technology, once it is transferred from abroad, as indicated by the growth of the country's output. Diffusion models have a methodological similarity with some of the models of industrial and economic growth which were developed in the 1930s by Kuznets and Schumpeter.

According to Schumpeter (1934), the diffusion process of major innovations is the driving force behind the trade cycle (the *long term Kondratieff cycle*). However, the forces driving the diffusion process per se are not made explicit. The conception is that the entrepreneur innovates and the attractiveness of attaining a similarly increased profit and cost reductions encourages others to imitate; this imitation representing a diffusion process.

Diffusion of technology can be defined as the process by which the use of an innovation spreads and grows. Diffusion is very important for the process of technological change. On the one hand, diffusion narrows the technological gap that exists between the economic units of an industry, and thus the rate of diffusion determines to a large extent the rate of technological change measured as the effect of an innovation on productivity increase in an industry. On the other hand, diffusion plays an important part in competitiveness process in the sense that diffusion deteriorates the competitive edge which is maintained by the originator of successful innovations. Schumpeter has classified technological change in the following steps:

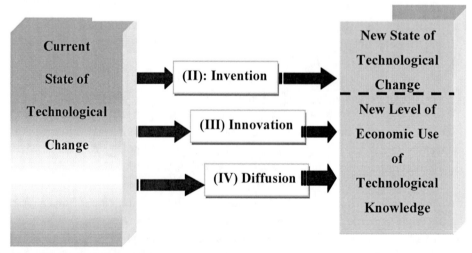

Figure 4.4. Process of Technological Change.

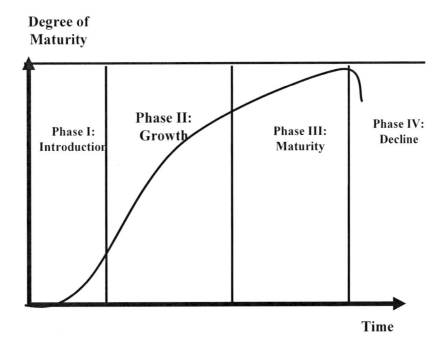

Figure 4.5. The Phases of Growth and the Diffusion.

(a) invention;
(b) innovation; and
(c) diffusion.

Diffusion is the last step in the economic impact of a new product or process. Diffusion is the stage in which a new product or process comes into widespread use.

Figure 4.5 indicates the importance of diffusion in the process of technological change, (Chen 1983). The *current state of technological knowledge* (phase I) gives rise to the second phase (II) of *invention*, however, sometimes it gives rise to *innovation* and *diffusion*. At the second phase, the results of *invention* can give rise to a *new state of technical knowledge*, where in this case a new phase is created and the cycle begins again. Most literature on diffusion is focused on the theoretical arguments underlying the traditional, *S-shaped epidemic diffusion curve*.

Figure 4.5 illustrates the different phases of the diffusion process, where improvements are achieved slowly in the first stage, then accelerate and finally slow down. Figure 4.4 (Malecki, 1991) shows diagrammatically the following diffusion phases:

(a) *phase I is the period of first introduction*, when the innovation has to perform adequately and break successfully into the market;
(b) *phase II is the period of rapid market growth*, once the product is basically defined and its market tested the focus shifts to the process of production;
(c) *phase III of maturity*, when market size and rate of growth are well known and the relationship between product and process has been optimised;
(d) *phase IV of decline*, when both the product and its process of production are standardised.

4.4.2. Epidemic Model and the Logistic Curve

Many diffusion models, i.e. Davies 1979, and Stoneman 1987, are based on the approach of the theory of epidemics. Epidemic models can be used to explain how innovation spreads from one unit to others, at what speed and what can stop it. The epidemic approach starts with assumption that a diffusion process is similar to the spread of a disease among a given population. The basic epidemic model is based on three assumptions:

(a) the potential number of adopters may not be in each case the whole population under consideration;
(b) the way in which information is spread may not be uniform and homogeneous;
(c) the probability to optimise innovation once informed is not independent of economic considerations, such as profitability and market perspectives.

The epidemic model is based on the idea that the spread of information about a new technology is the key to explaining diffusion. Epidemic models hypothesize that some firms adopt later than others because they do not have sufficient information about the new technology. According to this theory, initially, potential adopters have little or no information about the new technology and are therefore unable or disinclined to adopt it. However, as diffusion proceeds, non-adopters glean technical information from adopters via their day to day interactions with them, just as one may contract a disease by casual contact with an infected person. As a result, as the number of adopters grows, the dissemination of information accelerates, and the speed of diffusion increases. However, as the number of adopters exceeds the number of non-adopters, the speed of diffusion falls off. Importantly, the probability of a non-adopter becoming "infected" by contact with an adopter is not the same for every technology; it depends on characteristics of the technology such as profitability, risk, and the size of the investment required to adopt.

The spread of new technology among a fixed number of identical firms can be represented as follows: Let us assume that the level of diffusion is D which corresponds to m_t number of firms in a fixed population of n which have adopted the new innovation at time t and to $(n-m_t)$ firms that remaining as the potential adopters.

Let us assume the probability of an adoption is a constant term b. Then Dm_t, the expected number of new adopters between t and Dt, will be given by the product of this probability, (between one non-adopter and one adopter to lead to an adoption during the period of time D_t). The number of individuals contracting the disease between times t and t+1 is proportionate to the product of the number of uninfected individuals and the proportion of the population already infected, both at time t. The magnitude of b will depend on a number of factors, such as, the infectiousness of the disease and the frequency of social intercourse.

This is rationalised by assuming that each uninfected individual has a constant and equal propensity to catch the disease, from the contact with an infected individual and that the number of such contacts will be determined by the proportion of the population who is already infected (assuming homogeneous mixing). At each instant t, every individual can meet randomly with another member of population and then the expected number of encounters (between adopters and non-adopters) during the time Dt, is:

$$[m_t(n-m_t)]Dt$$

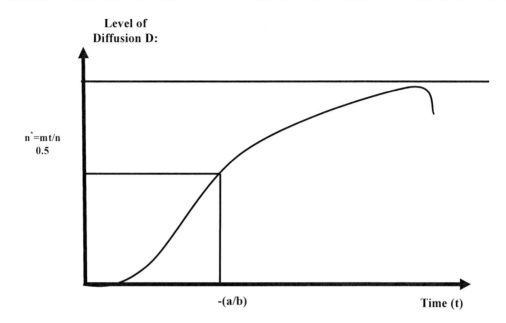

Figure 4.6. The Logistic Epidemic Curve.

It follows that Dm_t is equal to:

$$m_{t+1}-m_t=b[(n-m_t)m_t/n], (b>0)$$

where, the parameter b (usually called the *speed of diffusion* or the *rate of diffusion*). This is rationalised by assuming that each uninfected individual has a constant and equal propensity to catch the disease (as given by b) from the contact with an infected individual and the number of such contacts will be determined the proportion of the population who are already infected. If the period, is very small then the above last equation can be rewritten, as:

$$dm_t/dt[1/(n-m_t)]=bm_t/n$$

This differential equation has the following solution (*logistic function*):

$$m_t/n=\{1+\exp(-a-bt)\}^{-1}$$

New product variants enter into the market; products produced above average efficiency extend their market shares and below average products lose market shares and sometimes exit from the market. The epidemic model of technology diffusion is applied to depict this evolutionary process through which economic selection proceeds. The diffusion process is described by a complex equation, which is illustrated by the following simple logistic function (Gunnarsson Jan, Torsten Wallin, 2008).

Where a is a constant of integration,

If one plots m_t against the time t, the profile will follow an *S-shaped curve* (or the *sigmoid curve*). This is the well known logistic time curve. As we can see from Figure 4.6 it predicts that the proportion of the population which having contacted the disease will increase at an accelerating rate until 50%, when infection is attained at time t=-(a/b). Thereafter, infection increases at a decelerating rate and 100% infection is approached asymptotically.

The upper limit of the curve will be $m=\sqrt{n}$ (which itself has a maximum of 1, when t increases infinitely which follows from the assumption that all firms were potential adopters). The logistic curve has an infection point at $m_t=1/2$, where the adoption process accelerates up to a point where the half of the population of firms have adopted and decelerates beyond. Empirical tests are straightforward using the linear transformation:

$$\log[m_t/(n-m_t)]=a+bt,$$

There is a huge literature on the *law of logistic growth*, which must be measured in appropriate units. Growth process is supposed to be represented by a function of the form of the above third equation with t to represent the time. Different studies on plants and animals were found to follow the *logistic law*, even though these two variables cannot be subject to the same distribution. Population theory relies on logistic extrapolations. The only trouble with this theory is that not only the logistic distribution but also the normal, the Cauchy, and other distributions can be fitted to the same material with the same or better goodness of fit. Examining the logistic curve, we can summarise the following disadvantages:

(a) the infectiousness of the disease must remain constant over time for all individuals; that means, b must be constant, however, in the increasing resistance on the part of uninfected or a reduction in the contagiousness of the disease suppose that b falls over the time;
(b) all individuals must have an equal change of catching-up the disease.

That means, b is the same for all groups within the population. There are a number of other assumptions which may prove unrealistic for the logistic solution, (for instance, constant population is required).

4.4.3. The Probit Models

The probit analysis has already been a well-established technique in the study of diffusion of new products between individuals. This approach concentrates on the characteristics of individuals in a sector and is suitable not only to generate a diffusion curve, but also gives some indications of which firms will be early adopters and which late.

Given the difficulties which are associated with the linear probability model, it is natural to transform the original model in such a way that predictions will lie between (0,1) interval for all X. These requirements suggest the use of a *cumulative probability function* (F) in order to be able to explain a dichotomous dependent variable, (the range of the *cumulative probability function* is the (0,1) interval, since all probabilities lie between 0 and 1. The resulting probability distribution may be represented as:

$$P_i=F(a+bX_i)=F(Z_i)$$

Under the assumption that we transform the model using a *cumulative distribution function* (CDF), we can get the constrained version of the linear probability model:

$$P_i = a + bX_i$$

There are numerous alternative cumulative probability functions, but we will consider only two, the *normal* and the *logistic* ones. The probit probability model is associated with the cumulative normal probability function. To understand this model, we can assume that there exists a theoretical continuous index Z_i which is determined as an explanatory variable X. Thus, we can write:

$$Z_i = a + bX_i$$

The probit model assumes that there is a probability Z^*_i that is less or equal to Z_i, which can be computed with the aid of the *cumulative normal probability function*. The standardised cumulative normal function is written by the expression of the above last equation, that is, a random variable which is normally distributed with mean zero and a unit variance. By construction, the variable P_i will lie in the (0,1) interval, where P_i represents the probability that an event occurs. Since this probability is measured by the area under the standard normal curve, the more likely the event is to occur, the larger the value of the index Z_i will be. In order to be able to obtain an estimate of the index Z_i, we should apply in the above equation the inverse of the cumulative normal function of:

$$Z_i = F^{-1}(P_i) = a + bX_i$$

In the language of probit analysis, the unobservable index Z_i is simply know as *normal equivalent deviate* (n.e.d.) or simply as *normit*.

The central assumption underlying the probit model is that an individual consumer (or a firm/country) will be found to own the new product (or to adopt new innovation) at a particular time when the income (or the size) exceeds some critical level.

Let us assume that the potential adopters of technology differ according to some specified characteristic, z, that is distributed across the population as f(z) with a cumulative distribution F(z), as the Figure 4.7 illustrates. The advantage of the probit diffusion models is that relate the possibility of introducing behavioural assumptions concerning the individual firms (firms). The probit model also offers interesting insights into the slowness of technological diffusion process.

Let us consider that we have two set of innovations, the first group concerns the innovation A which follow a *cumulative lognormal diffusion curve* (this can be considered as the simple and the relative cheap innovation), while the second group concerns the innovation B which follow a *cumulative normal diffusion curve* (this can be considered as the more complex and expensive innovation):

$$P_t = N(\log t / m_D, s^2_D)$$

$$P_t = N(t / m_D, s^2_D)$$

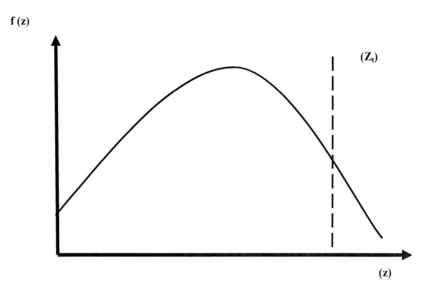

Figure 4.7. The Cumulative Distribution.

For estimation purposes, both the above equations can be linearized by the following transformation:

$$P_t = N(Z_t/0,1),$$

where: z_t may be defined as the *normal equivalent deviate or normit* of P_t, where given values for P_t, Z_t can be read off from the standard normal Tables.

Re-arranging the equations the last two equations in terms of the standard normal function, it follows that:

$$Z_t = (\log t - m_D)/s_D$$

$$Z_t = (t - m_D)/s_D$$

For empirical purposes, it must be remembered that P_t refers to a probability that a randomly selected firm has adopted the innovation at time t. This can only be measured by the proportion of firms having adopted m_t/n. However, to employ the variable Z_t as dependent variable in the regression equation, we will violate one of the assumptions of the standard linear regression model, which is the dependent variable and thus the disturbance term is not homoskedastic.

In fact, this problem is always encountered when is used the *probit analysis*. In the past, two alternative estimators have been advocated under these circumstances: the first concern the *maximum likelihood* and the second concerns the *minimum normit x^2 method*. In this context, the *minimum normit X^2 method* amounts the following weighted regressions

$$Z_t = a_1 + b_1 \log t$$

(for group A which corresponding to *cumulative lognormal*),

$$Z_t = a_2 + b_2 t$$

(for group B which corresponding to *cumulative normal*),

where: Z_i refers to the normal equivalent deviate of the level of diffusion (m_t/n) in year t where diffusion is defined by the proportion of firms in the relevant industry who have adopted.

Figure 4.7, (4.7(A), 4.7(B), and 4.7(C) parts), shows different possibly alternative time paths of diffusion between two group of innovations (5 A) and (5 B), which correspond to the theoretical cumulative lognormal and normal diffusion curves, (Davies, 1974). Figure (4.7A), in general shows the theoretical forms of these two model-equations.

Figures (4.7B) and (4.7C) shows the *fast* and *slow* curves which usually are based on the maximum and the minimum observed values, while the *average* curve merely correspond to the *typical* curve. These theoretical diffusion paths correspond to the diffusion of technologies in different industries (or countries).

4.4.4. Technological Substitution Models

A number of economists (such as Mansfield 1969, Sahal 1977a) consider diffusion as a disequilibrium phenomenon. Usually, when a new technology or a new method is introduced, it is less developed than the older with which it competes. Therefore, it is likely to have greater potential for improvement and for reduction in cost. The introduction of a new product or process broadens the range of choice of producers and consumers, and equilibrium is altered. In the real world, there is only a *gradual adjustment* over the course of time to the new equilibrium level. Figure 4.8 illustrates the alternative diffusion paths.

A simple formulation of this adjustment process would be to assume that the percentage adjustment in any period is proportional to the percentage difference between the actual level of adoption of innovation and the level which corresponds to the new equilibrium. The essence of the technological substitution hypothesis lies in the disequilibrium characteristic of diffusion process. We can assume that the system-wide disequilibrium caused by the gap in the use of two techniques. The equilibrium levels of the use of two techniques can be indicated by K_1 and K_2, while intra-equilibrium gaps can be denoted by:

$$(K_1-Y)/Y \text{ and } (K_2-Y)/X.$$

Particularly, we can assume that the use of one technique as a percentage of the other is some fixed proportion g of the percentage of intra-equilibrium gaps, that is:

$$\log f(t) - \log f'(t) = g[\log(X) - \log(Y)]$$

or, otherwise, using the differential equation of the well-known logistic function, we can find that:

$$\log f(t) - \log f'(t) = g[\log(K_2-X)/X - \log(K_1-Y)/Y]$$

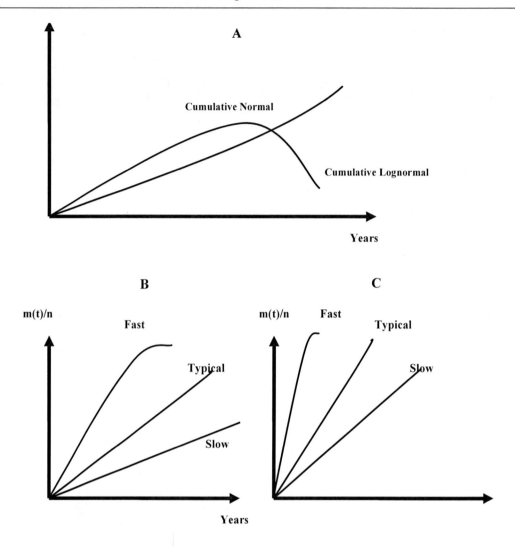

Figure 4.8. The Diffusion Paths. (B): Alternative Cumulative Lognormal Diffusion. Figure 4.8 (C): Alternative Cumulative Normal Diffusion.

where, $\log(K_2-X)/X = a_2 - b_2 t$ and $\log(K_1-Y)/Y = a_1 - b_1 t$ and a is the constant depending on the initial conditions, K is the equilibrium level of growth and b is the rate of growth parameter.

Another interesting result is that the coefficient g is a *measure of the speed* with which movement from an equilibrium to the other takes place. According to the previous analysis, the greater the disparity in the use of two techniques, the faster the speed the substitution will be. Using one technique as a proportion of the other, this can be indicated by f/f', and thus we can reach in the following equation:

$$\log(f/(1-f)) = a_1 + b_1 t$$

It can also be verified that the logistic curve is a symmetrical S-shaped curve with a point of infection at 0.5K. The higher the coefficient g, the less the difference between the rates of the adoption of the two techniques will be: $b = g(b_1-b_2)$, where: $a_1 = g(a_2-a_1)$, and $b_1 = g(b_1-b_2)$. For a more detailed analysis see Sahal and Nelson (1981) and Sahal (1980).

Moreover, assuming that X(t) is the adoption of new technique at the time t and Y(t) is the old technique at time t, then the fractional adoption of the new technique at time t is given by:

$$f(t) = X(t)/(X(t)+Y(t))$$

and

$$f'(t) = Y(t)/(X(t)+Y(t)),$$

so that $f(t) + f'(t) = 1$.

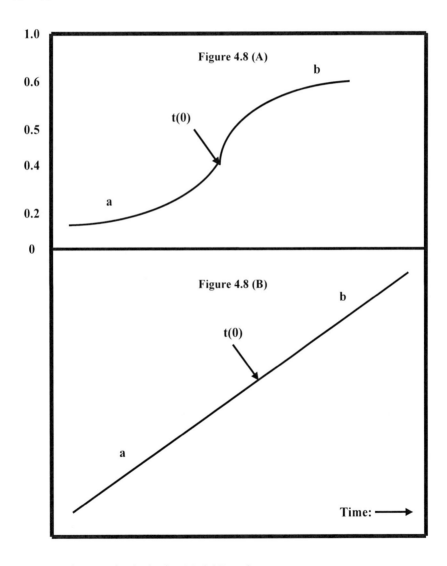

Graph 4.9. A General Form of Substitution Model Function.

Both X and Y can follow an S-shaped pattern of growth; see Sahal and Nelson (1981), and Sahal (1981). The simplicity of the model is that it contains only two parameters. Any substitution that has gained a few percent of the available market has shown economic viability and hence the substitution will proceed to 100 percent.

The substitutions tend to proceed exponentially in the early years (as for instance, with a constant percentage annual growth increment) and to follow an S-shaped curve. The simplest curve is characterised by two constants: the early growth rate and the time, at which substitution is half complete.

Figure 4.9 illustrates a similar analysis. According to this analysis, substituted fraction can be given by the relationship:

$$f=(1/2)[1+\tanh a(t-t_0)],$$

where: a is the half annual fractional growth in the early years and where t_0 is the time at which f=1/2. A more convenient form of the substitution expression can be given as:

$$f/(1-f)=\exp[2\ a(t-t_0)]$$

This expression allows us to plot substitution data in the form of f/(1-f) as a function of time on a *semilog function* which fit in a straight line. The slope of line is 2a, the time t_0 is found at f/(1-f)=1, as indicated by Figure 4.9.

4.5. SUMMARY CONCLUSIONS

Diffusion is the spread of a technology through a society or industry. The diffusion of a technology generally follows an S-shaped curve as early version of technology are rather unsuccessful, followed by a period of successful innovation with high levels of adoption, and finally a dropping off in adoption as a technology reaches its maximum potential in a market.

Technological progress has become virtually synonymous with long-run economic growth. It raises a basic question about the capacity of both industrial and newly industrialized countries to translate their seemingly greater technological capacity into productivity and economic growth. In literature, there are various explanations about the slow-down in productivity growth of EU countries. One source of the slow-down in productivity growth may be substantial changes in FDI, and in the industrial composition of output, employment, capital accumulation and resource utilization. The second source may be that technological opportunities have declined; otherwise, new technologies have been developed but the application of new technologies to production has been less successful. Technological factors act in a long-run way and should not be expected to explain medium-run variations in the growth of GDP and productivity.

Chapter 5

NATIONAL AND REGIONAL SYSTEMS OF INNOVATION

5.1. INTRODUCTION

Entrepreneurship and the relevant policies have played an important role for socio-economic and regional growth. Indeed, facilitating increasing rates of enterprise creation is an almost universal concern for local authorities who seek to accelerate development or reverse decline in localities, whether disadvantaged or prosperous. New enterprises can procure a range of benefits that contribute to local development, including: rises in employment and incomes; enhanced provision of services for consumers and businesses; and possibly, demonstration and motivational effects. Foreign direct investment contributed substantially to the transfer of new technologies and consequently to the modernisation and reorientation of the structure of the economies. The main bulk of technology transfer took place either through foreign direct investments (FDIs) (mainly through multinationals MNEs) or through *technological agreements* (for instance, licensing and joint ventures). *Mergers and acquisitions* have played a major role in this direction. Acquisitions have been used by foreign and domestic firms as a tool for strengthening their position in domestic or international markets.

Innovation is now recognised as a major source of competitiveness of firms and innovation systems. It is recognised as highly relevant to economic performance and sustainability and thus has been gaining more support and attention. This does not mean that innovation policy is immune from pressures for regulatory reform, shared with other policy areas. Innovation policy also needs to draw on evidence, be evaluated to be based on the best available knowledge and to become a learning process.

Archibugi and Michie (1997) concur:

"To understand technological change it is crucial to identify the economic, social, political and geographical context in which innovation is generated and disseminated. This space may be local, national or global. Or, more likely, it will involve a complex and evolving integration at different levels of local, national and global forces".

Hommen and Doloreux (2004) conclude:

"To develop a more comprehensive approach to understanding RIS, it will be necessary to consider failures as well as successes, non-localized as well as localized learning, and different modes of integration, both locally and globally. One possible line of inquiry might centre on the precise nature and the relative importance of localized and non-localized learning, relating these to the forms of knowledge accumulation that sustain the globalization of firms and the competitiveness of regions. On this basis, it would be possible to develop a more discriminating account of the conditions that enable some regions to adapt and generate certain forms of knowledge, more successfully than others".

Furthermore, innovation is a phenomenon that is relevant to a wide range of policies. For example, policies areas -such as education, environment, and Intellectual Property- have implications for innovation. Still policies whose fundamental concern is not innovation, have effects on innovation processes. These interrelations are often poorly understood, and this may have resulted in policy designs that are sub-optimal. Interactions between regulatory reform in all policy areas, the changing nature of innovation processes and the changing content of innovation policies need to be continually explored.

Government policies in new technologies and innovations aims exactly to this point: to reinforce technological capabilities in order to enhance productivity, competitiveness and economic growth of their countries. Government support is usually taken under the form of "direct" and "indirect" measures that is, different grant, loans, tax concessions, and equity capital.

This Chapter attempts to examine the structure and role of technological policy, the national and the regional systems of innovations and their implications on sustainable development and social change. This Chapter also deals with the entrepreneurship activities, the Foreign Direct Investments (FDIs), the transfer of technology and innovation activities.

5.2. ENTREPRENEURSHIP, FOREIGN DIRECT INVESTMENTS (FDIS) AND INNOVATION ACTIVITIES

Entrepreneurship is a complex subject of study and its characteristics, dynamics, determinants and manifestations differ across countries. The overall level of economic development is an important contextual distinction for the research on entrepreneurship, as it can take very different forms. Entrepreneurship in a Schumpeterian view is defined as an attitude of helping innovative ideas become reality by establishing new business models and at the same time replacing conventional business systems by making them obsolete ("creative destruction", Schumpeter). Schumpeter equated entrepreneurship with the concept of innovation applied to a business context:

> 'The entrepreneur is the innovator who implements change within markets through the carrying out of new combinations. The carrying out of new combinations can take several forms;
> - the introduction of a new good or quality thereof,
> - the introduction of a new method of production,
> - the opening of a new market,
> - the conquest of a new source of supply of new materials or parts,
> - the carrying out of the new organization of any industry.

The entrepreneurship research has identified a number of factors affecting the emergence and success of new enterprises. Many of these factors, at least indirectly, also relate to the attractiveness and image of entrepreneurship. Factors can be divided into personality and environmental characteristics. Personality factors presented in the literature include:

- risk-taking propensity to gain profits,
- locus of control,
- need for autonomy and independence,
- initiative,
- innovativeness and creativity,
- self-confidence and self-determination,
- tolerance for failure,
- tolerance for ambiguity,
- need for achievement,
- previous employment, and
- ability to learn.

Entrepreneurship plays a crucial role in innovative activity by serving as the mechanism by which knowledge spills over from the organization producing that knowledge, to the (new) organization commercializing it. While the conventional wisdom is derived from the Schumpeterian Hypothesis and assumption that scale economies exist in R&D effort, more recent theories and empirical evidence suggests that scale economies bestowed through the geographic proximity facilitated by spatial clusters seems to be more important than those for large enterprises in producing innovative output.

Contemporary theories of entrepreneurship generally focus on the decision-making context of the individual. Thus, while the entrepreneurship literature considers opportunities to exist exogenously, in the economics literature they are systematically and endogenously created through the purposeful investments in new knowledge. Of course, that the former is focusing on the cognitive context of the individual while the latter is concerned with the decision-making of the firm provides at least some reconciliation between these two different views.

Entrepreneurship for empirical measurement is a difficult task and the degree of difficulty involved increases exponentially when cross-country comparisons are involved. There is a vast literature and many studies attempt to measures entrepreneurship, such as:

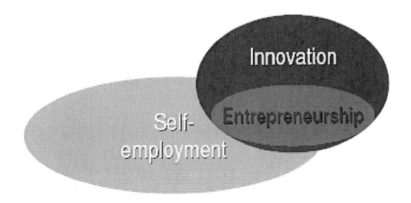

Figure 5.1. The Domain of Entrepreneurship and Innovation.

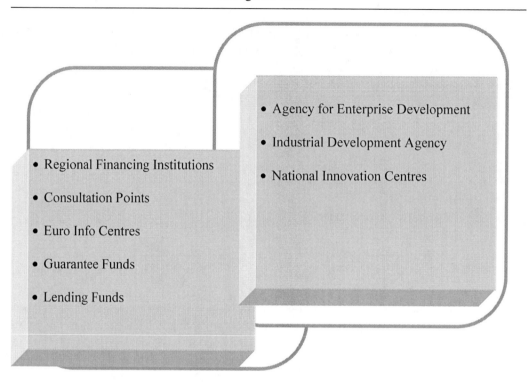

Figure 5.2. Integration Between Entrepreneurship and Innovation Policy.

- Audretsch, Carree, van Stel and Thurik (2002) use a measure of business ownership rates to reflect the degree of entrepreneurial activity. This measure is defined as the number of business owners, in all sectors excluding agriculture, divided by the total labour force.
- Other measures of entrepreneurship focus more on change that corresponds to innovative activity for an industry. Such measures include indicators of R&TD activity, the numbers of patented inventions, and new product innovations introduced into the market (Audretsch, 1995).
- Similarly, other measures of entrepreneurial activity focus solely on the criterion of growth. Firms exhibiting exceptionally high growth over a prolonged duration are classified as gazelles. For example, Holmes et al (1990) measures the number of gazelles to reflect entrepreneurship. Such measures of entrepreneurship must also be qualified for their narrow focus not only on a single unit of observation – enterprises – but also on a single measure of change – growth.
- Lundstrom and Stevenson (2001) followed the precedent of the Global Entrepreneurship Monitor (GEM) study (Reynolds et al., 2000) by defining and measuring entrepreneurship as "mainly people in the pre-startup, startup and early phases of business" (Lundstrom and Stevenson, 2001, p. 19).

Enterprise is at the heart of successful innovation, and not just in the private sector. Entrepreneurial attitudes - even if not precisely identical motivations – underpin much innovation in public sector organisations. Support for such enterprising attitudes in general should be fostered. Small and medium sized enterprises (SMEs) will continue to remain an important focus of innovative effort, and of policy interest. The two should be brought together: innovation support facilities can be built into systems that aim at supporting SMEs in general (European Commission, 2002). Figures 5.1 and 5.2 illustrate the main domain of entrepreneurship and innovation and also the integration between entrepreneurship and innovation policy.

Investment motives refer to economic advantages provided to foreign enterprises by a government, so that they are encouraged to locate in the specific potential host country. The motives of location choice can be categorized in four general categories:

Table 5.1. Categories and Type of Motives for FDIs

Motive categories	Type of motives
First Category: **Motives related to expected demand**	Market size or market potential
	Gross Domestic Product
	Population density
	Access to national and regional markets
	Barriers to international activity
Second Category: **Motives related to the factors of production cost**	Tenure of natural resources
	Access to low-cost labour
	Wage costs adjusted for Quality of human capital or labour productivity,
	Labour market conditions
	Production costs
	Specialized working force.
	Level of infrastructure
	Productivity rates
Third Category: **Motives related to the agglomeration effects**	Distance
	Availability and quality of infrastructure
	Economies of agglomeration
	Economic openness
	Capital market integration
	Peripheral or central location of the region
	Cost of transport
	Geographic degree of concentration
Fourth Category: **Motives related to public policies**	Policy liberalisation
	Policy toward FDI
	Political, economic and legal environment
	Institutional quality of the host country
	Macroeconomic stability
	Institutional stability
	Political stability
	General investment dangers

- motives related to the expected demand in a certain region,
- motives related to the factors of cost,
- motives related to the agglomeration effects, and
- the motives related to the public policies of attracting investment capital.

Table 5.1 illustrates the main categories and the types of motives for FDIs.

Efforts in the areas of FDIs and research activities have been associated in the economic literature with higher growth rates, increases in exports and trade, gains in productivity, growth in income and output, bigger business profits and lower inflation, international competitiveness. There are many aspects of technology transfer to be studied, such as through the direct investment, multinational corporations, joint-ventures and the licensing agreements.

Technology transfer has been variously defined. According to the definition provided by UNCTAD, it can be considered as: "Technology as the essential input to production which can embodied either in capital and in intermediate goods or in the human labour and in manpower or finally in information which is provided through markets", (United Nations).

We can also distinguish among *technology transfer*, *technology capacity* (that is, the flow of *knowledge* and the *stock of knowledge*, respectively), and *technology of innovation* (which indicates the type of technology that gives the capacity to the recipients country's to establish a new infrastructure or to upgrade obsolete technologies). Direct investment is a category in which an international investment made by a resident entity in one economy (direct investor) with the objective of establishing a lasting interest in an enterprise (or, otherwise, the direct investment enterprise) resident in another economy is classified. *Direct investment* involves both the initial transaction between the entities and all subsequent capital transactions between them and among affiliated enterprises, both incorporated and unincorporated. Innovation is about taking risks and managing changes. Some have defined it as «profitable change», others as economic exploitation of new ideas. A more business-related definition could be that innovation means harnessing creativity to invent new or improved products, equipment or services which are successful on the market and thus add value to businesses.

OECD recommends that direct investment flows be defined as: "A foreign direct investor may be an individual, an incorporated or unincorporated public or private enterprise, a government, a group of related individuals, or a group of related incorporated and/or unincorporated enterprises which has a direct investment enterprise – that is, a subsidiary, associate or branch – operating in a country other than the country or countries of residence of the foreign direct investor or investors".

Moreover, following the IMF definition, we can state that: "Direct investment refers to investment that is made to acquire a stake in an enterprise operating in an economy other than that of the investor, the investor's purpose being to have an effective voice in the management of the enterprise. The foreign entity or group of associate entities that makes the investment is termed the direct investor. The unincorporated or incorporated enterprise (a branch or subsidiary, respectively) in which a direct investment is made is referred to as a direct investment enterprise".

According to the OECD definition: "A foreign direct investor is an individual an incorporated or unincorporated public or private enterprise, a government, a group of related individuals, or a group of related incorporated and/or unincorporated enterprises which has a direct investment enterprise (that is a subsidiary, associated enterprise or branch operating in a country other than the country(ies) of residence of the direct investors)".

In addition, *Direct Investment Enterprises* defined as: "Incorporated or unincorporated enterprises in which a single foreign investor either controls ten per-cent or more of the ordinary shares or voting power of an incorporated enterprise (or the equivalent of an unincorporated enterprise) or has an effective voice in the management of the enterprise".

Finally, the OECD definition states that: "Direct investment flows are defined to include for subsidiary and associated companies: the direct investor's share of the company's reinvested earnings plus the direct investor's net purchases of the company's share and loans plus the net increase in trade and other short-term credits given by the direct investor to the company. For branches this includes the increase in unremitted profits plus the net increase in funds received from the direct investor. Finally, loans on short-term balances from fellow subsidiaries and branches to foreign direct investment enterprises, loans by subsidiaries to their direct investors and loans guaranteed by direct investors and defaulted as well as the value of goods leased by direct investors should be included in direct investment, with an exception only for the bank, deposits, bills and short term loans which should be excluded from direct investments".

A direct investment enterprise may be defined as an incorporated or unincorporated enterprise in which a foreign investor owns 10 per cent or more of the ordinary shares or voting power of an incorporated enterprise or the equivalent of an unincorporated enterprise. The numerical guideline of ownership of 10 per cent of ordinary shares or voting stock determines the existence of a direct investment relationship. Some countries may consider that the existence of elements of a direct investment relationship may be indicated by a combination of factors such as:

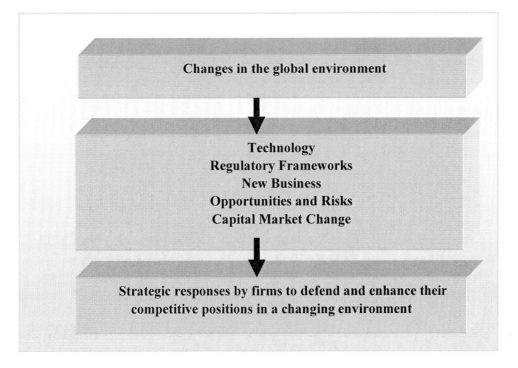

Figure 5.3. FDI, Innovation and Growth Process.

(a) representation on the board of directors;
(b) participation in policy-making processes;
(c) material inter-company transactions;
(d) interchange of managerial personnel;
(e) provision of technical information; and
(f) provision of long-term loans at lower than existing market rates.

The concept of Scientific and Technological Activities has been developed by OECD and UNESCO and EUROSTAT. According to "International Standardization of Statistics on Science and Technology", we can consider as scientific and technological activities as: "The systematic activities which are closely concerned with the generation, advancement, dissemination and application of scientific and technical knowledge in all fields of scientific and technology. These include activities on R&D, scientific and technical education and training and scientific and technological services".

Furthermore, we can distinguish R&D activities from Scientific and Technical Education and Training and Scientific and Technological Services. Whereas, "Scientific and Technical Education and Training activities comprising specialised non-university higher education and training, higher education and training leading to a university degree, post-graduate and further training, and organised lifelong training for scientists and engineers", while Scientific and Technological Services are considered as the following main categories: "Scientific and Technological Services comprise scientific and technological activities of libraries, museums, data collection on socio-economic phenomena, testing, standardization and quality control and patent and license activities by public bodies".

Figure 5.3 illustrates FDI, innovation and the growth process. There is a huge literature on the effects of innovation activities. However, only a small part of these studies their effects on a regional level. One of the major problems for the measurement of innovation activities is the availability of dissaggregate data and the lack of information in a regional level; this becomes more poignant for less advanced technological countries. According to the definition provided by UNCTAD, technology can be considered as: "the essential input to production which can embodied either in capital and in intermediate goods or in the human labour and in manpower or finally in information which is provided through markets" (United Nations, 1983).

It is well established that the accumulation of physical and human capital and advances in production efficiencies and technology lead to higher per capita income. Studies have typically found that approximately 60–70 percent of per capita growth in developing countries reflects increases in physical capital and another 10–20 percent is due to increases in education and human capital with the remaining 10–30 percent attributed to improved (total factor) productivity. Figure 5.4 illustrates the relationship and the effects of FDI and cross-border M&A to global socio-economic environment and at the firm level.

With FDI, the incumbent firm establishes a plant in another country, whereas with imitation, production in the other country is done by a rival firm (or firms). FDI, innovation, and imitation each typically require the investment of resources. Most innovation results from intentional efforts to develop new varieties of products, higher quality levels of existing products, or lower cost methods of production (process improvements).

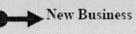
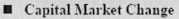

Figure 5.4. Cross Border FDI and M&A activity.

Mansfield et al (1981) finds that imitation costs average two-thirds of innovation costs for firms in the chemical, drug, electronics, and machinery industries. As the costs of a successful imitation tend to be lower than for the original innovation, the profits of a successful imitator can be lower (or shorter in duration) than for an innovator, but again imitators need to rewarded, through the expected profits from a successful imitation, for their imitation expenses. For FDI, the expected profits must rise by enough to compensate for the up front costs of shifting technology abroad. By shifting production abroad, FDI typically generates technology spillovers through demonstration effects. More can be learned about a technology when it is produced locally than when only the final product can be seen.

Findings have demonstrated both a positive effect of inward FDI on the productivity of local firms (Haskel, Keller & Yeaple, 2009) and a negative effect of inward FDI on the productivity of host country firms (Aitken & Harrison, 1999; Haddad & Harrison, 1993; Konings, 2001). Scholars have long recognized the potential for positive externalities from inward FDI in host economies (e.g., Caves, 1974; Buckley & Casson, 1976).

The development of technological capabilities is the outcome of a complex interaction of inventive structure with human resources, technology efforts and institutional factors. The incentive structure includes macroeconomic incentives, incentives from competition and factor markets; and the institutions includes market and non-market institutions such as legal framework, industrial institutions, and training and technology institutions. It is the interplay of all these factors in particular country settings that determines at the regional level, how well the regions employ the resources and develop their technological capabilities (Lall, 1992).

Foreign direct investment contributes to regional innovation in the following ways (Fu Xiaolan, 2007):

- R&D and other forms of innovation generated by foreign firms and R&D labs of MNEs increases the innovation outputs in the region directly.
- Spillovers emanated from foreign innovation activities may affect the innovation performance in the region they locate.
- FDI may affect regional innovation capacity through competition effect.

Market competition may also be a two-edged sword on innovation. Furthermore to greater R&D investments by MNEs and their affiliates, FDI may contribute to regional innovation capabilities by advanced practices and experiences in innovation management and thereby greater efficiency in innovation. The inward FDI, both into the industry and into the firm helps local firms increase their productivity, it hinders their innovativeness. Inward FDI helps firms operating at a point within the production possibility frontier become more efficient and move closer to that frontier, it does not help shift that frontier outward through innovation, which is critical to the growth of national economies. Substantial technology transfers are also associated with international migration and the diasporas of developing countries. Not all of these are positive. Even though 93 percent of university-educated individuals from developing countries return to or remain in their country of origin (Docquier and Marfouk 2004), the brain drain is a serious problem for a number of mostly small countries.

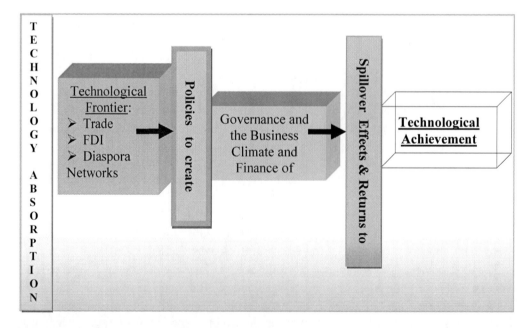

Figure 5.5. Domestic Absorptive Capacity and External Flows.

In summary, FDI impacts regional innovation capabilities in several ways.

- FDI may contribute to the overall regional innovation performance directly due to the greater innovation intensity in MNEs.
- FDI may contribute to regional innovation performance through greater innovation efficiency in MNEs.
- FDI may affect innovation capability of local indigenous firms through technological and managerial knowledge spillovers.
- The strength of the FDI effect on regional innovation capabilities depends upon the absorptive capacity of and the complementary assets in the domestic sector, the linkages between the foreign and the domestic sectors, and the technology content of the FDI.

Figure 5.5 illustrates a stylized description of how a developing country absorbs technology. As a first step, an economy is exposed to higher-tech business processes, products, and services through foreign trade; foreign direct investment; and contacts with its diaspora and other communications channels, including academia and international organizations (the large arrows at the top of the figure). The larger these flows, the greater the exposure of the economy to the global technological frontier (World Bank, 2008).

5.3. NATIONAL AND REGIONAL SYSTEMS OF INNOVATION

There is obviously a relationship between knowledge and economic development at the aggregate level of the economy. Over the last decades in high income-countries there has been a movement toward 'learning organisations' and 'networking' away from fordist and taylorist forms of organisation. Taylorist organisation refers to work situations where there is very little room for the worker to make decisions and where little learning takes place. Lean production learning includes job rotation and team-work but the degree of discretion and the scope of learning is limited. Finally, discretionary learning gives the employee wide discretion and offers rich learning opportunity (Lundvall, 2005).

Referring to the 'national production system', List pointed to the need to build national infrastructure and institutions in order to promote the accumulation of 'mental capital' and use it to spur economic development rather than just to sit back and trust 'the invisible hand' to solve all problems. It was a perspective and a strategy for the 'catching-up' economy of early 19th century Germany. The history and development of the innovation system concept indicates that it can be useful for analyzing less developed economies. Some of the basic ideas behind the concept 'national systems of innovation' go back to Friedrich List (List 1841) and they were developed as the basis for a German 'catching- up' strategy. His concept 'national systems of production' took into account a wide set of national institutions including those engaged in education and training as well as infrastructures such as networks for transportation of people and commodities (Freeman 1995).

Innovation, is a system that deal with technological innovation, learning (education and training), and economic development. Innovation, as socio-technical system, comprises two main divisions:

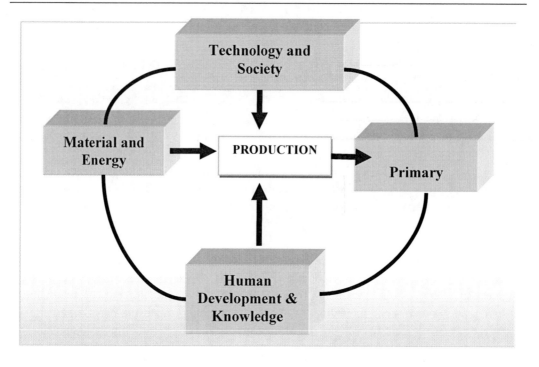

Figure 5.6. Technology, Society and Production.

- The social innovation (social structures, human resource development).
- Technological innovation (technical development).

Innovation as a socio-technical system, comprises two main structures:

- The Social Learning and
- Technological Innovation (Development).

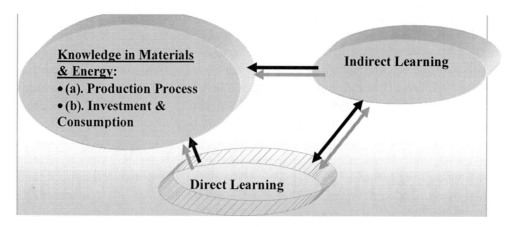

Figure 5.7. Knowledge and Learning Economy.

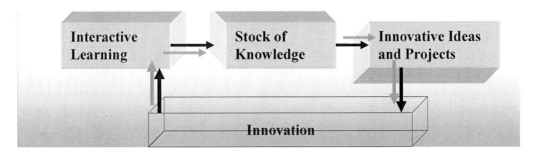

Figure 5.8. Learning and Innovation.

Technological innovation and economic development are also connected to each other. The interaction between technological innovation, social learning and economic development is crucial for the survival and growth of the systems of innovation, at the national or regional levels. The Interactive model demonstrates the main inter-connections between three systems: Society, Technology and Economy (Mahdjoubi Darius, (1998).

Figure 5.6 illustrates the flows of technology, society and production. In order to specify the characteristics of a learning economy it is useful to draw a distinction between the role of knowledge (as a kind of stock) and the role of learning (as a kind of flow) in economy. The idea of knowledge and learning as central and crucial aspects of economy and economic process may be pictured, as in Figure 5.7

In Figure 5.7 a distinction between learning as a deliberately organised process has been considered, for instance, some parts of the economy, for example universities, research institutes, and R&D departments are organised with the creation and utilisation of new knowledge in mind. But there is also learning going on in relation to "ordinary" economic activities.

A lot of learning may be described as more or less unintended by-products of the normal economic activities of procurement, production and marketing. These types of learning are referred to as direct learning and indirect learning, respectively. This distinction is made because heavy investments in direct learning as well as development of new ways to utilise indirect learning are characteristics of learning economy. The distinction is also useful because there are complementarities between these two types of learning. These complementarities may take the form of virtues circles. Learning by using a new type of machine tool may produce important information for the R&D department in the machine-tool producing firm. Improvements made on the basis of this information may lead to increased diffusion of improved machinery, which, again stimulates learning by using, etc.

In Figure 5.8 the role of learning and knowledge in economy is pictured in a very abstract and foot-lose way. Clearly some structures and actors are missing. In addition to being interactive, we regard learning to be partially cumulative. What one learns depends on what one has already known and therefore the production structure of economy affects its learning processes. The production structure of an economy consists not only of a tangible structure of buildings, equipment, etc., but also of a connected intangible structure of knowledge accumulated through production experiences.

Interactive learning, both direct and indirect, increases the stock of knowledge. As discussed above, this stock is diminished by different kinds of forgetting, Nevertheless, creative forgetting may create a feedback mechanism to learning and new knowledge. Entrepreneurs of different kinds use new knowledge to form innovative ideas and projects and some of these find their way into economy in the form of process and product innovations.

This means that there is a distinction to be made between production of knowledge and utilisation of knowledge. There is always a lot of knowledge around which is not put to use in economy. The ability to utilise existing knowledge is a crucial aspect of the learning economy which affects its dynamic efficiency, for example the generation of growth and employment. The whole process is very uncertain and only a small part of the new knowledge leads to innovative ideas and projects and only some of these are actually turned into innovations. These uncertainties in the process from learning to innovation are illustrated in Figure 5.9 by the insertion of selection mechanisms at different places.

We can use the term "innovation" rather broadly in order to include processes through which firms master and practice product designs and manufacture processes that are new to them, if not to the nation or even to the universe. We are adopting "innovation" to the actors that do research and development. The term "system" indicates something that is designed and built, but this concept is far from the orientation here. The term indicates a set of institutions whose interactions determine innovative performance. The term of "system" concept is a set of institutional actors that play major role in influencing the innovative performance. We are using the term "national system of innovations" in order to indicate policies that are related to research and technological activities planning, (both from a macro and micro economic view) in a country. Figure 5.10 illustrates the main goals and policy interventions of regional economic strategy.

Systems of innovation may be delimited in different ways; spatially-geographically, sectorally, and according to the breadth of activities they consider.

- Geographically defined innovation systems may be local, regional, national and supranational. This type of delimitation presumes that the area in question has a reasonable degree of 'coherence' or 'inward orientation' with regard to innovation processes.
- 'Sectorally' delimited systems of innovation only include a part of a regional, national or international system. They are delimited to specific technological fields (generic technologies) or product areas. They can be, but are not necessarily, restricted to one sector of production. Both 'technological systems' (Carlsson and Stankiewicz, 1995) and 'sectoral innovation systems' (Breschi and Malerba, 1997) belong to this category. Whether a system of innovation should be spatially or sectorally delimited – or both – depends on the object of study.

Freeman and the 'Aalborg- version' of the national innovation system-approach (Freeman 1987; Freeman and Lundvall 1988) aim at understanding 'the innovation system in the broad sense'. The definition of 'innovation' is broader. Innovation is seen as a continuous cumulative process involving not only radical and incremental innovation but also the diffusion, absorption and use of innovation and a wider set of sources of innovation is taken into account. On this aspect innovation is seen as reflecting, besides science and R&D, interactive learning taking place in connection with ongoing activities in procurement, production and sales. A wide definition of innovation should be used including product innovations (both material goods and intangible services) as well as process innovations (both technological and organizational ones).

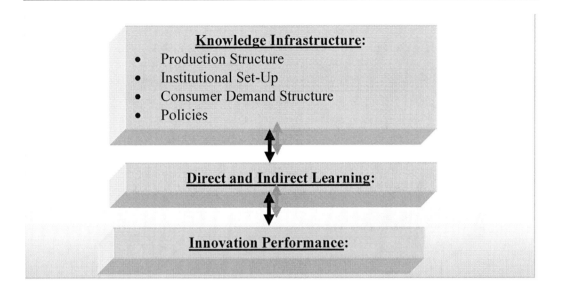

Figure 5.9. Main Factors Affecting Learning and Innovation in a National System of Innovation.

While there are competing conceptions regarding what constitutes the core elements of an innovation system, it might still be useful to see what the different definitions have in common.

- One common characteristic is the assumption that national systems differ in terms of specialization in production, trade and knowledge (Archibugi and Pianta 1992). The focus is here upon the co-evolution between what countries do and what people and firms in these countries know how to do well. This implies that both the production structure and the knowledge structure will change only slowly and that such change involves learning as well as structural change.
- Another common assumption behind the different approaches to innovation systems is that elements of knowledge important for economic performance are localized and not easily moved from one place to another.
- A common assumption behind the innovation system perspective is that knowledge is something more than information and that it includes tacit elements (Polanyi 1966). Important elements of knowledge are embodied in the minds and bodies of agents, in routines of firms and not least in relationships between people and organizations (Dosi 1999).
- One main point to the idea of innovation systems is a focus on interactions and relationships. The relationships may be seen as carriers of knowledge and interaction as processes where new knowledge is produced and learnt (Johnson 1992, Edquist and Johnson, 1997).
- The system of innovation approach is also associated with problems and weaknesses. One example is the term institution, which is used in different senses by different authors —some referring to social norms, such as trust, while others refer to types of organizations, such as universities.

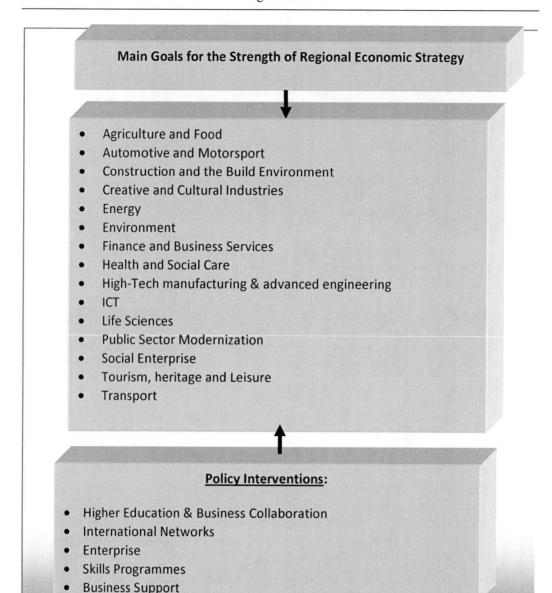

Figure 5.10. Regional Economic Strategy.

Another important point is that there is no agreement among scholars systems of innovation regarding what should be included in and what should be excluded from a '(national) system of innovation'. At can also be pointed out that 'systems of innovation', is not a formal theory, in the sense of providing propositions as regards established and stable relations between well defined quantitative variables. According to the World Bank (2002: 8), institutions have three main objectives: They channel information about market conditions, goods, and participants, they define and enforce property rights and contracts and they regulate competition. The overall structure of the functionality of National Systems of Innovation (NSI) is shown in the Figure 5.11.

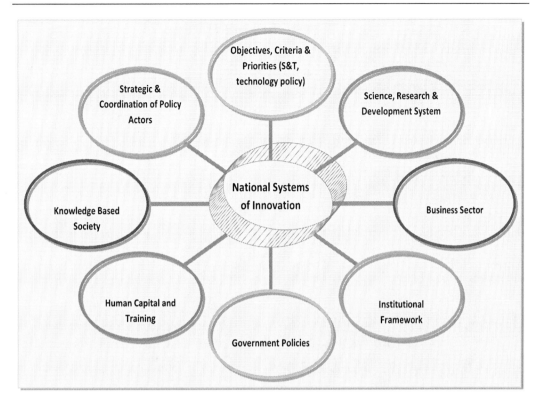

Figure 5.11. National Systems of Innovation (NSI).

Learning is the process of technical change achieved by diffusion and incremental innovation. The National Learning Systems should be centered in the activities, institutions, and relationships, associated to learning, rather than to innovation. Absorption and incremental innovation should, therefore, be the main focuses of studies of NLSs (National Learning Systems). Viotti (1997, Chapter 2, pp. 33-105) develops a much thorough analysis on the specificities of technical change in late industrializing economies, the proposed National Learning Systems' approach, and its methodological implications. Figure 5.12 illustrates the National and Regional Systems of Innovation and technical change.

Regions are considered to play a crucial role in the European Research Area, because they bring policy measures close to the citizen, thereby following the subsidiarity principle, and because they bridge the EU level and the local level (CEC, 2001a). In particular, the EU aims at stimulating innovative enterprises and the relationships within regional innovation networks. Regions can differ substantially with respect to their industrial specialisation, their connectedness with the national and global level, and in particular with respect to their potential to face national and global competition. Therefore, policy measures are best adapted to the region at hand.It makes sense to regionalize innovation policy for the following four reasons (Fritsch/Stephan, 2005):

(a) Innovation processes are taking place unevenly in geographic space.
(b) Innovation networks function differently in various regions.
(c) Innovation activity is crucial for economic development and growth on the regional as well as on the national level.

Systems of Technical Change

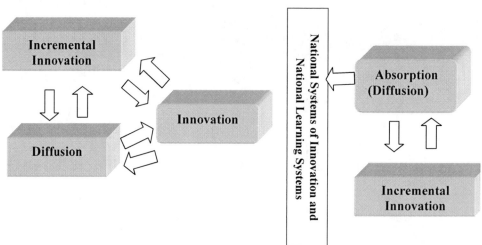

Figure 5.12. National Systems of Technical Change.

(d) Using various policy approaches in different regions enables countries to gain much more varied experiences, thereby enabling regions to learn from one another.

Recently, academics and policy makers have begun to refine the idea of national innovation systems, considering the utility of 'regional innovation systems' as both a theoretical concept and a policy objective (Cooke and Uranga et al, 1997 and 1998). Whilst the regional innovation systems perspective is clearly a development of the innovation systems literature, it can also be considered part of the 'new-regionalism'.

The concept of regional innovation system has been gaining much attention from policy makers and academic researchers since the early 1990s. The approach has received considerable attention as a promising analytical framework for advancing our understanding of the innovation process in the regional economy (Asheim *et al.*, 2003; Isaksen, 2002; Cooke *et al.*; 2002). The popularity of the concept of regional innovation system is closely related to the emergence of regionally identifiable nodes or clusters of industrial activity as well as the surge in regional innovation policies where the region is deemed as the most appropriate scale at which to sustain innovation-based learning economies (Asheim and Isaksen, 1997).

Most of the new contributions in regional economics are clearly indebted to the pioneering works and intuitions of Marshall, who stressed the importance of local externalities in favoring the geographical concentration of economic and innovative activities. The concept of regional innovation systems has no commonly accepted definitions, but usually is understood as a set of interacting private and public interests, formal institutions and other organizations that function according to organizational and institutional arrangements and relationships conducive to the generation, use and dissemination of knowledge (Doloreux, 2003). The basic argument is that this set of actors produce pervasive and systemic effects that encourage firms within the region to develop specific forms of capital that is derived from social relations, norms, values and interaction within the community in order to reinforce regional innovative capability and competitiveness (Gertler, 2003).

According to Cooke and Morgan (1998), a strict reading of the literature would suggest that only three regions are true regional innovation systems: Silicon Valley, Emilia-Romagna, and Baden-Württemberg. However, the variety of regional innovation systems provides a problem of definition and empirical validation. If the concept of regional innovation system is widely accepted in its specific form, and used to derive strategies and policies, the basis for the definition and existence remains obscure; at least the literature is not clear in what way a specific region can be labelled as an innovation system.

The regional innovation system is a normative and descriptive approach that aims to capture how technological development takes place within a territory. The approach has been widely adopted to underline the importance of regions as modes of economic and technological organization, and to reflect on the policies and measures aimed at increasing the innovative capacity of all kinds of regions.

As Asheim and Gertler (2004) point out:

"Regional innovation systems are not sufficient on their own to remain competitive in a globalizing economy. Production systems seem to be more important innovation system at the regional level. Thus local firms must also have access to national and supra national innovation systems, as well as to corporate innovation systems from the local firms that have been brought This line of reasoning is followed to a point where the regional innovation system expands beyond its own boundaries through a process of economic integration and globalization".

Many elements characterizing a national system could be, in principle, transferred to a smaller territorial scale and used also to define the RSI (Regional Systems of Innovation). The list includes:

- the internal organization of firms,
- interfirm relationships,
- role of the public sector and public policy,
- institutional set-up of the financial sector,
- R&D intensity and organization,
- institutional framework, for instance, regional governance structure, political, legal, fiscal, financial and educational arrangements, etc.,
- production system (including the competition and collaboration faced by firms, market structure, the division of labor, and the sectoral specialization,
- degree of openness and the capacity to attract the external resources core hierarchical forces taking into account the peculiarities of the different geographical scale.

In the schematic illustration, the external influences to a RSI come from other RSIs, from the NSI, and from international sources. Of these, the international institutions and policy instruments are becoming increasingly important, particularly in Europe. The influences from NSIs and from international sources mainly take the form of policy interventions, funding and subsidies for innovation, technology inputs received from outside the RSI and knowledge, resource and human capital flows from outside the RSI. Table 5.2 illustrates the illustrative proxies of the extent of innovative processes and interactions. Whereas, Table 5.3 illustrates some selected comparative studies for the Regional Systems of Innovation (RSI).

Table 5.2. Illustrative Proxies of the Extent of Innovative Processes and Interactions

- Existence and activity of demand activation schemes geared to activating demand for technological services among SMEs (e.g. research voucher schemes, student placement schemes, technological service schemes, etc.).
- Existence of science parks, new business incubators and business incubation programmes.
- Frequency and extent of technology exchanges between the knowledge creation and knowledge application sub-systems.
- Number and quality of personnel exchange and rotation arrangements between the knowledge creation and knowledge application sub-systems.
- Number and type of technology transfer mechanisms employed in the interaction between public sector research institutes and industrial companies.
- Number of new research and development projects started between public sector research institutes and industrial companies (e.g. SMEs).
- Number of researchers hired as part-time and full-time consultants by SMEs and large firms.
- Number of spin-off companies and other new units established to exploit research findings.
- The continuity and intensity of interactions between the knowledge generation and knowledge application sub-systems.
- The impact of technology intensive interactions on industrial companies.
- Usefulness and information content of interactions between sub-systems

Erkko Autio (1998) "Evaluation of RTD in Regional Systems of Innovation", *European Planning Studies*, Vol. 6, No. 2, pp. 131-140.

Table 5.3. Selected Comparative Studies for the Regional Systems of Innovation (RSI)

Study (Authors)	Study regions	Objectives	Main results/Lessons
Regional innovation systems: designing for the future (REGIS) (Cooke et al., 2000)	11 regions in the EU and in Eastern and Central Europe (Baden-Württemberg, Wallonia, Brabant, Tampere, Centro, Féjer, Lower Silesia, Basque country, Friuli, Styria, Wales)	Explore theoretically the key organization and institutional dimensions providing regional innovation system	Highly-detailed of different regions in terms of innovation performance potential for strong and weak regions
European Regional Innovation Survey (ERIS)	11 European regions (Vienna, Stockholm, Barcelona, Alsace, Baden,	Study the qualitative and quantitative assessment of determinants for innovation potential	Innovation activities and business innovation process can be viewed as a network process, in

(Sternberg, 2000)	Lower Saxony, Gironde, south Holland, Saxony, slovenia, south Wales)	of any region as well as the innovative linkages and networks between different players.	which business and interaction with other partners play a significant part.
SME policy and the regional dimension of innovation (SMEPOL) (Asheim et al., 2003; Tödlling and Kaufmann, 2001)	9 European regions (Northern Norway, South-eastern Norway, Upper Austria, Triangle region, Lombardy, Limburg, Wallonia, Valencia, Herfordshire)	Investigate how SMEs innovate and to what extent they are relying on other firms and organization in their innovation activities	Innovation activities of SMEs mainly related to incremental innovation and defensive strategy; Interactions are mainly with customers and suppliers; and innovation links of SMEs are more confined to the region
Nordic SMEs and regional innovation systems (Asheim et al., 2003)	13 Nordic regions (Oslo, Stockholm, Helsinki, Gothenburg, Malmö/Lund, Aalborg, Stavanger, Linköping, Jyväskyla, Horten, Jaeren, Salling, Icelandic regions	Explore the existence of similarities and differences between regional clusters of SMEs in different regions in the Nordic countries	In a Nordic cluster context, especially initiatives on social networking arrangements have proven to be a successful way to boost and secure social capital and trust. In addition, SMEs that mainly draw on a analytical knowledge base and innovate through science driven R&D (e.g. in biotech) tend to collaborate with global partners in search for new and unique knowledge. SMEs that mainly draw on a synthetic knowledge base and innovate through engineering based user-producer learning tend to collaborate more with regional partners.

Table 5.3. Continued

Regional clusters-driven innovation in Canada2 (Wolfe, 2003; Holbrook, and Wolfe, 2002)	9 regional case study cluster (*biomedica*l: Toronto, Montreal, Vancouver, Calgary; *multimedia*: Toronto, Montreal, Vancouver; *culture industries*: Toronto, Montreal, Vancouver; *photonics and wireless*: Ottawa, Waterloo, Calgary, Quebec; *ICT*: Ottawa, Atlantic regions; *wood products*: Kelowna, Quebec, Atlantic Canada; *food and beverage*: Toronto, Okanagan, Quebec, Atlantic Canada; *automobile and steel*: southern Ontario; *metal products*: Beauce	Identify the presence of significant concentrations of firms in the local economy and understand the process by which these regional-industrial concentrations of economic activity are managing in transition to more knowledge-intensive forms of production There	There are two main types of 'emerging' models of clusters: (1) the regional embedded and anchored regions where local knowledge/science base represents a major generator of new ,unique knowledge assets; (2) the 'entrepôt' regions where much of the knowledge base required for innovation and production is acquired through straightforward market transactions, often from non-local sources
Regional innovative clusters (OECD, 2001)	10 European regional clusters in Europe: ICT regional clusters in Finland, Ireland, Denmark, Spain, Flanders, and The Netherlands; mature regional clusters: agro-food cluster (Norway) and construction cluster (Denmark, The Netherlands, Switzerland).	Question the relevance of regional clusters in innovation policy	Regional clusters in every country/region has a unique clusters blends; regional clusters are variation and selection environments that are inherently different; regional clusters may transcend geographical levels

Source: Doloreux David and Saeed Parto (2004) "Regional Innovation Systems: A Critical Review", Working Paper.

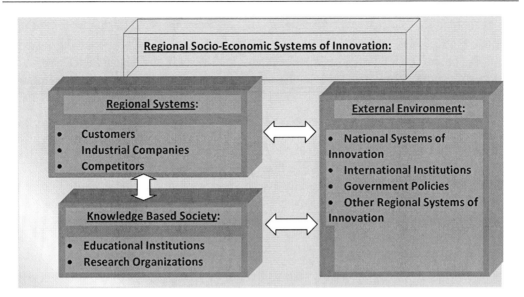

Figure 5.13. Schematic Illustration of the Structuring of RSIs.

Many studies of regional innovation systems are motivated by beliefs that the relation between technical advance and regional growth depends on the amount of technological knowledge in a region. We note that the Lisbon Strategy launched by the EU raises interesting policy questions about connections between technical advance and regional differences in growth. The concept of Regional System of Innovation (RSI) is distinctly different from that of National Systems of Innovation NSI. A schematic illustration of the structuring of RSIs is shown in the Figure 5.13. Figure 5.13 distinguishes between the two sub-systems that constitute the main building blocks of RSIs. These are the knowledge application and exploitation sub-system and the knowledge generation and diffusion sub-system. In the schematic illustration, the main external influences on RSIs take the form of NSI institutions and policy instruments, other RSIs, and international institutions and policy instruments.

The main functional sub-systems in RSIs are the knowledge generation and diffusion sub-system and the knowledge application and exploitation sub-system. The former consists mainly, but not exclusively, of industrial companies, while the latter comprises various (mostly public sector) institutions that are involved in knowledge creation and diffusion. The distinction between these two sub-systems largely corresponds to the division between public and private sectors and between non-commercial and commercial activities.

Thus, governments should pay more attention to the following points:

- to deal with multiple policy objectives in the establishment of priorities including their quantification;
- deal with uncertainty in the ex-ante assessment of cost and benefits for the proposed government-financed programmes;
- compare the cost-effectiveness of government intervention with other alternatives solutions; and
- identify the appropriate type of government intervention.

Technological policies aim to support and promote the new technologies through different "direct and indirect measures". "Direct measures" usually include different subsidies, or different favourable tax treatments for research and technological activities. "Indirect measures" are carried out in the pursuit of other policy objectives (for instance, competition policy, monetary, fiscal policies etc.), and, consequently, affect different research and technological activities.

The experience in most advanced countries shows that economic growth has been close related with that of technological growth and technological planning. The history of advanced technologically countries indicate that technology transfer has been essential contributed to industrialisation and to modernisation of the whole economy in new industrialised countries and advanced countries. However, most advanced technological countries import a substantial part of the technology that they use, as it happened to Japan and other European advanced technological member states.

Also, one important question is to examine the availability in human resources and the manner in which these resources are used. Universities and research institutes are important source that can be substantial contribute to the radical change in technological opportunities and infrastructure. Educational institutions can contribute to the introduction and diffusion of new techniques in different sectors. For many future employees they provide the first contact with techniques they will employ in their workplace.

Educational bodies and research institutions can often play a useful role in building up a core of expertise for a new industry itself before the industry becomes commercially viable. The industries that are based upon or associated with nuclear energy provide an example. Policies designed to alter the rate of economic growth directly tend to focus on enhancing the technological advances and the quality of labour force. The rate of technical change is affected by research expenditures and the rate of improvement of the quality of labour force is affected by investment in human capital (such as training, and education). The investment in human capital affects positively the rate of technical change. In general, (macro oriented) factors-the process of human resource formation, the inflow of foreign technologies, the government's industrial, trade and science/technology policies that shaped industrial structure and the direction of growth, and so on- set the stage for a rapid acquisition of technological capability. Table 5.4 illustrates the instruments of government policy that aim to support the industrial research and technological activities in comparison to several countries.

There is also a great deal of confusion about the meaning of "Appropriate technology". Several times, the word of appropriate technology has been used as synonymous with the suitable or "proper" technology. Therefore, appropriate technology can be understood as a technology that may be suitable to or proper in a particular community, area, region or country. Another problem with appropriate technology is that many people have been considering appropriate technology as an approach which is relevant only to the so-called "Less Developed or Poorer countries or South".

We can distinguish two views on appropriateness of technology. The first concerns policies devoted to indigenous produced technology, whereas the second concerns policies of appropriateness for technology transfer. Appropriate technology has to meet the basic criteria of comparable efficiency, performance and general production needs. The problem of appropriate technology is closely related to relevant strategies that each government follows. The problem of appropriate technology is also related to the availability of resources and the market size.

Table 5.4. Government Policy Instruments used to Support the Industrial R&D: (approx. Share Expenditures in Brackets)

United States:	Tax concessions (65%), grants (35%)(procurement)
Canada:	Grants (100%)(tax concessions not included)
Japan:	"Consignment" subsidies(40%),tax concessions(35%), grants(25%), equity capital(2.5%)
CEC:	Grants(100 %)(tax concessions not included)
Denmark:	Grants (some repayable)(80%),loans(20%)
France:	Grants(50%),repayable grants(25%),tax concessions(2.5%)
Germany:	Grants(90%), tax concessions(10%)
Greece:	Grants (infrastructure development)(100%)
Ireland:	Grants (100%)
Spain	Grants (100%)
United Kingdom:	Grants(65%), mixed grants+loans(35%)

Source: OECD, "Industrial Policy in OECD countries, annual".
Note: "Consigment" subsidies involve R&T in private industry and cooperative research projects.

Appropriate technology models offer many advantages for the socio-economic development particularly of developing countries, as for instance in the solution of rural employment problem, decentralisation and dispersal of industries in rural areas, encouragement of agro-industries, capital-saving and low costs, use of local resources, transfer of new skills and technical know-how, wide-dispersal of income, ecological balance, development of organisational-managerial and marketing skills. Labour intensive technologies tend to be available on a mass scale so that a large part of population can employ in these technologies. They also tend to use local resources in terms of material and energy that improve productive capacity on a sustained level of provided skills, encourage capital formation, research and technological capabilities. However, appropriateness of technology alone cannot guarantee effectiveness of small scale industries. Amongst other variables that play crucial role in determining the success of small industrial enterprises are the following: business management skills, technology use skills, resource supplies, regional and international climate, degree of monopolisation of industry areas and market volatility.

5.4. SUMMARY CONCLUSIONS

Technology transfer through FDI is an important factor on the process of economic development and economic performance. MNEs and FDIs are the main policy tools for the international technology transfer and the development of innovation activities in many countries. Multinationals also produce and control most of the world's advanced technology. About four fifths of the FDIs and the production of advanced technology originate in Japan, Germany, the United Kingdom, the USA and Switzerland.

Technology transfer through MNEs and FDIs lead to a geographical diffusion of technology and contribute substantially towards the development of research and innovation activities in less technologically advanced countries. Most of these countries lack the funds and opportunities to develop their own technologies, and they align on the policies of technology transfer through MNEs. However, multinationals transfer only the technologies that needed and have been developed abroad from the host laboratories. Ownership and control of new technologies from MNEs do not automatically imply the improvement and the development of research activities at a national level. Most empirical studies have emphasized the profits, the age and the amount of new technologies transferred by MNEs. Usually, the affiliated companies operate in a monopolistic market where new technologies give their its products a *quality advantage* and a higher market share. Long term foreign private capital flows have a complementary and catalytic role to play in building domestic supply capacity as they lead to tangible and intangible benefits, including export growth, technology and skills transfer, employment generation and poverty eradication. Policies to attract FDI are essential components of national development strategies.

Regional innovation policy may help stimulate firms, SMEs in particular, in less favoured regions to adopt improved production methods (for instance, quality and environmentally friendly processes, incorporation of technological developments and innovation management methods, etc), make new products and services and exploit new economic opportunities and markets, thus, using their regional innovation potential to the fullest in order to compete in the global economy.

Regional policy has to cope with fresh challenges, globalisation and rapid technological change in order to provide economic opportunities and quality jobs needed in less favoured regions. Today, innovation-gap is nearly twice as great as cohesion gap. Many of the causes of disparities among regions can be traced to disparities in productivity and competitiveness. Education, research, technological development and innovation are vital components of regional competitiveness. Inter-regional innovation-gap is not only of a quantitative nature but also of a qualitative one. There is a number of characteristics of regional innovation systems in less advance regions which make them less efficient, that is:

- Firms may not be capable of identifying their innovation needs or maybe unaware of the existence of a technical solution.
- There may be poorly developed financial systems in the area with few funds available for risk or seed capital, which are specifically adapted to the terms and risks of the innovation process in firms.
- There may be a lack of technological intermediaries capable of identifying and "federating" local business demand for innovation (and RTD&I) and channelling it towards sources of innovation (and RTD&I) which may be able to respond to these demands.
- Co-operation between the public and private sectors may be weak, and the area may lack an entrepreneurial culture which is open to inter-firm co-operation, leading to an absence of economies of scale and business critical mass which may make certain local innovation efforts profitable.
- Traditional industries and small family firms which have little inclination towards innovation may dominate. There may be a low level of participation in international RTD&I networks and a low incidence of large, multinational firms.

Given all the above, we believe that regional policy should increasingly concentrate its efforts on the promotion of innovation to prepare regions for the new economy and close the "technology gap" if it is to be successful in creating the conditions for a sustained (and sustainable) economic development process in less favoured regions. A stable economic, legal and institutional framework is crucial in order to attract foreign investment and to promote sustainable development through investment. In this regard, a conducive international financial environment is also crucial. Promoting a conducive macro-economic environment, good governance and democracy, as well as strengthening structural aspects of the economy and improved institutional and human capacities, are important also in the context of attracting FDI and other private external flows.

In setting different priorities, we should take into account different conditions of each country and each regions as well as different elements and objectives of other sectors. Education and the stock of knowledge, for instance, play an important role in influencing the rate of innovation and diffusion of technology. Usually, technological policy should aim to create a favourable "psychological climate" for the development of research and innovations; for instance, different financial incentives, the support in education and training programmes, to provide technical services etc.

The various objectives of technological policy may be subsumed under five headings:

- to improve the efficiency of the transfer of technology from foreign suppliers to the local users;
- increase the efficiency of operation of technology;
- strengthen the industrial base;
- develop the indigenous technological capability; and
- smooth adjustment forced by new technologies.

In addition, science and research policies should be oriented towards two main objectives:

- to assess the possibilities and needs of private and public enterprises with respect to research and technological activities.
- to choose those priority objectives that can delineate government technological action.

New technologies imply some direct and indirect effects or more specifically some micro effects (such as firms, and organisations) and macro effects (such as inter and intra-industrial and moreover regional effects) for the whole economy. New technologies play an important role is sectoral productivity, overall growth, employment, modernization, industrialisation, socioeconomic infrastructure and to competitiveness of a country. Principal effects on technological policy can are distinguished in demand and supply.

Small countries are likely to need a more comprehensive and oriented policy of co-operative innovative effort in order to develop their future capabilities and make the necessary choice for technological priorities. The participation of member states in the EU research and technological programmes can increase the opportunities for promotion and improvement of research activities, creation of new research institutions so to support innovation and diffusion of new technologies and, therefore, to improve the level of economic and regional growth and induce social development. In general, debates about the political response to innovation date back at the beginning of the industrial revolution. In particular, recent debates about biotechnologies suggest that knowledge-based economy may be associated with equally vociferous debate – and action.

The identification of key sectors or priority groupings must be accompanied with a framework for policy and decision-making. Interventions will differ according to the aspirations and needs of the sector. The set of interventions is likely to:

- Include rollout of a focused innovation centre and enterprise hub programme, centred on the areas of international quality expertise.
- Strength the links between enterprise and the knowledge base, through, for instance, R&D grants, spinout and licensing assistance.
- Support networks, skills initiatives and tailored business support packages, focused on needs and issues of certain sectors.
- Establish and overseeing international alliances, to ensure the international competitiveness and profile of what the region offers.
- Participate in the inter-regional initiatives, where there are sector synergies with other regions.
- Achieve the highest sustainable economic growth and employment and arising standard of living in member countries, while maintaining financial stability, and thus to contribute to the development of the world economy.
- Contribute to sound economic expansion in member as well as non-member countries in the process of economic development.
- Contribute to the expansion of world trade on a multilateral, non-discriminatory basis in accordance with international obligations.
- Ensure stable macroeconomic and framework conditions to underpin the entrepreneurial business environment.
- Ensure the reduction and simplification of administrative regulations and costs which fall disproportionately on SMEs.
- Promote an entrepreneurial society and entrepreneurial culture, in particular through education and training. Integrate entrepreneurship at all levels of the formal education system and ensure access to information, skills and expertise relating to entrepreneurship via "lifelong learning" programmes for the adult population. Promote the diffusion of training programmes by stimulating the private market's supply of such services and providing hands-on focused courses.
- Integrate the local development dimension into the promotion of entrepreneurship.
- Ensure that programmes in support of SMEs and entrepreneurship are realistic in terms of cost and are designed to deliver measurable results.
- Strengthen the factual and analytical basis for policymaking so that policy makers can take decisions in an informed manner based on empirical evidence.
- Increase the ability of women to participate in the labour force by ensuring the availability of affordable child care and equal treatment in the workplace. More generally, improving the position of women in society and promoting entrepreneurship generally will have benefits in terms of women's entrepreneurship.

- Support the emergence and maintenance of innovative clusters.
- Promote policy coherence at regional, national and international level. Work to support whole of government approaches so that trade and investment policies and standard setting are aligned with development co-operation objectives and policies.

Chapter 6

EUROPEAN INNOVATION POLICY AND REGIONAL CONVERGENCE

6.1. INTRODUCTION

Europe's overall economic performance experienced a significant weakening, after years of exceptional growth by European standards. The GDP of the European Union grew by 1.6% in 2001, a reduction of nearly 2% compared with that of 2000, when the highest growth rates of the last fifteen years were recorded. Economic growth gradually slowed down in 2002 and, more or less, stagnated in the first half of 2003. Most of the world's other main economies also experienced a slowdown and some of them even showed negative growth rates (for instance, real GDP actually declined). The US economy, after years of vigorous growth well ahead of the figures registered in the European Union, encountered near-stagnation in 2001. Japan, which had hardly recovered from the weak years before, reported economic growth very close to zero for the last two years.

Investment in research and development (R&D) rose in 2001 and into 2002, as did investment in software in several countries. Information and Communication Technology (ICT) continued to diffuse to households and businesses and electronic commerce continued to gain in importance, despite the slowdown in parts of the ICT sector. The growing role of knowledge is reflected in economic performance. In Australia, Canada, Finland, Ireland and the United States, the overall efficiency of capital and labour - Multi-Factor Productivity (MFP) - increased considerably over the 1990s, partly thanks to rapid technological progress and the effective use of ICT.

The trade-to-GDP ratio increased by about 2 percentage points over the 1990s in the United States and the European Union, although it remained stable in Japan.

- The E.U. accounted for 47% of total OECD patent applications to the EPO, significantly above the United States (28 %) and Japan (18 %).
- Among European countries, Germany had by far the largest share with 20.5% of total EPO applications, more than the combined shares of France, the United Kingdom, Italy and the Netherlands Patent applications from Korea, Ireland and Finland increased sharply over the 1990s (annual growth rates of 16 % or more).

Researchers are viewed as the central element of the R&D system. They are defined as professionals engaged in the conception and creation of new knowledge, products, processes, methods and systems and are directly involved in the management of projects. For those countries that compile data by qualification only, data on university graduates employed in R&D are used as a proxy. The number of researchers is here expressed in full-time equivalent (FTE) on R&D (for instance, a person working half-time on R&D is counted as 0.5 person-year) and includes staff engaged in R&D during the course of one year. Underestimation of researchers in the United States is due to the exclusion of military personnel in the government sector. The business enterprise sector covers researchers carrying out R&D in firms and business enterprise sector institutes. While the government and the higher education sectors also carry out R&D, industrial R&D is more closely linked with the creation of new products and production techniques as well as to the country's innovation efforts.

The White Paper on European Governance [COM (2001) 428] concerns the way in which the EU uses the powers given by its citizens. It proposes, "opening up the policymaking process to get more people and organisations involved in shaping and delivering EU policy. It promotes greater openness, accountability and responsibility for all those involved. The quality, relevance and effectiveness of EU policies depend on ensuring wide participation through the policy chain: from conception to implementation...". The European Commission requires effort from all the Institutions, central governments, regions, cities, and civil societies in the current and future Member States. The White Paper is primarily addressed to these actors – some of whom will be responsible for initiating reforms of governance in their own countries, regions and organizations. The proposals within the White Paper indicate:

- The EU must renew the Community method by following less of a top-down approach, and by complementing its policy tools more effectively with no legislative instruments.
- Better involvement and more openness implies provision of up-to-date, on-line information on preparation of policy through all stages of decision-making.
- There is a need to be a stronger interaction with regional and local governments and civil society. Member States bear the principal responsibility for achieving this, but the Commission has a role to play.
- This kind of development (in Governance) does not initially appear to have a direct bearing on innovation propensity. Nevertheless, it could influence the culture of public and private sector organizations, and the way they work together. It could stimulate the creation and growth of new kinds of knowledge-based companies, offering information, advice and support in new enhanced democratic or stakeholder processes.
- To improve the quality of its policies, the EU must first assess whether action is needed and, if it is, whether it should be at the EU level. Thus, the EU obligation ought to clarify and simplify proposed regulations and support schemes and determine if support can be decentralized.

This Chapter aims to analyse and examine the evaluation of the knowledge-based economy and the development of the EU's policy, and how it can be implemented to the member states and the effects on economic growth and integration. It also attempts to examine the role of knowledge-based economy and innovation policy and their effects on sustainable development and, more specifically, on economic integration, and regional development.

6.2. INNOVATION POLICY AND THE KNOWLEDGE BASED ECONOMY

The increasing recognition by policy makers and academics of the importance of "knowledge-based economy" for future output and employment growth has yet to be reflected in any policy action. On the one hand, the move towards an information society is likely to lead to substantial changes in the demand for various sorts of educational and skill requirement. The move into a creative Knowledge-Based Economy (KBE) has implications for innovation policy and a number of other policy areas. It is necessary to study these implications and associated developments in order to reach the Lisbon objectives and to be prepared for innovative economic activities. It is important to examine the extent to which relevant policy areas have already been utilised to advance innovation policy in Europe, and how they might become more useful in this respect. The KBE is thus at the fore of the strategy. It is both an interpretation of current socio-economic trends, an empirical hypothesis; and a vision of what Europe could become, a policy objective. Innovation is positioned as a central characteristic of a KBE that is successful in terms of being socially and environmentally sustainable.

Basic research plays an important role in the R&D system. It generates new knowledge and understanding that provide the foundation for applied research and development. Because basic research provides reliable information about areas of future applications, more intense knowledge generation through basic research could be seen as a way to enhance innovation activities.

Generally, basic research has been under mounting pressure during the past decade or so. Due to short-term needs and economic priorities, there has been a tendency towards increasing the share of applied research and development in total R & D expenditure. However, the situation is blurring with some countries making more resources available for basic research and others less. In many countries, basic research still has a high status in the agenda of science, technology and innovation policies. There are good reasons for that. For instance, the emerging science-based areas of biotechnology and nanotechnology are promising areas for future applications and commercial activities.

The Knowledge Innovation Assessment is an integrated design of ten diverse competencies essential in an innovation system:

Collaborative Process	Products/Services
Performance Measures	Strategic Alliances
Education/Development	Market Image/Interaction
Learning Network	Leadership/Leverage
Market Positioning	Computer/Communications

It is a lack of investment in human capital, not a lack of investment in physical capital that prevents poor countries from catching up with rich ones. Educational attainment and public spending on education are correlated positively to economic growth (Barro and Sala-i-Martin, 1995; Benhabib and Spiegel, 1994). School quality measured, for example, by teacher pay, student-teacher ratio, and teacher education is positively correlated to future earnings of the students. Education is important for explaining the growth of national income. Life-long learning is also crucial (Aghion et al., 1998). People with human capital migrate from places where education is scarce to places where it is abundant (Lucas, 1988). "Human capital flight" or "brain drain" can lead to a permanent reduction in income and growth of the country of emigration relative to the country of immigration. We need more technical graduates. R&D ability to innovate is a key competitive advantage

The meaning and scope of Innovation are defined in that Green Paper on Innovation (COM(95)688, which opened up a number of pathways. For the sake of efficiency, this *"First Action Plan"* refers to a limited number of priority initiatives to be launched very soon at Community level and includes a number of schemes put into action or announced since the launch of the Green Paper, identified as essential to the innovation process.

On 20 November 1996, the Commission adopted the First Action Plan for Innovation in Europe following the wide ranging public debate stimulated by the Green Paper on Innovation. The Action Plan provides a general framework for action at the European and member state level to support innovation process. A limited number of priority measures to be launched immediately by the Community, are identified. The plan also sets out these measures which have already been underway or which have been announced since the launch of the Green Paper. Two main areas for action have been identified:

- *Fostering an innovation culture:* education and training, easier mobility for researchers and engineers, demonstration of effective approaches to innovation in economy and in society, propagation of best management and organisational methods amongst businesses, and stimulation of innovation in the public sector and in government;
- *Establishing a framework conducive to innovation:* adaptation and simplification of the legal and regulatory environment, especially with respect to Intellectual Property Rights, and providing easier access to finance for innovative enterprises;

Gearing research more closely to innovation at both national and Community level: as far as action at the Community level is concerned, the Commission proposes to establish within the Research Framework a single, simplified horizontal framework to integrate "innovation" and "SME" dimensions. Outside of the Framework Programme, all Community instruments are to be mobilised to support innovation.

On the one hand, the Commission continues to investigate some of the long-term schemes identified in the Green Paper. On the other hand, it proposes to carry out a more detailed analysis of activities of the member states and of applicant countries, with their collaboration, with the aim of establishing, in a second phase, a common reference framework which will help to identify priority options and opportunities for cooperation.

Nevertheless, the Union's overall innovation performance continues to be disappointing. Europe as a whole must become more innovative if the strategic goal set at the Lisbon Summit of the European Council in March 2000 - the Union to become the most competitive and dynamic knowledge-based economy in the world - is to be achieved. The Commission targets five objectives:

- Coherence of innovation policies;
- A regulatory framework conducive to innovation;
- Encouragement of the creation and growth of innovative enterprises;
- Improvement a key interfaces in the innovation system;
- A society open to innovation.

Action at Community level, while respecting the rules of subsidiarity is necessary to draw up and enforce the rules of the game, particularly those on *competition, intellectual property rights* and the *internal market*. Innovation requires, first and foremost, a state of mind combining creativity, entrepreneurship, willingness to take calculated risks and an acceptance of social, geographical or professional mobility. Being innovative also demands an ability to anticipate needs, rigorous organisation and a capacity of meeting deadlines and controlling costs.

In particular, the means to act are:

- *Education and training.* At national level, continue reviewing courses and teaching methods, above all for their ability to stimulate creativity and a spirit of enterprise from the earliest age, and think about any changes which may be necessary for trainers' training. Member states should also continue to develop life long training. The Commission's contribution will be to set up a permanent "training and innovation" forum to stimulate the exchange of experience and best practice in this area.
- *Easier mobility of researchers and engineers to firms.* In the orientations the Framework Programme for Research, the Commission proposes a wide programme with the main objective to enhance human potential. It should in particular boost the efforts of the framework programme to arrange for transnational secondments of young researchers and engineers to businesses, in particular SMEs, to help with their innovation or technology transfer projects. Member states are invited to adopt similar measures and to set up the conditions in order to make this mobility a reality.
- *Demonstrate effective approaches to innovation in the economy and in society.* It is easier to make innovation acceptable and hence successful in the long run if citizens, industry, and their representatives are involved in the debate on the major technological choices to be made, and if employees, users and consumers take part in the process. The dissemination of good practice in this field shoul be strengthened. Moreover, the future framework programme for research should open up new approaches to demonstration, including technical, economic and social aspects, management and organisation, as well as fostering participation.
- (iv). *Propagate the best management and organisational methods amongst businesses.* More and more of the firms that succeed are "agile", pro-active and likely to forge cooperative links with external centres of expertise. At both national and Community level greater priority should be given to disseminate organisational innovations and use information and communication technologies in this field.
- (v). *Finally, stimulate innovation in the public sector and in government.* At national level, innovation training or awareness schemes for decision-makers and managers of projects and funds in the public domain need to be developed.

In the knowledge-based economies, the efficient systems are those which combine the ability to produce knowledge, those mechanisms which can disseminate it as widely as possible and the aptitude of the individuals, companies and organisations concerned to absorb and use it. The crucial factor for innovation is thus the link between research (the production of knowledge), training, mobility, interaction (the dissemination of knowledge) and the ability of firms, particularly SMEs, to absorb new technologies and know-how.

At the *national level*, several types of action are necessary, depending on the member state; the Commission may give assistance, where appropriate, by acting to:

- Facilitate the exchange of experiences between Member states and exploiting the results of these exercises in order to identify relevant leads at the Community level.
- Reinforce technology watch at European level within the framework of the European Science and Technology Observatory, set up by the RCC's Institute for Prospective Technological Studies as focal point for the Member states observatories.
- The Commission recommends that Member States establish a legal and practical framework which will foster this cooperation by:
  - providing opportunities to universities and researchers to spend some time in developing companies;
  - enabling universities and public research centres to exclusive contracts with industry so to take advantage results, including through financial holdings.

6.3. THE EUROPEAN INSTITUTIONAL FRAMEWORK AND THE INNOVATION ACTIVITIES

Innovation requires, first and foremost, a state of mind combining creativity, entrepreneurship, willingness to take calculated risks and an acceptance of social, geographical or professional mobility. Being innovative also demands an ability to anticipate needs, rigorous organisation and a capacity of meeting deadlines and controlling costs.

Greater priority should be given at both national and Community level to disseminate organisational innovations and use information and communication technologies in this field. The Commission aims to favour the use the instruments at its disposal (the framework programme, the Structural Funds and the training programmes) to this end.

The EU and the member states should first of all make efforts to improve the European patent system, making it more efficient, more accessible and less expensive. The public debate has confirmed the needs of users in this field. Many of the defects in the current situation stem from the coexistence of three patent systems in the EU: national, European and Community. The Commission recommends that Member States put in place instruments for assisting SMEs and universities in the event of litigation, to raise awareness in SMEs and to develop training schemes in this area. The Commission should needs to work on propagating good practice, facilitating its adoption -particularly with the support of pilot projects- and mobilising the Structural Funds and newer instruments such as the European Investment Fund (EIF).

This action should be guided by three objectives:

(a) investment in risk capital and equity needs encouragement. This applies particularly to start-up investment and innovative, high-growth firms, which are a major source of new jobs. Long term sources of funding (pension funds, life insurance, "business angels" and save-as-you-earn schemes) should be directed more towards risk investment.
(b) the conditions within which European capital markets for innovative, high-growth companies (such as the New Market Federation or EASDAQ) develop must be secured.
(c) interfaces between technological innovation and financial circles need to be strengthened. Support is needed for the transnational dissemination of good practice and the testing of new methods in this area. Furthermore, closer links between Community research and risk capital should improve the exploitation of the results of the research. Information and guidance service on this topic will be set up for those taking part in the framework programme.

6.3.1. Human Resources, Education and Training

Education, vocational training, further training, and concern for the skills level of the entire labour force are strong elements in innovation policies. However, educational budgets in member states are more decentralised than budget lines of most other innovation policy relevant actions. The observation that science subjects trail in popularity among school children and young people has become a concern to most member state governments.

The linkages between university level education and the enterprise sector: in this field most policies and measures aim to support the mobility of university graduates into their first jobs and promote the exchange of research staff.

6.3.2. Entrepreneurship and Innovation Activities

Recent national White Papers and Action Plans show the need to rationalise the framework conditions to support SMEs and industrial competitiveness. The following examples are categorised according to entrepreneurship and innovation finances. The excessive costs of patent protection in Europe compared with patent costs in the United States are addressed in most member states. The variety of measures demonstrates the difficulty in combining the benefits of protection (allowing a pay-back to the inventor and innovator) with the benefits of wider exploitation of new products, processes (in particular in biotechnology), or services. There is an uneven presence of adequate infrastructures to promote recent years' advances in the use of high quality norms and standards, not least in the field of services and in the application of total quality standards or design as a competition parameter.

Priorities differ among countries according to the current situation of the science, technology and innovation system in each country. Reallocation of government portfolios and departmental responsibilities are another indicator of policy development. The trend in several countries has been to maintain or raise the level at which R&D expenditure is co-ordinated with other industry relevant budgets.

Re-organisation at government level has been accompanied by restructuring of institutions as well. Intermediary institutions for the support of technology transfer and the co-operation among major research institutions are often organised as private non-profit entities outside the public sector.

6.3.3. Innovation, Growth and Employment

The new theories of growth (known as "endogenous") stress that development of know-how and technological change - rather than the mere accumulation of capital - are the driving force behind lasting growth. According to these theories, authorities can influence the foundations of economic growth by playing a part in the development of know-how, one of the principal mainsprings of innovation. Authorities can also influence the "distribution" of know-how and skills throughout economy and society, for instance, by facilitating the mobility of persons and interactions between firms and between firms and outside sources of skills, in particular universities, as well as ensuring that competition is given free rein and by resisting corporatist ideas.

Table 6.1. Some Factors Explain the American and Japanese Success

United States	Japan
• A more important research effort	• high level
• A larger proportion of engineers and scientists in the active population	• high level
• Research efforts better coordinated, in particular with regard to civilian and defence research (in particular in the aeronautic, electronic and space sectors).	• A strong ability to adapt terchnological information, wherever it comes from. A strong tradition of cooperation between firms in the field of R&D
• A close University - Industry relationship allowing the blossoming of a large number of high technology firms.	• An improving cooperation University / Industry, especially via the secondment of industrial researchers in Universities
• A capital risk industry better developed which invests in high technology. NASDAQ, a stock exchange for dynamic SMEs.	• Stable and strong relationships between finance and industry fostering long term benefits and strategies.
• A cultural tradition favourable to risk taking and to enterprise spirit, a strong social acceptation of innovation.	• A culture favourable to the application of techniques and on going improvement.
• A lower cost for filing licenses, a single legal protection system favourable to the commercial exploitation of innovations	• A current practice of concerted strategies between companies, Universities and public authorities
• Reduced lead time for firms creation and limited red tape	• A strong mobility of staff within companies.

Source: OECD, STAN database.

The relationship between innovation and employment is complex. In principle, technological progress generates new wealth. Product innovations lead to an increase in effective demand which encourages an increase in investment and employment. Process innovations, for their part, contribute to an increase in productivity of the factors of production by increasing production and/or lowering costs. In the course of time, the result is another increase in purchasing power, which promotes increased demand and, here again, employment. Table 6.1 illustrate some of the main factors explaining the American and Japanese success.

6.3.4. Innovation and the Convergence Process

Innovation is particularly important for the regions which lag behind in development. The SMEs, which make up virtually the entire economic fabric encounter special difficulties there, particularly with regard to financing. For instance, the actual interest rates are often 2-3 points higher than in the more developed regions, but also this happens quite often regarding cooperation opportunities, access to sources of technical or management skills, etc. The handicaps mount up, which indicates shortcomings in the operation of markets which can justify intervention by authorities. At national level, several types of action are necessary, depending on the member state; the Commission may give assistance where appropriate:

- *Firstly, develop a strategic foresight vision of research and its application.* Exercises such as "key technologies", "Delphi" or "Foresight" can contribute to directing collective efforts to sectors, areas or technologies, which are the most relevant the future. Member States which do not have any experience in that area ought to consider the opportunity of this type of approach. The Commission will act to:
  - facilitate the exchange of experiences between Member states and exploit the results of these exercises in order to identify relevant leads at the Community level;
  - reinforce technology watch at a European level within the framework of the European Science and Technology Observatory, set up by the RCC's Institute for Prospective Technological Studies as focal point for the Member states observatories.
- *Secondly, strengthen the research carried out by industry, in both absolute and relative terms*
- Member states are requested to draw up quantitative and ambitious objectives aiming to increase the share on the Gross Internal Product dedicated to research, to development and to innovation, in particular by encouraging research undertaken by industry (especially the one financed by enterprises or by governments within the limits allowed by article 92 of the Treaty). In Europe, the share of GDP devoted to research financed by industry, which offers more opportunities for exploitation, is on average 38% below that of the USA and 55% below that of Japan.
- *Thirdly, encourage strongly the start-up of technology-based firms ("campus companies", spin-offs, etc.).* The Commission recommends that member states step up the action they have been taking in this area and exploit the structures which have

proved effective in the field. Since 1997, it has been organised a thorough exchange with member states on this topic, involving leading players in the field.
- *Fourthly, intensify the cooperation between public, university and industrial research.* The Commission recommends that member states establish a legal and practical framework which will foster this cooperation by:
  - providing opportunities for universities and researchers to spend some of their time developing companies;
  - enabling universities and public research centres to incorporate exclusive contracts with industry so to take advantage of exploiting results, including through financial holdings.
- *Lastly, strengthen the capacity of SMEs so to absorb new technologies and know-how, whatever their origin.* Substantial effort needs to be made in this area. Member states should extend the scope of their measures to include the transfer of technologies of international origin. Companies, particularly SMEs, should have easier access to expertise at the highest level, European or worldwide, in technological, organisational or management methods.

Moreover, at national and regional level, the drive to rationalise innovation support organisations, as mentioned above, needs to be accompanied by measures empowering them to achieve critical mass and the necessary degree of professionalism. The Commission will intensify activities to create improved links among various national and regional innovation-support systems. The EU must make full use of the international dimension of innovation. Two-thirds of world innovations and scientific discoveries are made outside the EU, and most expanding markets are to be found outside Europe. In particular, this means:

- closer interaction of the framework programme with the COST and EUREKA cooperation frameworks;
- support for international industrial cooperation;
- intensified international cooperation on research and development with non-Member countries;
- stronger encouragement of entities in the countries concerned, through the possibilities offered by instruments such as TACIS, PHARE, MEDA, etc. in order to search for a stronger synergy with community research projects; and
- continued vigilance in international negotiations for aspects liable to affect European innovation and its outlets (such as intellectual property rights and anti-counterfeit measures).

The main effort must nevertheless be made at a local, regional or national level. The Commission proposes to analyse in more detail those activities which are the province of the member states, in collaboration with local governments, in order to establish a joint reference framework and so help them identify priority options and opportunities for cooperation.

6.3.5. Innovation and the Public Action

The Commission has clearly identified - first in the White Paper on Growth, Competitiveness and Employment, and then in its 1994 communication on An Industrial Competitiveness Policy for the European Union - that firms' capacity for innovation, and support for it from the authorities, are essential for maintaining and strengthening this competitiveness and employment. This Green Paper makes use of, adds to and extends that work with a view to arriving at a genuine European strategy for the promotion of innovation. While respecting the principle of subsidiarity, it has proposed the measures to be taken at both national and Community levels.

"In exercising their responsibilities, the authorities must promote the development of future-oriented markets and anticipate changes rather than react to them (...). The European Union must place its science and technology base at the service of industrial competitiveness and the needs of the market more effectively. Greater attention must be paid to dissemination, transfer and industrial application of research results and to bringing up to date the traditional distinction between basic research, pre-competitive research and applied research which, in the past, has not always allowed European industry to benefit from all the research efforts made." The Commission has paid attention to this aspect of updating in the new arrangements on research aid adopted in December 1995.

Strengthening the capacity for innovation involves various policies: industrial policy, RTD policy, education and training, tax policy, competition policy, regional policy and policy on support for SMEs, environment policy, etc. Ways must therefore be identified, prepared and implemented - in a coordinated fashion - the necessary measures covered by these various policies. There is widespread agreement on the need for a global approach to the problem, incorporating technological aspects, training, venture capital development and the legal and administrative environment.

The White Paper should be commended for its treatment of the many facets of public policy for a knowledge-economy. A key to success in knowledge-economy is a trained labour force. It is not surprising that so many countries have focused on improving their educational systems. Furthermore, we may observe the following points:

- First, in the long run, success in the knowledge economy requires creativity, higher order cognitive skills in addition to basic skills. Those countries that find ways of fostering this kind of creativity will, in the long run, be more successful in a competitive knowledge-economy.
- Second, also key to success in knowledge-economy is training in science and technology. There are good grounds for government subsidies to science education.
- Thirdly, one of the reasons that the education sector may not be as strong is due to limited competition.
- The Green Paper contributes to these two objectives by it wide-ranging debate, aiming to encourage the economic and social, public and private players. It touches upon the following:
- the *challenges of innovation* for Europe, its citizens, its labour force and its firms, against a background of globalisation and rapid technological changes;

- a *revaluation of the situation* of innovation policies and *the many obstacles to innovation*;
- •*proposals or lines of action,* while respecting the principle of subsidiarity, for government, regions and the European Union, aimed at removing the obstacles and contributing towards a more dynamic European society which is a source of employment and progress for its citizens.

6.4. THE EUROPEAN TECHNOLOGICAL POLICY

During the past quarter of a century or so, many arrangements for international economic integration have come into existence. The most important for the European Community is in reality an amalgamation of three separate communities: the European Coal and Steel Community (ECSC) established by the Treaty of Paris in 1952 and valid for fifty years. The European Economic Community (EEC) created in 1957 by the Treaty of Rome for an unlimited period and the European Atomic Energy Community (EURATOM) founded by another Treaty of Rome in 1957 and also of an unlimited duration.

The Treaty of Rome states that the aim of establishing the EEC is "to promote throughout the Community a harmonious development of economic activities, a continuous and balanced expansion, an increased stability, an accelerated raising of the standard of living and closer relations between its member states: (Article 2). In order to achieve this aim the EEC member states will consider their economic policy as a matter of common interest. They will consult with each other and with the Commission on measures to be taken in response to current circumstances (Article 103). With the EEC, the European integration reached a decisive stage in development providing a drastic form of integration: First of all, complete the customs union, the free movement of persons and capital, and finally, an integrated policy in a number of areas such as, agricultural policy, transportation, research and technological policies.

For many years, technological change has been widely considered as an *engine of growth* and an important factor in development process. Today, there is keen technological competition among the EEC, the USA and Japan. The aim is to reinforce technological capabilities and international competitiveness. European technology policy also aims to increase convergence among member states and to reduce disparities of the Community's less favoured regions. European technological policy is implemented through various rolling framework research programmes, which consist of various research projects and cover various sectors and scientific subjects.

Today, there is a large technological gap between advanced and less favoured regions within the EU. The countries of Europe have a long cultural and scientific tradition. Major scientific discoveries and the main developments in technology are products of European civilisation. The Treaty of Rome did not endow the Commission with explicit power to conduct research and technology policy. The Commission operated only through unanimous decisions of the Council of Ministers. In the first phase of the Community's research policy only eight articles from Euratom treaty were devoted to the promotion of research activities.

This treaty did not provide a framework for a general research policy. However, the Community's research activities were developed within this framework and provided the basis for the work is being done today. The ECSC and EEC treaties do not contain such detailed provisions as the Euratom treaty. During the first period 1953-1974 there was thus no clear common framework for Community's research policy. The Community's research programmes for this period concentrated mainly in the nuclear, steel and agricultural sectors. Only the Single European Act extended the Commission's competence in technological subjects and strengthened the Commission's role in these fields.

In 1965 three Communities (European Coal & Steel Community, Euratom and European Economic Community) set up a joint committee of their executive bodies to examine the merits of a Community for co-ordinated research and development programmes and to get prepared for a proposed meeting of the Councils of Ministers on this subject. In 1966, the Vice-president of EEC (M. Marjolin) addressed the issue of the importance of technology in the European Parliament. He proposed that scientific research should be regarded as an integral part of economic policy. At the same time, there was another proposition for a *technological Marshall aid* scheme that would have been based on NATO. Both aimed to fill out the existing technological gap. Finally, the *European Technological Community* was preferred.

Figure 6.1 illustrates the Gross Domestic Expenditures on Research and Development in relation to Gross Domestic Product for the mean of European Union, whereas Figure 5.3 illustrates the Business contribution to Gross Domestic Expenditures on Research and Development for the mean of European Union. However, the percentage of funds allocated for technological activities was still very low and corresponded only to 2% of the total Community's budget expenditures.

During the 1960s, several attempts were made to develop cross national research groupings. For instance, in 1962, Siemens, Olivetti, Elliott Automation (these later formed the core of ICL) and Bull tried to create a cross European research grouping. However, this attempt was unsuccessful. In 1969, the Eurodata consortiums, (ICL, CII, Philips, AEG, Telefuken, Saab and Olivetti), established the European Space Research Organisation (ESRO) for computer requirements, but this also failed.

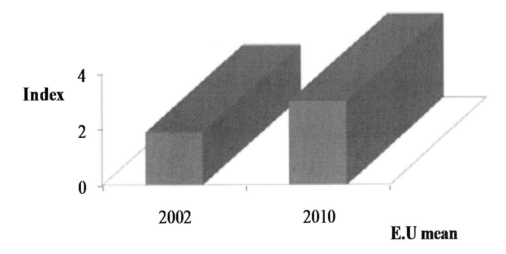

Source: EU.

Figure 6.1. Gross Domextic Expenditures on Research and Development in relation to GDP for EU mean.

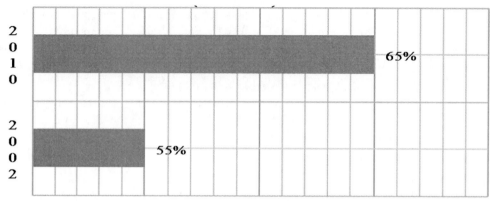

Source: E,U.

Figure 6.2. Business contribution to Gross Domestic on R&D (EU mean).

In 1960s, nuclear power was one of the most important areas of new technology; the Commission's power in this field derived from the Euratom treaty of 1957. At this period, four research centres were established and the areas of research extended to high temperature gas-reactors, nuclear ship propulsion and nuclear applications in medicine and agriculture. Later, in the early 1970s, the research that was undertaken at JRC (Joint Research Centres) focused on other fields, such as the environment, solar energy and materials. The most successful story in European collaboration during the 1960s and 1970s was in aerospace. In the 1970s, the European Space Agency (ESA) was developed with participation of all Western European countries. This helped create a *research space community* of scientists, engineers, policy makers and industrialists. In November 1971, the COST European programme in the field of Cooperation in Scientific and Technical research) was established. It consisted of nineteen OECD western European members (including Switzerland). COST was a useful framework to prepare and carry out pan-European projects in applied scientific research.

During 1974-1982, there was an unsteady technological policy without any apparent results. In this period, there was a tendency to increase the allocation of funds to R&T activities. In July 1978, the Commission launched FAST (Forecasting and Assessment in the field of Science and Technology) experimental programme. The main objective of FAST was to define the long-term priorities and objectives of the Community's technological policy. European technology slowed down after the energy crises of the 1970s, but it came into its own in the 1980s. The EUREKA project was launched in 1985, and by 1990 it had already reached total committed investment by governments, companies and research institutes of more than 8 billion €, deriving from almost 500 projects. Eureka membership encompasses the EC and EFTA countries and Turkey.

The Community's research programmes and EUREKA are complementary. In June 1991, there were 470 ongoing EUREKA projects in nine technology areas, which varied greatly in their scope and financial impact. Some EUREKA projects have through their size gained widespread awareness and have created a favourable image for initiative, as for example, JESSI, HDTV, and PROMETHEUS. However, the percentage of funds allocated for technological activities was still very low and corresponded only to 2% of the total Community's budget expenditures. The Community's expenditures allocated to JRC were about 25% of the Community's total research budget, these funds were allocated mostly to the four countries where the JRCs (Joint Research Centres) are located. In addition, the Community's *direct-order* research programmes are *more suitable* for the advanced technological member states.

Figure 6.2 illustrates the business contribution to Gross Domestic on R&D for EU mean. Until the end of the late 1980s, the Community's research policy was orientated mainly towards co-ordination of the national technology policies of member states rather than to pursue a coherent technology policy. Most of the criteria used by Community research policy were based on quality rather than our needs. However, during 1982-1990, a more coherent and clear technology policy began to develop. The European Single Act and the Treaty of Maastricht worked towards this direction. In 1987, things changed; the Single European Act (SEA) explicitly legitimised the Community dimension in scientific and technical co-operation within Europe by giving the Community formal power in the fields of research and technology. Articles 130f-130g of SEA embody a research and technology policy that enjoys equal status with other Community areas, such as economic, social and competition policy.

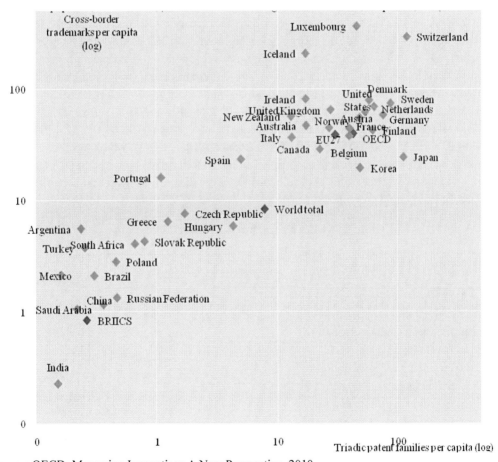

Source: OECD: Measuring Innovation: A New Perspective, 2010.

Figure 6.3. Patents and Trademarks per capita, 2005-2007, (average number per million population, G20 countries.

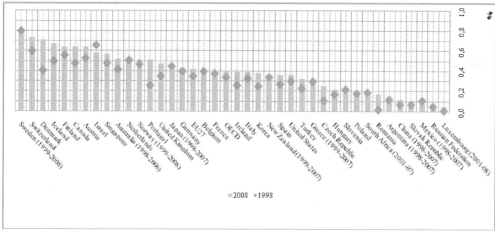

Source: OECD: Measuring Innovation: A New Perspective, 2010.

Figure 6.4. Higher education expenditure on R&D, 2008, as a percentage of GDP.

The SEA makes substantial amendments to the Treaty of Rome. It contains provisions that are intended to speed up European integration by completing the single market, strengthening economic and social cohesion and co-operation in financial matters. The European Single Act aims to develop the social and environment policies and to establish a genuine European research and technological Community. Figure 6.3 illustrates patents and trademarks per capita during the period 2005-2007 for EU member states. Triadic patent families refer to patent filed at the European Patent Office (EPO), the US Patent and Trademark Office (USPTO) and the Japan Patent Office (JPO) which protect the same invention. Counts are presented according to the priority date and the residence of the inventors. Figure 6.4 illustrates higher education expenditures on R&D as a percentage of GDP for EU and OECD member states.

Table 6.2. EU's Framework Research Programs

Focal areas:	Sum in m €:	Proportion of Total Budget
• *First Framework Programme (1984-1987):*		
• (1). Agricultural Competitiveness:	130	3.50
• (2). Industrial Competitiveness:	1060	28.20
• (3). Improving raw materials:	80	2.10
• (4). Improving energy resources:	1770	47.20
• (5). Stepping up development aid:	150	4.00
• (6). Improving working conditions:	385	10.30
• (7). Improving the S/T potential:	85	2.30
• (8). Horizontal action:	90	2.40
• Total Budget:	3750	100
• *Second framework programme (1987-1991):*		
• (1). Quality of Life:	375	6.90
• (2). Towards an Inf. society:	2275	42.30
• (3). Modernisation of industry:	845	15.60

• (4). Biological resources: • (5). Energy: • (6). S/T for development: • (7). Exploiting marine resources • (8). Improvement of S/T co-operation: • Total Budget (1)-(8): • R&D Programme already adopted or in hand: • Total Budget:	1173 280 80 80 288 5396 1084 6840	5.20 21.70 1.50 1.50 5.30 100
• *Third framework programme (1990-1994):* • Enabling Technologies: • (1). Information Technology & Communications: • (2). Industrial & material technologies: • Management Industrial Resources: • (1). Environment: • (2). Life Sciences & Technologies: • (3). Energy: • Management of Intellectual Resources: • (1). Human capital & mobility: • Total Budget:	3000 1200 700 1000 1100 700 7700	38.90 15.60 9.10 13.00 14.30 9.10 100
• *Fourth Framework programme (1994-1998):* • Area I: Technology & demonstration of R&D programmes: • Area II: Cooperation of non-EC countries & Intern. Organisation: • Area III: Circulating and exploiting research funding: • Area IV: Improving training and mobility for researchers: • Horizontal support measures: • Total Budget:	11600 1400 700 1000 (1600) 14700	78.91 9.52 4.76 6.80 100
• *Fifth Framework programme (1999-2002):* • Research, technological development and demonstration activities:	10843	72,4
• Confirming the International Role of Community's Research:	475	3,2
• Promotion of Innovation and Encouragement of SME participation:	363	2,5
• Improving human research potential and the socio-economic knowledge base:	1280	8,6
• Joint Research Centre (JRC):	739	4,9
• Indirect Actions: Research and Training in the Field of Nuclear Energy:	979	6,6
• Direct Actions: Joint Research Centre (JRC):	281	1,8

Note: Horizontal support measures can be applied to four activities. The framework programmes aimed to promote the international competitiveness of European industry and to reinforce economic and social cohesion.
Source: CEC, "EC Research Funding", Brussels, Belgium.

The principles introduced by the Single European Act are repeated, confirmed and extended in the text agreed at Maastricht. The Treaty of Maastricht (1992) gives a double perspective to technological policy. The co-ordination of national technological policies essentially ceases to be entrusted solely to the good intentions of member states. Now, there should be mutual consistency between national and Community policies.

The Community's research policy is implemented with specific programmes. In the 1980s, the first step towards the direction of Community research policy was the formulation of the first framework program (1984-1987). This introduced the medium term planning of research activities at an EC level. The Community's research programs concern the following:

(a) research and technological programs of JCR centres;
(b) *direct order* research programs which are in collaboration and in co-financing with governments of the member states;
(c) training research programs; and
(d) international research programs.

The research framework programs aim to strengthen the international competitiveness of European industry in high technology sectors and more specifically as against the USA and Japan. The first framework programme covered seven high priority areas, and these formed the basis for a large number of projects in industry, universities and research centres. The second framework programme started in September 1987. About 60% of the funds of the second framework programme were allocated to industrial research.

However, most funds were intended to promote the introduction of new technologies to traditional industrial sectors (such as engineering and construction). The decisive breakthrough to a comprehensive political strategy on technology sectors came with the second and third framework programmes. The second (1987-1991) and the third (1990-1994) research framework programmes were based on the Single European Act. In April 1990, the Council of Ministers adopted the third framework programme (1990-1994), which overlapped the second framework programme by two years. The total appropriation of ECU 5.7 billion falls for the third framework programme into two parts: (a) 2.5 b € for 1990-1992 and (b) 3.2 b € for 1993-1994.

Table 6.3. A Comparison of Framework programmes of R&T Activities, (percentages)

	1984-1987	1987-1991	1990-1994
A. Information & communication technologies	25	42	39
B. Industrial & Materials Technologies	11	16	16
C. Environment	7	6	9
D. Life Science & Technologies	5	9	13
E. Energy	50	23	14
F. Human Capital	2	4	9
Total (%)	100	100	100

Source: CEC, DGXII/A1, (Quinn, Copol 90, EC).

Table 6.2 indicates a sectoral breakdown for the Community framework research programmes. Since 1984, there has been rapid growth of the Community's research expenditures. The amount which is included in these figures corresponds to the previous proposed resource allocation of four activities: evaluation, co-ordination, concentration and JRC (Joint Research Centre). It should be noticed that the representative budget figures in the framework programmes correspond to the Community's financial contribution only. If we take into account national contributions, then the total budget would be approximately doubled. The research framework programmes consist of various projects that work on a competitive basis, which implies that the participation of each country depends upon the criteria of *quality and strength of applicants*.

The Commission proposed a total amount of 14,700 m € for the fourth research programme (1994-1998). The fourth programme complies with the provisions Treaty of Maastricht and therefore covers all the Community's research and demonstration activities. International scientific co-operation will now be part of the program, and some research activities that were outside the third framework program will be included in the new one. The objectives of the Community's framework programmes are to:

(a) enhance European industrial competitiveness;
(b) set up a vast unified market by promoting standardisation and open procurement;
(c) improve the effectiveness of the Community's scientific and technical co-operation;
(d) promote agricultural competitiveness;
(e) speed up the marketing of new technologies by carrying out programmes for the application of information technologies;
(f) help the least favoured regions of Community (LFR) obtain access to new technologies;
(g) encourage SMEs and continuing education and training.

Table 6.3 compares the first, second and third research framework programmes. As we can see on the one hand, information technologies receive more attention and account for about 40% of the total budget. On the other hand, research in the energy sectors has declined from 50% in the first programme to only 14 % for the third. In addition, life sciences and industrial and material technologies have increased their participation and account for about 13% and 16% respectively. In the 1990s, the Community's research plans are to enforce *joint research*. In the long-term, these plans aim to change the approach of co-operation between theoretical and industrial research, by providing a *new learning environment*. The main problem for less favoured member states is the poor rate of diffusion of new technologies and lack of access to information networks related to new techniques and to new technologies. The Community aims to emphasise these points and to accelerate the diffusion of technologies between and within the member states.

For instance, the SPRINT programme was established in order to reinforce dissemination activities. SPRINT accounted for 90 m € during 1989-1993. However, in reality, SPRINT represented a total expenditure of 180 m € as it supported the total cost of an activity up to a maximum level of 50%, while the remaining expenditures were contributed by participants. Similarly, the research framework programmes have specific sections concentrated on dissemination of information and diffusion of new technologies. Table 6.4 illustrates the emerging technologies for the EU vis-avis USA and Japan. Tables 6.5 and 6.6 illustrate the allocation of the whole funds by objective and the allocation of funds by member states, respectively.

The European Union Framework Programme currently the 6th (FP6) is implemented for the time period 2002 until 2006 (CEC, 2002). The FP6 concentrates on research and innovation, human resources and mobility as well as research infrastructures in order to build a science and technology network in the EU, for instance, the European Research Area. It does so by connecting actions on the national and the regional level as well as on the EU level. Innovation is being built into regional policy to an increasing extent. Reforms to the Structural Funds for 2000-06 have increased the possibilities for financing measures linked to innovation. For example, the European Regional Development Fund (ERDF) can now contribute to, "financing the transfer of technology, including in particular the collection and dissemination of information, common organization between enterprises and research establishments and financing the implementation of innovation in enterprises" and supporting RTD "with a view to promoting the introduction of new technologies and innovation and the strengthening of research and technological development capacities contributing to regional development" (CEC, 2000, p.134). The links between innovation policy and regional policy have been recognized. Regional Innovation and Technology Transfer Strategies (RITTS), funded through the Innovation and SMEs programme, and Regional Innovation Strategies (RIS), funded through the ERDF, have been jointly managed by Enterprise DG and Regional Policy DG. Because of the different sources of funding RITTS projects can be located throughout the EU and EEA while the RIS projects are confined to those regions entitled to ERDF assistance. The Regional Policy DG has invited all current RIS and eligible RITTS regions to submit proposals for ERDF assistance.

Table 6.4. Emerging technologies

Europe	Vis-a-Vis the USA	Vis-a-Vis Japan
Ahead:	Digital imaging technology Flexible computer-integrated manufacturing	Flexible computer-integrated manufacturing Software engineering technologies
Level:	Advanced semiconductors High-density data storage Sensor technology Advanced materials Software engineering technologies	Artificial intelligence Digital imaging technology Sensor technology Superconductors Biotechnology Medical equipment
Behind	Artificial intelligence High-performance computers Optoelectronics Biotechnology Medical equipment	Advanced semiconductors High-performance computers High-density data storage Optoelectronics Advanced materials

Source: Korres G. (2003).

Table 6.5. Allocation of Community Structural Funds for Various Objectives

	Allocation in billions of Euro	% of the Structural Funds budget	% reserved for transitional support
Objective 1	135,9	69,70%	4,30%
Objective 2	22,5	11,50%	1,40%
Objective 3	24,05	12,30%	-
Fisheries: (outside of Objective 1)	1,11	0,60%	-

Source: European Union.

Table 6.6. Allocation of Community Structural Funds for the Member States

Member State	Objective 1	Transitional support ex-Objective 1	Objective 2	Transitional support ex-Objective 2 & 5b	Objective 3	Fisheries Instrument (outside Obj. 1)	Total
Belgium	0	625	368	65	737	34	1829
Denmark	0	0	156	27	365	197	745
Deutschland	19229	729	2984	526	4581	107	28156
Greece	20961	0	0	0	0	0	20961
Spain	37744	352	2533	98	2140	200	43087
France	3254	551	5437	613	4540	225	14620
Ireland	1315	1773	0	0	0	0	3088
Italy	21935	187	2145	377	3744	96	28484
Lux.	0	0	34	6	38	0	78
Netherl.	0	123	676	119	1686	31	2635
Austria	261	0	578	102	528	4	1473
Portugal	16124	2905	0	0	0	0	19029
Finland	913	0	459	30	403	31	1836
Sweden	722	0	354	52	720	60	1908
UK	5085	1186	3989	706	4568	121	15635
EUR15	127 543	8411	19733	2721	24050	1106	183 564
	Mill. €	Million €	Mill. €	Million €	Million €	Million €	Mil. €

(1) Including PEACE (2000-2004).
(2) including the special programme for the Swedish coastal areas.
Source: European Union, www.eu.int/eurostat

Within the Structural Funds the so-called innovative actions are the particularly important instrument for EU regional innovation policy (CEC, 2001a and 2001b). The innovative actions are partly financed by the European Regional Development Funds (ERDF) and partly financed by the regions and countries themselves. Innovative actions are meant to give the regional policy makers the possibility to manage risk and change inherent in innovation as well as to exploit the synergies between regional policy and other EU policies, in particular those, which support innovative activities on the regional level and the emergence of the European Research Area (ERA). Innovative actions are an experimental tool that explores the future orientation of the least-developed regions of the EU, in particular the Objective 1 regions, for instance, regions with less than 75% of the EU average per capita income and Objective 2 regions, for instance, regions that experience structural difficulties (CEC, 2001b). Every region participating in innovative actions works with a thematic network that takes into account the specific characteristics of the region. Core aim of these networks is facilitate interregional exchanges and collective learning processes. In particular, they aim at regional economies based on knowledge and technological innovation and on information and communication technologies at the service of regional development. The European' action plan covers successively some aspects linked to the effectiveness of support for research and to improvement of framework conditions:

- Improving the effectiveness of support for research and innovation;
- Redirecting public resources towards research and innovation;
- Improving framework conditions for research and innovation.

Cohesion is strong on the part of both national and supranational political processes in Europe. During the period 1994-1999, Structural Funds allocated money to regions on the basis of six "objectives", (Sapir 2003):

- supporting development and structural adjustment of regions whose development is lagging behind. They received 68% of the funds. In 1999, 24.6% of the EU population lived in regions that received objective 1 funding from the EU.
- helping frontier regions or parts of regions seriously affected by industrial decline.
- combating long-term unemployment and facilitating the integration into working life of young people and of persons exposed to exclusion from the labour market.
- facilitating the adaptation of workers to structural change.
- speeding up the adjustment of agricultural structures as part of CAP reform (Objective 5a), facilitating the development and structural adjustment of rural areas (Objective 5b).
- (since 1995) promoting the development and structural adjustment of regions with low population density.

The Cohesion Fund as such, which only exists since 1993, has a national rather than regional focus and targets those member states (Greece, Spain, Ireland and Portugal) whose GDP *per capita* is lower than 90% of the EU average and that are following a programme of economic convergence.

For the period 2000-2006, the Agenda 2000 package allocates a total of €213 billion to cohesion policy. Of this, about €195 billion (European Commission 2002d: 226) are allocated to the Structural Funds and €18 billion to the Cohesion Fund which still targets Greece, Spain, Ireland (only till 2003) and Portugal. If one adds in the €22 billion earmarked for new Member States in the period 2004-2006, the total cohesion effort comes to €236 billion for the whole period, or about 34% of the total EU expenditure (Sapir, 2003).

Agenda 2000 made a major effort to simplify the Structural Funds, which for the period 2000-2006 are divided into just three objectives (instead of six as previously), (Sapir, 2003) :

- development and structural adjustment of regions lagging behind (formerly objectives 1, 5a, 5b and 6): about 70% of the Structural Funds;
- development of border regions and regions in industrial decline (formerly objective 2);
- adaptation and modernisation of education and training systems (formerly objectives 3 and 4).
- Cohesion policy can be disaggregated in three main parts:
- objective 1 funds, which have a clear regional focus, which target the low-income EU regions across member states and which represent about 65% of the total cohesion policy;
- other objectives, which have a horizontal focus and which represent about 25% of total cohesion spending;
- cohesion funds, which have a clear national focus, which target the low-income Member States and which represent about 10% of the total cohesion policy;

To sum up, we can say that there were at least three major benefits from technological collaboration within European Community:

(a) cost savings for both research and production;
(b) reinforced competitiveness as against USA and Japan;
(c) technological convergence of member states.

6.5. EUROPEAN INNOVATION POLICY AND REGIONAL COHESION IN EUROPE

The European Council of Barcelona (March 2002) emphasized the importance of research and innovation by setting the goal of increasing the level of expenditure in research and development to 3% of GDP by 2010. While investing more in R&D is one part of the equation, another is better co-ordination of European research. This has been initiated through the creation of the European Research Area (ERA) and related policy actions, such as the "benchmarking of national research policies". The ERA is the broad heading for a range of linked policies attempting to ensure consistency of European research and facilitate the research policies of individual member states in order to improve the efficiency of European research potentialities.

The Lisbon strategy becomes all the more important (Spring Report: European Commission, 2003d, p.29). As decided by the Heads of State and Governments at the Lisbon Summit in 2000, this strategy aims to transfer the European Union by 2010 into "the most competitive and dynamic knowledge-based economy in the world capable of sustainable economic growth with more and better jobs and greater social cohesion". The set of measures and decisions taken then, better known as "the Lisbon strategy", entail reforms in three main dimensions:

(a) Further consolidation and unification of the European economic environment;
(b) Improvement of the creation, absorption, diffusion and exploitation of knowledge; and
(c) Modernisation of the social model.

Thus not only does the Lisbon strategy remain Europe's overall roadmap to higher and sustainable economic growth but also do European policy-makers acknowledge that the progress needs to be accelerated for growth recovery.

Education, research and innovation are some of the main means to achieve the overall Lisbon objective. Recognizing the pivotal role of education and training, the European Council invited Ministers of Education "to reflect on the concrete future objectives of education systems" and to concentrate on "common concerns and priorities". Hereby the Lisbon Council launched an unprecedented process in the area of education and training helping member states to develop their own policies progressively by spreading best practice and achieving greater convergence towards the main EU goals. Both from a theoretical and empirical point of view, there is a broad recognition among economists and policy-makers of the impact of human capital, R&D, technological progress and innovation on productivity and economic growth.

Europe is, however, still under-investing in knowledge and skills. The EU-25 is still lagging far behind the US and Japan in R&D investment and the exploitation of technological innovations; in many domains the gap is still widening. If we are to consolidate economic recovery and enhance long-term competitiveness, efforts should therefore be maintained and increased.

Today, it is widely agreed that research and technological advancement together with the availability of a highly skilled labour force are among the key factors for innovation, competitiveness and socio-economic welfare. Likewise, the capacity to exploit knowledge has become a crucial element for the production of goods and services. In 2000, the Lisbon European Council agreed upon the objective to make Europe the most competitive and dynamic knowledge based economy in the world. To reach the objective, the Barcelona Council in March 2002 set the specific target to increase the average level of R&D expenditure in the EU from 1.9% of GDP to 3% by 2010, of which two thirds should be funded by the private sector.

The "R&D intensity' indicator compares countries" R&D expenditure with their GDP. It also facilitates comparisons of the R&D activities between countries. R&D expenditure broken down by main sources of funds reveals information on the structure of financing and the relative importance of different sources in the national R&D system. The section also deals with the role of government in R&D financing, and expenditure on basic research. In terms of the absolute volume of R&D investment compared to the three economic blocks (EU-15, US, Japan), both the EFTA countries (€10 billion; PPS 7 billion, in 2001) and the 13 Acceding countries (€5 billion; PPS 9 billion) are comparatively small investors. Table 6.7 illustrates the Relative Activity Index (RAI) by EU-15 for the time-span 1996-2008.

The situation has certainly improved for the US. While the US suffered from diminishing publication numbers and shares during the late 1990s, it has managed to grow in both categories since 2000. It may be too early to speculate about changes in trends. However, the capabilities of the US in terms of scientific production should not be underestimated.

High technology products represented almost one-third of American exports in 1990 (31%), more than one-quarter of Japanese exports (27%) and less than one-fifth of European exports (17%). Table 6.8 illustrates the development of export market shares between 1970 and 1990 on the basis of two broad industry groupings, as well as for total manufacturing trade. The first grouping reflects *technological intensity* and the second the major factors that affect the *competitiveness* of particular industries.

Table 6.7. Relative Activity Index (RAI) by EU-15, 1996-2008

	Engine-ering	Physics, Astro-physic Astronomy	Mathematics, Statistics & Computer Sciences	Chemistry	Earth & Environ-mental Sciences	Life Sciences
Greece	+		+		+	
Poland		+		+		
Bulgaria		+		+		
Latvia		+		+		
Italy		+				
Slovenia	+			+		
Cyprus						
Tu rkey	+					
Germany		+		+		
Russia		+		+		
Estonia		+			+	
Slovakia				+		
Spain				+		
Czech Republic				+		
France						
Japan+			+			
Israel						
UK						
US						
Austria						
Switzerland						
Denmark					+	
Belgium						
Norway					+	+
Ireland						
Iceland					+	+
Finland						+
Sweden						+

Source: DG Research, Key Figures 2003-2004.

Table 6.8. Export Market Shares by Type of Industry(*) & RCA in manufacturing exports(**)

	Total man.	High techn (***)	Medium technol.	Low technol.	Resour. intens.	Labour intens.	Scale intens.	Special. supplier	Science based
Un. States									
1970:	17.8	28 (159)	19 (110)	11.9 (67)	14.1 (79)	10.2 (58)	15.5 (97)	21 (123)	34 (194)
1980:	15.7	25 (160)	16 (106)	11.0 (70)	12.2 (78)	12.6 (80)	12.5 (79)	18 (118)	32 (204)
1990:	14.8	23 (161)	13.2 (89)	11.0 (74)	13.3 (90)	9.3 (63)	11.5 (78)	16 (110)	26 (181)
Japan									
1970:	9.7	12 (124)	7.6 (78)	10 (113)	3.2 (33)	12 (132)	13 (139)	10 (105)	6.1 (63)
1980:	11.7	15 (130)	12 (106)	8 (75)	2.6 (22)	8.6 (73)	17 (151)	15 (135)	6.6 (56)
1990:	12.8	19 (149)	14 (113)	5 (44)	2.3 (18)	6.2 (48)	16 (125)	19 (156)	12.2 (95)
Bel./Lux									
1970:	5.5	2.4 (44)	5.2 (95)	7.0 (127)	6.0 (109)	7.4 (135)	7.1 (129)	2.9 (52)	2.3 (42)
1980:	5.4	2.6 (49)	5.5 (102)	6.6 (123)	6.6 (122)	8.0 (149)	6.2 (115)	2.7 (50)	3.1 (58)
1990:	5.0	2.0 (40)	5.8 (116)	6.2 (124)	5.6 (113)	7.9 (159)	6.6 (132)	2.3 (47)	2.6 (53)
Denmark									
1970:	1.5	1.1 (73)	0.9 (62)	2.2 (149)	2.9 (197)	1.4 (97)	0.7 (50)	1.5 (97)	1.0 (69)
1980:	1.4	1.0 (77)	0.8 (58)	2.2 (161)	2.6 (195)	1.5 (111)	0.6 (46)	1.2 (92)	1.0 (77)
1990:	1.4	1.1 (78)	0.8 (59)	2.4 (171)	2.7 (195)	1.8 (128)	0.7 (51)	1.3 (92)	1.1 (82)
Greece:									
1970:	0.2	0.0 (15)	0.1 (60)	0.3 (174)	0.4 (221)	0.2 (115)	0.2 (96)	0.0 (10)	0.1 (35)
1980:	0.4	0.1 (18)	0.2 (39)	0.3 (210)	1.0 (247)	0.7 (184)	0.2 (43)	0.1 (15)	0.2 (44)
1990:	0.3	0.1 (18)	0.1 (33)	0.8 (252)	0.8 (250)	0.9 (294)	0.1 (39)	0.1 (18)	0.1 (18)
Ireland									
1970:	0.4	0.3 (72)	0.1 (22)	0.7 (191)	1.0 (274)	0.5 (136)	0.1 (25)	0.1 (26)	0.3 (85)
1980:	0.7	0.8 (117)	0.4 (58)	1.0 (143)	1.3 (183)	0.7 (109)	0.4 (58)	0.4 (53)	1.0 (145)
1990:	1.0	1.8 (181)	0.5 (54)	1.1 (107)	1.5 (150)	0.7 (66)	0.5 (48)	0.7 (68)	2.3 (232)
Italy:									
1970:	6.5	5.0 (78)	6.4 (99)	7 (109)	4.8 (74)	11 (185)	5.1 (78)	7.5 (117)	4.5 (69)
1980:	7.0	4.6 (66)	6.3 (91)	8 (128)	5.9 (84)	13 (199)	5.7 (81)	7.4 (106)	4.0 (57)
1990:	7.3	4.6 (63)	6.6 (90)	10 (140)	6.4 (87)	16 (227)	5.4 (74)	7.7 (106)	4.1 (56)

Spain: 1970: 1980: 1990:	1.0 1.7 2.3	0.4 (37) 0.8 (47) 1.2 (53)	0.6 (63) 1.5 (86) 2.4 (102)	1.6 (163) 2.5 (142) 3.0 (132)	1.8 (184) 2.3 (133) 3.1 (134)	1.3 (132) 1.9 (112) 2.4 (104)	0.8 (82) 2.1 3.1 (134)	0.6 (56) 1.1 (62) 1.3 (59)	0.3 (32) 0.7 (42) 1.2 (52)
Un Kingd. 1970: 1980: 1990:	9.2 8.8 7.5	9 (105) 11 (127) 9 (123)	10 (117) 9 (109) 7 (97)	7.4 (81) 7.1 (80) 6.9 (91)	7.1 (78) 7.8 (88) 6.3 (83)	10 (115) 10 (115) 7 (97)	8.6 (94) 7.1 (81) 7.0 (93)	10 (112) 9 (104) 7 (98)	10 (118) 14 (163) 11 (147)

Source: OECD, "Industrial Policy OECD countries", annual review chapter III.
(*) Calculated on the basis of US dollars.
(**) Revealed Comparative Advantage (RCA) for a particular industry (or industry grouping) is defined as the ratio of the shares of the country's exports in that industry in its total manufacturing exports to the share of total exports by that industry (or industry grouping) in OECD manufacturing exports. With exports denoted by X for a country k, the RCA of an industry i is given by: $100.([X_{ik}/\Sigma X_{ik}]/[\Sigma X_{ik}/\Sigma X_{ik}])$.
(***)The definition of high-technology sectors depends upon the following three criteria: (a) R&D expenditure; (b) scientific and technical employment staff; and (c) the nature of the sector products.

In total manufacturing, except for the early 1980s, Germany has had the highest overall export market share during the past two decades, fluctuating between 16% and 18%, slightly above that of the United States. The United Kingdom has lost ground steadily from over 9% in the early 1970s to 7.5% in 1990.

The shares of Italy and Belgium remained stable at about 7% and 5%, respectively. Greece nearly doubled its export market share for total manufacturing but remains at 0.3% of the OECD market. Share of export markets provide a description of the evolving structure of OECD exports, the pattern of international specialisation, however is best examined through indicators such as *revealed comparative advantage* (RCA). Table 6.12 indicate in brackets *revealed comparative advantage* for the period between 1970 and 1990. RCA is an indicator showing the relative specialisation and performance. It provides information about the export specialisation of a country and about comparative advantage in the past. It can be defined as the share of the exports of the industry in the total manufacturing exports of the country divided by the share of total OECD exports of the industry in total OECD manufacturing exports. With exports denoted by X for a country k, the RCA of an industry i is given by:

$$100.([X_{ik}/\Sigma X_{ik}]/[\Sigma X_{ik}/\Sigma X_{ik}])$$

However, Revealed Comparative Advantage neglects intrafirm exchanges. By definition, the average value of RCA for a particular industry in the OECD area is 100. Values greater than 100 indicate that the country's exports are specialised in that industry. In the high technology industrial groups, only four countries had a relative specialisation in 1990, United States (161), Japan (149), United Kingdom (123) and Ireland (181); Ireland has increased its specialisation in computers, while the United States specialised in aerospace. Japan, Belgium, Germany and U.K. are specialised in the medium technology industries, while the small economies such as Greece and Portugal have a comparative advantage in the low technology group and in the labour intensive industries. Figure 6.5 illustrates GDP per head during the period 1995-2005 for EU regions.

Furthermore, the results of the European Innovation Scoreboard, (2009 & 2010), the innovation and R&T performance for EU member' states are the followings:

- Denmark, Finland, Germany, Sweden, Switzerland and the UK are the Innovation leaders, with innovation performance well above that of the EU27 and all other countries.
- Austria, Belgium, France, Ireland, Luxembourg and the Netherlands are the Innovation followers, with innovation performance below those of the innovation leaders but above that of the EU27.
- Cyprus, Czech Republic, Estonia, Greece, Iceland, Italy, Norway, Portugal, Slovenia and Spain are the Moderate innovators with innovation performance below the EU27 where the first 4 countries show a better performance than the last 6 countries.

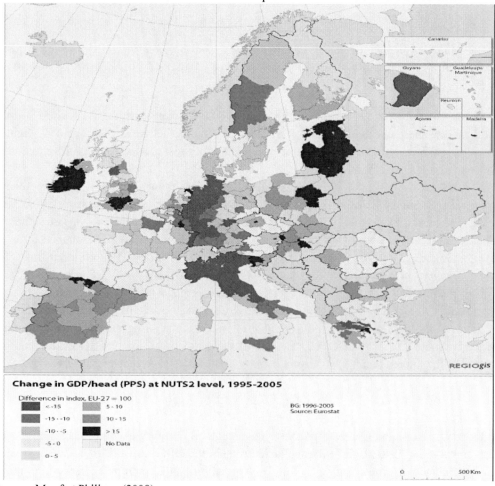

Source: Monfort Philippe (2009).

Figure 6.5. GDP/head (EU-27=100): Change in GDP per head, EU-27 NUTS 2 regions, 1995-2005.

Table 6.9. Innovation Growth Leaders

Group	Growth rate	Growth leaders	Moderate Growers	Slow growers
Innovation Leaders	1.6%	• Switzerland (CH)	• Germany (DE), • Finland (FI)	• Denmark (DK), • Sweden (SE), • United Kingdom • (UK)
Innovation followers	2.0%	• Ireland (IE),	• Austria (AT) Belgium (BE) • France (FR),	• Luxembourg • (LU), Netherlands • (NL)
Moderate innovators	3.6%	• Cyprus (CY), • Portugal (PT)	• Czech Republic • (CZ), Estonia • (EE), Greece • (GR), Iceland • (IS), Slovenia (SI)	• Italy (IT), Norway • (NO), Spain (ES)
Catching up countries	4.1%	• Bulgaria • (BG), • Romania • (RO)	• Latvia (LV), • Hungary (HU), • Malta (MT), • Poland (PL), • Slovakia (SK), • Turkey (TR)	• Croatia (HR), • Lithuania (LT)

Source: European Innovation Scoreboard, 2009.

- Bulgaria, Croatia, Hungary, Latvia, Lithuania, Malta, Poland, Romania, Slovakia and Turkey are the Catching-up countries. Although their innovation performance is well below the EU average, this performance is increasing towards the EU average over time with the exception of Croatia and Lithuania.

According to the results of the European Innovation Scoreboard, (2009 & 2010), for the innovation and R&T performance for the Innovation followers we observe that only Ireland and Austria have managed to grow faster than the EU27. These countries are the growth leaders within the Innovation followers. Of the Moderate innovators seven countries have grown faster than the EU27, but three countries have shown a slower progress: Italy, Norway and Spain. The growths leaders here are Cyprus and Portugal. Of the Catching-up countries two countries have actually grown at a slower pace than the EU27: Lithuania and Croatia. Bulgaria and Romania are the growth leaders also showing the overall fastest rate of improvement in innovation performance. The Innovation leaders and the Innovation followers have the smallest variance in their performance across the different dimensions. This suggests that high levels of performance require countries to perform relatively well over all the dimensions of innovation. For the Innovation followers performance in firm investments is a relative weakness. Table 6.9 illustrates the innovation growth leaders.

According to the results of the European Innovation Scoreboard, (2009 & 2010) for the innovation and R&T performance the US is performing better than the EU27 in 12 indicators, only in S&E graduates, Trademarks, Technology Balance of Payments flows and Medium-high and high-tech manufacturing employment is the EU27 performing better. Overall there is a clear performance gap in favor of the US, with the US showing a better performance in Enablers, Firm activities and Outputs. But the US innovation lead is declining, as its innovation performance has grown at an annual rate of 0.95% while the EU27 is growing at an annual rate of 2.65%. It is striking that the EU outperforms the US in growth performance in all of the indicators except Business R&D, EPO patents and PCT patents. The EU27 is closing the performance gap with the US in Tertiary education, Researchers, Public R&D, Venture capital, Broadband subscribers, Public-private co-publications, Knowledge-intensive services employment and Medium-high and high-tech manufacturing exports. The EU27 is increasing its lead in S&E graduates, Trademarks, Technology Balance of Payments flows and Medium-high and high-tech manufacturing employment. The US is slightly improving its lead in Business R&D, EPO patents and PCT patents. The EU is making a great effort in developing and coordinating innovation policies, adopting a joint innovation framework based on common legal bases (Art. 157 and 163-173 of EU Treaty), policy plans (Lisbon Strategy), programmes of action (R&D Framework Programmes), and networks, all conforming the European Research Area (ERA)

Following the results of the European Innovation Scoreboard, (2009 & 2010) for the innovation and R&T performance, Japan is performing better than the EU27 in 12 indicators, only in Trademarks, Technology Balance of Payments flows, Knowledge-intensive services employment and Knowledge-intensive services exports is the EU27 performing better. Overall there is a clear performance gap in favor of Japan, with Japan showing a better performance in Enablers, Firm activities and Outputs. The Japanese innovation lead is however decreasing, as its innovation performance has grown at 1.65% while the EU27 is growing at an annual rate of 2.65%. The EU27 is closing the performance gap with Japan in S&E graduates, Tertiary education, Researchers, Public R&D, Broadband subscribers, Public-private co-publications and Medium-high and high-tech manufacturing exports. The EU27 is increasing its lead in Trademarks, Technology Balance of Payments flows and Knowledge-intensive services employment. Japan is improving its lead in Business R&D, EPO patents, PCT patents and Medium-high and high-tech manufacturing employment and Japan is marginally closing the gap in Knowledge-intensive services exports.

6.6. THE EUROPEAN REGIONAL SYSTEMS OF INNOVATION

Regional differences remain the prime sources of competitive advantage. A long-term approach to development of regional knowledge economies must therefore combine local (regional) bottom-up approaches with global or European top-down approaches. There is no contradiction between global and local approaches to development of knowledge- economy. Regional policy should evolve from supporting general R&D efforts towards innovation promotion. It should also change the emphasis from a "technology-push" a "demand-pull" approach, to identify and understand the demand for innovation in firms in the less favoured regions. Technological transfer is essential for regions which lag behind. It might even be more important than the development of indigenous R&D activities in the weaker regions. Regional policy should facilitate the identification, adaptation and adoption of technological developments elsewhere in a specific regional setting. It might be less costly, avoid duplicating previous errors and reinventing the wheel. Regional policy should facilitate technology transfer and the flow of knowledge across regions, maximising the benefit of the European dimension by facilitating access from less favoured region's economic actors to international networks of "excellence" in this field. They encourage regions to take actions such as:

(a) Promoting innovation, new forms of financing (for instance, venture capital) to encourage start-ups, specialised business services, technology transfer,
(b) interacting between firms and higher education/research institutes,
(c) encouraging small firms to carry out R&D for the first-time,
(d) networking and co-operating in industry,
(e) developing human skills.

The theoretical framework for the concept can be found mainly in the work of Cooke and his colleagues. According to the author the first references to the term appeared at the beginning of the nineties and their evolution has its origin in two major theoretical currents. The first current originates in research on technological innovation, particularly that which refers to National Systems of Innovation (Lundvall, 1992); the second results from advances in theories of regional development. The discussion of National Systems of Innovation emphasizes the importance of innovations on national processes of development. These innovations are the result of the interaction between firms, clients, and government and research institutions, constituting an environment that is favourable to the learning of new ways of producing and of organizing production. One of the matters that is emphasized in this type of research are the processes through which this learning takes place and the roles carried out by the different actors that are involved.

In 1997, the OECD proposed a more general strategy set for all (not just for less favoured) regions. Although this was not specifically focused on Information Society issues, it has clear and direct relevance with knowledge-economy. The OECD study (1997) looked at the concept of *regional competitiveness* to explain why some regions successfully develop clusters and networks, a wide variety of manufacturing activities and of services for businesses and consumers, along with educational, research and cultural institutions, and why some must grapple with industrial and institutional imbalance and a lack of resources necessary to adapt. A territory's indigenous capacity of development is linked with the productivity of enterprises, their ability to join networks, the skills of the labour force and the strength of institutional resources. Such an approach stresses the (mainly) endogenous task of creating networks, partnerships and cooperation within the region, and five important strategies are recommended in this context:

(a) To use regional policies for human resource development;
(b) To give a demand-driven focus to human resource development;
(c) To base competitiveness on the development of partnerships;
(d) To reinforce economic efficiency by policies of equity; and
(e) To develop regional governance in order to consolidate national policies.

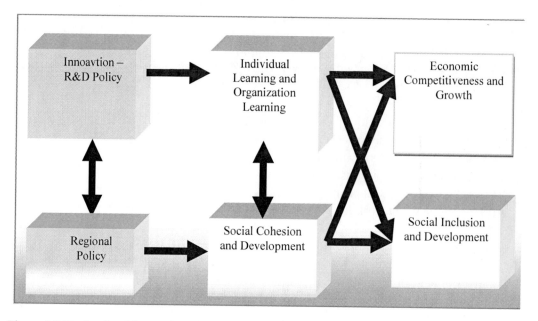

Figure 6.6. Regional and Innovation Policies towards the Learning Economy.

Strategies (a) and (b) were subsequently refined into one of the most important current policy and strategy approaches to the development of regions in a knowledge-economy context, the *learning region*, (OECD, 2001a). This emphasises the essential role of skills and competencies in enhancing innovative capacity and regional competitiveness. The *learning region* concept is seen as a heuristic framework for analysing key relationships and developing effective strategies for regional policy.

It is argued that a *learning region* need not necessarily be high-tech (Maskell and Törnqvist, 1999), and that it can be based upon one or more traditional manufacturing sectors. Malmberg and Maskell (1999) argue that the *learning region* permits the acquisition of monopoly rents, so that they become the basis of comparative advantage based on the local available resources and resource immobility.

Figure 6.6 illustrates regional and innovation policies for the learning economy. Morgan (1997) and Maskell and Törnqvist (1999) define a *learning region* as one where an industrial cluster becomes a collective learning system, a concept drawing heavily on Lundvall's concept of national systems of innovation, fleshed out at local and regional levels. Morgan (1997) and Maskell and Törnqvist argue that in such regions, learning organisations develop at three levels:

- at an intra-firm level,
- at an inter-firm level between firms interacting within a cluster,
- at the institutional level, through public intervention to support organisational innovation in business services, research and training.

The EU is one of the most prosperous economic areas in the world but the disparities between its member states are striking, even more so if we look at the EU's various 250 regions. To assess these disparities, we must first of all measure and compare the levels of wealth generated by each country, as determined by their gross domestic product (GDP)

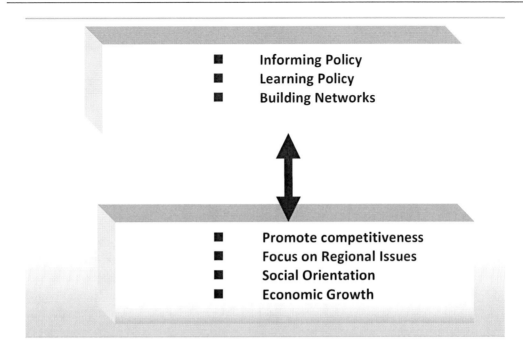

Figure 6.7. Main Objectives for the Regional Policy Planning.

For instance, in Greece, Portugal and Spain, average per capita GDP is only 80% of the Community average. Luxembourg exceeds this average by over 60 percentage points. The ten most dynamic regions in the Union have a GDP almost three times higher than the ten least developed regions. The European Union's regional policy is based on financial solidarity inasmuch as part of member states' contributions to the Community budget goes to the less prosperous regions and social groups. For the 2000-2006 period, these transfers will account for one third of the Community budget, or €213 billion. More analytically:

- € 195 billion will be spent by the four Structural Funds (the European Regional Development Fund, the European Social Fund, the Financial Instrument for Fisheries Guidance and the Guidance Section of the European Agricultural Guidance and Guarantee Fund);
- € 18 billion will be spent by the Cohesion Fund.
- 70% of the funding goes to regions whose development is lagging behind. They are home to 22% of population of the Union (Objective 1);
- 11.5% of the funding assists economic and social conversion in areas experiencing structural difficulties. 18% of the population of the Union lives in such areas (Objective 2);
- 12.3% of the funding promotes the modernisation of training systems and the creation of employment (Objective 3) outside the Objective 1 regions where such measures form part of the strategies for catching up.
-

There are also four Community Initiatives seeking common solutions to specific problems, namely Interreg III for cross-border, transnational and interregional cooperation, Urban II for sustainable development of cities and declining urban areas, Leader for rural development through local initiatives, and Equal for combating inequalities and discrimination in access to the labour market. Figure 6.7 illustrates some of the most popular objectives of regional policy. Table 6.14 illustrates the R&ST profile of European member states. Finally, Figure 6.8 illustrates the European Regional Innovation Performance Groups. However, the main findings of the 2009 Regional Innovation Scoreboard are:

- There is considerable diversity in regional innovation performances. The results show that all countries have regions at different levels of performance. The most heterogeneous countries are Spain, Italy and Czech Republic where innovation performance varies from low to medium-high.
- The most innovative regions are typically in the most innovative countries. Noord-Brabant in the Netherlands is a high innovating region located in an Innovation follower country. Praha in the Czech Republic, Pais Vasco, Comunidad Foral de Navarra, Comunidad de Madrid and Cataluρa in Spain, Lombardia and Emilia-Romagna in Italy, Oslo og Akershus, Agder og Rogaland, Vestlandet in Norway are all medium-high innovating regions from Moderate innovators. The capital region in Romania, Bucuresti – Ilfov, is a medium-low innovating region in a Catching-up country.
- Regions have different strengths and weaknesses. There are no straight forward relationships between level of performance and relative strengths, it can be noted that many of the "low innovators" have relative weaknesses in the dimension of Innovation enablers which includes Human resources.
- Regional performance appears relatively stable since 2004. Most of the changes are positive and relate to Cataluρa, Comunidad Valenciana, Illes Balears and Ceuta (Spain), Bassin Parisien, Est and Sud-Ouest (France), Unterfranken (Germany), Κφzιp- Dunαntϊl (Hungary), Algarve (Portugal) and Hedmark og Oppland (Norway).

Table 6.10 illustrates annual data on employment in technology and knowledge intensive sectors at the European regional level for the period 2001-2008. Furthermore, Table 6.11 illustrates the business enterprise R&D expenditures for European member states for the period 2000-2007. Finally, Table 6.12 illustrates the research and scientific and technological profile of European member states.

Table 6.10. Annual Data on Employment in Technology and Knowledge-Intensive Sectors at the Regional Level, (2001 - 2008)

	2001	2002	2003	2004	2005	2006	2007	2008
Belgium	4052,202	4064,850	4065,722	4135,282	4224,965	4255,881	4371,384	4437,400
Région de Bruxelles-Capitale / Brussels Hoofdstedelijk Gewest	341,964	352,002	350,560	360,229	370,361	366,443	381,874	396,391
Vlaams Gewest	2504,801	2514,159	2498,606	2558,853	2600,765	2623,062	2691,772	2725,085
Région Wallonne	1205,437	1198,689	1216,556	1216,200	1253,840	1266,377	1297,738	1315,924
Bulgaria	2751,652	2796,909	2866,366	2963,968	2976,328	3105,647	3248,547	:
Severna i iztochna Bulgaria	:	:	1435,406	1459,278	1474,087	1527,609	1579,883	:
Yugozapadna i yuzhna centralna Bulgaria	:	:	1430,960	1504,689	1502,241	1578,038	1668,663	:
Czech Republic		4675,415	4726,717	4697,844	4676,045	4757,288	4820,998	4914,664	4994,595

Czech Republic	4675,415	4726,717	4697,844	4676,045	4757,288	4820,998	4914,664	4994,595
Denmark	2716,926	2739,337	2703,250	2741,257	2751,006	2804,193	2803,720	2853,536
Danmark	2716,926	2739,337	2703,250	2741,257	2751,006	2804,193	2803,720	2853,536
Germany (including ex-GDR from 1991)								
Baden-Württemberg	4932,526	4980,367	4948,881	4916,347	5109,820	5095,018	5291,960	5408,974
Bayern	5909,225	5871,841	5809,677	5779,126	5924,425	6032,149	6172,849	6279,083
Berlin	1460,631	1446,973	1412,930	1403,635	1438,407	1457,873	1490,723	1517,115
Brandenburg	1126,041	1113,992	1100,982	1092,325	1127,689	1170,585	1200,315	1223,536
Bremen	274,470	265,742	269,364	257,327	262,051	272,836	286,103	288,865
Hamburg	811,072	790,602	781,896	773,529	802,486	823,665	854,288	860,824
Hessen	2784,277	2759,851	2724,897	2683,996	2774,696	2816,932	2828,205	2882,750
Mecklenburg-Vorpommern	738,152	725,649	716,176	690,075	730,875	751,120	754,013	782,138
Niedersachsen	3397,904	3383,996	3363,029	3310,523	3409,412	3478,204	3572,066	3613,677
Nordrhein-Westfalen	7616,843	7552,681	7462,856	7359,527	7647,937	7798,202	7965,512	8107,425
Rheinland-Pfalz	1782,906	1776,298	1789,072	1731,583	1812,270	1869,302	1910,923	1931,992
Saarland	436,784	437,051	421,528	424,331	432,138	436,851	445,018	455,429
Sachsen	1854,343	1806,408	1792,086	1764,184	1823,046	1860,383	1911,038	1947,944
Sachsen-Anhalt	1049,648	1044,502	1030,542	1000,063	1029,947	1066,374	1083,795	1090,425
Schleswig-Holstein	1233,952	1216,759	1235,628	1203,795	1255,683	1289,056	1311,318	1328,638
Thüringen	1067,683	1049,202	1015,778	1019,969	1016,441	1048,884	1060,825	1089,436
Estonia	576,007	581,178	589,124	595,223	607,410	646,262	655,347	656,546
Eesti	576,007	581,178	589,124	595,223	607,410	646,262	655,347	656,546
Ireland	1716,107	1757,414	1787,159	1829,990	1922,099	2066,508	2088,210	2100,198
Éire/Ireland	1716,107	1757,414	1787,159	1829,990	1922,099	2066,508	2088,210	2100,198
Greece	4097,236	4182,227	4278,188	4322,848	4361,232	4443,385	4500,357	4548,686
Voreia Ellada	1304,188	1306,666	1342,895	1345,044	1346,838	1383,669	1394,671	1399,586
Kentriki Ellada	887,103	919,653	946,647	914,902	940,051	958,548	971,152	981,540
Attiki	1472,019	1528,313	1551,555	1618,063	1629,062	1658,641	1683,658	1718,046
Nisia Aigaiou, Kriti	433,926	427,595	437,091	444,838	445,281	442,527	450,876	449,514
Spain								
Noroeste	1591,914	1604,846	1666,261	1686,099	1769,780	1835,405	1883,938	1908,892
Noreste	1716,677	1740,844	1802,711	1840,265	1940,299	1988,214	2034,433	2042,180
Comunidad de Madrid	2347,539	2486,714	2567,453	2700,230	2855,897	2976,293	3052,615	3062,149
Centro (ES)	1874,233	1917,386	1983,044	2021,432	2170,341	2240,682	2326,952	2318,660
Este	4940,865	5026,011	5240,579	5496,817	5807,825	6061,070	6232,755	6226,616
Sur	2903,585	3070,061	3188,814	3314,406	3575,781	3751,863	3896,059	3823,750
Canarias (ES)	695,691	743,821	783,053	797,213	835,908	878,503	914,929	860,519
France								
Île de France	5100,056	5024,117	4915,279	4977,803	5053,454	5036,689	5226,778	5336,046
Bassin Parisien	4075,326	4055,220	4324,153	4301,036	4339,040	4328,918	4378,341	4468,224
Nord - Pas-de-Calais	1418,306	1448,214	1505,347	1505,284	1507,296	1497,015	1491,604	1470,324
Est	2268,811	2298,282	2161,710	2124,520	2212,340	2207,859	2203,107	2269,238
Ouest	3081,624	3140,522	3284,654	3366,506	3325,808	3436,483	3397,121	3530,707
Sud-Ouest	2541,897	2569,207	2601,591	2606,481	2688,115	2682,237	2804,840	2909,006
Centre-Est	2851,928	2861,695	2964,978	2992,709	3084,331	3023,760	3132,705	3135,513

Table 6.10. Continued

	2001	2002	2003	2004	2005	2006	2007	2008
Méditerranée	2323,263	2466,618	2678,441	2731,982	2754,360	2822,255	2900,721	2919,526
Italy								
Nord-Ovest	6342,900	6446,384	6570,483	6583,467	6682,536	6802,070	6855,835	6924,967
Nord-Est	4594,387	4683,387	4753,442	4809,957	4865,914	4972,442	5035,631	5109,331
Centro (IT)	4315,085	4395,421	4490,497	4562,679	4564,852	4656,727	4773,629	4846,601
Sud	4125,969	4209,193	4234,085	4382,469	4338,729	4400,318	4408,606	4384,282
Isole	1927,131	1961,339	1946,994	2051,552	2064,444	2107,921	2100,178	2087,795
Cyprus	308,080	313,470	324,664	334,269	346,083	355,620	376,182	380,442
Cyprus	308,080	313,470	324,664	334,269	346,083	355,620	376,182	380,442
Latvia	960,043	987,323	1003,766	1021,236	1033,681	1087,089	1117,982	1124,505
Latvia	960,043	987,323	1003,766	1021,236	1033,681	1087,089	1117,982	1124,505
Lithuania	1370,004	1420,054	1469,177	1436,089	1473,431	1497,262	1531,919	1518,110
Lithuania	1370,004	1420,054	1469,177	1436,089	1473,431	1497,262	1531,919	1518,110
Luxembourg (Grand-Duché)	185,307	188,131	186,849	188,397	193,511	195,203	202,858	202,315
Luxembourg (Grand-Duché)	185,307	188,131	186,849	188,397	193,511	195,203	202,858	202,315
Hungary	3858,986	3867,516	3923,977	3894,140	3901,463	3929,972	3926,190	3879,435
Közép-Magyarország	1173,397	1187,997	1201,043	1220,200	1238,917	1241,096	1249,093	1246,872
Dunántúl	1234,468	1240,079	1262,058	1234,724	1238,613	1245,748	1235,653	1219,645
Alföld és Észak	1451,121	1439,441	1460,876	1439,216	1423,933	1443,128	1441,444	1412,917
Malta	147,344	148,784	148,681	145,951	148,410	151,565	156,301	160,288
Malta	147,344	148,784	148,681	145,951	148,410	151,565	156,301	160,288
Netherlands	8057,512	8169,743	8116,339	8089,369	8100,483	8165,909	8347,596	8512,748
Noord-Nederland	794,545	821,748	822,913	815,426	813,150	813,056	837,971	852,100
Oost-Nederland	1681,932	1703,988	1711,343	1695,226	1697,874	1719,211	1774,826	1812,064
West-Nederland	3826,882	3843,349	3797,370	3800,689	3834,227	3860,231	3934,691	4007,081
Zuid-Nederland	1754,153	1800,659	1784,713	1778,028	1755,233	1773,411	1800,109	1841,503
Austria	3692,194	3661,082	3739,926	3647,665	3818,288	3920,419	4014,487	4076,383
Ostösterreich	1576,919	1533,948	1564,592	1531,600	1578,503	1638,885	1677,885	1708,397
Südösterreich	762,170	765,176	781,992	749,829	805,049	815,796	831,154	846,792
Westösterreich	1353,105	1361,958	1393,341	1366,237	1434,735	1465,737	1505,448	1521,194
Poland								
Region Centralny	3185,249	3005,148	2909,066	2958,883	3082,211	3240,681	3522,860	:
Region Poludniowy	2829,109	2755,109	2715,647	2841,653	2899,649	2967,670	3035,564	:
Region Wschodni	2673,346	2639,600	2594,064	2487,354	2597,583	2627,280	2810,445	:
Region Pólnocno-Zachodni	2225,536	2138,144	2237,159	2217,381	2219,562	2236,300	2287,451	:
Region Poludniowo-Zachodni	1305,507	1269,067	1211,344	1249,195	1353,248	1422,349	1502,973	:
Region Pólnocny	1975,845	1958,933	1947,502	1885,633	1915,902	1910,088	2041,500	:
Portugal	5023,149	5071,144	5029,836	5046,734	5040,795	5071,549	5075,786	5100,159
Continente	4819,665	4858,169	4816,362	4829,228	4819,434	4847,840	4853,339	4871,842
Região Autónoma dos Açores (PT)	96,313	100,745	100,203	104,125	104,926	107,152	106,838	110,700
Região Autónoma da Madeira (PT)	107,171	112,229	113,271	113,382	116,435	116,558	115,610	117,617
Romania		9564,988	9367,856	9282,930	9114,581	9290,987	9353,328	9369,122
Macroregiunea unu	2515,746	2312,639	2185,168	2115,574	2096,921	2159,776	2153,625	2155,084
Macroregiunea doi	3185,299	2904,936	2927,355	2918,810	2825,774	2828,248	2850,339	2829,152
Macroregiunea trei	2597,343	2398,105	2382,610	2392,867	2366,790	2453,307	2486,367	2517,621
Macroregiunea patru	2208,364	1949,308	1872,723	1855,678	1825,095	1849,657	1862,997	1867,265

Slovenia	909,363	917,137	893,292	941,458	944,714	955,505	978,167	:
Slovenia	909,363	917,137	893,292	941,458	944,714	955,505	978,167	:
Slovakia	2114,992	2110,950	2166,298	2147,950	2214,675	2301,710	2357,017	2432,906
Slovakia	2114,992	2110,950	2166,298	2147,950	2214,675	2301,710	2357,017	2432,906
Finland	2402,940	2406,433	2400,696	2383,980	2424,758	2460,750	2491,664	2530,895
Manner-Suomi	2389,210	2393,151	2386,440	2370,555	2411,281	2446,807	2476,881	2515,971
Åland	13,730	13,283	14,256	13,424	13,477	13,943	14,783	14,924
Sweden	4339,353	4347,859	4351,836	4310,748	4346,701	4429,443	4540,666	:
Östra Sverige	1691,892	1685,388	1685,065	1663,087	1686,029	1707,360	1745,802	:
Södra Sverige	1855,035	1866,900	1879,711	1865,474	1877,379	1926,670	1971,445	:
Norra Sverige	792,427	795,571	787,059	782,187	783,293	795,413	823,419	:
United Kingdom								
North East (ENGLAND)	1065,619	1069,563	1070,137	1097,908	1113,040	1151,286	1154,172	1150,630
North West (ENGLAND)	3037,726	3020,166	3101,346	3113,107	3133,661	3156,297	3152,940	3135,562
Yorkshire and The Humber	2244,194	2256,816	2303,019	2354,662	2368,349	2410,555	2397,480	2432,057
East Midlands (ENGLAND)	1962,728	2003,327	2024,645	2071,356	2081,375	2132,152	2107,535	2170,543
West Midlands (ENGLAND)	2406,293	2442,619	2430,044	2446,307	2497,465	2497,159	2468,623	2454,205
East of England	2668,737	2668,030	2678,030	2724,069	2745,778	2721,434	2744,072	2815,453
London	3479,402	3504,309	3477,689	3523,406	3519,636	3594,867	3616,379	3750,200
South East (UK)	4019,574	4036,518	4031,182	4010,255	4059,513	4116,696	4120,677	4161,909
South West (ENGLAND)	2354,440	2390,598	2396,439	2424,740	2478,872	2482,228	2487,938	2571,840
Wales	1213,122	1220,611	1303,503	1321,148	1295,726	1310,036	1337,596	1345,322
Scotland	2340,970	2335,182	2385,367	2413,097	2433,139	2436,071	2537,911	2523,882
Northern Ireland	697,377	710,567	736,784	708,644	736,420	766,298	784,522	783,264
Iceland	158,057	156,418	157,479	156,378	159,857	167,848	175,527	177,056
Ísland	158,057	156,418	157,479	156,378	159,857	167,848	175,527	177,056
Norway	2275,916	2293,208	2264,872	2273,164	2282,627	2352,988	2434,170	2513,686
Norge	2275,916	2293,208	2264,872	2273,164	2282,627	2352,988	2434,170	2513,686
Switzerland	3920,127	3945,309	3937,943	3939,005	3959,564	4032,731	4099,896	4204,928
Switzerland	3920,127	3945,309	3937,943	3939,005	3959,564	4032,731	4099,896	4204,928
Croatia	:	1513,731	1528,390	1574,537	1563,398	1575,629	1604,542	1627,451
Hrvatska	:	1513,731	1528,390	1574,537	1563,398	1575,629	1604,542	1627,451
Former Yugoslav Republic of Macedonia, the	:	:	:	:	:	569,792	589,254	:
Poranesna jugoslovenska Republika Makedonija	:	:	:	:	:	569,792	589,254	:
Turkey	:	:	:	:	:			
Istanbul	:	:	:	:	:	2620,107	3541,851	3653,462
Bati Marmara	:	:	:	:	:	795,442	1069,781	1026,502
Ege	:	:	:	:	:	2349,105	3031,837	2961,903
Dogu Marmara	:	:	:	:	:	1525,440	1998,865	2052,309
Bati Anadolu	:	:	:	:	:	1506,522	2058,164	2190,796
Akdeniz	:	:	:	:	:	2117,325	2849,582	2866,036
Orta Anadolu	:	:	:	:	:	824,899	1082,316	1021,030
Bati Karadeniz	:	:	:	:	:	1255,798	1624,179	1642,135
Dogu Karadeniz	:	:	:	:	:	979,646	1216,493	1273,083
Kuzeydogu Anadolu	:	:	:	:	:	505,489	623,954	685,347
Ortadogu Anadolu	:	:	:	:	:	672,167	856,966	839,961
Güneydogu Anadolu	:	:	:	:	:	915,694	1166,146	1245,897

Source: Eurostat.

Table 6.11. Business Enterprise R&D Expenditure (2000 - 2007)

Indicators	\multicolumn{8}{c}{Millions of euro (from 1.1.1999)/Millions of ECU (up to 31.12.1998)}
	2000	2001	2002	2003	2004	2005	2006	2007
European Union (27 countries)	110557	115689	119126	119815	123018	127098	137431	146241
Belgium	3589	3921	3662	3608	3732	3776	4129	4337
Bulgaria	15	15	15	18	24	23	31	43
Czech Republic	446	501	586	618	701	914	1165	1248
Denmark	2596	2934	3198	3355	3332	3477	3628	3752
Germany (including ex-GDR from 1991)	35600	36332	36950	38029	38363	38651	41148	43003
Estonia	8	16	17	23	32	47	67	82
Ireland	842	900	988	1105	1210	1330	1560	:
Greece	202	278	287	313	317	357	367	353
Spain	3069	3261	3926	4443	4865	5485	6558	7454
France	19348	20782	21839	21646	22523	22503	23915	24872
Italy	6239	6661	7057	6979	7293	7856	8210	8525
Cyprus	5	5	7	9	10	12	14	16
Latvia	15	14	17	13	21	30	57	41
Lithuania	16	27	17	23	29	32	53	66
Luxembourg (Grand-Duché)	337	:	:	379	393	408	485	495
Hungary	180	220	250	255	297	362	435	492
Malta	:	:	3	4	16	18	21	21
Netherlands	4458	4712	4543	4804	5071	5169	5480	5840
Austria	:	:	3131	:	3556	4160	4449	4891
Poland	432	474	238	284	327	440	477	535
Portugal	258	330	334	338	400	462	725	988
Romania	103	109	111	118	130	163	215	272
Slovenia	167	197	215	209	254	243	291	299
Slovakia	94	101	95	93	86	97	93	100
Finland	3136	3284	3375	3528	3683	3877	4108	4513
Sweden	:	8118	:	7886	7667	7725	8754	8805
United Kingdom	18884	19260	19830	18319	18665	19464	20985	23544
Iceland	142	153	160	142	:	187	212	219
Norway	:	1814	1946	1960	1821	1987	2204	2488
Switzerland	5065	:	:	:	6257	:	:	:
Croatia	:	:	115	114	144	129	109	141
Turkey	465	395	367	301	394	774	901	1407
Russian Federation	2087	2829	3176	3353	3780	4458	5643	6807
United States	216502	225566	205021	177443	167458	181785	197252	193501
China (excluding Hong Kong)	:	8499	10066	10256	12761	16417	21325	25744
Japan	109181	105364	98059	89783	88272	93137	91271	:
Korea (Republic of) (South)	9871	10651	11059	10765	11950	14604	17604	:

Source: Eurostat.

Table 6.12. R&ST Profile of European Member States

Country Performance
Belgium
For Belgium, one of the Innovation followers, innovation performance is above the EU27 average but the rate of improvement is below that of the EU27. Relative strengths, compared to the country's average performance, are in Linkages & entrepreneurship, Innovators and Economic effects and relative weaknesses are in Firm investments and Throughputs.
Bulgaria
Bulgaria is one of the Catching-up countries with an innovation performance well below the EU27 average but the rate of improvement is one of the highest of all countries and it is a growth leader within the Catching-up countries. Relative strengths, compared to the country's average performance, are in Human resources, Finance and support and Economic effects and relative weaknesses 5 years, Throughputs and Finance and support have been the main drivers of the improvement in innovation performance, in particular as a result from strong growth in Private credit (19.8%), Broadband access by firms (22.0%), Community trademarks (69.6%) and Community designs (24.1%). Performance in Economic effects has hardly grown, in particular due to a decrease in New-to-market sales (-5.7%) and New-to-fi rm sales (-3.1%) are in Linkages & entrepreneurship and Throughputs Over the past
Czech Republic
The Czech Republic is among the group of Moderate innovators with innovation performance below the EU27 average but the rate of improvement is above that of the EU27. Relative strengths, compared to the country's average performance, are in Firm investments, Innovators and Economic effects and a relative weakness is in Throughputs.
Denmark
For Denmark, one of the Innovation leaders, innovation performance is well above the EU27 average but the rate of improvement is not only below that of the EU27 but virtually zero. Relative strengths, compared to the country's average performance, are in Human resources, Finance and support and Throughputs and relative weaknesses are in Firm investments, Innovators and Economic effects. Over the past 5 years, Human resources, Finance and support and Throughputs have been the main drivers of a stagnating innovation performance
Germany
Germany is one of the Innovation leaders with innovation performance considerably above the EU27 average and the rate of improvement is also above that of the EU27. Relative strengths, compared to the country's average performance, are in Innovators and Economic effects and relative weaknesses are in Human resources, Finance and support and Throughputs.
Estonia
For Estonia, one of the Innovation followers, innovation performance is just below the EU27 average but the rate of improvement is above that of the EU27. Relative strengths, compared to the country's average performance, are in Finance and support, Firm investments, Linkages & entrepreneurship and Innovators and relative weaknesses are in Throughputs.
Ireland
Ireland is in the group of Innovation followers, with an innovation performance above the EU27 average. It's rate of improvement just below that of the EU27. Relative strengths, compared to the country's average performance, are in Human resources and Economic effects and relative weaknesses are in Firm investments and Throughputs

Table 6.12. Continued

Greece
For Greece, one of the Moderate innovators, innovation performance is below the EU27 average and the rate of improvement is above that of the EU27. Relative strengths, compared to the country's average performance, are in Linkages & entrepreneurship, Innovators and Economic effects and relative weaknesses are in Firm investments and Throughputs. Over the past 5 years, Finance and support, Throughputs and Economic effects have been the main drivers of the improvement in innovation performance, in particular as a result from strong growth in Venture capital (24.1%), Broadband access by firms (35.4%), Community designs (34.2%) and New–to-market sales (32.8%). Performance in Firm investments has worsened, due to a decrease in Business R&D expenditures (- 4.5%) and Non-R&D innovation expenditures (-22.7%).
Spain
For Spain, one of the Moderate innovators, innovation performance is below the EU27 average and the rate of improvement is also below that of the EU27. Relative
strengths, compared to the country's average performance, are in Finance and support and Economic effects and relative weaknesses are in Firm investments and Linkages & entrepreneurship.
France
France is in the Innovation followers group of countries with an innovation performance above the EU27 average but the rate of improvement is below that of the EU27. Relative strengths, compared to the country's average performance, are in the
Enablers (Human resources, Finance and support), and Outputs (Innovators and Economic effects) and relative weaknesses are in Firm activities (Firm investments, Linkages & entrepreneurship and Throughputs). Over the past 5 years, Human resources, Finance and support and Throughputs have been the main drivers of the improvement in innovation performance, in particular as a result from growth in S&E and SSH doctorate graduates (7.3%), Private credit (4.5%) and Technology Balance of Payments flows (7.1%). Performance in Economic effects has decreased, in particular due to a decrease in Employment in medium-high & high-tech manufacturing (-1.2%) and Medium-high & high-tech manufacturing exports (-1.2%).
Italy
For Italy, one of the Moderate innovators, innovation performance is below the EU27 average and the rate of improvement is also below that of the EU27. Relative strengths, compared to the country's average performance, are in Finance and support and Economic effects and relative weaknesses are in Human resources, Firm investments and Linkages & entrepreneurship.
Cyprus
Cyprus is a growth leader among the group of Innovation followers, with an innovation performance just above the EU27 average and a rapid rate of improvement. Relative strengths, compared to the country's average performance, are in Finance and support, Linkages & entrepreneurship and Innovators and relative weaknesses are in Human resources and Throughputs. Over the past 5 years there has been strong growth in Finance and support, Linkages & entrepreneurship and Throughputs which have been the main drivers of the improvement in innovation performance, in particular as a result from strong growth in S&E and SSH doctorate graduates Broadband access by firms (22.6%), Innovative SMEs collaborating with others (12.3%), Public-private co-publications (22.1%), EPO patents (13.1%) and Community designs (15.3%). Performance in Innovators has worsened (- 4.3%).

Latvia
For Latvia, one of the Catching-up countries, innovation performance is well below the EU27 average but the rate of improvement is above that of the EU27. Relative strengths, compared to the country's average performance, are in Human resources and Finance and support and relative weaknesses are in Linkages & entrepreneurship, Throughputs and Innovators.

Lithuania
Lithuania is among the group of Moderate innovators, with an innovation performance well below the EU27 average and a rate of improvement above that of the EU27. Relative strengths, compared to the country's average performance, are in Human resources, Finance and support and Linkages & entrepreneurship and relative weaknesses are in Firm investments, Throughputs and Innovators

Luxembourg
Luxembourg is one of the Innovation followers, innovation performance is above the EU27 average but the rate of improvement is slightly below that of the EU27. Relative strengths, compared to the country's average performance, are in Finance and support, Throughputs and Innovators and relative weaknesses are in Human resources, Firm investments and Linkages & entrepreneurship.

Hungary
Hungary is in the group of Moderate innovators with an innovation performance well below the EU27 average but a rate of improvement above that of the EU27. Relative strengths, compared to the country's average performance, are in Economic effects and relative weaknesses are in Throughputs and Innovators

Malta
Malta is one of the Moderate innovators, innovation performance is below the EU27 average but the rate of improvement is above that of the EU27. Relative strengths, compared to the country's average performance, are in Finance and support and Economic effects and relative weaknesses are in Human resources, Linkages & entrepreneurship and Innovators

Netherlands
The Netherlands is one of the Innovation followers. Its innovation performance is just above the EU27 average but the rate of improvement is below that of the EU27. Relative strengths, compared to the country's average performance, are in Finance and support and Linkages & entrepreneurship while relative weaknesses are in Firm investments and Innovators.

Austria
For Austria, among the group of Innovation followers, innovation performance is above the EU27 average and the rate of improvement close to that of the EU27. Relative strengths, compared to the country's average performance, are in Firm investments, Linkages & entrepreneurship and Innovators and relative weaknesses are in Human resources and Finance and support.

Poland
Poland is among the group of Moderate innovators, with an innovation performance considerably below the EU27 average but an above average rate of improvement. Relative strengths, compared to the country's average performance, are in Human resources, Firm investments and Economic effects and relative weaknesses are in Linkages & entrepreneurship, Throughputs and Innovators.

Table 6.12. Continued

Portugal
For Portugal, one of the Moderate innovators, innovation performance is below the EU27 average but the rate of improvement is three times that of the EU27 making it a growth leader within the group of Moderate innovators. Relative strengths, compared to the country's average performance, are in Finance and support and Innovators while relative weaknesses are in Firm investments and Throughputs.
Romania
Romania is one of the growth leaders among the Catching-up countries, with an innovation performance well below the EU27 average but a rate of improvement that is one of the highest of all countries. Relative strengths, compared to the country's average performance, are in Innovators and Economic effects and relative weaknesses are in Finance and support and Throughputs.
Slovenia
For Slovenia, one of the Innovation followers, innovation performance is just below the EU27 average but the rate of improvement is above that of the EU27. Relative strengths, compared to the country's average performance, are in Human resources, Finance and support, Innovators and Economic effects and relative weaknesses are in Firm investments and Throughputs.
Slovakia
For Slovakia, one of the Catching-up countries, innovation performance is well below the EU27 average but the rate of improvement is above that of the EU27. Relative strengths, compared to the country's average performance, are in Firm investments and Economic effects and relative weaknesses are in Finance and support, Linkages & entrepreneurship, Throughputs and Innovators.
Finland
For Finland, one of the Innovation leaders, innovation performance is well above the EU27 average and the rate of improvement is also above that of the EU27. Relative strengths, compared to the country's average performance, are in Human resources and Firm investments and relative weaknesses are in Throughputs and Innovators.
Sweden
Sweden is one of the Innovation leaders and the best performing EU Member State, although its rate of improvement is below that of the EU27. Relative strengths, compared to the country's average performance, are in Human resources, Finance and support and Firm investments and relative weaknesses are in Throughputs and Innovators.
United Kingdom
For the UK, one of the Innovation leaders, innovation performance is above the EU27 average but the rate of improvement is negative and below that of the EU27. Relative strengths, compared to the country's average performance, are in Human resources, Finance and support, Firm investments and Linkages & entrepreneurship and relative weaknesses are in Throughputs, Innovators and Economic effects. Over the past 5 years, Finance and support has been the main driver of the improvement in innovation performance, in particular as a result from strong growth in Broadband access by fi rms (14.9%). Performance in Linkages & entrepreneurship, Innovators and Economic effects has worsened, in particular due to a decrease in Newto-market sales (-12.7%) and New-to-fi rm sales (-10.7%). Performance in Firm investments and Throughputs has hardly improved.

Croatia
For Croatia, one of the Catching-up countries, innovation performance is well below the EU27 average and its rate of improvement is above that of the EU27. Relative strengths, compared to the country's average performance, are in Innovators and Economic effects and relative weaknesses are in Firm investments and Throughputs.
Serbia
For Serbia, one of the Catching-up countries, innovation performance is well below the EU27 average. Relative strengths, compared to the country's average performance, are in Economic effects and relative weaknesses are in Linkages& entrepreneurship, Throughputs and Innovators.
Turkey
For Turkey, one of the Catching-up countries, innovation performance is well below the EU27 average and the rate of improvement is more than three times that of the EU27. Relative strengths, compared to the country's average performance, are in Finance and support, Innovators and Economic effects and relative weaknesses are in Human resources, Firm investments and Throughpu
Norway
For Norway, one of the Moderate innovators, innovation performance is below the EU27 average and the rate of improvement is also below that of the EU27. Relative strengths, compared to the country's average performance, are in Human resources and Finance and support and relative weaknesses are in Firm investments, Throughputs and Innovators.
Switzerland
Switzerland has the highest overall level of innovation performance and its rate of improvement is also above that of the EU27. Relative strengths, compared to the country's average performance, are in Throughputs and Innovators and relative weaknesses are in Linkages & entrepreneurship and Economic effects.

Source: European Innovation Scoreboard, 2010.

Using data from European Innovation Scoreboard, we can define the growth for each country c per indicator i as y_{ic}^{t}/y_{ic}^{t-1}, as for instance is the ratio between the non-normalised values for year t and year t-1. In order to minimize the effect of growth outliers on the overall growth rate, these ratios are restricted to a maximum of 2 (such that growth in an individual indicator is restricted to 100%) and 0.5 (such that a decrease in an individual indicator is limited to -50%). We may aggregate these indicator growth rates between year t and year t-1 using a geometric average to calculate the average yearly growth rate τ_c^t:

$$1+\tau_c^t = \prod_{i=1}\left(\frac{y_{ic}^t}{y_{ic}^{t-1}}\right)^{w_i}$$

Furthermore, we can then calculate for each country c the average annual growth rate in innovation performance as the geometric average of all yearly growth rates: 1 + Innovation

$$\text{Growth Rate}_c = \prod_t \left(1+\tau_c^t\right)^{w_i}$$

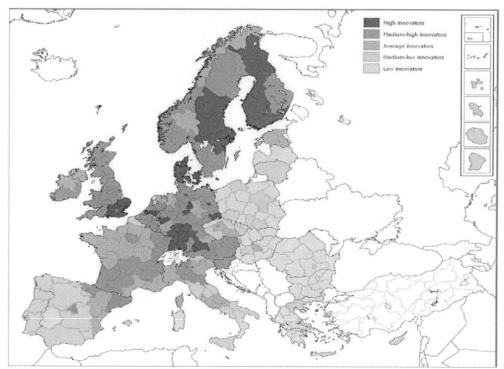

Source: European Innovation Scoreboard, 2010.

Figure 6.8. European Regional Innovation Performance Groups.

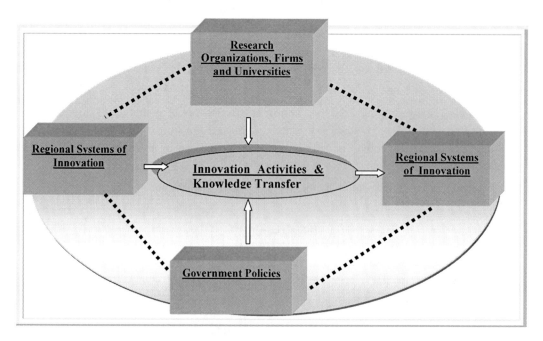

Figure 6.9. The Regional Systems of Innovation.

where $t\varepsilon[2004,2008]$ and each average yearly growth rate receives the same weight w_t. The average annual growth rate in innovation performance does not measure the change in the SII but the average change in the 29 innovation indicators. The average growth rates calculated over a five-year period. Figure 6.9 illustrates the determinant factors of regional systems of innovation.

"Europe Strategy 2020" is a 10-year growth strategy proposed by the European Commission in March 2010 for reviving the economy of the European Union to become a smart, sustainable and inclusive economy. The Commission identifies three key drivers for growth, to be implemented through concrete actions at EU and national levels:

- Smart growth (fostering knowledge, innovation, education and digital society),
- Sustainable growth (making production more resource efficient while boosting competitiveness) and
- Inclusive growth (raising participation in the labour market, the acquisition of skills and the fight against poverty).

Finally, we can summarize the following results, according to the INNOMETRICS, (2009):

- There is considerable diversity in regional innovation performances. The results show that all countries have regions at different levels of performance. This emphasizes the need for policies to reflect regional contexts and for better data to assess regional innovation performances. The most heterogeneous countries are Spain, Italy and Czech Republic where innovation performance varies from low to medium-high.
- The most innovative regions are typically in the most innovative countries. Noord-Brabant is a high innovating region located in an "Innovation follower" country (the Netherlands).
    - Praha in the Czech Republic, Pais Vasco, Comunidad Foral de Navarra, Comunidad de Madrid and Cataluña in Spain, Lombardia and Emilia-Romagna in Italy, Zahodna Slovenija in Slovenia, and Oslo og Akershus, Sør-Østlandet, Agder og Rogaland, Vestlandet and Trøndelag in Norway are all medium-high innovating regions from moderate innovators and catching up countries.
    - The capital regions in Hungary and Slovakia show an innovation level at the EU average but are located in catching up countries whose overall innovation performance is well below average.
- Regional performance appears relatively stable since 2004. The pattern of innovation is quite stable between year 2004 and 2006, with only a few changes in group membership. More specifically, most of the changes are positive and relate to Cataluña, Comunidad Valenciana, Illes Balears, and Ceuta (Spain), Bassin Parisien, Sud-Ouest (France), Unterfranken (Germany), Közép-Dunántúl (Hungary), Algarve (Portugal), and Hedmark og Oppland (Norway). Longer time series data would be needed to analyse the dynamics of regional innovation performance and how this might relate to other factors such as changes in GDP, industrial structure and public policies.

Table 6.13 summarizes the changes in innovation performance for European regional groups. The performance results appear, between 2004 and 2006, the following 16 changes in group membership. Innovation is a priority of all European Union member states and various policy measures and support schemes for innovation have been implemented. Innovation is the cornerstone of the EU Lisbon strategy again emphasized by the EU Barcelona' conclusions. Innovation and S&T policy are key elements of several other EU policies, such as the "EU Green paper on entrepreneurship". The EU has cited insufficient innovation capacity as a key factor for the EU's underperformance in productivity growth. Innovation policy must go beyond the model of R&D as a source of innovation to more complex models of an interconnected system of mutually interacting institutions in a given environment.

Table 6.13. Changes in Regional Groups for Innovation Performance

Regions	2004	2006
BE2 Vlaams Gewest	High innovator	Medium-high innovator
DE26 Unterfranken	Medium-high innovator	High innovator
ES51 Cataluña	Average innovator	Medium-high innovator
ES52 Comunidad Valenciana	Medium-low innovator	Average innovator
ES53 Illes Balears	Low innovator	Medium-low innovator
ES63 Ciudad Autónoma de Ceuta (ES)	Low innovator	Medium-low innovator
FR2 Bassin Parisien	Medium-low innovator	Average innovator
FR4 Est	Average innovator	Medium-high innovator
FR6 Sud-Ouest	Average innovator	Medium-high innovator
ITG2 Sardegna	Medium-low innovator	Low innovator
HU21 Közép-Dunántúl	Low innovator	Medium-low innovator
PL11 Lódzkie	Medium-low innovator	Low innovator
PL31 Lubelskie	Medium-low innovator	Low innovator
PL61 Kujawsko-Pomorskie	Medium-low innovator	Low innovator
PT15 Algarve	Low innovator	Medium-low innovator
NO02 Hedmark og Oppland	Medium-low innovator	Average innovator

Source: INNOMETRICS: (2009).
Notes: Based on regional data availability the analysis will cover at most 201 regions for all EU Member States and Norway at different NUTS levels as follows (cf. RIS Methodology report):
- NUTS 1: 3 regions from Austria, 3 regions from Belgium, 2 regions from Bulgaria, 9 regions from France, 9 regions from Germany, 3 regions from Greece, 1 region from Hungary, 2 regions from Spain, 12 regions from UK.
- NUTS 2: 8 regions from Czech Republic, 4 regions from Finland, 29 regions from Germany, 1 region from Greece, 6 regions from Hungary, 2 regions from Ireland, 17 regions from Italy, 12 regions from the Netherlands, 7 regions from Norway, 16 regions from Poland, 5 regions from Portugal, 8 regions from Romania, 2 regions from Slovenia, 4 regions from Slovakia, 17 regions from Spain, 8 regions from Sweden.
- 1 merged region for Greece (Anatoliki Makedonia Thraki GR11, Dytiki Makedonia GR13 and Thessalia GR14), 2 merged regions for Italy (Valle d'Aosta ITC2 and Piemonte ITC1; Molise ITF2 and Abruzzo ITF1), 1 merged region for Portugal (Região Autónoma dos Açores PT2 and Região Autónoma da Madeira PT3).
- Denmark, Estonia, Cyprus, Latvia, Lithuania, Luxembourg and Malta will be included at the country level.

Table 6.14 illustrates the Objectives of the European Regional Innovation Strategy for the period 2010-2013. The EU' strategy towards regional innovation policy should emphasize in the following points:

- Enhance the scientific & innovation framework and the related structural changes
- Encourage and expand the creation and growth of innovative enterprises
- Improve the key interfaces in the innovation system

Table 6.14. Objectives of the European Regional Innovation Strategy 2010-2013

\multicolumn{3}{c}{**Regional Innovation Strategy 2010-2013**}
\multicolumn{3}{c}{**General Objective: Increase of innovation and competitiveness of the Regions**}
\multicolumn{3}{c}{**Pillars:**}
I	II	III
Economy Based on Knowledge *Objective:* Transition of the regions into the region based on knowledge and the centre for innovation.	**Innovation Culture** *Objective:* Improvement of intangible environment supporting innovations (culture, attitudes, norms and behaviour patterns, human capital) and the increase of the susceptibility of local authorities and society to innovations.	**Innovative Management** *Objective:* Higher efficiency and innovativeness in the development process support.
\multicolumn{3}{c}{**Priorities:**}
• Increased financial support, especially from the state, on R&D • Enhancing regional R&D potential and the effectiveness of the R&D institutions. • Support to development of high technology industries • Transition of traditional industries into the more scientific-based • Development of information society and knowledge-based economy services	• Promotion of innovation and entrepreneurship • Education for innovation	• Durable partnership • Anticipating the future • Effective mechanisms of implementation

Source: ec.europa.eu/regional_policy/conferences/od2006/doc

- To create an "open society" for sciences and innovation;
- Competitiveness of economy must grow to a satisfactory level;
- Enhance competitiveness and development through science and technology system (S&T);
- Enforce the linkages between theoretical and empirical research (universities and industries) and increase the demand and funds allocated to S&T activities from SMEs and industry;
- Explore the available human resources and increase the mobility, both within public S&T system and between public S&T and industry;
- Support the networking and international S&T cooperation;
- Increase the public S&T investments and funding;
- Establish a suitable information system that would provide well-structured data available for evaluation, benchmarking and monitoring for S&T activities;
- Enforce the financing of R&D activities by companies and exploit R&D results within the public RDIs and universities;
- Regional economies based on knowledge and technological innovation, helping less favoured regions to raise their technological level. It is seen as essential that efforts are made to try and establish co-operation between the public sector and bodies responsible for RTDI and business, so that efficient regional innovation systems can be created. "It is a matter of establishing an environmental and a regional institutional framework which will promote, by reinforcing human capital, the creation, dissemination and integration of knowledge within the productive fabric as a principle source of innovation and competitive advantage" (CEC, 2001, p.7);
- The Regional Innovation and Technology Transfer Strategies (RITTS projects) offered mechanisms and incentives to create regional dialogue in geographically, institutionally or culturally fragmented regions;
- The Regional Innovation and Technology Transfer Strategies (RITTS projects) promoted the development of a concept of innovation broader than linear technology transfer, and it helped to raise this higher on the agenda;
- The Regional Innovation and Technology Transfer Strategies (RITTS projects) assisted many regions to clarify the components of their innovation support infrastructures, and to develop actions to rationalise them and augment their visibility." (Enterprise DG, 2001, p.63);
- E-Europe-regio, the information society at the service of regional development. In the context of the e-Europe initiative, the aim is to ensure that the less-favoured regions are in a good position to take advantage of the opportunities offered by the information society;
- Regional identity and sustainable development promoting regional cohesion and competitiveness through an integrated approach to economic, environmental, cultural and social activities. This recognises the importance of local assets in developing a sustainable and competitive economy;
- Upgrade the patent applications and exploitation towards an e-economy.

6.7. SUMMARY CONCLUSIONS

Extracting sufficient benefits from public investment in science and R&D is a core task for governments. Links between science and industry are not equally developed across countries. Science is also of increasing importance if countries want to benefit from the global stock of knowledge. It is particularly important for government-funded research to continue to provide the early seeds of innovation. The shortage of private-sector product and R&D cycles carries the risk of under-investment in scientific research and long-term technologies with broad applications.

Most of the efforts of the last thirty years in innovation and R&D activities have been directly linked to the following policies:

- In the 1980s, attention towards Japan: technology pouch (Framework Program);
- In 2000s, attention towards USA: competitiveness push: (Lisbon Strategy);
- Today, attention towards importance of ICT, sustainability, social innovation and demand pull measures (Europe 2020).

This Chapter has analyzed the situation of EU member states from the perspective of indicators, showing their relative position in respect of the knowledge-based economy as well as their competitive position. It has been argued that in order to make Europe more competitive - or even simply maintain its current competitive position, sustained growth and employment levels - Europe needs to invest in production of new knowledge, in application of new technology, and ultimately in the people that will be able to put the new knowledge and technology to use.

According to the Community's plans, the following criteria are essential for the selection and implementation in technological policy:

(a) research must contribute to strengthen the economic performance, social cohesion and competitiveness of the Community's areas and moreover to secure their *convergence*;
(b) research must contribute to the achievement of the common market and to unification of European scientific and technical areas, in order to establish uniform norms and standards.

Decision making in technology policy has been largely transferred to the Community level; the scope for national decision making has been reduced, while the responsibility of Community has increased correspondingly. The Community's action for small member states in technological activities should be reconsidered carefully, in order to achieve a higher level of efficiency. They should be more targeted and concentrated. The various *research measures* can be combined with other financial instruments and institutional regulations to create a significant size of action and to have a more favourable effect on the productive capabilities of these countries.

The Community's research framework programmes have been launched to meet the specific needs of the weaker member states. Financial and technological flows through the CSFs and the Community's research programmes should be expected to reduce the disparities between member states and to expand the opportunities for the LFRs (Less Favoured Regions).

In the light of these remarks, Community technological policy has to be reinforced and oriented on several fronts:

- Establish a coherent technological policy;
- Target and concentrated more effectively on the technological capabilities of the small member states. A co-ordination with the broader Community instruments and resources (CSFs) can create a much more favourable effect on the productive capabilities of these countries;
- The traditional industries that are quite an important factor for the weaker states should be supported by appropriate research and technological programmes;
- The Community could envisage specific programmes for technological diffusion in the small member states;
- Human capital formation should have a particular position in the Community policies vis-a-vis the smaller countries. The Community's technological policy aims to enhance the international demand for research activities and consequently to reinforce the weak internal market demand of the small member states. This creates the opportunity to expand activities that otherwise would probably have remained at much lower levels;
- Investment in knowledge – research and development expenditure, education, software – and venture capital investment, for instance, spending patterns in the perspective of the knowledge economy;
- Technology policy has been relatively successful in certain fields like telecommunications or traffic control systems. In other fields, like microelectronics and computers, the results have been mixed.

Looking first at scientific and technological output, the EU is still ahead of the US and Japan in its share of scientific publications, but lags behind in most of the other performance indicators, especially patents. There is, nonetheless, a substantial variation within the EU and certain EU member states often score better than the US and Japan (most notably Sweden and Finland), yet the overall situation in the EU-15 is far from satisfactory. There is considerable empirical evidence that investment in research and technological development and innovation (R&D) has a positive correlation with the level of economic development. Efforts in the area of R&D have been associated with higher growth rates, increases in exports and trade, gains in productivity, growth in income and output, bigger business profits and lower inflation, international competitiveness, etc in economic literature. Given the correlation between innovation and R&D efforts, and regional economic development, closing the interregional R&D gap in the EU becomes a requirement for reducing the cohesion gap, which is the primary objective of regional policy. Less favoured regions spend comparatively lower levels of public funds on innovation and, on top of this, having greater difficulties in absorbing these funds than more developed regions.

EU cohesion policy is the second largest item in the EU budget, making up about 35% of total expenditure. Cohesion policy is translated into financial disbursements via its two main instruments: the Structural Funds and the Cohesion Fund, with the former accounting for roughly 90% and the latter for 10% of the total. Prior to 1989, EU cohesion policy was relatively unstructured and financially much smaller.

Moreover, the European research and innovation policy has adopted an approach oriented more towards innovation than technological excellence as such, better addressing the deficiencies of less favoured regions as a result. An improvement in the interaction between the deployment of the Structural Funds and research policy is important for acceleration of the "catching up" of lagging regions. Structural Funds can provide the necessary support for firms and research institutes in the latter to participate on equal terms in future research programmes.

New technologies imply some direct and indirect effects or more specifically some micro effects (such as firms, and organisations) and macro effects (such as inter and intra-industrial and moreover regional effects) for the whole economy. New technologies play an important role to sectoral productivity, overall growth, employment, modernization, industrialisation, socioeconomic infrastructure and to competitiveness of a country. The principal effects for technological policy can be distinguished in demand and supply sides. Technical change and innovation activities have an important role for growth and sustainable development. There is a huge literature on the role and economic impact of invention and innovation activities; many studies investigate the relationship between productivity, technical change, welfare, growth and regional development. Local produced technologies may affect and determine the rate of regional growth.

In the literature there are various explanations for the slow-down in productivity growth for E.U. countries. One source of the slow-down may be substantial changes in the industrial composition of output, employment, capital accumulation and resource utilization. The second source of the slow down in productivity growth may be that technological opportunities have declined; otherwise, new technologies have been developed but the application of new technologies to production has been less successful. Technological factors act in a long run way and should not be expected to explain medium run variations in the growth of GDP and productivity. The countries that are technologically backward have a potentiality to generate more rapid growth even greater than that of the advanced countries, if they are able take advantage of new technologies which have already employed by technological leaders.

The Community's technology policy has the following objectives:

- industrial modernisation and competitiveness;
- quality and productivity improvements in agriculture;
- dissemination of new technologies;
- exploitation of human and natural resources;
- a better quality of life;
- regional convergence.

The Community's research programmes also attempt to establish co-operation between *theoretical research* through the different research bodies of the public sector (such as research institutes and universities) and *industrial research* through private enterprises. We can summarise the main conclusions and policy implications of this Chapter as follows: technology policy has been heavily concerned with the external gap of the EEC vis-a-vis

Japan and USA. However, the same size of gap also exists among EC countries. It is true that technological competition among Japan, the USA and European Community is intense. Moreover, one tends to find most of the Acceding countries in a position of catching up from relatively low levels of S&T output. Although there are some noticeable encouraging tendencies in several Acceding countries, one can expect that with the enlargement of the European Union the "European Paradox" will be, at least temporarily, further accentuated. In other words, in relation to its enlarged population, the EU-25's strong performance in science will contrast increasingly with its weaker development and commercialization of technology.

However, Europe still needs to exploit better its scientific and technological output, notably in terms of selling its high-tech goods on world markets. While its share of high-tech exports has grown slightly since the mid-1990s, the EU still had a lower market share than the US in 2001. Indeed, 2001 was a difficult year for the high-tech sector, and the ability of industry to withstand this correction will be a crucial factor in a number of countries. Moreover, this is a highly competitive market no longer restricted to the major developed countries. Over the past decade, we have seen developing Asian producers emerge as important players in high-tech market niches. A number of Acceding countries are also growing rapidly in their exports of high-tech, due in part to inflows of foreign investment.

The slowing down of EU-15 investment in the knowledge-based economy is likely to be reflected sooner or later in a significant decline in its performance. This trend underlines the urgency of implementing the Lisbon Strategy. In particular, the EU needs to increase its efforts, so as to give renewed impetus to the catching up of some countries with the rest of the EU-15 and to close the gap as soon as possible with the US.

- In 2000, approximately 3.4 million researchers were engaged in research and development (R&D) in the EU area. This corresponds to about 6.5 researchers per thousand employees, a significant increase from the 1991 level of 5.6 researchers per thousand.
- Among the major OECD regions, Japan has the highest number of researchers relative to total employment, followed by the United States and the European Union. However, around 38% of all OECD-area researchers reside in the United States, 29% in the European Union and 19% in Japan.
- In 2000, approximately 2.1 million researchers (about 64% of the total) were employed by the business sector in the OECD area.
- In the major economic zones, the share of business researchers in the national total differs widely. In the United States, four out of five researchers work in the business sector but only one out of two in the European Union.
- Finland, the United States, Japan and Sweden are the only countries where business researchers in industry exceed 6 per thousand employees; in the large European economies, they are only 3 or 4 per thousand employees.
- Portugal, Greece and Poland have a low intensity of business researchers (fewer than 1 per thousand employees in industry). This is mainly due to national characteristics; in these countries, the business sector plays a much smaller role in the national innovation system than the higher education and government sectors. Business sector R&D expenditure in these countries accounts for only 25-35% of total R&D expenditure.

- Countries in Central and in the previous Eastern Europe have been affected by the reduction in numbers of business researchers in the 1990s, although the trend has reversed in the Czech Republic and Hungary in the past few years.

We can summarize some of the main findings:

- In terms of scientific publications Europe's strong growth seems to have halted. Actual numbers are still rising, but the EU share of world publications is declining, whereas the US share is recovering.
- Per head of population, the EU generates fewer patents with a high economic value (so-called 'Triadic patents') than the US and Japan.
- The EU is lagging behind the US in its share of patents in biotechnology and information and communications technology.
- There has been a slight increase in the EU share of global exports of high-tech products in value terms between 1996 and 2001. Japan's share fell sharply in 2001 hit by falling sales of electronic goods.
- Since the middle of the 1990s, the EU has stopped catching up with the US in terms of labour productivity, reflecting a relatively weaker innovation performance.
- Large disparities persist among EU countries in high-tech manufacturing. Japan outperforms the EU in high-tech manufacturing indicators while the Central European Acceding countries perform better than the EU average.
- The production of scientific research and technological know-how increasingly depends on research conducted in other countries. Indicators of cross-border co-authorship of scientific articles and co-invention of patents seek to shed light on this trend.
- Scientific collaboration with advanced countries is generally much more widespread than with smaller ones. Researchers in 160 countries co-authored at least 1% of their internationally co-authored papers with US researchers. The United Kingdom, France and Germany also play a leading role in international scientific collaboration.
- By late of 1990s, about 6% of patents were the result of international collaborative research. Several factors may affect the degree of a country's internationalization in science and technology: size, technological endowment, geographical proximity to regions with high research activity, language, industrial specialization, existence of foreign affiliates, etc.
- Internationalization tends to be higher in smaller European countries. For example, 56 % of Luxembourg's patents have foreign co-inventors and 30 % of Iceland's and Belgium's. International cooperation in science and technology is also relatively high in Poland, the Czech Republic and the Slovak Republic.
- International collaboration in patenting is lower in EU than in USA. In Japan, international co-operation in science and technology is rather limited.

7. POLICY PERSPECTIVES

Innovation is a central element of the Lisbon objective. It is well known that innovation is a central element of economic performance. The first generation of innovation policy was based on the idea of a linear process for the development of innovations. This process begins with laboratory science and moves through successive stages till the new knowledge is built into commercial applications that diffuse in the economic system. The emphasis of policy was on fostering critical directions of scientific and technological advance, and enhancing the flow of knowledge down along the innovation chain. The second generation policy recognizes the complexity of the innovation system, with many feedback loops between the different two-stages" of the process as outlined in the first generation model. Even though the second generation policies still have to be embedded in many agencies, the contours of a new generation of innovation policy are now becoming apparent. Such a new generation of policy would emphasise the benefits of co-ordinating actions in policy areas, and making innovation – and innovation-friendly policies – one of the core principles of this. Thus the "third generation innovation policy" would place innovation at the heart of each policy area..

As the economy has moved from the industrial age to the information age, the driving force of innovation has excited some and frightened others. Innovation and the competitive spirit of the free enterprise system have always made jobs, and even entire industries, obsolete. United States has entered the information age, and brain power has surpassed motor skill as the economy's most valuable labor resource. The pace of technology dissemination across countries has picked up considerably over the past 100 years, and most technologies are available at some level in most countries, but the extent to which technologies are available differs enormously. Many developing countries made progress in closing the technology gap with advanced countries during the 2010s. However, despite more rapid improvement in technological achievement among the poorest countries, enormous gaps in technological achievement remain.

Technological progress can spur development by lowering the costs of production and enabling the exploitation of increasing returns to scale. By improving the efficiency with which existing products are produced, new technologies can open up the possibility of increasing output and, assuming that markets are available, taking advantage of previously unexploited increasing returns to scale.

Technological progress in one sector can create new economic opportunities in other sectors. Lower production costs can create whole new products, or even sectors. The benefits of a new technology can extend well beyond the immediate sector or good in which the technology exists. Technology can yield quality improvements.

Such improvements can enable a developing country to penetrate more demanding consumer and intermediate markets. Measuring technology directly is difficult, mainly because, unlike pencils or automobiles, technology has no easily counted physical presence. Some indexes emphasize inputs into technological advancement, such as education levels, numbers of scientists and engineers, and expenditures on research and development (R&D) or R&D personnel, for example, the index of innovation capability put out by the United Nations Conference on Trade and Development. Other indexes also incorporate information on the diffusion of technologies and on indicators of innovation, such as the number of patents granted. The technology achievement index, published by the United Nations Development Programme is an example. Still other indexes focus on outputs, such as the share of high-tech activities in manufacturing value added and exports, for instance, the index of competitive industrial performance published by the United Nations Industrial Development Organization. Some indexes focus more on the mechanisms by which technological progress is achieved (Sagasti 2003) or by which technological learning occurs (Soubattina 2006). For example, the national innovative capacity index reflects government and firm-level policies associated with successful innovation (Porter and Stern 2003).

The clear dominance of high-income countries in the number of scientific and technical journal articles published, the number of patents. Not all countries need to be on the cutting age of global technological advance, but every country needs the capacity to understand and adapt global technologies for local needs. When a country reviews its technology policies, a useful starting point is a realistic assessment of its current situation in technological progress.

National Systems of Innovation (NSI), introduced recently, has had a strong appeal to those interested in understanding the connections between technical change, growth and development of late industrializing economies The National Systems of Innovation (NSI) approach has much in common with the methodological perspectives of the social psychological pragmatist school of Chicago and not least with the ideas of George Herbert Mead (Mjøset 2002). The concept of national systems of innovation, (NSIs) was first introduced by Freeman and Lundvall (Lundvall, 1986, 1992; Freeman, 1987), even though somewhat similar concepts had been discussed earlier. Lundvall gives no clear-cut definition for the concept of NSI, even though his book focuses on them. Freeman, on the other hand, gives a definition, defining NSIs as: "... the network of institutions in the public and private sectors whose activities and interactions initiate, import, modify, and diffuse new technologies ...".

Economic growth depends increasingly on "innovation" and on "regions". Regions are going to acquire ever increasing role in the contexts of national innovation strategies. Freeman (19871) considers "the national systems of innovation as the 'network of institutions in the public and private sector whose activities and interactions initiate, import, modify and diffuse new technologies." National systems of technological innovation involve those institutions that determine the rate and direction of technological development, the rate at which local or foreign innovations are commercialized, and learning process. The concept of national system of innovation is much wider than a network of scientific and technical institutions. It also involves the production system and a continuous process of learning. Lundval, another researcher on innovation believes "a system of innovation is constituted by elements and relationships which interact in the production, diffusion, and use of new and economically useful knowledge". A national system of innovation encompasses, but not limited to, the elements and relationships either located within or rooted inside the borders of a national state. Lundval (1992) indicates that 'the national system of technological innovation is larger than the R&D system. For example, it includes not only the system of technology diffusion and the R&D system but also institutions and factors determining how new technology affects productivity and economic growth. The system of technological change is, of course, less comprehensive than the society as a whole. Following Freeman and the 'Aalborg- version' of the national innovation system-approach (Freeman 1987; Freeman and Lundvall 1988) aims at understanding 'the innovation system in the broad sense'. According to this definition, 'innovation' is broader. Innovation is seen as a continuous cumulative process involving not only radical and incremental innovation but also the diffusion, absorption and use of innovation and a wider set of sources of innovation is taken into account. Innovation is seen as reflecting, besides science and R&D, interactive learning taking place in connection with ongoing activities in procurement, production and sales. On this context, a wide definition of innovation should be used including product innovations (both material goods and intangible services) as well as process innovations (both technological and organizational ones). Policies to stimulate innovation need to take account of changes in the global economy and the transformation of innovation processes. To transform invention into innovation successfully requires a range of complementary activities, including organisational changes, firm-level training, testing, marketing and design. Innovation today encompasses much more than research and development (R&D), although R&D remains vitally important. Innovation rarely occurs in isolation; it is a highly interactive process of collaboration across a growing and diverse network of stakeholders, institutions and users. The knowledge creation, diffusion, and accumulation processes taking place in innovation systems are often highly complex, diffuse and unpredictable, and it is often a practical impossibility to measure them accurately and objectively. The evaluation of innovation *systems* is more complex than the evaluation of single policy interventions.

European regions vary considerably, and countries vary considerably in terms of the diversity of their regions. In the past the focus of regional policy tended to be on ensuring a high standard of basic infrastructure. In particular, EU regional policy aims to ensure that all regions can take full advantage of the single market and economic and monetary union. Recently, much greater emphasis has been placed on capacity building and the promotion of innovation.

The promotion of innovation is a major concern at regional, national and supranational level, since there is a wide consensus about the benefits of innovation on social an economic progress. The implementation of innovation policies has been adopted at European level from a common perspective, based on common legal bases, policy plans and structures. There is plenty of empirical evidence that science and technology are the key drivers of economic growth and there is direct correlation between S&T utilization and economic competitiveness and overall social welfare. The S&T and innovation policy must design a friendly and supportive environment to encourage and maximize benefits. It must not only focus on technology creation but also on technology diffusion, adaptation and transfer into the business environment, since these mechanisms are more frequently the factors for development.

The Treaty establishing the European Community sets economic and social cohesion as one of the main priorities of the Union. This priority is established by the EU cohesion policy whose objectives are defined by Articles 2 and 4, and Title XVII of the Treaty. According to

Article 2, cohesion policy should contribute to « *promote economic and social progress as well as a high level of employment, and to achieve balanced and sustainable development* ». Article 158 adds « *in particular, the Community aims to reduce the disparities between the levels of development of the different regions and the backwardness of the least favoured regions or islands, including rural areas* »

Article 2 of the Treaty on European Union states: *"to promote economic and social progress and a high level of employment...in particular... through the strengthening of economic and social cohesion"*. Article 158 contains a more explicit definition: *"In order to promote its overall harmonious development, the Community shall develop and pursue its actions leading to the strengthening of its economic and social cohesion. In particular, the Community shall aim at reducing disparities between the levels of development of the various regions and the backwardness of the least favored regions or islands, including rural areas."*

Cohesion policies can be grouped into the following categories, (Sapir, 2003):

- Convergence policy aims to promote the regional convergence by allocating development funding to countries and regions on a non-competitive basis.
- Social policy targets towards an employment policy and to enhance the labor market policy.
- Innovation policy, although not conceived as an instrument has been turning into one over time.

Growth enhancement is the main concern. In particular, we can specify two types of capital expenditure that are likely to have the greatest impact on growth:

- human capital investment (R&D, education and training) and
- physical capital investment (infrastructure).

The EU convergence fund should act as a catalyst for both types of capital expenditure so as to sustain high investment rates without crowding out domestic investment. Comparison and benchmarking across member states can be of significant help to assess what are the most effective ways of supporting the growth and convergence.

Follow the Sapir' report the recommendation principles for new policy includes:

- To expand the process of economic growth and social development. On this aspect, there is a need to revise some features of the current macroeconomic policy setting and to redesign cohesion policies at both the EU and national levels.
- Well-structuring the market regulations and competitiveness for labor, capital, goods and services in order to enhance the growth process.
- The EU economic policy should aim to foster growth and improve the cohesion.

The European innovation strategy is built around five priorities for government action, which together can underpin a strategic and broad-based approach to promoting innovation:

- empowering people to innovate;
- unleashing innovation in firms;
- creating and applying knowledge;
- applying innovation to address global and social challenges; and
- improving the governance and measurement of policies for innovation.

In particular, the main policy principles for innovation are based on the following lines:

- Empowering people to innovate.
- Education and training systems should equip people with the foundations to learn and develop the broad range of skills needed for innovation in all of its forms, and with the flexibility to upgrade skills and adapt to changing market conditions. To foster an innovative workplace, ensure that employment policies facilitate efficient organisational change.
- Enable consumers to be active participants in the innovation process.
- Foster an entrepreneurial culture by instilling the skills and attitudes needed for creative enterprise.
- Unleashing innovations.
- Ensure that framework conditions are sound and supportive of competition, conducive to innovation and are mutually reinforcing.
- Mobilise private funding for innovation, by fostering well-functioning financial markets and easing access to finance for new firms, in particular for early stages of innovation. Encourage the diffusion of best practices in the reporting of intangible investments and develop market-friendly approaches to support innovation.
- Foster open markets, a competitive and dynamic business sector and a culture of healthy risk taking and creative activity. Foster innovation in small and medium-sized firms, in particular new and young ones.
- Creating and applying knowledge.
- Provide sufficient investment in an effective public research system and improve the governance of research institutions. Ensure coherence between multi-level sources of funding for R&D.
- Ensure that a modern and reliable knowledge infrastructure that supports innovation is in place, accompanied by the regulatory frameworks which support open access to networks and competition in the market. Create a suitable policy and regulatory environment that allows for the responsible development of technologies and their convergence.
- Facilitate efficient knowledge flows and foster the development of networks and markets which enable the creation, circulation and diffusion of knowledge, along with an effective system of intellectual property rights.
- Foster innovation in the public sector at all levels of government to enhance the delivery of public services, improve efficiency, coverage and equity, and create positive externalities in the rest of the economy.
- Applying innovation to address global and social challenges.

- Improve international scientific and technological co-operation and technology transfer, including through the development of international mechanisms to finance innovation and share costs.
- Provide a predictable policy regime which provides flexibility and incentives to address global challenges through innovation in developed and developing countries, and encourages invention and the adoption of cost-effective technologies.
- To spur innovation as a tool for development, strengthen the foundations for innovation in low income countries, including affordable access to modern technologies. Foster entrepreneurship throughout the economy, and enable entrepreneurs to experiment, invest and expand creative economic activities, particularly around agriculture.
- Improving the governance and measurement of policies for innovation.
- Ensure policy coherence by treating innovation as a central component of government policy, with strong leadership at the highest political levels. Enable regional and local actors to foster innovation, while ensuring co-ordination across regions and with national efforts. Foster evidence-based decision making and policy accountability by recognising measurement as central to the innovation agenda.

We can summarize some of our recommendations, (EBAN, 2010):

- The EU convergence policy should focus on low-income countries rather than low income regions. The EU convergence fund should be allocated to a country on the basis of its GDP per capita level. The principle of conditionality should be systematically strengthened.
- A country's eligibility for the EU convergence fund should be re-assessed at the end of each programming period. A country should be declared eligible for renewal only if it meets the income requirement and has met the conditionality criterion on the use of previously allocated money.
- Priority should be given to improving the administrative capacity of Member States.
- Investment in human and physical capital.
- Create co-investment funds through public & private partnerships at a European level is essential, in order to develop local financial communities.
- Encourage member states to create or increase special fiscal incentives for investments in young innovative companies.
- Remove obstacles to cross-border investments by venture capital funds through mutual recognition and a stronger and more transparent regulatory framework to conduct cross-border investments.
- Lighter regulation in the early-stage investment market.
- Organize financing of SMEs and helping to support networking between those actors.

8. BIBLIOGRAPHY

Abbing, M.R., and Schakernaad, J. (1990), *Joint R&D Activities of Firms in European Cost-Sharing Programmes.* Maastricht: MERIT.

Abramovitz, M. (1956), Resource and output trends in the United States since 1870, *American Economic Review*, vol. 46, p.p.: 5-23.

Abramovitz M. (1986), "Catching-up, foreign ahead and falling behind", *Journal of Economic History,* vol. 46.

Abramowitz, M. and David, P. (1996), "Technological change and the rise of intangible investments: The US economy's growth path in the Twentieth Century", in Foray, D. and Lundvall B.-Å. (eds.), *Employment and growth in the knowledge-based economy*, Paris, OECD.

Academia Europaea, (2000), *Responses from the Academia Europaea to the Communication from the European Commission, January* (2000) at http://albert.hep.ph.ic.ac.uk/~bttrwrth/aeresponse.html

Acemoglu, Daron, (2002), "Technical Change, Inequality, and the Labor Market." *Journal of Economic Literature* 40: 7–72.

Acs, Zoltan J. (2002), *Innovation and the Growth of Cities*, Edward Elgar.

Acs, Zoltan J. and David B. Audretsch (eds.), (1991), *Innovation and Technological Change: An International Comparison*, Ann Arbor: University of Michigan Press.

Acs, Z. J., & Audretsch, D. B. (1993), Analyzing Innovation Output Indicators: The US Experience. In A. Kleinknecht & D. Bain (Eds.), *New concepts in innovation output measurement.* (pp. 10-41): New York: St. Martin's Press; London: Macmillan Press.

Acs ZJ, FitzRoy F, Smith I (1999), "High technology employment, wages and university R&D spillovers: Evidence from US cities". *Economics of innovation and new technology* volume 8, No: 1-2, p.p.: 57-78.

Acs, Z. J., Anselin, L., & Varga, A. (2002), Patents and innovation counts as measures of regional production of new knowledge. *Research Policy, 31*(7), 1069- 1085.

Acs, Zoltan J., and David J. Storey, (2004), "Introduction: Entrepreneurship and Economic Development," *Regional Studies*, 38(8), 871-877.

Acs, Zoltan J., and Attila Varga, (2005), "Entrepreneurship, Agglomeration and Technological Change," *Small Business Economics*, 24(3), 323-334.

Acs, Zoltan J. and Catherine Armington, (2006), *Entrepreneurship, Geography and American Economic Growth*, Cambridge: Cambridge University Press.

Agell, J., T. Lindh and H. Ohlson (1997), "Growth and the public sector: A critical review essay", *European Journal of Political Economy*, No. 13, pp. 33-52.

Agell, J., T. Lindh and H. Ohlson (1999), "Growth and the public sector: A reply", *European Journal of Political Economy*, 15, pp. 359-66.

Aghion P., Howitt P. (1992), "A Model of Growth through Creative Destruction", *Econometrica*, 60(2), pp. 323-351.

_____ . (1998), *Endogenous Growth Theory*, MIT Press, Cambridge (USA).

Aghion, P. and P. Howitt (1998), *Endogenous Growth Theory*, Cambridge, Mass.: The MIT Press.

Aghion, P., C. Meghir and J. Vandenbussche (2003), 'Growth, Education and Distance to the Technological Frontier', mimeo.

Ahmad N. (2003), "Measuring Investment in Software", *STI Working Paper 2003/6*, OECD, Paris, www.oecd.org/sti/working-papers

Aigner D.J., Lovell C.A.K., Schmidt P. (1977), Formulation and estimation of stochastic frontier production functions. *Journal of Econometrics* 6:21—37.

Agrawal, Ajay K., Devesh Kapur, and John McHale (2007), "Brain Drain or Brain Bank? The Impact of Skilled Emigration on Poor-Country Innovation." Unpublished paper. *University of Toronto, Rotman School of Management, Ontario*.

Aitken, B. J. & Harrison, A. E. (1999), Do Domestic Firms Benefit from Direct Foreign Investment? Evidence from Venezuela, *American Economic Review*, 89(3): 605-618.

Aked N.H. and Gummett P.J. (1976), "Science and technology in the European Communities: the history of the cost projects", *Research policy*, No: 5, p.p.: 270-294.

Alderman, Harold, John Hoddinott, and Bill H. Kinsey (2006), "Long Term Consequences of Early Childhood Malnutrition." *Oxford Economic Papers* 58 (3): 450–74.

Alesina, Alberto (1996), "Budget deficits and budget institutions", *National Bureau of Economic Research, Working Paper* No. 5556, May.

Alexander, R.J. (1997), "Inflation and Economic Growth: Evidence from a Growth Equation", *Applied Economics*, 29(2), pp. 233-38.

Almus, M., Czarnitski, D. (2003), The effects of public R&D subsidies on firms' innovation activities: The case of Eastern Germany. *Journal of Business and Economic Statistics*, 21(2), pp. 226-236.

Amable B. (1994), "Endogenous Growth Theory, Convergence and Divergence", in Silverberg G, Soete L. (eds) *The Economics of Growth and Technical Change*, MIT Press, Cambridge (USA).

Amendola G. and Perrucci A. (1990), *Specialization and competitiveness of Italian industry in high technology products*, Rome, ENEA.

_____ . (1992), "European patterns of specialization in high technology products: a new approach", in *Proceedings of the joint EC-Leiden conference on science and technology indicators*, Leiden, DSWO Press.

_____ . (1985), "The diffusion of an organizational innovation. international data telecommunications and multinational industrial firms", *International Journal of Industrial Organisation*, vol.3, pp:109-118.

_____ . (1986), "The international diffusion of new information technologies", *Research Policy*, vol.15, pp:139-147.

_____ . (1988), *New information technology and industrial change: the Italian case*, Dordrecht, Kluwer.

_____. (1989a), "A failure inducement model of research and development expenditures, the Italian evidence in the early eighties", *Journal of Economic Behaviour and Organization*.

_____. (1989b), "The role of technological expectations in a mixed model of international diffusion of process innovations", *Research Policy*, October.

_____. (1990), "Profitability and imitation in the diffusion process of innovations", *Rivista Internazionale di Science Economiche e Commerciali*, February.

Amemiya, T. (1985), *Advanced Econometrics*, Basic Blackwell.

American Association for the Advancement of Science (2003), "Long-delayed '03 budget provides historic increases for R&D", *Science* and *Technology in Congress,* March, volume 1, Nos: 6-7.

Amin, A., Wilkinson, F. (1999), "Learning, proximity and industrial performance: an introduction", *Cambridge Journal of Economics*, vol. 23, p.p.: 121-125.

Amin, A. and Cohendet, P. (2004), *The architectures of knowledge: Firms, capabilities and communities*, Oxford, Oxford University Press.

Anand, B.N. and T. Khanna (2000), "The Structure of Licensing Contracts", *The Journal of Industrial Economics*, 48(1), 103-135.

Andersen, B, Howells, J, Hull, R, Miles, I, and Roberts, J (eds.) (2000), Knowledge and Innovation in the New Service Economy Aldershot, Elgar.

Andreasen, L E, B Coriat, F den Hertog and R Kaplinsky (eds.) (1995), Europe's next Step: Organisational Innovation, Competition and Employment Ilford, Frank Cass.

Andres, J. and I. Hernando (1997), "Does inflation harm economic growth? Evidence for the OECD", *NBER Working Paper* No. 6062.

Anselin,L., A. Varga and Zoltan J. Acs, (2000), "Geographic and Sectoral Characteristics of Academic Knowledge externalities," *Papers in Regional Science*, 79(4), 435-443.

Antonelli, C. (1990), Induced adoption and externalities in the regional diffusion of new information technology, *Regional Studies* 24, 31-40.

Antonelli, C. (1991), *The diffusion of advanced telecommunications in developing countries,* Paris, OECD.

Antonelli, C. (1993), Investment and adoption in advanced telecommunications, *Journal of Economic Behavior and Organization* 20, 227-246.

Antonelli, C. (1995), *The economics of localized technological change and industrial dynamics,* Kluwer, Boston.

Antonelli, C. (1999), *The microdynamics of technological change*, Routledge, London.

Antonelli, C. (2001), *The microeconomics of technological systems,* Oxford University Press, Oxford.

Antonelli, C. (2003*), The economics of innovation, new technologies and structural change,* Routledge, London.

Antonelli, C., Petit, P. and Tahar, G. (1992), *The economics of industrial modernization*, Academic Press, Cambridge.

Appel, Michael (1992), Werner Sombart. Theoretiker und Historiker des modernen Kapitalismus. Marburg, Metropolis-Verlag.

Armstrong, H. (1995), "An Appraisal of the Evidence from Cross-sectional Analysis of the Regional Growth Process within the European Union", en *Convergence and Divergence Among European Regions, European Research in Regional Science*, vol. 5, p.p.: 40-65. Ed. H. W. Armstrong y R. W. Vicherman, Pion Limited, London.

Andersen,B, Howells, J., Hull, R., Miles, I., and Roberts, J. (eds.) (2000), *Knowledge and Innovation in the New Service Economy,* Aldershot, Elgar.

Antonelli C., P. Petit and G. Tahar (1990), "The diffusion of interdependent innovations in the textile industry", *Structural Change and Economic Dynamics*.

Antonelli C., P.Petit and G. Tahar (1992), *The Economics of Industrial modernization*, Academic Press.

Arbache, Jorge Saba, Andy Dickerson, and Francis Green (2004), "Trade Liberalization and Wages in Developing Countries." *Economic Journal* 114:F73–F96.

Archibugi, Daniele and Mario Pianta (1992), *The Technological Specialization of Advanced Countries*, Dordrecht: Kluwer Academic Publishers.

Archibugi, D., Michie, J. (1997), *Innovation Policy in a global economy.* Cambridge: Cambridge University Press.

Archibugi, Daniele and Bengt-Åke Lundvall (eds.) (2000), *The Globalising Learning Economy: Major Socio-Economic Trends and European Innovation Policy*, Oxford: Oxford University Press.

Archibugi, Daniele, and Alberto Coco (2005), "Measuring Technological Capabilities at the Country Level: A Survey and a Menu for Choice." *Research Policy* 34: 175–94.

Ark, B. van, (1993), "Comparative Levels of Manufacturing Productivity in Postwar Europe: Measurement and Comparisons", *Oxford Bulletin of Economics and Statistics* vol. 52, p.p.: 343-374.

Ark, B. van, and D. Pilat (1993), "Productivity Levels in Germany, Japan, and the United States: Differences and Causes", *Brookings Papers Microeconomics*, vol. 2, p.p.:1-69.

Arlington, VA. June. Kaufmann, Daniel, Aart Kray, and Massimo Mastruzzi. (2007), "Governance Matters: Governance Indicators for 1996–2006." World Bank Policy Research Working Paper No. 4280, World Bank, Washington, DC.

Arnold L.G. (1998), "Growth, Welfare and Trade in an Integrated Model of Human-Capital Accumulation and Research", *Journal of Macroeconomics*, 20(1), pp. 81-105.

Arocena, Rodrigo and Judith Sutz (2000), *Interactive Learning Spaces and Development Policies in Latin America*, DRUID working papers, No. 00-13.

Arora, A, Fosfuri, A, & Gambardella, A (2002), Markets for Technology: the economics of innovation and corporate strategy MIT Press, Cambridge Ma, 2002, ISBN 0-262-01190-5.

Arrow, K. (1962), *The Economic Implications of Learning by Doing.* Review of Economic Studies 29, 155-173.

Arrow K.J. Hollis B. Chenery, Minhas B.S. and R. M. Solow (1961), "Capital-Labour substitution and economic efficiency", *Review of Economics and Statistics*, vol.63, No:3, August, pp:225-247.

Artis, Michael (1996), "Alternative transitions to EMU", *The Economic Journal*, Vol. 106, No. 437, p.p.: 1005-1015.

Arvanitis, S. and Hollenstein, H. (2001), The determinants of the adoption of advanced manufacturing technology, *Economics of Innovation and New Technology* 10, 377-414.

Arvis, Jean-François, Monica Alina Mustra, John Panzer, Lauri Ojala, and Tapia Naula. (2007). *Connecting to Compete: Trade Logistics in the Global Economy.* Washington, DC: World Bank.

Arundel, A. (2007), Innovation Survey Indicators: What Impact on Innovation Policy? In D. Organisation for Economic Co-operation and (Ed.), *Science, Technology and Innovation*

Indicators in a Changing World: Responding to Policy Needs (pp. 49-64) Paris and Washington, D.C.: Organisation for Economic Co operation and Development.

ASEAN (1999), *ASEAN Investment Report 1999: Trends and Developments in Foreign Direct Investment*, ASEAN Secretariat, Jakarta.

Asheim, B. and M. Gertler (2004), Understanding regional innovation systems. in Jan Fagerberg, David Mowery and Richard Nelson *Handbook of Innovation* . Oxford: Oxford University Press

Asheim, B. T., & Isaksen, A. (2002), Regional Innovation Systems: The Integration of Local 'Sticky' and Global 'Ubiquitous' Knowledge. *Journal of Technology Transfer, 27*(1), 77-86.

Asheim, B., Isaksen, A., Nauwelaers, C. and F. Tötdling (2003), *Regional innovation policy for small-medium enterprises*, Cheltenham, UK and Lyme, US : Edward Elgar.

Atkinson, A.B. and Stiglitz, J.E. (1969), A new view of technological change, *Economic Journal* 79, 573-578.

Atkinson, A.B. (2007), "Distribution and growth in Europe – the empirical picture: a long-run view of the distribution of income", in Eu 2007 Conference.

Atkinson Robert D., Kenan Patrick Jarboe (1998), *The Case for Technology in the Knowledge Economy: R&D, Economic Growth, and the Role of Government*, Washington, DC: Progressive Policy Institute.

Atrostic, B.K., J. Gates, and Ron Jarmin (2000a), "Measuring the *Electronic Economy: Current Status and Next Steps*," U. S. Census Bureau.

Atrostic, B.K., A. Colecchia, and B. Pattinson (2000b), "Defining and Measuring *Electronic Commerce:* A Discussion Paper," *Paper presented to the Working Group on Statistics on the Information Society, Eurostat*, January.

Auerbach, A. J. (1979), "Wealth Maximization and the Cost of Capital", *Quarterly Journal of Economics*, August, p.p.: 433-66.

_____ . (1983), "Corporation Taxation in the United States", *Brookings Papers on Economic Activity*, Vol. 2, Washington D.C., Brookings Institution, p.p.: 451-513.

_____ . (1991), New Firm Survival and the Technological Regime, *Review of Economics and Statistics*, 73 (03), August, 441-450.

_____ . (1995), *Innovation and Industry Evolution*, Cambridge: MIT Press.

Audretsch, David B., and Maryann P. Feldman, (1996), "R&D Spillovers and the Geography of Innovation and Production. *American Economic Review* 86 (4): 253–73.

——— . (2004), "Knowledge Spillovers and the Geography of Innovation." In *Handbook of Urban and Regional Economics*, vol. 4, ed. J. V. Henderson and J. F. Thisse, 2,713–39. New York: North Holland.

Audretsch, David B. and Roy Thurik (2001), What's New about the New Economy? Sources of Growth in the Managed and Entrepreneurial Economies, *Industrial and Corporate Change*, 10(1), 267-315.

Audretsch, David B. and Roy Thurik (2002), *Linking Entrepreneurship to Growth,* OECD STI Working Paper, 2081/2.

Audretsch, David B. Martin A. Carree, Adriaan J. van Stel and A. Roy Thurik (2002), Impeded Industrial Restructuring: The Growth Penalty, *Kyklos* 55(1), 81-98.

Audretsch, David B., Roy Thurik, Ingrid Verheul and Sander Wennekers (2002), *Entrepreneurship: Determinants and Policy in a European-U.S. Comparison*, Boston: Kluwer Academic Publishers.

Autio, E. (1998), Evaluation of RTD in regional systems of innovation. European Planning Studies, 6(2), 131-140.

Ayyagari, M., and R. Kosova (2006), *Does FDI Facilitate Domestic Entrepreneurship? Evidence from the Czech Republic.* Washington, DC: George Washington University, School of Business.

Backhaus, Jürgen (ed). (1996), *Werner Sombart Social Scientist.* 3 vols., Marburg : Metropolis-Verlag

Bailey, Martha J. (2006), "More Power to the Pill: The Impact of Contraceptive Freedom on Women's Labor Supply." *Quarterly Journal of Economics* 121 (1): 289–320.

Baily, M. N. and A. K. Chakrabarti (1988), *Innovation and the productivity crisis,* Washington, DC: Brooking Institution.

Bankable Frontier Associates (2007), "Financial Service Access and Usage in Southern and East Africa: What Do FINSCOPE™ Surveys Tell Us?"

Bankable Frontier Associates (2007), http://www.bankablefrontier.com Accessed October.

Barker, T., Köhler, J. (1998), *Equity and Ecotax Reform in the EU: Achieving a 10 per cent Reduction in CO2 Emissions Using Excise Duties.* Fiscal Studies 19, 375–402.

Barker, T., Pan, H., Köhler, J., Warren, R., Winne, S. (2006), *Decarbonizing the Global Economy with Induced Technological Change: Scenarios to 2100 using E3MG.* The Energy Journal, Special Issue: Endogenous Technological Change and the Economics of Atmospheric Stabilisation, 241–258.

Barkley Rosser, J. (Ed.) (2003), Complexity in Economics, Cheltenham, Edwar and Elgar.

Barrios, S. and Strobl, E. (2005), "The Dynamics of Regional Inequalities", *Economic Papers of the European Commission,* 229, Brussels.

Barro R.J. (1991), "Economic Growth in a Cross Section of Countries", *Quarterly Journal of Economics,* 106, pp. 407-443.

_____. (1998), "Notes on Growth Accounting", *NBER Working Paper* No. 6654, Cambridge, MA.

Barro, Robert J. and Lee, Jong-Wha (1993), 'International comparisons of educational attainment', *NBER Working Paper 4349,* National Bureau of Economic Research, Cambridge, MA.

Barro, Robert J., and Jong Wha Lee. (2000), "International Data on Educational Attainment: Updates and Implications." Center for International Development Working Paper No. 42, April.

Barro R.J., Sala-i-Martin X. (1992), "Convergence", *Journal of Political Economy,* 100, pp. 223-251.

_____. (1995), *Economic Growth,* McGraw-Hill, New York.

_____. (1997), "Technological diffusion, convergence and growth", *Journal of Economic Growth, vol. 2,* p.p.: 1-26.

Basile, R., Nardis, S. and Girardi, A. (2005), "Regional Inequalities and Cohesion Policies in the European Union", http://www.camecon.com/services/europe/Downloadable%20files/isae%20paper.PDF (2006/01/06).

Bassanini Andrea, Stefano Scarpetta and Ignazio Visco, (2000), *Knowledge, Technology and Economic Growth: Recent Evidence from OECD Countries,* Economics Department Working Papers No: 259, OECD, Paris.

Battese, G.E., and T.J. Coelli, (1988), "Prediction of Firm-Level Technical Efficiencies with a Generalized Frontier Production Function and Panel Data", Journal of Econometrics 38, p.p.: 387-399.

Baumol, W. (1986), "Productivity Growth, Convergence and Welfare." *American Economic Review .vol.* 76, p.p.: 1072–1085.

Baumol, W., Nelson, R. and Wolff, N. (eds.) (1988), *Convergence of Productivity: Cross-National Studies and Historical Evidence*. New York: Oxford University Press.

Behrman, Jere, and Mark Rosenzweig (2004), "Returns to Birthweight." *Review of Economics and Statistics* 86 (2): 586–601.

Belsley, D., E.Kuh, and Welsch, R., (1980), *Regression Diagnostics: Identifying Influential Data and Sources of Collinearity*, John Wiley and Sons, New York.

Benassy J.P. (1998), "Is there Always Too Little Research in Endogenous Growth with Expanding Product Variety?", *European Economic Review*, 42(1), pp. 61-69.

Ben-David, D. (1994), "Convergence Clubs and Diverging Economies", *CEPR*, No. 922, London.

Benhabib J., Jovanovic B. (1991), "Externalities and Growth Accounting", *American Economic Review*, vol. 81, No: 1, p.p.: 82-113.

Benhabib J. and Spiegel M. (1994), "The role of human capital in economic development: evidence from aggregate cross-country data", *Journal of Monetary Economics*, vol. 34, p.p.: 143-73.

Benvignati A.M.: (1982), "*The relationship between the origin and diffusion of industrial innovation*", Economica, vol.49, p: 313-323.

Bergsman, J. and Shen, X. (1997), "Foreign Direct Investment in Developing Countries: Progress and Problems." *Finance and Development vol.* 32(4) p.p.: 6–8.

Bergson (Burk) Abraham (1936), "Real Income, Expenditure proportionality, and Frisch's New Method of Measuring utility", *Review of Economic Studies*, vol. 4:1, October, p.p.: 33-52.

Van Bergeijk P.A.G., van Hagen G.H.A., de Mooij R.A., van Sinderen J. (1997), "Endogenizing Technological Progress: The MESEMET Model", *Economic Modelling*, 14, pp. 341-367.

Berkhout, A. J. (2000), *New Science in a New Society, cyclic interaction between knowledge and innovation*, T U Delft, December 2000.

Bernard and Jones (1996a), "Comparing apples to oranges: productivity convergence and measurement across industries and countries", American Economic Review, vol. 86, pp.1216-1238.

_____ . (1996b), "Technology and Convergence", *The Economic Journal*, 106, pp. 1037-1044.

_____ . (1996c), "Productivity Across Industries and Countries: Time Series Theory and Evidence", *Review of Economics and Statistics*, vol. 78, p.p.: 135-146.

Berndt Ernst R. (1976), "Reconciling Alternative Estimates of the Elasticity of Substitution", *Review of Economics and Statistics*, vol. 58:1, February, pp: 59-68.

_____ . (1980), "U.S. Productivity Growth by Industry, 1947-1973: Comment" in John W. Kendrick and Beatrice N. Vaccara, editors, New Development in Productivity Measurement and Analysis, Chicago: The University of Chicago Press for the National Bureau of Economics Research, p.p.: 124-136.

_____. (1991), *The practice of Econometrics: classic and contemporary*, Addison-Wesley publishers.

Berndt E.R. and D. W. Jorgenson (1973), *Production structure*, in *U.S. Energy Resources and Economic Growth*, (ed.) Dale W.Jorgenson and Hendrik S. Houthakker, Energy Policy Project, Washington D.C.

Berndt E.R. and L. R. Christensen (1973), "The translog function and the substitution of equipment, structures, and labour in U.S. manufacturing 1929-68", *Journal of Econometrics*, vol.1, pp:81-114.

Berndt E.R. and David O. Wood (1975), "Technology, prices and the derived demand for energy", *Review of Economics and Statistics*, vol.56, No:3, August, p.p.:259-268.

Berndt E.R. and Savin N.E. (1975), "Estimation and hypothesis testing in singular equation systems with autoregressive disturbances", *Econometrica*, vol.43, September/November, pp: 937-957.

Berndt, Ernst, and Mohammed S. Khaled (1979), "Parametric Productivity Measurement and Choice Among Flexible Functional Forms," *Journal of Political Economy*, Vol. 87 p.p.: 1220-45.

Berndt E.R. and Waverman L. (1979), *Empirical analysis of dynamic adjustment models of the demand for energy in U.S. manufacturing industries 1947-1974*, Final Report, Electric Power Research Institute, Palo Alto CA.

Berndt E.R. and Field F. C. (1981), *Modelling and measuring natural resource substitution*, MIT Press, Cambridge, Massachusetts.

Berndt E.R. and Triplett J. (1990), "Productivity and economic growth", chapter 3 pp: 19-119 in Jorgenson D. (ed.) *Fifty years of economic measurement studies in income and wealth*, NBER, pp. 19~119.

Berndt E.R. and Morrison K. (1995), "High-tech capital formation and economic performance in U.S. manufacturing industries: an exploratory analysis", *Journal of Econometrics*, vol.65, p.p.: 9-43.

Bernstein J.I (1989), "The Structure of Canadian Inter-Industry R&D Spillovers and the Rate of Return to R&D", *Journal of Industrial Economics*, 37, pp. 315-28.

Bernstein J.I., Nadiri M.I. (1988), "Interindustry R&D Spillovers, Rates of Return and Production in High-Tech industries", *The American Economic Review*, vol.78, No2, pp. 429-34.

Bernstein J.I., Nadiri M.I. (1991), "Product Demand, Cost of Production, Spillovers, and the Social Rate of Return to R&D", NBER Working Paper, No3625.

Besant-Jones, John (2006), "Reforming Power Markets in Developing Countries: What Have We Learned?" Energy and Mining Sector Board Discussion Paper 19. World Bank,Washington, DC.

Bhalla, A. and A. Fluitman (1985), "Science and technology indicators and socio-economic development", *World Development*, vol.13, no. 2.

Biehl, D, et al (1986), "The contribution of infrastructure to regional development". *Comisión de las Comunidades Europeas*, Luxemburg.

Bienaymé, A. (1986), The Dynamics of Innovation. International, *Journal of Technology Management* vol. 1, p.p.: 133-159.

Binswanger H.P.: (1974), "The measurement of technical change with many factors of production", *American Economic Review*, vol.64, No:6, pp:964-976.

Binswanger H.P., Vernon W.R. (1978), *Induced innovation: technology, institutions and development*, The Johns Hopkins University press.

Bitros G. and Korres G (2002), *Economic Integration: Limits and Prospects*, Macmillan-Palgrave Press, London.

Blaug, Mark (1963), "A Survey of the Theory of Process Innovations", in: Rosenberg (ed.) 1971, pp. 86-113.

Blinder, Alan (2000), "The Internet and the New Economy", *The Internet Policy Institute*, January.

Blomstrom, M., A. Kokko, and M. Zejan (2000), *Foreign Direct Investment: Firm and Host Country Strategies*. London: Macmillan.

Böhringer, C. (1998), *The synthesis of bottom-up and top-down in energy policy modeling.* Energy Economics 20, 233–248.

Böhringer, C., Rutherford, T.F. (2006), *Combining Top-Down and Bottom-Up in Energy Policy Analysis: A Decomposition Approach.* ZEW Discussion Paper 06-007, Centre for European Economic Research, Mannheim.

Boskin, M. J. and L. J. Lau (1992), "Capital, technology and Economic growth", in Rosenberg, Landau and Mowery (eds) *Technology and the wealth of nations* (Stanford, CA: Stanford University press).

Bosworth, B. and Collins, S. M. (2003), The Empirics of Growth: An Update. *Brookings Papers on Economic Activity* 2003, no. 2: 113-206.

Boulding, K. E. (1981), *Evolutionary Economics*. Sage, Beverly Hills.

_____. (1985), *The World as a Total System*, Beverly Hills: Sage Publications.

_____. (1991), "What is evolutionary economics?", *Journal of Evolutionary Economics*, Vol. 1, No. 1.

Bovenberg A.L., de Mooij R. (1997), "Environmental Tax Reform and Endogenous Growth", *Journal of Public Economics*, 63, pp. 207-237.

Bovenberg A.L., Smulders S.A. (1996), "Transitional Impacts of Environmental Policy in an Endogenous Growth Model", *International Economic Review*, 37(4), pp. 861-893.

Braczyk, H.-J., Cooke, P., Heidenreich, M. (Eds.) (1998), *Regional Innovation Systems. The Role of Governances in a Globalised World*, UCL Press, London.

Breschi, S. and Malerba, F. (1997), "Sectoral Innovation Systems-Technological Regimes, Schumpeterian Dynamics and Spatial Boundaries", in Edquist, C. (ed.) (1997) *Systems of Innovation: Technologies, Institutions and Organizations*. Pinter Publishers/Cassel Academic.

Breschi, S., Livoni, F. (2001), "Localised knowledge spillovers vs. innovative milieux: knowledge 'tacitness' reconsidered", *Papers in Regional Science*, vol. 80, p.p.: 255-273.

Briceno-Garmendia, Cecilia, Antonio Estache, and Nemat Shafik, (2004), "Infrastructure Services in Developing Countries: Access, Quality, Costs and Policy Reform." Staff Working Paper 3468. World Bank, Washington, DC.

Brown, D. K., (1991), "Tariffs and Capacity Utilization by Monopolistically Competitive Firms", *Journal of International Economics*, vol. 30, p.p.: 371-381.

Brown L.A.: (1981), *Innovation diffusion: a new perspective*, (eds.), Methuen publishers.

Brown R.S. and Christensen L. R. (1981), "Estimating elasticities of substitution in a model of partial static equilibrium: an application to U.S. agriculture 1947 to 1974" in Berndt and Field (eds.) *Modelling and measuring natural resources substitution*.

Brynjolfsson, E. and L. Hitt, (1995), "Computers as a Factor of Production: The Role of Differences Among Firms," *Economics of Innovation and New Technology*, vol. 3, May, p.p.: 183-199.

Brynjolfsson, E. and S. Yang, (1996), " Information Technology and Productivity: A Review of the Literature", *Advances in Computers*, vol. 43, p.p.: 179-214.

Buckley, P. J. & Casson, M. (1976), The Future of the Multinational Enterprise. London, UK: Holmes & Meier.

Buckley, P. J., Dunning, J. H., & Pearce, R. D. (1977), The Influence of Firm Size, Industry, Nationality, and Degree of Multinationality on the Growth and Profitability of the World's Largest Firms, 1962–1972. Weltwirtschaftliches Archiv (Review of World Economics), 114(2): 243-257.

Buigues, P., and Sapir, A. (1993), Community Industrial Policies, in P. Nicolaides (ed.), *Industrial Policy in the European Community: A Necessary Response to Economic Integration?*, p.p.: 21-37, Dordrecht etc.: Nijhoff.

Bureau of Labor Statistics (1997), *Handbook of Methods: Productivity Measures: Business Sector and Major Subsectors*," Chapter 10, BLS Bulletin 2490, April 1997, pp. 89-102, www. stats.bls.gov/mprhome.htm

Burton-Jones, A. (1999), *Knowledge Capitalism*, Oxford, Oxford University Press.

Bush, V. (1945), Science, the Endless Frontier: A Report to the President, from http://www.nsf.gov/od/lpa/nsf50/vbush1945.htm

Busom, I. (2000), An empirical evaluation of the effects of R&D subsidies. *Economic Innovation and New Technology*, 9, pp. 111-148.

Camagni R. (1985), "Spatial diffusion of pervasive process innovation", *Papers of the Regional Science Association*, vol.58.

Canepa A. and Stoneman, P. (2004), Comparative international diffusion: Patterns Determinants and Policies, *Economics of Innovation and New Technology* 13, 279-298.

Cappelen, A., F. Castellacci, J. Fagerberg and B. Verspagen (2003), The Impact of EU Regional Support on Growth and Convergence in the European Union, in *Journal of Common Market Studies*, 41 (4), 621- 644.

Caracostas, P., Soete, L. (1997), "The Building of Cross-Border Institutions in Europe: Towards a European System of Innovation?" In: Edquist, C. (Ed.): *Systems of Innovation. Technologies, Institutions and Organizations*, Pinter, London, p.p.: 395-419.

Carlsson, B (Ed.) (1995), *Technological Systems and Economic Performance: The Case of Factory Automation*, Kluwer, Dordrecht.

Carlsson, B., & et al. (2002). Innovation Systems: Analytical and Methodological Issues. Research Policy, 31(2), 233-245.

Carlsson, B. and Stankiewicz R. (1995), "On the nature, function and composition of technological systems", in Carlsson, B. (ed.) (1995) *Technological Systems and EconomicPerformance. The Case of Factory Automation*. Kluwer, Dordrecht.

Caselli, Francesco, and Wilbur John Coleman II (2001), "Cross-Country Technology Diffusion: The Case of Computers." *American Economic Review Papers and Proceedings* 91 (2): 328–35.

Castells, M. (1996), *The Rise of the Network Society*, Blackwell, Oxford.

Castro, E.A., Jensen-Butler, C.N. (1991), *Flexibility and the neo classical model in the analysis of regional growth*, Institute of Political Science, University of Aarhus, Denmark.

_____ . (2002), "Demand for information and communication technology based services and regional economic development", *Papers in Regional Science, 2002.*

Caves, Richard E. (1998), "Industrial Organization and New Findings on the Turnover and Mobility of Firms, *Journal of Economic Literature,* Vol. XXXVI (December), pp. 1947-1982.

Caves, R. E. (1974), Multinational Firms, Competition, and Productivity in Host-Country Markets. Economica, 41(162): 176-193.

Caves, R. E. (1996), Multinational Enterprise and Economic Analysis. New York: Cambridge University Press.

Caves D.W. and Christensen L.R. and Diewert W.E. (1982a), "The Economic theory of index numbers and the measurement of input, output and productivity", *Econometrica*, vol. 50, p.p.: 1393-1414.

_____ . (1982b), "Multilateral Comparisons of Output, Input, and Productivity using Superlative Index Numbers", *The Economic Journal*, vol. 92, p.p.: 73-86.

Caves D.W. and Christensen L.R. and Swanson J. A. (1980), "Productivity in U.S. railroads, 1951-1974", *Bell Journal of Economics*, vol.11, No:1, p.p.:166-181.

Caves D.W. and Christensen L.R. and Tretheway M.W. (1984), "Economics of Density versus economics of scale: why truck and local airline costs differ", *Rand Journal of Economics*, vol.15, No: 4, p.p.:471-489.

Cellini, R. (1997), "Growth Empirics: Evidence from a Panel of Annual Data", *Applied Economic Letters*, 4, pp. 347-351.

Cellini, R., M. Cortese and N. Rossi (1999), "Social Catastrophes and Growth", *mimeo*.

Centre for Economic Planning and Research (C.E.P.R.), *The financing of Greek manufacture*", (by Tsoris N.).

_____ . (1985), *Innovation in Greek manufacturing*", (by Skoumai S. and Kazis), Athens.

_____ . (1986a), *Foreign investment in Greece*, (by Georganta Z., Manos K. et), Athens, Greece.

_____ . (1986b), *Licensing and industrial development: the case of Greece*, (by Kazis and Perrakis), Athens, Greece.

Centre for European Policy Studies (CEPS) (2004), Can Europe Deliver Growth ? The Sapir Report and Beyond, by Jacques Pelkmans and Jean-Pierre Casey, Report No:45, Brussels.

Chaloupek, Günther (1995), "Long-term economic perspectives compared : Joseph Schumpeter and Werner Sombart". In *The European Journal of the History of Economic Thought* 2:1(Spring)

Chaloupek, Günther (1996), "Long Term Economic Trends in the Light of Werner Sombart's Concept of 'Spätkapitalismus'". In: Backhaus 1996, Vol.2, pp. 163-178.

Chambers R. G. (1988), *Applied production analysis*, Cambridge University Press, New York.

Chandra, Vandana. ed. (2006), *Technology, Adaptation and Exports: How Some Developing Countries Got It Right.* Washington, DC: World Bank.

Chandra, Vandana, and Shashi Kolavalli (2006), "Technology, Adaptation and Exports: How Some Developing Countries Got It Right." In *Technology, Adaptation and Exports: How Some Developing Countries Got It Right*, ed. Vandana Chandra, 1–48. Washington, DC: World Bank.

Chen E (1983), "The diffusion of technology", chapter 4 in *Multinational corporations, technology and employment*, Macmillan press.

Chen, Derek H. C., and Carl J. Dahlman, (2004), "Knowledge and Development: A Cross-Section Approach." Policy Research Working Paper 3366. World Bank, Washington, DC.

Chenery H and Srinivasan (1989), *Handbook of development economics*, vol.2, (chapter 30), Amsterdam, North Holland.

Chenery H., Shishido S. and Wtanabe T. (1962), The pattern of Japanese growth, 1914-1954, *Econometrica* vol.30, No.1, January.

Chenery H. (1986), "Growth and transformation" in Kubo Y, Robinson Sherman & M. Syrquin (ed) *Industrialization and growth: a comparative study*, Oxford University Press.

Chenery H., Lewis J., De Melo J. and Robinson S. (1986), "Alternative routes to development", chapter 11 in Kubo Yuji, Robinson Sherman and Syrquin M. (ed.) *Industrialization and growth: a comparative study*, Oxford University Press.

Chesnais, F. (1988), Technical Co-operation Agreements Between Firms, *STI Review*,
OECD, Paris.

Chesbrough, H. (2003), *Open Innovation*, Harvard Business Press, Cambridge, Massachusetts.

_____ . (2006), *Open Business Models*, Harvard Business Press, Cambridge, Massachusetts.

Chesbrough, H. and D.J. Teece (2002), "Organizing for Innovation: When is Virtual Virtuous?", *Harvard Business Review*.

Chesbrough, H., W. Vanhaverbeke and J. West (2006), *Open Innovation: Researching a New Paradigm*, Oxford University Press.

Chinn, Menzie D., and Hiro Ito. (2006), "What Matters for Financial Development? Capital Controls, Institutions and Interactions." *Journal of Development Economics* 81 (1): 163–92.

Christensen L.R., Jorgenson D.W. and Lau L. J. (1970), "U.S.real product and real factor input 1929-1967", *Review of Income and Wealth, vol. 16*, p.p.:19-50.

Christensen, Laurits R., Dale W. Jorgenson, and Lawrence J. Lau (1971), "Conjugate Duality and the Transcendental Logarithmic Function," *The Review of Economics and Statistics*, vol. 53 p.p.: 255-56.

Christensen, L.R., Jorgenson D.W. and Lau L.J. (1973), Transcendental logarithmic production frontiers, *Review of Economics and Statistics* 55 (1973), pp. 28–45.

Christensen L.R., D. W. Jorgenson and Lau L.J. (1975), "Transcendental logarithmic production frontiers", *Review of Economic Studies*, volume 55, February, pp:28-45.

Christensen L.R. and Greene W. H. (1976), "Economies of scale in U.S. electric power generation", *Journal of Political Economy*, vol.84, No:4, part 1, p.p.:655-676.

Christensen, J.L. and Lundvall, B.-Å. (2004), Product innovation, interactive learning and economic performance, Amsterdam, Elsevier.

Clarke, L., Weyant, J., Edmonds, J. (2006a), *On the sources of technological change: What do the models assume?* Energy Economics.

Clarke, L., Weyant, J., Birky, A. (2006b), *On the sources of technological change: Assessing the evidence.* Energy Economics 28, 579-595.

Clarysse, B., Muldur, U (2001), "Regional cohesion in Europe? An analysis of how EU public RTD support influences the techno-economic regional landscape", in *Research Policy*, Vol. 30, No. 2, p.p.: 275-296.

Cobb C.W. and Douglas P.H. (1928), "A theory of production", *American Economic Review*, Supplement vol.18, No:1, March, p.p.:139-165.

Coe D.T. and Helpman E. (1993), "International R&D spillovers", *NBER Working Paper*, No: 4444, August, Cambridge, MA.

_____. (1995), "International R&D Spillovers", *European Economic Review*, 39(5), pp. 859-887.

Coelli, T., Rao, D. S. P. & Battese, G. (1998), *An Introduction to Efficiency and Productivity Analysis* (Boston, MA, Kluwer).

Coelli, T.J., Rao, D.S.P., O'Donnell, C.J., Battese, G.E. (2005), *An Introduction to Efficiency and Productivity Analysis,* 2nd Edition, Springer.

Cohen, W. M., Levinthal, D. A. (1989), Innovation and Learning: The Two Faces of R&D, *Economic Journal*, vol. 99, p.p.: 569-596.

Comin, Diego, and Bart Hobijn (2004), "Cross-Country Technology Adoption: Making the Theories Face the Facts." *Journal of Monetary Economics* 51(1): 39–83.

Commission of the European Communities, CEC (1980), *The European Community's research policy*, Brussels, Belgium.

_____. (1982), *The current state of European research & development*, Brussels, Belgium.

_____. (1983a), *Towards a European research and science strategy*, Brussels, Belgium.

_____. (1983b), *The Community and small & medium sized enterprises*, Brussels, Belgium.

_____. (1983c), *The Europe, United States and Japan controversy*, Brussels, Belgium.

_____. (1983d), *European Economy No 15-18*, July, Brussels, Belgium.

_____. (1984), *The European Community and new technologies*, Brussels, Belgium.

_____. (1985a), *European Research Policy*, Brussels, Belgium.

_____. (1985b), *The European Community and culture*, Brussels, Belgium.

_____. (1985c), *The European Community research policy*, Brussels, Belgium.

_____. (1985d), *Community R&D policy up to 1984*, Brussels, Belgium.

_____. (1985e), *ERDF in figures*, Brussels, Belgium.

_____. (1985f), *The regional location pattern of new information technology production in the community: national and regional report-Greece*, (by Tsipouri L.), , Brussels, Belgium.

_____. (1986a), *New technologies in Europe*, Brussels, Belgium.

_____. (1986b), *National regional development aid*, Economic and Social Consultative Assembly, Brussels, Belgium.

_____. (1986c), *Incentives for industrial R&D and innovation*, second edition, Brussels, Belgium.

_____. (1986-1987), *Research and Technological development in less favoured regions of the Community*, (STRIDE), final reports, (two volumes), Brussels, Belgium.

_____. (1987a), *The Single European Act*, Brussels, Belgium.

_____. (1987b), *Research and technological development for Europe*, Brussels, Belgium.

_____. (1988a), *Research and technological development policy*, Brussels, Belgium.

_____. (1988b), *Technology in Europe*, 1988-1991, Eurotech, Brussels.

_____. (1988c), *Science, research and the European Community*, Brussels, Belgium.

_____. (1988d), *Science and technology in EEC member states*, Brussels, Belgium.

_____. (1988e), *Science and technological policy, scientific potential policies in EEC member states*, Brussels, Belgium.

_____. (1988f), *Small countries, science and technology and EC cohesion*, FAST programme II (1984-1987), exploratory dossier 14, Brussels, Belgium.

_____. (1988g), *Comparison of scientific and technological policies of Community member states-Greece*, (by Fragakis Ch.), CREST, copol, Brussels, Belgium.

_____. (1989a), *Science and technology for Europe*, JRC, Brussels, Belgium.

_____. (1989b), *Managing technological change: a key element in technology transfer*, Brussels, Belgium.

_____. (1989c), *Statistical analysis of extra-EUR12 trade in high technology products*, Eurostat, Brussels, Belgium.

_____. (1989d), *First survey on state aid in the European Community*, Brussels, Belgium.

_____. (1989e), *Guide to the reform of the Community's structural funds*, Brussels, Belgium.

_____. (1989f), *European economy No 41*, July, Brussels, Belgium.

_____. (1989g), *Science, technology and society in Europe*, FAST II, report, Brussels, Belgium.

_____. (1989h), *European Communities-Financial reports 1986-1990*, different issues, Brussels, Belgium.

_____. (1989i), *The regional impact of Community policies*, European parliament papers, Brussels, Belgium.

_____. (1989j), *Enterprises in the European Community*, Brussels, Belgium.

_____. (1989-1990), *The Community budget in figures*, Brussels, Belgium.

_____. (1990a), *SPRINT-innovation & technology transfer-Fifth annual report 1988*, Brussels, Belgium.

_____. (1990b), *Trends in scientific R&TD in the EEC*, (by A.Quinn), Brussels, Belgium.

_____. (1990c), *Community Support Framework 1989-1993, Greece(objective 1)*, Brussels, Belgium.

_____. (1990d), *An empirical assessment of factor shaping regional competitiveness-the problem regions*, Brussels, Belgium.

_____. (1990e), *The regional impact of Community policies*, European parliament papers, Brussels, Belgium.

_____. (1990 and 1991), *EC research funding*, second & third editions, Brussels, Belgium.

_____. (1991a), *European Community direct investment 1984-1988*, Eurostat, Brussels, Belgium.

_____. (1991b), *Globalisation and the small less advanced Countries: the case of Greece*, FAST, vol.21, (by T.Giannitsis), University of Athens, April, Brussels, Belgium.

_____. (1991c), *A new strategy for social and economic cohesion after 1992*, European parliament papers, Brussels, Belgium.

_____. (1991d), *Government financing of R&D 1980-1990*, Eurostat, Brussels, Belgium.

_____. (1991e), *Guide to Community initiatives 1990*, first edition, Brussels, Belgium.

_____. (1991f), *Second survey on state aid in European Community in the manufacturing and certain other sectors*, Brussels, Belgium.

_____. (1991g), *Annual report of the implementation of the reform of the structural funds-1989*, Brussels, Belgium.

_____. (1991h), *European scenarios on technological change and social and economic cohesion*, FAST, vol.16,(by Cadmos), June, Brussels, Belgium.

_____. (1991i), *Aid element of government R&D contracts*, Brussels, Belgium.

_____. (1991j), *Prospects for anthropocentric production systems in Greece*, FAST/MONITOR, vol.17, (by Papadimitriou Z.), July.

_____. (1991k), *Archipelago Europe-islands of innovations: the case of Greece*", FAST/MONITOR, vol.28,(by Halaris G. Kyrtsoudi M., Nikolaidis E. and Philippopoulos P.), December.

_____. (1991l), *General reports on the activities of European Communities*, 1989, 1990 & 1991", Brussels, Belgium.

_____. (1992a), *Information and communications technologies in Europe 1991*, Brussels, Belgium.

_____. (1992b), *Research after Maastricht: an assessment-a strategy*, Brussels, Belgium.

_____. (1992c), *IMP-Progress report for 1990*, SEC(92)690 Final, Brussels, Belgium.

_____. (1992d), *SPRINT-The European network for technological inter-firm co-operation*, Brussels, Belgium.

_____. (1992e), *A specific programme for R&TD and demonstration in the field of agriculture and agro-industry, a list of financed projects*, Brussels, Belgium.

_____. (1992f), *The Community's Structural Interventions*, Statistical Bulletin No 3, Brussels, Belgium.

_____. (1992g), *Second annual report on the implementation of the reform of the Structural Funds*, Brussels, Belgium.

_____. (1992h), *European economy*, No 25, Chapter 4, Brussels, Belgium.

_____. (1993), *An Integrated Approach to European Innovation and Technology Diffusion Policy - a Maastricht Memorandum*, Brussels/Luxembourg.

_____. (1995), *Small and Medium-Sized Enterprises, a Dynamic Source of Employment, Growth and Competitiveness in the European Union*, report at European Council, December, Brussels/Luxembourg.

_____. (2000), Presidency Conclusions of the Lisbon European Council, March, mimeo: Commission of the European Communities, Brussels.

_____. (2001a), The Regional Dimension of the European Research Area, October, mimeo: Commission of the European Communities, Brussels.

_____. (2001b), The Regions and the New Economy. Guidelines for Innovative Actions Under the ERDF in 2000-2006, January, mimeo: Commission of the European Communities, Brussels.

_____. (2002), The Sixth Framework Programme in Brief, December, mimeo: Commission of the European Communities, Brussels.

Commission of the European Communities, International Monetary Fund, Organisation for Economic Co-operation and Development, United Nations, World Bank (1993), *System of National Accounts -SNA 1993*, Brussels/Luxembourg, New York, Paris, Washington D.C.

Commission on Intellectual Property Rights (2002), Integrating Intellectual Property Rights and Development Policy, London: Department for International Development; Available at: : http://www.iprcommission.org

Commission Staff Working Paper (2000), Report on the Implementation of the Action Plan to Promote Entrepreneurship and Competitiveness Terms of Reference SEC(2000) 1825 Brussels, European Commission.

Cooke, P. (1992), "Regional Innovation Systems: Competitive Regulation in the New Europe", *Geoforum*, Vol. 23, No. 3, p.p.: 365-382.

_____. (1998), Introduction: Origins of the Concept. In: Braczyk, H.-J., Cooke, P., Heidenreich, M. (Eds.): *Regional Innovation Systems. The Role of Governances in a Globalised World*, UCL Press, London, 2-25.

_____. (2001), Regional Innovation Systems, Clusters, and the Knowledge Economy. Industrial and Corporate Change, 10(4), 945-974.

Cooke, P. and K. Morgan (1994), The regional innovation system in Baden-Württemberg, *International Journal of Technology Management*, 9: 394-429.

Cooke, Philip, Uranga, Mikel Gomez and Etxebarria, Goio, (1997) 'Regional innovation systems: Institutional and organizational dimensions', *Research Policy*, Vol. 26 Issue 4/5, p475-91.

Cooke, P., Morgan, K. (1998), *The associational economy: firms, regions, and innovation.* Oxford: Oxford University Press.

Cooke, P., Boekholt, P., Tödtling, F. (2000), *The governance of innovation in Europe.* London: Pinter.

Cooke, P., Clifton, N., Huggins., R (2001), *Competitiveness and the knowledge economy*, ESRC "Social Capital and Economic Performance", Project Research Paper 1, Centre for Advanced Studies, Cardiff University, UK, January.

Cooke, P., & Memedovic, O. (2003), *Strategies for Regional Innovation Systems: Learning Transfer and Applications.* Vienna, Austria: United Nations Industrial Development Organization.

Cooke, P., Heidenreich, M., & Braczyk, H. (2004), Regional Innovation Systems: The Role of Governance in a Globalized World. New York: Routledge.

Cornwell, C., P. Schmidt and R.C. Sickle (1990), "Production Frontiers with Cross-Sectional and Time-Series Variation in Efficiency Levels". - Journal of Econometrics 46, 185-200.

Costello, D. M., (1993), "A Cross-Country, Cross-Industry Comparison of Productivity Growth", *Journal of Political Economy*, vol. 101, p.p.: 207-222.

Costello, A., Watson, F. and Woodward, D. (1994), *Human Face or Human Facade? Adjustment and the Health of Mothers and Children.* London: Institute of Child Health Occasional Paper.

Cowles, M.G. (1994), "Organizing Industrial Coalitions". *Paper presented at the Sussex European Institute Seminar 'Industrial Networks in the EC*, 13-15 October.

Cuadrado, J.R. (1994), "Regional disparities and territorial competition in the EC", en *Moving Frontiers: Economic Restructuring, Regional Development and Emerging Networks*, Eds. J.R. Cuadrado, P. Nijkamp, P. Salva, Hants, UK, p.p.: 3-23.

Czarnitzki, D., Fier, A. (2001), Do R&D Subsidies Matter? - Evidence from the German Service Sector, *ZEW Discussion Paper* No. 01-19. ZEW, Mannheim.

Dahlman, Carl J., Bruce Ross-Larson, and Larry E. Westphal (1987), "Managing Technological Development: Lessons from the Newly Industrialising Countries." *World Development* 15 (6): 759–75.

Dalum, B., Johnson, B. and Lundvall, B.-Å. (1992), "Public Policy in the Learning Society", in Lundvall, B.-Å., ed, *National Systems of Innovation*, Pinter Publishers, London.

Danciu Aniela, Goschin Zizi (2010), "Innovation Assesment in the European Union: National and Regional Approaches", Working Paper, Bucharest Academy of Economic Studies.

Dasgupta, P. and Stiglitz, J.E. (1980a), "Industrial Structure and the Nature of Innovative Activity," *Economic Journal*, vol. 90, June 1980, pp. 266-293.

_____. (1980b), "Uncertainty, Market Structure and the Speed of R&D", *Bell Journal of Economics*, vol. 11(1), Spring.1-28.

_____. (1988), "Potential Competition, Actual Competition and Economic Welfare," *European Economic Review*, vol. 32, May p.p.: 569-577.

Davenport, T. and L. Prusak (1998), *Working Knowledge*, Boston: Harvard Business School Press.

David P.A. (1969), "A contribution to the theory of diffusion", *Research Center in Economic Growth, Stanford University*.

_____. (1975), *Technical choice, innovation and economic growth*, Cambridge University Press, New York and London.

_____. (1985), Clio and the Economics of QWERTY, *American Economic Review* 75, 332-37.

Davidson R and Mackinnon G.J. (1993), *Estimation and inference in Econometrics*, Oxford University Press.

David P.A. and Van de Klundert T. (1965), "Biased efficiency growth and capital-labour substitution in the U.S., 1899-1960", *American Economic Review*.

Davidson R and Mackinnon G.J. (1993), *Estimation and inference in Econometrics*, Oxford University Press.

Davies S. (1979), *The diffusion of process innovations*, Cambridge University Press.

_____. (1979), "Diffusion innovation and market structure" in Sahal D. (eds.) *Research, Development and Technological Innovation*, Lexington, Massachussetts.

De Bresson, C., Amesse, F. (1991), Networks of Innovators: A Review and Introduction to the Issue, *Research Policy, Vol.* 20, p.p.: 363-379.

Debreu, G. (1951), The coefficient of resource utilization, *Econometrica* 19(3), 273 - 292.

Dedrick, J, and K.L. Kraemer, (1999), "Compaq Computer: Information technology in a company in transition," *Working Paper, Center for Research on Information Technology and Organizations*, University of California at Irvine, available at www.crito.uci.edu

Dedrick, J., K.L. Kraemer and T. Tsai (1999), "Acer: An IT company learning to use information technology to compete," *Working Paper, Center for Research on Information Technology and Organizations*, University of California at Irvine, available at www.crito.uci.edu

De Gregorio, J. (1996), "Inflation, Growth and Central Banks: Theory and Evidence", *mimeo*.

De la Fuente (1995), "Catch-up, growth and convergence in the OECD", *CEPR*, Discussion Paper, No. 1274, London.

_____. (1997), "The empirics of growth and convergence", *Journal of Economic Dynamics and Control*, vol. 21, p.p.: 23-77.

De La Fuente, A. and R. Domenech (2000), "Human capital in growth regressions, how much difference does data quality make?", CSIC, Campus de la Universidad Autonome de Barcelona, *mimeo*.

Deming, W. E. (1982), *Out of the Crisis. Cambridge*, MIT Center for Advanced Engineering Study.

_____. (1994), *The New Economics for Industry, Government, Education*, Cambridge: MIT Center for Advanced Engineering.

Denison E. F. (1962), *The sources of economic growth in the United States*, Washington, Committee for Economic Development.

_____. (1967), *Why growth rates differ: post-war experience in nine Western countries*, Washington, D.C. Brookings Institution.

Denny M., and Pinto C. (1978), "An aggregate model with multi-product technologies", in *Production economics: a dual approach to theory and applications* (ed.) Melvyn Fuss and Daniel McFadden, North Holland, Amsterdam.

Denny M., Fuss M., and Waverman L. (1981), "The substitution possibilities for energy: evidence from U.S. and Canadian manufacturing industries", in *Modelling and measuring natural resource substitution*, (ed.) Ernst R. Berndt and Barry C. Field, MIT Press, Cambridge, Massachusetts.

Denny M., and Fuss M. (1983), "A general approach to intertemporal and interspatial productivity comparisons", *Journal of Econometrics*, vol.23, No:3, December, p:315-330.

Department for Trade and Industry (1998a), *Our Competitive Future: Building the Knowledge-Driven Economy*, London: Cm 4176.

Department for Trade and Industry (1998b), *Our Competitive Future: Building the Knowledge-Driven Economy: Analytical Background*, London.

Dicken, P. (1998), *Global Shift: Transforming the World Economy*, Third Edition. The Guilford Press, New York.

Diewert W.E. (1971), An application of the Shepard duality theorem: a generalised linear production function", *Journal of Political Economy*, vol.79, No:3, May/June, pp:482-507.

_____. (1974), Applications of duality theory, in *Frontiers of quantitative economics*, ed. Michael Intriligator and David A. Kendrick, vol.2, Amsterdam, North-Holland.

_____. (1976), "Exact and superlative index numbers", *Journal of Econometrics*, vol.4, p.p.:115-145.

_____. (1982), "Duality approaches to microeconomic theory" in *Handbook of Mathematical Economics* eds. Kenneth J. Arrow and Michael D. Intriligator, vol.2, North Holland.

_____. (1992), "The Measurement of Productivity", *Bulletin of Economic Research*, vol. 44, p.p.: 163-198.

Diewert W.E. and Wales T.J. (1987), "Flexible functional forms and global curvature conditions", *Econometrica*, vol.55, No:1, January, p.p..:43-68.

_____. (1995), "Flexible functional forms and tests of homogeneous separability", *Journal of Econometrics*, vol.67, p.p.:295-302.

Diez, J. R. (2002), Metropolitan innovation systems: A comparison between Barcelona, Stockholm, and Vienna. *International Regional Science Review*, 25(1), 63-85.

Dixit A., Stiglitz J. (1977), "Monopolistic Competition and Optimum Product Diversity", *American Economic Review*, 67, pp. 297-308.

Dixit, A. K. (1996), *The Making of Economic Policy: A Transaction-Cost Politics Perspective*, Cambridge: MIT Press.

Dluhosch, B., (2000), *Industrial Location and Economic Integration*, Cheltenham: Edward Elgar.

Docquier, Frederic, and Abdeslam Marfouk, (2004), "Measuring the International Mobility of Skilled Workers (1990–2000)." Policy Research Working Paper Series 3381. World Bank, Washington, DC. Easterly, William, and Ross Levine. 2001. "It's Not Factor Accumulation: Stylized Facts and Growth Models." *The World Bank Economic Review* 15(2):177–219.

Dollar, D., and Wolff E. N. (1993), *Competitiveness, Convergence, and International Specialization*, MIT Press, Cambridge, MA.

Doloreux, D. (2004), Innovative Networks in Core Manufacturing Firms: Evidence from the Metropolitan area of Ottawa. *European Planning Studies*. 12 (2)..

_____. (2003), Regional innovation systems in the periphery: The case of the Beauce in Québec (Canada). *International Journal of Innovation Management*. 7 (1) : 67-94.

_____. (2002a), What we should know about regional systems of innovation? *Technology in Society: An International Journal*. 24: 243-263.

_____. (2002b), Characterizing the regional innovation systems in Sweden: A tentative typology based on a description of responses to the Community Innovation Survey II. *Nordisk Samhällsgeografisk Tidskrift* 34 (1): 69-92.

Doloreux David and Saeed Parto (2004), "Regional Innovation Systems: A Critical Review", Working Paper.

Dosi Giovanni (1982), "Technological Paradigms and Technological Trajectories: A Suggested Interpretation of the Determinants and Directions of Technical Change", *Research Policy*, VOL. 11, No. 3.

_____. (1984), *Technical change and Industrial Transformation: the theory and the application to the semiconductor industry*, MacMillan Press ltd.

_____. (1988), "Sources, procedures, and microeconomic effects of innovation", *Journal of Economic Literature*, vol. XXVI, September, p.p.: 1120-1171.

_____. (1999), 'Some Notes on National Systems of Innovation and Production and Their Implication for Economic Analysis', in Daniele Archibugi, Jeremy Howells, and Jonathan Michie (eds.), *Innovation Policy in a Global Economy*, Cambridge: Cambridge University Press.

Dosi G., Freeman C., Nelson R., Silverberg G., and Soete L. (1988), *Technical change and economic theory*, Pinter Publishers, London.

Dosi, G. and Orsenigo, L. (1988), "Coordination and transformation: an overview of structures, behaviours and change in evolutionary environments" in Dosi, Freeman, Nelson, Silverberg and Soete (eds.), *Technical Change and Economic Theory*, Pinter Publishers, London & New York.

Dosi G., Pavitt, K. and Soete L. (1990), *The economics of technical change and international trade*, London, Harvester, Wheatsheaf.

Dowrick, S., (1992), "Technological Catch Up and Diverging Incomes: Patterns of Economic Growth 1960-1988", *Economic Journal*, vol. 102, p.p.: 600-610.

Dowrick, S., Nguyen, D.T. (1989), "OECD Comparative Economic Growth 1950-85: Catch-Up and Convergence", *American Economic Review*, vol. 79, p.p.: 1010-1030.

Drakopoulos Stylianos (2002), "A Model for Regional Development and the Learning Economy", Archieve of Economic History, vol. 14, No: 2, Athens.

_____. (2004), "Community Structural Funds and Regional Cohesion in Europe", Archieve of Economic History, Athens.

Dunning, J.H. (1993), Governments and Multinational Enterprises: From Confrontation to Co-operation? in L. Eden, E. H. Potter (ed.), *Multinationals in the Global Political Economy*, p.p.: 59-83. New York: St. Martins Press.

_____. (2000), (ed.) *Regions, Globalisation & the Knowledge-Based Economy*, Oxford, Oxford University Press.

Durlauf S.N. and Quah D.T. (1999), "The new empirics of economic growth", *Centre for economic Performance Discussion Paper*, No. 384, Final version February 1999.

Dutz, Mark A., (ed.) (2007), *Unleashing India's Innovation: Toward Sustainable and Inclusive Growth.* Washington, DC.

Easterly, William, and Ross Levine, (2001), "It's Not Factor Accumulation: Stylized Facts and Growth Models." *The World Bank Economic Review* 15(2):177–219.

Eaton, Jonathan, and Samuel Kortum, (1996), "Trade in Ideas: Patenting and Productivity in the OECD." *Journal of International Economics* 40: 251–78.

_____ . (2001), "Trade in Capital Goods." *European Economic Review* 45 (7): 1195–235.

EBAN (2010), *Early Stage Investing: An asset class in support of the EU strategy for growth and jobs: A recipe for the EU to become one of the world's most-dynamic early - stage investment markets*, White Paper 2010.

EBRD (1999), *Transition Report Update*, April, Luxembourg.

ECLAC (1999), *Foreign Investment in Latin America and the Caribbean*, ECLAC, Santiago.

Edlin, A. and Stiglitz, J.E. (1995), "Discouraging Rivals: Managerial Rent-Seeking and Economic Inefficiencies." *American Economic Review*, vol. 85 No: 5, December, and also NBER Working Paper 4145, 1992.

Edquist, C. (1997a), *Systems of Innovation. Technologies, Institutions and Organizations*, Pinter, London.

Edquist, C. (1997b), Systems of Innovation Approaches - Their Emergence and Characteristics. in: Edquist, C. (Ed.): *Systems of Innovation. Technologies, Institutions and Organizations*, Pinter, London, Washington, 1-35.

Edquist, C. and Johnson, B. (1997), "Institutions and Organizations in Systems of Innovation", in Edquist, C. (ed.) (1997) *Systems of Innovation: Technologies, Institutions and Organizations*. Pinter Publishers/Cassell Academic.

Edquist, C., Hommen, L., McKelvey, M. (2001), *Innovation and employment – process versus product innovation*, Edward Elgar, Cheltenham, UK.

El Elj M. (1997), "Specific R&D, Domestic and Foreign Technological Spillovers and Productivity in Major OECD Countries: Causality Tests and Estimation Based on Heterogenous Panel Data", E3ME-Working Paper no1.2, Work package 4.3, CCIP/ERASME..

Elam, M. (1995), "The National Imagination and Systems of Innovation", Paper prepared for the Systems of Innovation Research Network Meeting, Söderköping, Sweden, September 7-10, 1995.

Englander, S. and A. Gurney (1994), "Medium-term determinants of OECD productivity", *OECD Economic Studies*, No. 22, Spring.

Enos, John, and W. H. Park. (1987), *The Adoption and Diffusion of Imported Technology.* London: Croom Helm.

Enterprise DG (2000), 'Innovation in a knowledge-based economy', *Innovation and Technology Transfer (Special Edition)*, Nov. 2000.

Enterprise DG (2001), Building an Innovative Economy in Europe, European Commission Enterprise DG (2002), "Business Impact Assessment Pilot Project - Final Report: Lessons Learned and The Way Forward", Enterprise Working Paper of March 2002 available from http://europa.eu.int/comm/enterprise/regulation/bia/ppbia_en.htm

Enterprise DG (2002), "Business Impact Assessment Pilot Project - Final Report: Lessons Learned and The Way Forward", Enterprise Working Paper From http://europa.eu.int/comm/enterprise/regulation/bia/ppbia_en.htm

Epstein, G. (1995), "International Profit Rate Equalization and Investment: An Empirical Analysis of Integration, Instability and Enforcement." In Epstein, G. and Gintis, H. (eds.) *Macroeconomic Policy After the Conservative Era: Studies in Investment, Saving and Finance*. Cambridge: Cambridge University Press.

Ergas, H. (1987), "Does technology policy matter?", in B.R.Guile, H.Brooks (eds.), *Technology and global industry. Companies and nations in the world economy*, p.p.: 191-245. Washington, D.C.: National Academy Press.

Erkko Autio (1998), "Evaluation of RTD in Regional Systems of Innovation", *European Planning Studies*, Vol. 6, No. 2, pp. 131-140.

Esben Andersen and Bengt-Åke Lundvall (1988), 'Small National Innovation Systems Facing Technological Revolutions: An Analytical Framework', in Christopher Freeman and Bengt-Åke Lundvall, *Small Countries Facing the Technological Revolution*, London: Pinter Publishers.

Ethier, W., (1982), "National and International Returns to Scale in the Modern Theory of International Trade", *American Economic Review*, vol. 72, p.p.: 389-405.

Etzkowitz, Henry and Loet Leydesdorff (2000), 'The Dynamics of Innovation: From National Systems and 'Mode 2' to a Triple Helix of University-Industry-Government Relations', Introduction to the special 'Triple Helix' issue, *Research Policy*, Vol. 29, No. 2: 109-123.

EU KLEMS Database, March (2007), http://www.euklems.net

European Central Bank (2002b), 'Recent Findings of Monetary Policy Transmission in the Euro Area', *Monthly Bulletin*, October.

European Commission: http://www.innovating-regions.org/download/ritts-ris-brochure.pdf

_____. http://trendchart.cordis.lu/tc_policy_measures_overview.cfm

_____. http://ec.europa.eu/comm/regional_policy

_____. http://ec.europa.eu/regional_policy/atlas2007/fiche/it_en.pdf

_____. http://www.innovating-regions.org/network/whoswho/new_map_search.cfm

_____. http://ec.europa.eu/eu2020/index_en.htm

European Commission (1985), 'Completing the Single Market: White Paper', COM(85) 314.

European Commission (1988a), *The Economics of 1992*, European Economy No. 35, Office for Official Publications of the EC: Luxembourg.

_____. (1998b), *Risk Capital: A Key to Job Creation in the European Union*, SEC(1998) 522.

_____. (1994), *The European Report on Science and Technology Indicators 1994*, Report EUR 15897 EN. Luxembourg.

_____. (1995a), 'Fourth Survey on State Aid in the European Union in the Manufacturing and Certain Other Sectors', in Griffith, R. (2000).

_____. (1995b), *Green Paper on Innovation*, COM (95) 688, December 1995.

_____. (1997a), *Green Paper on the Community patent and Patent System in Europe*, COM (97) 314 final 24 June 1997.

_____. (1997b), *Green Paper on the Community patent and patent system in Europe*, COM (97) 314 final 24 June 1997.

_____. (1999), *Italy's Slow Growth in the 1990s: Facts, Explanations and Prospects*, European Economy–Reports and Studies No. 5, Office for Official Publications of the EC: Luxembourg.

_____. (2000a), *Towards a European research area: Communication from the Commission*, COM(2000)6, European Commission, Luxembourg.

_____. (2000b), *The Regions in the New Economy – Guidelines for Innovative Measures under the ERDF in the Period 2000-06*, Draft Communication from the Commission to the Member States, Brussels 11/07/00.

_____. (2000c), *The Regions in the New Economy*, Fact Sheet, Brussels 14/07/00.

_____. (2000d), *The new programming period 2000-2006: methodological working papers*, Working Paper 3, "Indicators for monitoring and evaluation: an indicative methodology", *DG Regional Policy*, Brussels.

_____. (2000e), *11th annual report on the Structural Funds, 1999*, Brussels, 13.11.2000, COM(2000)698 final.

_____. (2000f), Communication from the commission *Research and technological development activities of the European Union*, Annual Report http://europa.eu.int

_____. (2000g), *11th Annual Report on the Structural Funds*, COM (2000) 698 final.

_____. (2000h), *Towards a European Research Area", Communication from the Commission to the Council, the European Parliament, the Economic and Social Committee and the Committee of the Regions*, COM(2000)6 http://www.europarl.eu.int /

_____. (2000i), *Public Finances in EMU – 2000*, European Economy–Reports and Studies No. 3, Office for Official Publications of the EC: Luxembourg.

_____. (2001a), *Competitiveness Report 2001*, Commission staff working paper, SEC (2001) 1705 - available at: http://europa.eu.int/comm/enterprise/enterprise_policy/competitiveness/doc/competitiveness_report_2001/

_____. (2001b), "Environment 2010: Our future. Our Choice" the sixth Environment Action Plan, *Proposal for a decision of the European Parliament and f the Council*, COM(2001)31 final European Commission (2001c) The Regions and the New Economy, COM (2001) 60-005.

_____. (2001c), "A mobility strategy for the European Research Area", *Communication from the Commission* COM (2001) 331. European Commission, Brussels.

_____. (2001d), *European Competitiveness Report 2001*, European Commission, Brussels.

_____. (2001e), "On implementation of the Risk Capital Action Plan (RCAP)", *Communication from the European Commission* COM (2001) 506. European Commission, Brussels.

_____. (2001f), *Second Report on Economic and Social Cohesion*, European Commission, Brussels.

_____. (2001g), *Unity, Solidarity, Diversity for Europe, its People and its Territory: Second Report on Economic and Social Cohesion*, Office for Official Publications of the European Communities: Luxembourg.

_____. (2001h), *Financial Report 2000*, Office for Official Publications of the European Communities: Luxembourg.

_____. (2001i), 'The Economic Impact of Enlargement', Enlargement Papers No. 4, June.

_____. (2001j), *Compte de gestion et bilan financier afférents aux opérations du budget de l'exercice 2000*, SEC(2001) 528.

_____. (2001k), *Company Taxation in the Internal Market*, Commission Staff Working Paper, SEC(2001) 1681.

_____. (2002a), *Human Capital in a global and knowledge-based economy*, European Commission, Brussels.

_____. (2002b), *Innovation Tomorrow: innovation policy and the regulatory framework: making innovation an integral part of the broader structural agenda*, Louis Lengrand & Associés, Innovation Papers, No: 28, Luxembourg.

_____. (2002c), *Nineteenth Annual Report on Monitoring the Application of Community Law (2001)*, COM(2002) 324 final, June.

_____. (2002d), *The EU Economy 2002 Review*, European Economy No. 6, Office for Official Publications of the EC: Luxembourg.

_____. (2002e), *Strengthening the Coordination of Budgetary Policies*, COM (2002) 668, November.

_____. (2002f), *European Union Public Finance*, Office for Official Publications of the European Communities: Luxembourg.

_____. (2003a), Investing in research: an action plan for Europe, *Communication from the Commission* COM (2003) 226. European Commission, Brussels.

_____. (2003b), "Researchers in the European Research Area: One profession, multiple careers", *Communication from the Commission* COM (2003) 436. European Commission, Brussels.

_____. (2003c), "The role of the universities in the Europe of knowledge", *Communication from the Commission* COM (2003) 58. European Commission, Brussels.

_____. (2003d), *"Employment in Europe"*, European Commission, DG Employment, Brussels.

_____. (2003e), "Choosing to Grow: Knowledge, innovation and jobs in a cohesive society", *Report to the Spring European Council, 21 March 2003 on the Lisbon strategy of Economic, social and environmental renewal* COM (2003) 5. European Commission, Brussels.

_____. (2003f), *Commission's Paper launching an initiative for growth on 9 July* 2003 SEC(2003)813, European Commission, Brussels.

_____. (2003g), *Communication from the Commission: An initiative for growth for the European Union through investment in networks and knowledge. Interim Report to the European Council* (26 September, 2003), European Commission, Brussels.

_____. (2003g), *Choosing to Grow: Knowledge, Innovation and Jobs in a Cohesive Society*, Report to the Spring European Council, 21 March 2003 on the Lisbon Strategy of Economic, Social and Environmental Renewal', COM(2003) 5 final, January.

_____. (2003h), *Commission Staff Working Paper in Support to the Report from the Commission to the Spring European Council in Brussels* (COM(2002) 5 final) ("The Spring Report"): Progress on the Lisbon Strategy', SEC(2003) 25, January.

_____. (2003i), *Second Progress Report on Economic and Social Cohesion*, COM(2003) 34 final.

_____. (2003j), *Public Finances in EMU – 2003*, European Economy, Reports and Studies No 3, Office for Official Publications of the EC: Luxembourg.

_____. (2003k), *Single Market News: 10th Anniversary Special*, Directorate General Internal Market.

_____. (2006a), *Innovating Regions in Europe*, RITTS/RIS Network, Brussels, Belgium.

_____. (2006b), *European Innovation Scoreboard 2006. Comparative Analysis of Innovation Performance*, Brussels, Belgium.

_____. (2007), *Science, Technology and Innovation Key Figures 2003-2004, 2007*, Brussels, Belgium.

_____. (2009a), *Enterprise and Industry European innovation scoreboard 2008 Comparative analysis of innovation performance*, Brussels.

_____. (2009b), European Research Area, 7th Framework Program, Brussels.

_____. (2010), *European innovation scoreboard 2009 Comparative analysis of innovation performance*, Brussels.

Eurostat, New Cronos and COMEXT – databases. http://epp.eurostat.cec.eu.int/pls/portal

European Convention (2003), 'Draft Treaty Establishing a Constitution for Europe', CONV 820/03, submitted by the President of the Convention to the European Council meeting in Thessaloniki on 20 June.

European Commission / DG Research (2003a), *Third European Report on Science and Technology Indicators 2003: Towards a Knowledge-based Economy*. European Commission, Brussels.

_____. (2003b), *"She Figures" Women and Science Statistics and Indicators*. European Commission, Brussels.

_____. (2004), *Key Figures 2003-2004: Towards a European Research Area Science, Technology and Innovation*. European Commission, Brussels.

European Council (2003), *Presidency Conclusions of the Thessaloniki European Council, 19 and 20 June 2003*. European Council, Brussels.

European Science Foundation (2003), "New structures for the support of high-quality research in Europe". *An ESF Position Paper,* April 2003.

European Investment Bank (EIB), *Annual reports*, different issues, Luxembourg.

Eurostat, New Cronos and COMEXT – databases. http://epp.eurostat.cec.eu.int/pls/portal

Eurostat (1991), *R&D and Innovation Statistics: Lena Tsipouri's Paper on the Regional Dimension of R&D and Innovation Statistics*, Brussels, Belgium.

_____. (1991), *R&D and Innovation Statistics: Final Draft Report by Dr. David Charles on the Regional Dimension of R&D and Innovation Statistics*, Brussels, Belgium.

_____. (1995), *European System of Accounts - ESA 1995*, Luxembourg.

_____. (1996), *Regional Statistics of R&D and Innovation*, Brussels, Belgium.

_____. (1996), *Research and Development*, Brussels, Belgium.

_____. (2002a), *Research and development: Annual statistics, data 1990-2000*. Eurostat, Luxembourg.

_____. (2002b), *Science and technology in Europe. Statistical pocketbook, data 1990-2000* (2002). Eurostat, Luxembourg.

Eurostat/OECD (1995), *Manual on the Measurement of Human Resources Devoted to S&T*, Canberra Manual, Paris.

Evangelista (1999), *Knowledge and Investment*. Edward Elgar, Cheltenham.

_____. (2000), Sectoral patterns of technological change in services, *Economic Innovation and New Technology* 9, 183–221.

Evangelista R., Sandven T., Sirilli G. and Smith K. (1998), Measuring innovation in European industry, *International Journal of Economic Business* 5, 311–33.

Evangelista R., Iammarino S., Mastrostefano V. and Silvani A. (2001), Measuring the regional dimension of innovation: lessons from the Italian innovation survey, *Technovation* 21(11), 733–45.

Evangelista, R., & et al. (2002), Looking for Regional Systems of Innovation: Evidence from the Italian Innovation Survey. *Regional Studies, 36*(2), 173-186.

Evans, P. and Karras, G. (1994), "Are government activities productive? Evidence from a panel of U.S. States", *The Review of Economics and Statistics*, vol. 1, p.p.: 1-11.

Fabricant, S. (1954), *Economic progress and economic change* (Princeton, NJ: Princeton University Press).

Fageberg J.(1987), "A technology gap approach to why growth rates differ", in *Research policy*, vol.16, pp.87-99.

_____. (1988), "Why growth rates differ" chapter 20 in Dosi G., Freeman Ch., Nelson R., Soete L. et (ed.) *Technical change and Economic theory*.

_____. (1991), "Innovation, catching-up and growth" in OECD (ed.) *Technology and productivity-the challenge for Economic Policy*, Paris.

_____. (1994), "Technology and international differences in growth rates", *Journal of Economic Literature*, September, volume XXXII, No:3.

_____. (1995), "User-producer interaction, learning and comparative advantage", *Cambridge Journal of Economics*, vol.19, pp:243-256.

_____. (1996), "Technology, Policy Growth - Evidence and Interpretation", *NUPI Working Paper* no 546, March 1996.

Fagerberg J. and Verspagen B. (1996), "Heading for divergence. Regional growth in Europe reconsidered", *Journal of Common Market Studies*, vol. 34, p.p.: 431-48.

Fagerberg, J., Verspagen, B. and Caniëls, M. (1996), "Technology, growth and unemployment across European regions", *NUPI Working Paper*, No. 565, December 1996, Oslo.

Faini, R., Clavijo, F. and Senhadj-Semlali, A. (1989), "The Fallacy of Composition Argument: Does Demand Matter for LDCs' Manufacturers Exports?" Centro Studi Luca d'Agliano/Queen Elizabeth House Development Studies Working Paper No. 7.

Fare, R., Grosskopf, S. Norris, M. and Zhang, Z. (1994) Productivity Growth, Technical Progress, and Efficiency Change in Industrialized Countries. *The American Economic Review*. 84 (1) 66-83.

Fare, R., Grosskopf, S. and Lovell, C. A. K. (1985), *The Measurement of Efficiency of Production*. Boston: Kluwer-Nijhoff, Boston.

Faria, A.P., Fenn, P., and Bruce, A. (2002), Determinants of the adoption of flexible production technologies: Evidence from Portuguese manufacturing industry, *Economics of Innovation and New Technology* 11, 560-580.

Farrell, M. (1957). The Measurement of Productive Efficiency, *Journal of the Royal Statistical Society Series A (General)*, 120 (3), 253-281.

Fink, Carsten, (2005), "Intellectual Property Rights and U.S. and German International Transactions in Manufacturing Industries." In *Intellectual Property Rights and Development: Lessons from Recent Economic Research*, ed. Carsten Fink and Keith Maskus, 75–110. Washington, DC: World Bank.

Fischer, M.M. (1999), The Innovation Process and Network Activities of Manufacturing Firms, in: Fischer, M.M., Suarez-Villa, L. Steiner, M. (Eds.): *Innovation, Networks and Localities*, Springer, Berlin, p.p.: 11-27.

Fischer, M. M., Revilla Diez, J., & Snickars, F. (2001), *Metropolitan innovation systems: Theory and evidence from three metropolitan regions in Europe*. In association with Attila Varga. Advances in Spatial Science. Heidelberg and New York: Springer.

Folster, S. and M. Henrekson (2000), "Growth Effects of Government Expenditure and Taxation in Rich Countries", *Stockholm School of Economics, Working Paper* No. 391, June.

Foray, D. (2000), *The economics of knowledge*, Cambridge Massachussets, The MIT-press.

Foray, D. and Lundvall, B.-Å. (1996), "The Knowledge-based Economy: From the Economcs of Knowledge to the Learning Economy", in *Employment and Growth in the Knowledge-based Economy*, OECD Documents, OECD, Paris.

Ford, R. and P. Poret (1991), "Infrastructure and Private-Sector Productivity", *OECD Economic Studies*, No. 17, pp. 63-89.

Fosfuri, A., M. Motta, and T. Ronde, (2001), "Foreign Direct Investment and Spillovers through Workers' Mobility." *Journal of International Economics* 53: 205–22.

Førsund, F. and L. Hjalmarsson (1974), "On the Measurement of Productive Efficiency". Swedish Journal of Economics 76 (2), 141-154.

_____ . (1987), "Analyses of industrial structure: A Putty-Clay Approach." The Industrial Institute for Economic and Social Research, Almqvist and Wiksell International, Stockholm.

Foster, Lucia, J. Haltiwanger, and C.J. Krizan (1998), "Aggregate Productivity Growth: Lessons from Microeconomic Evidence", *NBER Working Paper* 6803, November.

Freeman C. (1974), *The economics of industrial innovation*, Penguin.

_____ . (1982), *Technological Infrastructure and International Competitiveness*, unpublished paper for the OECD Expert Group on Science, Technology, and Competitiveness.

_____ . (1984), *Long waves in the world economy*, Pinter, London.

_____ . (1987a), *Technology Policy and Economic Performance: Lessons from Japan*, London: Pinter Publishers.

_____ . (1987b), *Innovation,* New Palgrave Dictionary.

_____ . (1990), *The Economics of Innovation*, Elgar, Aldershot.

_____ . (1991), Networks of Innovators: A Synthesis of Research Issues, *Research Policy,* vol.20, p.p.: 499-514.

_____ . (1992a), *Economics of Hope. Essays on Technical Change, Economic Growth and the Environment*, Pinter Publishers, London.

_____ . (1992b), "Technology, progress and the quality of life" in *The Economics of Hope. Essays on Technical Change, Economic Growth and the Environment*, London and New York: Pinter Publishers.

_____ . (1994), "The economics of technical change: a critical survey, *Cambridge Journal of Economics*, vol.18, p.p.: 463-514.

_____ . (1995), "The national system of innovations in historical perspective", *Cambridge Journal of Economics*, vol.19, no: 1, p.p.: 5-24.

Freenan C. and Soete L. (1987), *Technical Change and Full Employment*. Blackwell, Oxford.

Freeman, Christopher and Bengt-Åke Lundvall (eds.) (1988a), *Small Countries Facing the Technological Revolution*, London: Pinter Publishers.

Freeman, C. and Perez, C. (1988b), "Structural Crises of Adjustment, Business Cycles and Investment Behaviour" in Dosi et al (eds), *Technical Change and Economic Theory,* London: Pinter Publishers.

Freeman C. and Soete L. (1990), *New explorations in the economics of technical change*, Pinter, London.

Freeman C. and Foray D: (1993), *Technology and the wealth of nations*, Pinter, London.

Fried, H.O., C.A.K. Lovell, S.S. Schmidt (2008), Efficiency and Productivity, in: H. Fried, C.A.K. Lovell, S. Schmidt (eds) *The Measurement of Productive Efficiency and Productivity Change,* New York, Oxford University Press, 3-91.

_____ . (eds.) (1993), *The Measurement of Productive Efficiency: Techniques and Applications.* New York: Oxford Univ. Press.

Friedman, Thomas. (2007), "If IT Merged with ET." *International Herald Tribune,* October 31.

Frisch R.: (1935), "The principle of substitution: an example of its application in the chocolate industry", *Nordisk Tidsskrift for Teknisk Okonomi,* vol.1, No:1, p.p.:12-27.

Fuss M., McFadden D., and Mundlak Y. (1978), "A survey of functional forms in the economic analysis of production", chapter II in Fuss M. A., McFadden D. et al. (eds.) *Production economics: a dual approach to theory and applications,* North Holland, Amsterdam.

Fu Xiaolan (2007), "Foreign Direct Investment, Absorptive Capacity and Regional Innovation Capabilities: Evidence from China", OECD, Global Forum on International Investment, (International Investment and Innovation), Paris.

Galbraith, John K. (1956), *American Capitalism: The Concept of Coutervailing Power,* revised edition, Boston, MA: Houghton Mifflin.

Gallant A. Ronald (1987), *Nonlinear Statistical Models,* New York, John Willey and Sons.

Garcia Perez Francisco, Byungchae Jin, and Robert Salomon (2010), "Does Inward Foreign Direct Investment Increase the Innovative Productivity of Local Firms?", Working Papers.

Gellman Research Associates, (1976), *Indicators of International Trends in Technological Innovation,* prepared for the National Science Foundation.

Geroski, P. (2001), Models of technology diffusion, *Research Policy* 29, 603-625.

Gertler, M., Wolfe, D., & Garkut, D. (1998), The dynamics of regional innovation in Ontario. In J. de la Mothe & G. Paquet (Eds.), *Local and Regional Systems of Innovation* (pp. 211-238). New York: Springer-Verlag.

Gertler, M., Wolfe, D., Garkut, (2000), No place like home? The embeddedness of innovation in a regional economy. *Review of international Political Economy,* 7 (4): 688-718.

GGDC University of Groningen: Groningen Growth and Development Centre, 60-Industry Database, http://www.ggdc.net

Giannitsis, T. (1991), "Licensing in a newly industrializing country:the case of Greek manufacturing", *World Development,* vol.19, No.4.

Giorno Claude, Pete Richardson and Wim Suyker (1995), *Technical Progress, Factor Productivity and Macroeconomic Performance in the Medium-Term,* OECD Economics Department, Working Papers, No: 157, Paris.

Gilbert, R. J. and Newbery, D.M.G. (1982), "Preemptive patenting and the Persistence of Monopoly", *American Economic Review,* vol. 72, p.p.: 514-526.

Gillespie, A., Richardson, R. and Cornford, J. (2001), "Regional development and the new economy", *Paper presented to the European Investment Bank Conference,* Luxembourg, January.

Gittleman M. and Wolf E.N. (1995), "R&D activity and cross-country growth comparisons", *Cambridge Journal of Economics,* vol.19, pp: 189-207.

Glewwe, Paul, Hanan G. Jacoby, and Elizabeth M. King (2001), "Early Childhood Nutrition and Academic Achievement: A Longitudinal Analysis." *Journal of Public Economics* 81 (3:) 345–68.

Godin, B. (2004), "The knowledge-based economy: conceptual framework or buzzword?" *The Journal of Technology Transfer*, vol. 29.

Goel R.(1990), "The substitutability of Capital-Labour and R&D in US manufacturing", *Bulletin of Economic Research* 42-No:3.

Goldman, Melvin, and Henry Ergas, (1997), "Technology Institutions and Policies: Their Role in Developing Technological Capability in Industry." Technical Paper 383. World Bank, Washington, DC.

Gollop, Frank M., and Mark J. Roberts (1981), "The Sources of Growth in the U.S. Electric Power Industry," in Cowing, Thomas G., and Rodney E. Stevenson, editors, Productivity Measurement in Regulated Industries, New York: Academic Press, p.p.: 107-143.

Gomulka S. (1971), *Incentive activity, diffusion and the stages of economic growth*, Institute of Economics, Aarhus.

_____ . (1990), *The theory of technological change and economic growth*, Routledge, London.

Görg, Holger, and David Greenaway (2004), "Much Ado about Nothing? Do Domestic Firms Really Benefit from Foreign Direct Investment?" *World Bank Research Observer* 19 (2): 171–97.

Goulder, L.H., Schneider, S. (1999), *Induced technological change and the attractiveness of CO2 abatement policies.* Resource and Energy Economics, 21, 211–253.

Goulder, L.H., Mathai, K. (2000), *Optimal CO2 Abatement in the Presence of Induced Technological Change.* Journal of Environmental Economics and Management 39, 1–38.

Grahl J and Teague P. (1988), "The EUREKA project and the industrial policy of the European Community", *International Review of Applied Economics*.

_____ . (1990), *1992-The big market: the future of European Community*, Lawrence and Wishart publishers.

Greenan, N., and J. Mairesse (1996), "Computers and Productivity in France: Some Evidence", *NBER Working Paper* No. 5836.

Greenwald, B. and Stiglitz, J.E. (1986), "Externalities in Economics with Imperfect Information and Incomplete Markets," *Quarterly Journal of Economics*, May, p.p.: 229-264.

Greenwood, J., Z. Hercowitz and P. Krusell (1997), "Long-Run Implications of Investment-Specific Technological Change", *American Economic Review*, Vol. 87, pp. 342-362.

Greenwood, J. and B. Jovanovic (1999), "Accounting for Growth", in: C. Hulten (ed.), *Studies in Income and Wealth: New Directions in Productivity Analysis*, Chicago: University of Chicago Press for NBER.

Gregersen, B., Johnson, B., Kristensen, A. (1994), "Comparing National Systems of Innovation. The Case of Finland, Denmark and Sweden" in Vuori, S. and Vuorinen, P. (eds.), *Explaining Technical Change in a Small Country*, Heidelberg, Physica-Verlag.

Gregersen, B., Johnson, B. (1997), Learning Economies, Innovation Systems and European Integration, *Regional Studies*, vol. 31, No: 5, p.p.: 479-490.

Grether, J. M. (1999), "Determinants of Technological Diffusion in Mexican Manufacturing: A Plant-Level Analysis." *World Development* 27 (7): 1287–98.

Griliches, Z. (1957), Hybrid corn: An exploration in the economics of technological change, *Econometrica* 25, 501-522.

_____. (1963), "The Source of Measured Productivity Growth: US Agriculture, 1940-1960", *Journal of Political Economy*, Vol. 71, pp. 331-46.

_____. (1973), "Research expenditures and growth accounting" in B. R. Williams (ed.) *Science and technology in economic growth*, New York: John Wiley.

_____. (1979), "Issues in Assessing the Contribution of R&D in Productivity Growth", *Bell Journal of Economics*, vol. 10, pp. 92-116.

_____. (1980), "R&D and the productivity slow down", *American Economic Review*, vol.70, May, No2.

_____. (1987), "Productivity: Measurement Problems", in J. Eatwell, M. Milgate and P. Newman (eds), *The New Palgrave: A Dictionary of Economics*, New York: Stockson Press.

_____. (1988a), *Technology, education and productivity* in Basil Blackwell, Oxford.

_____. (1988b), "Productivity Puzzles and R&D: Another Explanation", *Journal of Economic Perspectives*, 2(4), pp. 9-21.

_____. (1990), Patent Statistics as Economic Indicators - A Survey. *Journal of Economic Literature, 28*(4), 1661-1707.

_____. (1992), "The Search for R&D Spillovers", *Scandinavian Journal of Economics*, 94, p.29-48.

Griliches, Z. and Jorgenson, D.W. (1966), Sources of measured productivity change: capital-input, *American Economic Review*, vol. 56, p.p.: 50-61.

Griliches Zvi and Lichtenberg F. (1984), "*R&D and productivity growt at the industry level: Is there still a relationship ?*", chapter 21, in Griliches Zvi (ed.) "*R&D, patents & productivity*", Harvard University Press.

Grossman G.M., Helpman E. (1989), "Endogenous product cycles", *NBER Working Paper*, No: 2913, Cambridge, MA.

_____. (1991a), "Quality Ladders in the Theory of Growth", *Review of Economic Studies*, 58, p.p. 43-61.

_____. (1991b), *Innovation and Growth in the Global Economy*, MIT Press, Cambridge (USA).

_____. (1994), "Endogenous Innovation in the Theory of Growth", *Journal of Economic Perspectives*, vol. 8, No: 1, p.p.: 23-44.

_____. (2007a), Advertising, in-house R&D, and growth, Oxford Economic Papers.

_____. (2007b), How to promote R&D-based growth? Public education expenditure on scientists and engineers versus R&D-subsidies, Journal of Macroeconomics.

Grossman, H.J. and Lucas, R.F. (1974), "The Macroeconomic Effects of Productive Public Expenditures", *The Manchester School of Economics and Social Studies*, vol. 42, p.p.: 162-170.

Grubel, H.G., and Llyod, P.J. (1975), *Intra-Industry Trade: The Theory and Measurement of International Trade in Differentiated Products.* New York: John Wiley.

Grupp, H., & Mogee, M. E. (2004), Indicators for national science and technology policy: How robust are composite indicators? *Research Policy, 33*(9), 1373-1384.

Guellec, Domininque, and Bruno van Pottelsberge de la Potterie, (2004), "From R&D to Productivity Growth: Do the Institutional Settings and the Source of Funds of R&D Matter?" *Oxford Bulletin of Economics and Statistics* (July): 353–78.

Guerrieri, P., and C. Milana, (1998), "High-Technology Industries and International Competition." In *Trade Growth and Technical Change*, ed. D. Archibugi and J. Michie, 188–207. Cambridge, U.K.: Cambridge University Press.

Günther Chaloupek (2009), *Technological change and economic development in Werner Sombart's concept of economic system*, 13th Annual Conference of the European Society for the History of Economic Thought, Thessaloniki, April 23-26, 2009.

Gunnarsson Jan, Torsten Wallin (2008), "An Evolutionary Approach to Regional Systems of Innovation", Discussion Papers, Department of Economics, University of Copenhagen.

Guy Crauser (2000), "Regional Innovation Policy under the new Structural Funds" in *Innovating Regions in Europe* (RIS-RITTS Network), II Plenary Meeting, Madrid, Director General, DG Regional Policy, European Commission 15 June 2000.

Gwatkin, Davidson R., Shea Rustein, Kiersten Johnson, Eldaw Suliman, Adam Wagstaff, and Agbessi Amouzou. (2000), *Socio-economic Differences in Brazil*. Washington, DC: World Bank. http:// www.worldbank.org/poverty/health/data/index. htm#lcr.

Haddad, M. & Harrison, A. E. (1993), Are There Positive Spillovers from Direct Foreign Investment?: Evidence from Panel Data for Morocco. *Journal of Development Economics*, vol. 42(1): 51-74.

Håkansson, H. (1987), *Industrial Technological Development: A Network Approach.*, Croom Helm, London.

Hall, J. L. (2007), Developing historical 50-state indices of innovation capacity and commercialization capacity. *Economic Development Quarterly, 21*(2), 107-123.

_____ . (2009), Adding Meaning to Measurement Evaluating Trends and Differences in Innovation Capacity among the States. *Economic Development Quarterly, 23*(1), 3-12.

Hall H.P. (1988), "The theory and practice of innovation policy: an overview", *Greek Economic Review*.

Hall, B. and Khan, B. (2003), *Adoption of a new technology*, NBER Working paper No.9730.

Hall R.E. and Jones C.I. (1999), Why do some countries produce so much more output per worker than others?, *Quarterly Journal of Economics*, vol. 114, p.p.: 83-116.

Halter, A.N., H.O. Carter, and J.G. Hocking (1957), "A Note on the Transcendental Production Function," *Journal of Farm Economics*, p.p.: 466-74.

Haltiwanger, John and Ron Jarmin (1999), "A Measuring the Digital Economy", in E. Byrnjolfsson and B. Kahin (eds.) *Understanding the Digital Economy,* MIT Press.

Hanoch, G. (1975), "The elasticity of scale and the shape of average costs", *American Economic Review*, vol.65, pp:492-7.

Hansson, P. and M. Henrenkson (1994), "A new framework for testing the effect of government spending on growth and productivity", *Public Choice* 81, pp. 381-401.

Hanushek, Eric A., and Ludger Woessmann, (2007), "The Role of Education Quality in Economic Growth." Working Paper 4122. World Bank, Washington, DC.

Hariolf Grupp (1995), "Science, high technology and the competitiveness of EU countries", *Cambridge Journal of Economics*.

Harrigan, J. (1995), "Factor Endowments and the International Location of Production: Econometric Evidence for the OECD, 1970-1985", *Journal of International Economics*, vol. 39, p.p.: 123-141.

_____ . (1997a), "Technology, Factor Supplies and International Specialization: Estimating the Neoclassical Model", *The American Economic Review*, vol. 87, p.p.: 475-494.

_____. (1997b), "Cross-Country Comparisons of Industry Total Factor Productivity: Theory and Evidence", *Federal Reserve Bank of New York Research Paper*, No: 9734.

Harrison, G., Rutherford, T., and Tarr, D. (1995), "Quantifying the Uruguay Round." In Martin, W. and Winters, A. (eds.) *The Uruguay Round and the Developing Countries*. Washington, D.C.: World Bank Discussion Paper No. 307.

Haskel, Jonathan E., and Matthew J. Slaughter, (2002), "Does the Sector Bias of Skill-Biased Technical Change Explain Changing Skill Premia?" *European Economic Review* 46: 1757–83.

Haskel, J. E., Pereira, S. C., & Slaughter, M. J. (2007), Does Inward Foreign Direct Investment Boost the Productivity of Domestic Firms? Review of Economics and Statistics, 89(3): 482-496.

Hayami, Y. and Ruttan, V.M. (1970), Agricultural productivity differences among countries, *American Economic Review*, vol. 60, p.p.: 895-911.

Hayami, Y. and Ruttan, V.M. (1985), *Agricultural development: an international perspective*, Baltimore, Johns Hopkins University Press.

Hayek, F.A. von ((1937), 'Economics of knowledge', *Economica*, 4: 33-54.

Heady Earl and John L. Dillon (1961), Agricultural Production Functions, Ames, Iowa: Iowa State University Press.

Hellenic Industrial Development Bank (1991), "*Incentives for investments in Greece-Law 1892/90*".

Helpman, E. (ed.) (1998), *General purpose technologies and economic growth*, MIT Press Cambridge.

Helpman, E., and Krugman P. (1985), *Market Structure and Foreign Trade*, MIT Press, Cambridge, MA.

Herzenberg, S. A., Alic, J. A., Wial, H. (1999), "Toward a Learning Economy", in *Issues in Science and Technology*, Winter 1998-1999, p.p.: 55-62.

Hicks, J. R. (1932), *The Theory of Wages*. Macmillan.

_____. (1935), "A suggestion for simplifying the theory of money", *Econometrica*, vol.2, pp:1-19.

_____. (1946), *Value and capital*, Oxford University Press.

_____. (1963), *The theory of wages*, second edition, (first edition 1932), Macmillan, London.

_____. (1965), *Capital and Growth*, Oxford University Press.

_____. (1994), "Adjusting to Technological Change", *Canadian Journal of Economics*, 27(4), pp. 763-775.

Hirschman, Albert O. (1958), *The Strategy of Economic Development*, Clinton: Yale University Press.

_____. (1981), *Essays in Trespassing: Economics to politics and beyond*, Cambridge: Cambridge University Press.

Hjalmarsson, L. (1973), "Optimal Structural Change and Related Concepts", *Swedish Journal of Economics*, vol. 75 (2), p.p.: 176-192.

Hodbay M: (1989), "The European semiconductor industry: resurgence & rationalisation", *Journal of Common Market Studies*, vol.XXVIII, No 2.

Hoekman, Bernard, Keith E. Maskus, and Kamal Saggi, (2005), "Transfer of Technology to Developing Countries: Unilateral and Multilateral Policy Options." *World Development* 33 (10): 1587–1602.

Hoen, A.R. (1999), *An Input-Output Analysis of European Integration*, Capelle aan de IJssel: Labyrint Publication.

Holbrook, A., and Salazar, M. (2004). Regional Innovation Systems within A Federation: Do national policies affect all regions equally? *Innovation: Management, Policy & Practice*, 6(1), 50-64.

Holmes, Thomas J. and James A. Schmitz, Jr. (1990). "A Theory of Entrepreneurship and its Application to the Study of Business Transfers, *Journal of Political Economy*, 98(4), 265-294.

Hollanders, H., (2006) *European Regional Innovation Scoreboard* (2006 RIS).

Hommen, L. and Doloreux, D. (2004), Bring back labour in: a 'new' point of departure for the regional innovation approach. In Flensburg, P., Hörte, S.A. and Karlsson, K. Knowledge spillovers and knowledge management in industrial clusters and industrial networks. London: Edward Elgar Publisher.

Hooper, P. and Larin, K.A. (1989), "International Comparisons of Labor Costs in Manufacturing", *Review of Income and Wealth Series*, vol. 35, No: 4, December.

Hotelling H. (1932), "Edgeworth's taxation paradox and the nature of demand and supply functions", *Journal of Political Economy*, vol.40, p.p.:577-616.

Hou, Chi-Ming, and San Gee. (1993), "National Systems Supporting Technical Advance in Industry: The Case of Taiwan." In *National Innovation Systems: A Comparative Analysis*, ed. Richard R. Nelson, 384–413. New York: Oxford University Press.

Howitt, Peter, and David Mayer-Foulkes, (2005), "R&D, Implementation, and Stagnation: A Schumpeterian Theory of Convergence Clubs." *Journal of Money, Credit, and Banking* 37 (1).

Hudson, R. (1999), 'The Learning Economy, the Learning Firm and the Learning Region: A Sympathetic Critique of the Limits to Learning', *European Urban and Regional Studies*, vol. 6, No: 1, p.p.: 59-72.

Hughes, A. (2003). 'Knowledge Transfer, Entrepreneurship and Economic Growth: Some Reflections and Implications for Policy in the Netherlands'. University of Cambridge Centre for Business Research Working Paper no.273.

Hughes, A. and Scott, M. (2007), 'Transforming Complementary assets into productivity' *Stern Management Review*.

IEA (2000), *Experience Curves for Energy Technology Policy*. Paris, OECD.

I.M.F. *Various publications for data collection.*

IMF (2000), *Balance of Payments Statistics,* Washington.

IMF/OECD (1999), *Report on the Survey of Implementation of Methodological Standards for Direct Investment,* Washington.

Inditex (2005). Inditex Group: downloads. www.inditex.com/en/downloads/Press_Dossier_05.pdf.

Inditex (2007), *Annual Report.*

Informal Seminar of Industry and Research Ministers (2002), "Fostering Innovation: The European Research and Innovation Area", S'Agaró-Girona, 1-2 February 2002.

Inklaar, O´Mahoney, Timmer Robert Inklaar, Mary O´Mahoney, Marcel Timmer (2003), "ICT and Europe's Productivity Performance, Industry-level Growth Account Comparison with United States, Research Memorandum GD-68. Groningen

Growth and Development Centre, University of Groningen, December 2003, 78 pp. http://www.ggdc.net/pub/online/gd68(online).pdf

Inklaar, R., Timmer, M.P., van Ark, B. (2007), *Mind the Gap! International Comparisons of Productivity in Services and Goods Production.* German Economic Review 8, 281–307.

INNOMETRICS (2009), *Regional Innovation Scoreboard (RIS) 2009*, by Hugo Hollanders – MERIT1, Stefano Tarantola – JRC2, Alexander Loschky – JRC2, December 2009. This report is accompanied by the "Regional Innovation Scoreboard 2009 Methodology report.

Ioannides Y.M. and Caramanis M.C. (1979), "Capital-labour substitution in a developing country: the case of Greece", *European Economic Review*, Vol.12.

Ireland N. and Stoneman P. (1986), *Technological Diffusion, Expectations and Welfare*, Oxford Economic Papers, vol. 38, p.p.: 283-304.

Isaksen, A. (2001), Building Regional Innovation Systems: Is Endogenous Industrial Development Possible in the Global Economy? *Canadian Journal of Regional Science*, 24(1), 101-120.

_____. (2003), Knowledge-intensive industries, clustering, and regional development. The software industry in Norway. *Urban Studies.*

Islam N. (1998), Growth empirics: a panel data approach – A reply, *Quarterly Journal of Economics*, vol. 113, p.p.: 325-9.

_____. (1995), Growth empirics: a panel data approach, *Quarterly Journal of Economics*, vol. 110, p.p.: 1127-70.

Jaffe, Adam B., (1986), "Technological Opportunity and Spillovers of R&D: Evidence from Firms' Patents, Profits and Market Value," *American Economic Review*, 76, 984-1001.

_____. (1989), "Real Effects of Academic Research," *American Economic Review,* 79(5), 957-970.

Jaffe, A., Palmer, K. (1996), *Environmental Regulation and Innovation: A Panel Data Study.* NBER Working Paper 5545, National Bureau of Economic Research, Cambridge, Massachusetts.

Jamas, T. (2007), *Technical Change Theory and Learning Curves: Patterns of Progress in Electricity Generation Technologies.* The Energy Journal 28, 51–71.

Javorcik, Beata Smarzynska (2004), "Does Foreign Direct Investment Increase the Productivity of Domestic Firms? In Search of Spillovers through Backward Linkages." *American Economic Review* 94 (3): 605–27.

_____. (2006), "Technological Leadership and the Choice of Entry Mode by Foreign Investors." In *Global Integration and Technology Transfer*, ed. B. Hoekman and B. Javorcik, 179–206. New York: Palgrave Macmillan.

_____. (2007), "Foreign Direct Investment and International Technology Transfer: What Do We Know? What Would We Like to Know?" Unpublished paper. World Bank, Washington, DC.

Jefferson, T. (1984), *No Patent on Ideas: Letter to Isaac McPherson, August 13, 1813,* in Writings. New York, Library of America: p.p.: 1286-94.

Jefferson, Gary H., Thomas G. Rawski, and Yifan Zhang, (2007), "Productivity Growth and Convergence Across China's Industrial Economy." Draft. Brandeis University, Waltham, Mass.

Johannisson, B. (1991), "University Training for Entrepreneurship: Swedish Approaches", *Entrepreneurship and Regional Development*, vol. 3, p.p.: 67-82.

Johansen L. (1972), *Production Functions*, Amsterdam, North Holland.

Johnson, Björn (1992), 'Institutional learning', in Bengt-Åke Lundvall (ed.), *National Innovation Systems: Towards a Theory of Innovation and Interactive Learning*, London: Pinter Publishers.

_____ . (1997), "Systems of Innovation: Overview and Basic Concepts", In: Edquist, C. (Ed.) *Systems of Innovation, Technologies, Institutions and Organizations*. Pinter, London, p.p.: 36-40.

Johson, B., Kristensen, A., Christensen, J. L., Mulvad, M. and Storgaard, L. (1991), "Modes of usage and diffusion of new technologies and new knowledge - the case of Denmark", FAST programme, Commission of the European Comunities.

Johnson, Björn and Bengt-Åke Lundvall (1992), 'Closing the Institutional Gap?', *Revue D'Economie Industrielle*, No. 59.

Johnson, B. and Gregersen, B. (1995), "Systems of Innovation and Economic Integration", *Journal of Industry Studies*, 2, No. 2, pp. 1-18.

Johnson, D. K. (2002), 'Learning-by-licensing': R&D and technology licensing in Brazilian invention, *Economics of Innovation and New Technology* 11, 163-177.

Johnson, B. and Lundvall B.-Å. (2003), 'National Systems of Innovation and Economic Development', in *Putting Africa First – The Making of African Innovation Systems*, in Muchie, M., Gammeltoft, P. and Lundvall, B.-Å., Aalborg: Aalborg University Press.

Johnson Björn, Charles Edquist, Bengt-Åke Lundvall (2003), *Economic Development and the National System of Innovation Approach*, Chapter 7 in *Handbook of Innovation*, edited by Fagerberg, Mowery and Nelson, to be published by Oxford University Press in 2004, and also with Björn Johnson and Bengt-Åke Lundvall: "National Systems of Innovation and Economic Development", chapter 1 in Putting Africa First – The Making of African Innovation Systems, edited by Muchie, Gammeltoft and Lundvall, to be published 2003 by Aalborg University Press.

Jones C.I. (1995), "Time Series Tests of Endogenous Growth Models", *Quarterly Journal of Economics*, 110, pp. 495-525.

_____ . (1995), "R&D-Based Models of Economic Growth", *Journal of Political Economy*, 103, pp. 759-784.

_____ . (1997), "Convergence Revisited", *Journal of Economic Growth*, 2, p.p.: 131-153.

_____ . (1997), "Population and Ideas: A Theory of Endogenous Growth", NBER Working Paper, no6285.

Jones, Charles I. (1997). *Introduction to Economic Growth*. W.W. Norton

Jones C.I., Williams J.C. (1996), "Too Much of a Good Time? The Economics of Investment in R&D", Standford Unibersity Working Paper, unpublished.

Jorgenson, D.W. (1963), "Capital Theory and Investment Behaviour", *American Economic Review*; Vol. 53, No. 2, May.

_____ . (1966), "The Embodiment Hypothesis", *Journal of Political Economy*; Vol. 74, No. 1, pp. 1-17.

_____ . (1988), "Productivity and Economic Growth," *Mimeo, Washington Meeting of the Conference on Research and Income and Wealth, National Bureau of Economic Research*, Cambridge, Mass.

_____ . (1990), "Productivity and Economic Growth", in: E.R. Berndt and J.E.Triplett, eds., *Fifty Years of Economic Measurement*, University of Chicago Press, Chicago.

Jorgenson, D.W. and Griliches Z. (1967), The explanation of productivity change, *Review of Economic Studies*, vol. 34, p.p. 249-183.

Jorgenson, D. and Jean-Jacques Laffont (1974), "Efficient estimation of non-linear stimultaneous equations with additive disturbances", *Annals of Economic and Social Measurement*, October, p.p.: 615-640.

Jorgenson D.W. and Fraumeni B.M. (1983), "Relative prices and technical change", in *Quantitative Studies on Production and Prices*, Wurzburg-Wien.

Jorgenson D.W., Gollop F.M. and Fraumeni B.M. (1987), "Productivity and U.S. economic growth", Chapter 9, *Growth in Aggregate Output*, Harvard University Press.

Jorgenson, D. W., and Kuroda M., (1990), "Productivity and International Competitiveness in Japan and the United States, 1960-1985", in: C. R. Hulten, ed., *Productivity Growth in Japan and the United States*, University of Chicago Press, Chicago.

Jorgenson, D. W., Kuroda, M. and Nishimizu M. (1987), "Japan-U.S. Industry-Level Productivity Comparisons, 1960-1979", *Journal of the Japanese and International Economies*, vol. 1, p.p.: 1-30.

Jorgenson D.W. and Landau R. (1989), *Technology and capital formation*, MIT Press, Cambridge, Massachusetts.

Jorgenson D.W., and Wilcoxen P.J. (1990), "Environmental Regulation and U.S. Economic Growth", *Rand Journal of Economics*, vol. 21, pp. 314-340.

Jorgenson, D. and K. Stiroh (1995), "Computers and Growth", *Economics of Innovation and New Technology*, vol. 3, May, p.p.: 295-316.

Jorgenson, D.W. and K.J. Stiroh (2000), "Raising the Speed Limit: U.S. Economic Growth in the Information Age", May, *Brookings Papers on Economic Activity*.

Jorgenson, D. W., Hob, M. S., Stiroh, K. J. (2003), Lessons from the US growth resurgence, *Journal of Policy Modeling*, 25: 453–470.

Joskow, P.L., Rose, N.L. (1985), The Effects of Technology Change, Experience, and Environmental Regulation on the Construction Cost of Coal-burning Generating Units. *Rand Journal of Economics* 16(1), 1119–1135.

Jovanovic B. and Lach S. (1993), *Diffusion Lags and Aggregate Fluctuations*, NBER Working Paper N. 4455.

Judge, G.G., W.E. Griffiths, R.C. Hill, and T.C. Lee (1980), *The Theory and Practice of Econometrics* (New York: John Wiley and Sons, 1980).

Kalt J.P.(1978), "Technological change and factor substitution in the United States:1929-1967", *International Economic Review*, vol.19, No:3, October, p:761-773.

Kamien M.I., Schwartz N.L. (1969), "Induced Factor Augmenting Technical Progress from a Microeconomic Viewpoint", *Econometrica*, 37(4), pp. 668-684.

Kamien, Morton I. and Nancy L. Schwartz, (1975), "Market Structure and Innovation: A Survey", *The Journal of Economic Literature,* 13, 1-37.

Kannankutty, Nirmala, and Joan Burrell (2007), "Why Did They Come to the United States? A Profile of Immigrant Scientists and Engineers." *Info Brief*. National Science Foundation: Directorate for Social Behavioural and Economic Sciences.

Kaplinsky R. (1990), *The economies of small: appropriate technology in a changing world*, London, Intermediate technology publications.

Kapur, Devesh, (2001), "Diasporas and Technology Transfer." *Journal of Human Development* 2 (2): 265–86.

Kapur, Devesh, and John McHale, (2005), *Give Us Your Best and Brightest: The Global Hunt for Talent and Its Impact on the Developing*.

Katz, M.L. and Shapiro, C. (1986), Technology adoption in the presence of network externalities, *Journal of Political Economy* 94, 822-841.

Kaufmann, Daniel, Aart Kray, and Massimo Mastruzzi (2007), "Governance Matters: Governance Indicators for 1996–2006." World Bank Policy Research Working Paper No. 4280, World Bank, Washington, DC.

Kaufman, Leslie (1999), "A Big Names Lead in Holiday Internet Sales", *The New York Times* on the Web, Technology, http://www.nytimes.com/library/tech99/12/biztech/articles/02shop.html

Kearns, David and David Nadler (1992), *Prophets in the Dark*, New York: Harper Business.

Keller A. (1990), "Econometrics of technical change: techniques and problems", in Hackl P.(ed.) *Statistical analysis and forecasting of economic structural change*, chapter 23, International Institute for Applied Systems Analysis.

Keller, Wolfgang, (1998), "Are International R&D Spillovers Trade Related? Analyzing Spillovers among Randomly Matched Trade Partners."*European Economic Review* 42: 1469–81.

_____ . (2004), "International Technology Diffusion." *Journal of Economic Literature* 42 (September): 752–82.

Keller, W. and Yeaple, S. R. (2009), Multinational Enterprises, International Trade, and Productivity Growth: Firm-Level Evidence from the United States. Review of Economics and Statistics, 91(4): 821-831.

Kendrick J. W. (1961), *Productivity trends in the United States*, Princeton University press.

_____ . (1984), *International comparisons of productivity and causes of the slowdown*, Cambridge, Mass. Ballinger.

_____ . (1991), 'Total factor productivity - what it does not measure: an overview', in OECD, *Technology and productivity: the challenge for economic growth* pp. 149~57, (Paris: OECD).

_____ . (1992), "The translog production function and variable returns to scale", Review of Economics and Statistics, 74 (3), August 1992, pp. 546-552.

_____ . (1977), "Capital-Labour substitution in a developing country: the case of Greece: Comments and some new results", *European Economic Review*, vol.9, p:379-382.

_____ . (1978), "Specification of the elasticity of substitution function within a cost-minimization CES production function framework", Economic Appliquee XXIX, April 1-28.

_____ . (1978), "Biased efficiency growth and capital-labour substitution in Greek manufacturing", the *Quarterly Review of Economics and Business*, pp:27-37.

_____ . (1979), *Patterns and sources of growth in Greek manufacturing*, Athens, Greece.

Kim H.Y. (1992), "The translog production function and variable returns to scale", *Review of Economics and Statistics*, vol. 74, No: 3, August, p.p.: 546-552.

King, Robert G., and Ross Levine, (1994), "Capital Fundamentalism, Economic Development, and Economic Growth." *Carnegie-Rochester Conference Series on Public Policy* 40:259–92.

Kinoshita, Yuko, (2000), "R&D and Technology Spillovers via FDI: Innovation and Absorptive Capacity." William Davidson Institute Working Paper No. 349. Available at SSRN: http://ssrn.com/abstract=258194.

Kirat, T., Lung, Y. (1999), "Innovations and Proximity. Territories as Loci of Collective Learning Processes", *European Urban and Regional Studies, vol.* 6, No: 1, p.p.: 27-38.

Kitsos, C. P. and Hatzikian, J. (2005), *Sequential techniques for innovation Indexes. ISPIM, Porto*, Portugal, May.

Kitsos, C. P., Korres, G. Hatzikian, J. (2005), Innovation Activities in Greec: A Statistical and Empirical Approach. *18th Greek Statistical Meeting*, May, Greece.

Kitsos, C. P., Hadjidema, S. Korres, G. (2005), The Determinant Factors of the Female Entrepreneurship in Greek Enterprises. *18th Greek Statistical Meeting*, Greece.

Kleinknecht, Alfred, (1987), "Measuring R&D in Small Firms: How Much Are We Missing?", *Journal of Industrial Economics*, 36(2), 253-256.

Kleinknecht, Alfred and Bart Verspagen, (1989), "R&D and Market Structure: The Impact of Measurement and Aggregation Problems," *Small Business Economics,* 1(4), 97-302.

Kleinknecht, A., van Montfort, K., & Brouwer, E. (2002), The Non-trivial Choice between Innovation Indicators. *Economics of Innovation and New Technology, 11*(2), 109-121.

Klenow, Peter J., and Andrés Rodriguez-Clare (2004), "Externalities and Growth." Working Papers Series 11009. National Bureau of Economic Research, Cambridge, MA. http://www.nber.org/papers/w11009.

Kline, S. J., & Rosenberg, N. (1986), An Overview of Innovation. In R. Landau & N. Rosenberg (Eds.), *The positive sum strategy: Harnessing technology for economic growth* (pp. 275-305). Washington, D. C.: National Academy Press.

Kmenta, J. (1986), *Elements of Econometrics*, Macmillan, New York.

Kneller, R., M. Bleaney and N. Gemmell (1998), "Growth, public policy and the government budget constraint: evidence from OECD countries", *University of Nottingham, School of Economics*, Discussion Paper No. 98/4.

Knox Lovell, C.A. (1993), Production Frontiers and Productive Efficiency, in *The measurement of productive efficiency : Techniques and applications,* ed. Fried, H.O., Knox Lovell, C.A., Schmidt, S. S., Oxford University Press, 1993.

Kokkelenberg, Edward C. and Sang V. Nguyen (1987), "Forecasting Comparison of Three Flexible Functional Forms," Proceedings of the Business and Economic Statistics Section, *American Statistical Association*, p.p.: 57-64.

_____ . (1989), "Modelling Technical Progress and Total Factor Productivity: A Plant Level Example," *Journal of Productivity Analysis*, p.p.: 21-42.

Kokkinou A. (2010a), A study in theory and models of Data Envelopment Analysis, *The Journal of World Economic Review,* Vol. 5, No. 1, pp. 1-12.

Kokkinou A. (2010b), A note on Theory of Productive Efficiency and Stochastic Frontier Models, *European Research Studies Journal,* Vol. XIII, Issue 4, 2010.

Kokkinou A. (2010c), *Inside to the Productive Efficiency: Theory and Models,* European Asian Economics, Finance, Econometrics and Accounting Science Association Conference, September 2010, China.

Konings, J., (2001), The Effects of Foreign Direct Investment on Domestic Firms: Evidence from Firm-Level Panel Data in Emerging Economies. *Economics of Transition*, 9(3): 619.

Koopmans, T. C. (1951), An analysis of production as efficient combination of activities. in T. C. Koopmans, ed., *Activity Analysis of Production and Allocation*. Cowles Commission for Research in Economics, Monograph 13, Wiley, New York.

Koopmans T. C. and Montias, J. M. (1971), "On the Description and Comparison of Economic Systems" in Eckstein, A. (ed.), *Comparison of Economic Systems*, University of California Press, Berkeley, Los Angeles, London.

Kopp, R.J. (1981), Measuring Technical Efficiency of Production: A comment, *Journal of Economic Theory*, 25, 450-52.

Korres G. M. (1996), *Technical change and Economic Growth: an empirical evidence from European countries*, Avebury-Ashgate, London.

_____ . (1996), "Sources of structural change: an input-output decomposition analysis", *Journal of Applied Economic Letters*, Vol. 3, No: 11, November.

_____ . (1998), "An Overview on Theory of Diffusion Models", *Journal of Science, Technology and Development*, University of Strathclyde-Management School, Vol. 16, No: 1, May.

_____ . (1998), "Productivity and technical change on EEC countries", *Cyprus Journal of Science and Technology*, Vol. 1, No: 4, February

_____ . (1999), "An Implementation of Generalized Production Function to Greek Industry", *Journal Southwestern Economic Review*, Vol. 26, No: 1, Spring, University of Arkansas.

_____ . (2000), "Some insights of Endogenous Technical Change and Economic Growth", *Journal Archives of Economic History*, Special Issue, p.p.: 63-71.

_____ . (2001), "An estimation of technical change and productivity using a translog function for Greek industrial sectors", *Journal Southwestern Economic Review*, Vol. 28, No: 1, p.p.: 55-75, Spring.

_____ . (2002), "Technical Change, Diffusion and Innovation in a Context of a Growth Model", in ed. Paraskevopoulos et. *Globalization and Economic Growth*, University of Toronto and APF/ Press Canada, p.p.: 111-122.

_____ . (2002), "The Institutional development and the Harmonization of technological policy on the European Community", in eds. Bitros G. and Korres G., *Economic Integration: Limits and Prospects*, Macmillan-Palgrave Press.

_____ . (2002), "Technical change and productivity in European member states: an explanation of why growth rates are different", in in eds. Bitros G. and Korres G,. *Economic Integration: Limits and Prospects»*, Macmillan-Palgrave Press.

_____ . (2007), (eds.), *Regionalization, Growth and Economic Integration*, Springer-Physica-Verlag Press, Germany.

────── . (2007), "Industrial and Innovation Policy in Europe: the Effects on Growth and Sustainability", Bulletin of Science, Technology and Society.

Korres G. and Bitros G. (2002), *Economic Integration: Limits and Prospects*, Macmillan-Palgrave Press, London.

Korres G., Chionis D. and Tsamadias C. (2004), "An Inter-Comparison Study of labour Productivity in the European Union and the United States, 1979-2001", *Applied Econometrics and Quantitative Studies, IJAEQS*, Vol. 1-4.

Korres G., and Drakopoulos St. (2002), "Globalization, Foreign Direct Investment (FDI) and International Inequality", Applied Research Review, Vol. 7, No: 1, p.p.:. 201-222.

Korres G., Drakopoulos St. and Polychronopoulos G. (2004), "Regional Cohesion and Innovation Activities: A measurement on the capacity of E.U. States", Review of Economic Science.

Korres G., and Iwsifidis Th. (2002), "The impact of Foreign Direct Investment and Technical Change on Regional Growth", in *CD of the European Regional Science Association (ERSA)*, University of Dortmund – Germany.

_____ . (2003), "Technical Change, Productivity and Economic Growth", in *CD of the European Regional Science Association (ERSA)*, University of Jyvaskyla – Finland.

_____. (2006), "Meta-Production Function: A Review on Theory and Evidence", in the *Journal of Statistical Review*, Vol. 1.

_____. (2007), "A Note for the Role of Foreign Direct Investment, and Technical Change in Regional Growth", in the *Journal Management Sciences and Regional Development*.

_____. (2007), "Foreign Direct Investment, Technical Change and Regional Growth", in the *Journal Management Sciences and Regional Development*.

Korres G., Kitsos Ch. και Chatsidima St., (2005), "Inside to the Knowledge Based Economy: Looking for the Effects of Innovation and the Entrepreneurship Activities on Regional Growth", in the *International Journal of Knowledge, Culture and Change Management*, Vol. 5, Issue 4.

_____. (2006), "Innovation Activities: a Study for the Determinant Factors and the Role of Female Entrepreneurship in Greek Enterprises", in a book of *Sixth Conference Proceedings of the International Statistical Association*.

Korres G., Liargkovas P. και Tsamadias C., (2007), "Regional Disparities and the Effects of Innovation Activities on Regional Integration", in ed. Korres G. *Regionalisation, Growth and Economic Integration*, Springer, Germany.

Korres G., Lionaki I., and Polychronopoulos G., (2003), "The Role of Technical Change and Diffusion in the Schumpeterian Lines", in eds. Jurgen Backhaus *Joseph Alois Schumpeter: Entrepreneurship– Style and Vision*, Kluwer Academic Publishers, p.p.: 293-312.

Korres G. and Paraskevopoulos Y. (1996), "The role and the impact of Community's technological policy to European economic integration", in eds. Paraskevopoulos Chr., Grinspun and Georgakopoulos Th., *Economic Integration and Public Policy in the European Union*, York University in Toronto/Canada, Edwar και Elgar.

Korres G. and Paraskevopoulos Y. and Geraniotakis E. (1997), "European Mediterranean and Technological policy and the effects on growth and employment", in a book of *International Conference Proceedings of the European Association of Labour Economics*, Vol. VI.

Korres G., Patsikas St. και Polychronopoulos G. (2002), "A knowledge based economy, the socio-economy impact and the effects on regional growth", in the *International Journal of Informatica Economica*, No: 1, p.p.: 5-12.

Korres G., and Polychronopoulos G. (2003), "A Review on Theory of Productivity, Technical Change and Growth", in a book of *a Conference Proceedings of the Quantitative Methods in Industry and in Commercial Firms, Technological Educational Institute of Athens*, p.p.: 279-291.

_____. (2003), "Looking at the Framework of Statistical Measurement on Innovation Activities", in a book of *a Conference Proceedings of the Quantitative Methods in Industry and in Commercial Firms, Technological Educational Institute of Athens*, p.p.: 435-450.

_____. (2004), "Some Aspects for the Measurement of the Development Process: The Human Development Index", in a book of *an International Conference Proceedings of Europe and the Regional Inequalities, Technological Educational Institute of Epirus*, p.p.: 58-80.

_____. (2007), "Entrepreneurship and the Role of Information Economy", in *Journal of Archieves of Economic History*.

Korres G., Polychronopoulos G. and Rigas C. (2001), "A Note on the Choice of a Flexible Functional Form", in a book of *Fourteenth Conference Proceedings of the International Statistical Association*, p.p.: 605-612.

Korres G. and Rigas C. (1997), "Technological Substitution Models, Diffusion Policy and Economic Integration in EEC countries", in a book of *International Conference Proceedings of the Maastricht ISINI-Papers*, Vol. II, edited by G. Meijer, W. J. M. Heijman, J.A.C. Van Ophem and B. H. J. Verstegen, p.p.: 321-337.

_____ . (1999), "Reseacrh and Development, Statistical Measurement and the Regional Dimension of Innovation Activities", in a book of *Twelveth Conference Proceedings of the International Statistical Association*.

Korres G., Tsombanoglou G. (2003), "National System of Innovations in E.U., Institutional Harmonization and the effects on Sustainable Development", in a *CD- Proceedings, Defining and Measuring Knowledge, New Economy Statistical Information System (NEsis Project)* Luxemburg.

_____ . (2005), "The Knowledge Based Economy and the European National Policy of Innovation", in the *The Cyprus Journal of Sciences*, Vol. 3.

_____ . (2005), *Technical Change, Social Policy and Development: Innovation Activities and Employability in Europe*, Gutenberg publishers (in Greeks), Athens.

Kouvaritakis, N., Soria, A., Isoard, S. (2000), *Modelling energy technology dynamics: methodology for adaptive expectations models with learning by doing and learning by searching.* International Journal of Global Energy Issues 14, 1–4.

Kraemer, K.L., J. Dedrick and S. Yamashiro (1999), "Refining and extending the business model with information technology: Dell Computer Corporation", *Working Paper, Center for Research on Information* Technology and Organizations, University of California at Irvine, available at www.crito.uci.edu

Krugman P.R. (1979), "A Model of Innovation, Technology Transfer, and the World Distribution of Income", *Journal of Political Economy*, 87, pp. 253-266.

Krugman, Paul, (2000). "Technology, Trade and Factor Prices." *Journal of International Economics* 50: 51–71.

Krieger L, Mytelka and Delapierre M. (1987), "The alliance strategies of European firms in the information technology industry and the role of ESPRIT", *Journal of Common Market Studies*, vol. 25, No 2.

Kubo Y. (1985), "A cross-country comparison of interindustry linkages and the role of imported intermediate inputs", *World Development*, vol.13, December, p.p.: 1287-1298.

Kubo Y. and Robinson S. (1984), *Sources of industrial growth and structural change: a comparative analysis of eight economies*, in UNIDO (ed.) The proceedings of the seventh international conference on input-output techniques.

Kugler, Maurice, (2006). "Spillovers from Foreign Direct Investment: Within or between Industries?" *Journal of Development Economics* 80 (2): 444–77.

Kuhn, Thomas Samuel (1996). *The Structure of Scientific Revolutions*, 3rd edition. University of Chicago Press.

Kui-Yin, Cheung, and Ping Lin, (2007), "Spillover Effects of FDI on Innovation in China: Evidence from the Provincial Data." http://ssrn.com/ abstract=419020. Accessed November 15, 2007.

Kumbhakar, S., A. Heshmati and L. Hjalmarsson (1997), "Temporal Patterns of Technical Efficiency: Results from Competing Models", *International Journal of Industrial Organisation*, vol. 15, p.p.: 597-616.

Kumbhakar, S.C. and C.A.K. Lovell (2000), *Stochastic Frontier Analysis*, Cambridge University Press.

Kuznets, S.S. (1971), *Economic growth of nations*, Cambridge, M.A. Harvard University Press.

_____. (1973), *Population, Capital and Growth: selected essays*, New York, W.W.Norton.

Kuznetsov, Yevgeny, (2006), "Leveraging Diasporas of Talent: Towards a New Policy Agenda." In *DiasporaNetworks and the International Migration of Skills*, ed. Yevgeny Kuznetsov, 221–37. Washington, DC: World Bank Institute.

Lahiri Kajal and Geoffrey H. Moore (1992), *Leading Economic Indicators: New approaches and forecasting records*, Cambridge University Press.

Lai, Edwin L. C. (1998), "International Property Rights Protection and Rate of Product Innovation." *Journal of Development Economics* (February): 133–53.

Lall, S., (1992), 'Technological capabilities and industrialization', *World Development*, 20 (2), pp. 165-186.

_____. (1996), *Learning From the Asian Tigers – Studies in Technology and Industrial Policy*. London: Macmillan.

_____. (2000), "The Technological Structure and Performance of Developing Country Manufacturing Exports, 1985–98." *Oxford Development Studies* 28 (Part 3): 337–69.

_____. (2001), "Competitiveness Indices and Developing Countries: An Economic Evaluation of the Global Competitiveness Report." *World Development* 29 (9): 1501–25.

_____. (2003), "Indicators of the Relative Importance of IPRs in Developing Countries." Issue Paper 3. UNCTAD-ICTSD Project on IPRs and Sustainable Development.

Landau R. (1983), "Government expenditure and economic growth: a cross country study", *Southern Economic Journal*, January, p.p.: 783-792.

Landau D. (1986), "Government expenditure and economic growth in the Less Developed Countries: an empirical study for 1960-1980", *Economic Development and Cultural Change*, vol.35, October, p.p.:35-75.

Landau R. (1989), "Technology and capital formation", chapter 12 in (ed). *Technology and capital formation* by Jorgenson D. and Landau R., MIT press.

Lau L. J. (1978), "A note on the compatibility of a system of difference equations and a time-independent linear equation", *Economic Letters*, vol.1, No:3, pp:243-247.

Lau L.J., Lin W., and Yotopoulos P.A. (1978), "The linear logarithmic expenditure system", *Econometrica*, vol. 46, p:840-868.

Lau L.J. and Yotopoulos P.A. (1989), "The meta-production function approach to technological change in world agriculture", *Journal of Development Economics*, October, vol. 31, pp:241-269.

Lau L.J., Jamison D.T. and Louat F.F. (1990), "Education and productivity in developing countries: an aggregate production function approach", mimeo, *Stanford University*.

Leamer, E. E. (1978), *Specification Searches,* John Wiley and Sons, New York.

Lederman, Daniel, and William F. Maloney, (eds.) (2007), *Natural Resources, Neither Curse nor Destiny.* Palo Alto, CA: Stanford University Press.

Lederman, Daniel, and Laura Saenz, (2005), "Innovation and Development Around the World, 1960–2000." *Policy Research Working Paper* 3774. World Bank, Washington, DC.

Lee, J-W. (1995), "Capital goods imports and long-run growth", *Journal of Development Economics*, 48, pp. 91-110.

Lee, K., M.H. Pesaran and R. Smith (1996), "Growth and convergence in a multi-country empirical stochastic Solow model", *Journal of Applied Econometrics*, 12, pp. 357-392.

Lee, Jeong-Yeon, and Edwin Mansfield, (1996), "Intellectual Property Protection and U.S. Foreign Investment." *Review of Economics and Statistics.* 78 (2): 181–86.

Lee, Y.H. and P. Schmidt (1993), "A Production Frontier Model with Flexible Temporal Variation in Technical Efficiency", in The Measurement of Productive Efficiency Techniques and Applications, eds., Fried H., C.A.K.Lovell, and S.S. Schmidt, Chapter 8, p.p.: 237-255, Oxford Academic Press.

Lee K., Pesaran M.H. and Smith R. (1998), "Growth empirics: a panel data approach – A comment", *Quarterly Journal of Economics*, vol. 113, p.p.: 319-24.

Lehmann, J.P. (1992), *France, Japan, Europe, and industrial competition: the automotive case*, International Affairs, vol. 68, No. 1.

Leibovitz, J. (2003), Institutional Barriers to Associative City-region Governance: The Politics of Institution-building and Economic Governance in 'Canada's Technology Triangle', in: Urban Studies, 40 (13), 2613-2642.

Lengrand, L. (2002), *Innovation Tomorrow* Office for Official Publications of the European Communities, ISBN 92-894-4549-1.

Leontief W. (1953), "*Dynamic analysis*", chapter 3 in *the studies in the structure of the American Economy*, Oxford University Press.

Levin R.C. (1988), "Appropriability, R&D spending and technological performance", *American Economic Review*, vol.78, p.p.: 424-428.

Lequiller F., Ahmad. N., Varjonen S., Cave W. and Ahn K.H. (2003), "Report of the OECD Task Force on Software Measurement in the National Accounts", *Statistics Directorate Working Paper,* 2003/1, OECD, Paris;

Levin, Richard C. and Peter C. Reiss, (1984), "Tests of a Schumpeterian Model of R&D and Market Structure", in Zvi Griliches (ed.), *R&D, Patents, and Productivity*, Chicago, IL: University of Chicago, 175-208.

Levine R. and David Renelt (1990), *Cross-country studies of growth and policy: methodological, conceptual and statistical problems*, World Bank, Washington.

Lichtenberg F., van Pottelsberghe de la Potterie B. (1996), "International R&D Spillovers: A Re-examination", NBER Working Paper No5668.

Link, Albert N. (1987), *Technological Change and Productivity Growth* Chur, Switzerland: Harwood Academic Publisher.

Lipsey, Richard G., and Kenneth Carlaw (1996). A Structuralist View of Innovation Policy, in: Howitt, Peter (ed.), *The Implications of Knowledge-Based Growth for Micro-Economic Policies.* Calgary: University of Calgary Press: 255-333.

Lipsey, Robert E., and Fredrik Sjoholm (2005), "The Impact of Inward FDI on Host Countries: Why Such Different Answers?" In *Does Foreign Investment Promote Development?*, ed. Theodore H. Moran, Edward M. Graham, and Magnus Blomstrom. Washington, DC: Institute for International Economics.

List, Friedrich (1841), Das Nationale System der Politischen Ökonomie, Basel: Kyklos, (translated and published under the title: The National System of Political Economy' by Longmans, Green and Co., London 1841).

López-Bazo, E, Vayá, E. Mora, A. and Suriñach, J. (1999), "Regional Economic Dynamics and Convergence in the European Union", *The Annals of Regional Science*, vol. 22, No: 3, p.p.: 1-28.

Löschel, A. (2002), *Technological change in economic models of environmental policy: a survey.* Ecological Economics 43, 105-126.

Lucas R.E. Jr. (1967), "Tests of a Capital-Theoretic Model of Technological Change", *Review of Economic Studies*, pp. 175-189.

_____. (1969), "Labour-Capital Substitution in U.S. Manufacturing" in Arnold C. Harberger and Martin J. Bailey eds. *The Taxation of Income from Capital*, Washington, D.C.: The Brooking Institution, pp: 223-274.

_____. (1988), "On the Mechanics of Economic Development", *Journal of Monetary Economics*, 22, pp. 3-42.

Lumenga-Neso, A., M. Olarreaga, and M. Schiff (2005), "On 'Indirect' Trade-Related R&D Spillovers and Growth." *European Economic Review* 49 (7): 1785–98.

Lundstrom, Anders and Louis Stevenson (2001), *Entrepreneurship Policy for the Future*, Stockholm: Swedish Foundation for Small Business Research.

Lundvall, B.-Å. (1988), Innovation as an Interactive Process: From User-producer Interaction to the National System of Innovations. In: Dosi, G., Freeman, C., Nelson, R., Silverberg, G., Soete, L. (Eds.) *Technical Change and Economic Theory*, Pinter, London, p.p.: 349-369.

_____. (1992a), "User-Producer Relationships, National Systems of Innovation and Internationalization", in Lundvall, B.Å. (ed.) (1992) *National Systems of Innovation*. Pinter Publishers, London.

_____. (ed.) (1992b), *National Systems of Innovation,* Pinter Publishers, London.

_____. (1992c), *National Systems of innovations: towards a theory of innovation and interactive learning*, Pinter Publishers, London.

Lundvall, B.Å. and Johnson, B. (1994), "The Learning Economy", *Journal of Industry Studies,* Vol. I, No. 2.

Lundvall, Bengt-Åke and Susana Borras (1998), *The Globalising Learning Economy: Implications for Innovation Policy*, DG XII-TSER, Bruxelles: The European Commission.

Lundvall Bengt-Åke, (2005), "Innovation systems, national learning patterns and economic development", Working Paper, Third Globelics Conference Pretoria.

Luther, Martin (1523), "Concerning Secular Authority", in *Readings in Political Philosophy*, ed. F. W. Coker, p.p.: 306-29. New York: Macmillan.

Mackay, R.M., Probert, S.D. (1998), *Likely market-penetration of renewable-energy technologies.* Applied Energy 59, 1–38.

Maddala G.S. (1987), *Limited dependent and quality view variables in Econometrics*, Econometric Society Monographs, Cambridge University Press.

Maddison, Angus (1987), "Growth and Slowdown in Advanced Capitalist Economies," *The Journal of Economic Literature*, vol. 25, p.p.: 649-698.

Mahdjoubi Darius, (1998), "Mapping the Regional Innovation Systems", Working Paper.

Malebra, F. (2002), Sectoral systems of innovation and production, *Research Policy*, 31(2), pp. 247-264.

_____. (2004), *Sectoral systems of innovation: Concepts, issues and analyses of six major sectors in Europe*. Cambridge; New York and Melbourne: Cambridge University Press.

Malecki E. J. (1991), *Technology and economic development: the dynamics of local regional and national change*, (eds.) Longman Scientific and Technical.

_____. (1997), *Technology & Economic Development*, second edition, Longman, Essex.

_____. (1997), *Technology and Economic Development. The Development of Local, Regional and National Competitiveness*, Harlow (UK): Addison Wesley Longman.

Malecki, E.J., Oinas, P. (Eds.) (1999a), *Making Connections: Technological Learning and Regional Economic Change*, Ashgate, Aldershot.

Malecki, E.J., Oinas, P., Ock Park, S. (1999b), On Technology and Development. In: Malecki, E.J., Oinas, P. (Eds.): *Making Connections. Technological Learning and Regional Economic Change. Ashgate*, Aldershot 261-275.

Malmquist, Sten (1953), "Index Numbers and Indifference Surfaces", *Trabajos de Estatistica* 4, pp. 209-242.

Maloney, William (2006), "Missed Opportunities: Innovation and Resource-Based Growth in Latin America." Unpublished report. World Bank, Washington, DC.

Manjon Juan Vicente Garcva (2010), "A Proposal of Indicators and Policy Framework for Innovation Benchmark in Europe", Journal of Technological Management Innovation 2010, Volume 5, Issue 2.

Mankinw N.G., Romer D., Weil D.N. (1992), "A Contribution to the Empirics of Economic Growth", *Quarterly Journal of Economics*, vol. 107, No: 2, p.p.: 407-437.

Mansfield E. (1961), "Technical Change and the Rate of Imitation," *Econometrica*, 29, pp. 741-765.

_____. (1968), *Economics of technological change*, Norton, New York.

_____. (1969), *Industrial research and technological innovation: an econometric analysis*, (eds.), Longman & Green Publishers.

_____. (1977), *The production and application of new industrial technology*, W. W Norton publishers.

_____. (1988), "The speed of cost of industrial innovation in Japan and the United States: external vs. internal technology", *Management Science*, vol. 34, No: 10.

_____. (2003), *Microeconomics Theory and Applications*, 11th edition. W. W. Norton.

Mansfield, E., Romeo, A., Schwartz, M., Teece, D., Wagner, S., Brach, P. (1982), *Technology Transfer, Productivity and Economic Policy*, Norton and Co., New York.

Maskell, P., Malmberg, A. (1999), "The Competitiveness of Firms and Regions. 'Ubiquitification' and the Importance of Localized Learning", *European Urban and Regional Studies*, vol. 6, No: 1, p.p.: 9-25.

Maskell P, Malmberg A (1999), "Localised learning and industrial competitiveness", *Cambridge Journal of Economics, vol.* 23, p.p.: 167-185.

Maskus, K. E., (1991), "Comparing International Trade Data and Product and National Characteristics Data for the Analysis of Trade Models", in: P. Hooper and J. D. Richardson, eds., *International Economic Transactions: Issues in Measurement and Empirical Research*, University of Chicago Press for the NBER, Chicago.

Martin, W., and D. Mitra. (2001), "Productivity Growth and Convergence in Agriculture and Manufacturing." *Economic Development and Cultural Change* 49 (2): 403–23.

Marx, Karl (1867), Das Kapital Volume 1, Marx/Engels Werke, Vol 23, Berlin: Dietz Verlag.

May K.O. (1966), "Quantitative growth of the mathematical literature", *Science* vol.154, p.p.:1672-1673.

McAleavey, P.C. (1994), Who is the operative subject of EC Regional Policy? The cases of Scotland and North Rhine-Westphalia in U. Bullmann (Ed.), *Die Politik der dritten Ebene: Regionen im Europa der Union*, p.p.: 79- 90. Baden-Baden: Nomos.

McKenzie, D. J. (2003), "Measure Inequality with Asset Indicators." Working Paper 042. Cambridge, MA: Harvard University, Center for International Development, Bureau for Research and Economic Analysis of Development.

McDonald, A., Schrattenholzer, L. (2001), *Learning rates for energy technologies.* Energy Policy 29, 255–261.

McFadden Daniel (1978), *"Production Economics: A Dual Approach to Theory and Applications"*, volume 1, Amsterdam: North-Holland.

_____. (1978a), "Cost revenue and profit functions", chapter I.I in Fuss M. and McFadden D. (eds.) *Production economics: a dual approach to theory and applications*, vol. 1, North Holland, Amsterdam, pp:1-109.

_____. (1978b), "The general linear profit function", chapter II.2 in Fuss M. and McFadden D. (eds.) *Production economics: a dual approach to theory and applications*, vol. 1, North Holland, Amsterdam,pp:269-286.

Meeusen, W. and van Den Broeck,. J. (1977), Efficiency estimation from Cobb – Douglas Production Functions with Composed Error. *International Economic Review*, 18, 2: 435 – 444.

Meghnaddesai, Sakikofukuda-Parr, Claes Johansson and Fransiscosagasti (2002), Measuring the Technology Achievement of Nations and theCapacity to Participate in the Network Age, Journal of Human Development, vol.3, No.1, pp. 95-122.

Mendoza, E., G. Milesi-Ferretti and P. Asea (1997), "On the effectiveness of tax policy in altering long-run growth: Harberger's superneutrality conjecture", *Journal of Public Economics*, 66, pp. 99-126.

Mera, K. (1973), "Regional production functions and Social Overhead Capital: An Analysis of the Japanese Case", *Regional and Urban Economics*, vol. 3: p.p.:157-186.

Merton R. (1981), "Fluctuations in the rate of industrial invention", *Quarterly Journal of Economics*, vol.49, p.p.: 454-474.

Meripa (2007*), Indicators and Benchmarking Tools Benchmarking Innovation Performance of Regions*. Emilia-Romagna Region.

Mesenbourg, Thomas L. (2000), *Measuring Electronic Business*, presentation to COPAFS, March 10, http://www.census.gov/econ/www/index.html.

Messner, S. (1997), *Endogenised Technological Learning in an Energy Systems Model.* Journal of Evolutionary Economics 7, 291–313.

Metcalfe, J.S. (1981), Impulse and diffusion in the study of technical change, *Futures* 13, 347-359.

_____. (1987), *Technical Change*, in: the New Palgrave, London New York 1987, Vol. 4, pp. 617-620.

_____. (1990), "The diffusion of innovation: an interpretative survey", in Dosi et al. (eds.) *Technical change and economic theory.*

Metcalfe J.S. and Gibbons M.: (1991) "The diffusion of the new technologies a condition for renewed economic growth", in OECD (eds.) "*Technology and productivity-the challenge for economic policy*", Paris.

_____ . (1996), "The Economic Foundations of Technology Policy: Equilibrium and Evolutionary Perspectives", in Stoneman (ed.) (1996).

_____ . (1997a), *Evolutionary economics and creative destruction*, Routledge, London.

_____ . (1997b), 'Technology systems and technology policy in an evolutionary framework, in Archibugi, D. and Michie, J. (Eds.) Technology, Globalisation and Economic Performance, Cambridge University Press, Cambridge.

Metcalfe, J. Stanley (1995), The Economic Foundations of Technology Policy: Equilibrium and Evolutionary Perspectives, in: Stoneman, Paul (ed.), Handbook of the Economics of Innovation and Technological Change. Oxford and Cambridge, MA, USA: Blackwell.

Metcalfe, J. Stanley, and Luke Georghiou (1997), Equilibrium and Evolutionary Foundations of Technology Policy. CRIC Discussion Paper No. 3, The University of Manchester, Manchester: mimeo.

Middlemas, K. (1994), "Informal Politics: Power without Sovereignty". *Paper presented at the Sussex European Institute Seminar 'Industrial Networks in the EC,* 13-15 October.

Millard, J. (1999), "New Methods of Work: Experience from the Fourth Framework Programme", *Paper given to the Socio-Economic Preparatory Conference for the Fifth Framework Programme*, Paris, 23 February.

Miller, Grant (2005), "Contraception as Development? New Evidence from Family Planning in Colombia." Working Paper 11704. National Bureau of Economic Research, Cambridge, MA.

Miller, S.M. and F.S. Russek (1997), "Fiscal structures and economic growth at the state and local level", *Public Finance Review*, Vol. 25, No. 2.

Ministry of Education and Science (2000), *A summary of Government Bill "Research and Renewal"*, 2000/01:3. Ministry of Education and Science, Stockholm.

Ministry of Education, Culture, Sports, Science and Technology of Japan (2002), *Science and Technology Basic Plan. http://mext.go.jp/english/org/science*

Mitra, Raja M. (2007), "India's Emergence as a Global R&D Center." Working Paper R2007:012, Swedish Institute for Growth Policy Studies, Stockholm.

Mjøset, Lars (2002), *An Essay on the Foundations of Comparative Historical Social Science*, ARENA Working Paper, No. 22, Oslo: ARENA.

Mizen, Paul and Brian Tew (1996), "Proposals to ensure a smooth transition to European Monetary Union by 1999", *The World Economy*, Vol. 19, No. 4, July, p.p.: 387-406.

Mohnen P. (1994), "The Econometric Approach to R&D Externalities", in Cahiers de Recherche du Departement des Sciences Economiques de l'UQAM, No9408.

Molle W. (1990), *The Economics of European Integration: Theory, Practice, Policy*, Dartmouth Publishing Company Ltd, England, p.p.: 417-438.

Monfort Philippe (2009), *Regional Convergence, Growth and Interpersonal Inequalities across EU*, Working Paper, Directorate General Regional Policy European Commission.

Montgomery, M. R., K. Gragnolati, A. Burke, and E. Paredes (2000), "Measuring Living Standards with Proxy Variables." *Demography* 37: 155–74.

Morgan, K. (1997), "The Learning Region: Institutions, Innovation and Regional Renewal", *Regional Studies,* vol. 31, No: 5, p.p.: 491-503.

Morrison C. J. (1987), "Quasi-fixed inputs in U.S. and Japanese manufacturing: a generalized Leontief restricted cost function approach", *The Review of Economics and Statistics*.

Morrison, C. J., (1993), *A Microeconomic Approach to the Measurement of Economic Performance*, Springer-Verlag, New York.

Morrison, Catherine, R., and W. Erwin Diewert (1987), "New Techniques in the Measurement of Multifactor Productivity." Paper presented at the National Bureau of Economic Research Spring Meeting of the Productivity Workshop, March 20.

Mowery, David C. and Joanne E. Oxley (1995), 'Inward Technology Transfer and Competitiveness: the Role of National Innovation Systems', *Cambridge Journal of Economics*, Vol. 19, No. 1.

Myrdal, Gunnar (1968), *Asian Drama, An Inquiry into the Poverty of Nations*, New York: Penguin Books.

Myers, M. B., Rosenbloom, R. S. (1996), Rethinking the Role of Industrial Research. In: Rosenbloom, R. S., Spencer, W. J. (Eds.): *Engines of Innovation: US Industrial Research at the End of an Era*, Harvard Business School Press, Boston, p.p.: 209-228.

Mytelka, L.K. (1993), Strengthening the Relevance of European Science and Technology Programmes to Industrial Competitiveness: The Case of ESPRIT. In M. Humbert (ed.), *The impact of globalization on Europe's firms and industries*, p.p.: 56-63. London: Pinter.

Nadiri, M.I. (1993), "Innovations and Technological Spillovers", *NBER Working Paper* No. 4423.

Nasbeth L. and Ray F.G. (1974), "*The diffusion of new industrial processes: an international study*", (eds.) Cambridge University Press.

National Science Board (1975), *Science Indicators 1974*, Washington, D.C.: Government Printing Office.

National Science Foundation (1986), *National Patterns of Science and Technology Resources 1986*, Washington, D.C.: Government Printing Office.

_____. (2002), *National Science Board, Science and engineering indicators 2002*, vol. 1, National Science Foundation, Arlington, VA.

Naxakis Charis (1996), "The globalization on Products, Markets and Technology", Oikonomika Xronika, No 94.

Nelson, Richaed (1959), "The simple economics of basic economic research", *Journal of Political Economy*, vol. 67, pp. 323-348.

_____. (1964), "Aggregate Production Functions and Medium-Run Growth Projections", *American Economic Review*, Vol. 54, pp. 575-606.

_____. (1973), "Recent Exercises in Growth Accounting: New Understanding or Dead End?", American Economic Review 73, pp. 162-68.

_____. (1981), "Research on productivity growth and productivity differences: Dead ends and new departures", *Journal of Economic Literature*, vol. XIX, September, p.p.: 1209-1064.

_____. (1993), *National innovation systems: a comparative analysis*, Oxford University Press.

_____. (1995), "Recent Evolutionary Theorizing About Economic Change", *Journal of Economic Literature*, vol XXXIII, number 1, March 1995.

Nelson, R.R., and S.G. Winter (1982), *An Evolutionary Theory of Economic Change*, Cambridge, MA: The Belknap Press of Harvard University Press.

Nelson, Richard R., Merton J. Peck, and Edward D. Calacheck (1987), *Technology, Economic Growth, and Public Policy*, Washington, D.C.: Brookings.

Nelson, Richard R. (ed.) (1993), *National Innovation Systems: A Comparative Analysis*, Oxford: Oxford University Press.

Nerlove Marc (1963), "Returns to Scale in Elasticity Supply " in Carl Christ ed. *Measurement in Economics: Studies in Mathematical Economics and Econometrics in Memory of Yehuda Grunfeld*, Stanford, California, Stanford University Press, pp: 167-198.

_____ . (1967), "Recent empirical studies of the CES and Related Production Functions" in Murray brown ed., *The Theory and Empirical Analysis of Production*, Studies in Income and Wealth, vol. 32, New York, Columbia University Press for the National Bureau of Economic Research, pp: 55-122.

NESTA (2009), *The Innovation Index Measuring the UK's investment in innovation and its effects,* Index report: November 2009, United Kingdom.

Nicolaides, P. (1993), "Industrial Policy: The Problem of Reconciling Definitions, Intentions and Effects", in P. Nicolaides (ed.), *Industrial Policy in the European Community: A Necessary Response to Economic Integration?*, p.p.: 1-17. Dordrecht etc.: Nijhoff.

Nicoletti, Giuseppe, Stefano Scarpetta, and Olivier Boylaud (1999), "Summary Indicators of Product Market Regulation with an Extension to Employment Protection Legislation." Economics Department Working Papers 226. Organisation for Economic Co-operation and Development, Paris.

Noisi, J., Saviotti, P., Bellon, B., Crow, M. (1993), "National Systems of Innovation", in *Search of a Workable Concept, Technology in Society*, vol. 15, No: 2, p.p.: 207-227.

Nonaka, I. Takeuchi, H. (1995), *The Knowledge-Creating Company. How Japanese Companies Create the Dynamics of Innovation*, Oxford University Press, New York, Oxford.

Nordhaus, W. (1994), *Managing the Global Commons: The Economics of Climate Change.* The MIT Press, Cambridge, Massachusetts.

_____ . (2002), *Modelling Induced Innovation in Climate Change Policy.* In: Technological Change and the Environment, edited by A. Grubler, N. Nakicenovic and W. Nordhaus, Washington, DC: Resources for the Future Press.

Norworthy J.R. (1984), "Growth accounting and productivity measurement", *Review of Income and Wealth*, vol.30, No: 3, pp:309-329.

_____ . (1990), "Cost function estimation and the additive general error model", *Unpublished working paper*, April, Renssalaer Polytechnic Institute, Department of Economics, Troy.

Norworthy J.R., and Malmquist, D.H. (1983), "Input measurement and productivity growth in Japanese and U.S. manufacturing", *American Economic Review*, vol.73, pp:947-967.

Norworthy J.R., and Jang S.L. (1992), *Empirical measurement and analysis of productivity and technical change: Applications in High technology and service industries*, in series of Tinbergen J., Jorgenson D.W. and Laffont J.J., Contributions to Economic analysis, North Holland publications.

Nourzad, F. and M.D. Vrieze (1995), "Public Capital Formation and Productivity Growth: Some International Evidence", *Journal of Productivity Analysis*, 6, pp. 283-295.

OECD, STAN and National Accounts databases.

OECD (1963), *Proposed Standard Practice for Surveys of Research and Development: The Measurement of Scientific and Technical Activities*, Directorate for Scientific Affairs, DAS/PD/62.47, Organisation for Economic Co-operation and Development, Paris.

_____. (1968a), *Statistical Tables and Notes* ("International Statistical Year for Research and Development: A Study of Resources Devoted to R&D in OECD Member countries in 1963/64"), Vol. 2, Organisation for Economic Co-operation and Development, Paris.

_____. (1968b), *Fundamental research and the universities*, Organisation for Economic Co-operation and Development, Paris.

_____. (1970), *Proposed Standard Practice for Surveys of Research and Experimental Development: The Measurement of Scientific and Technical Activities*, DAS/ SPR/70.40, Directorate for Scientific Affairs, Organisation for Economic Co-operation and Development, Paris.

_____. (1976), *Proposed Standard Practice for Surveys of Research and Experimental Development: "Frascati Manual"*, The Measurement of Scientific and Technical Activities Series, Organisation for Economic Co-operation and Development, Paris.

_____. (1979), *Trends in Industrial R&D in Selected OECD Member Countries 1967-1975*, Organisation for Economic Co-operation and Development, Paris.

_____. (1981a), *Proposed Standard Practice for Surveys of Research and Experimental Development: "Frascati Manual 1980"*, The Measurement of Scientific and Technical Activities Series, Organisation for Economic Co-operation and Development, Paris.

_____. (1981b), *The measurement of scientific and technical activities: Frascati Manual 1980*, Organisation for Economic Co-operation and Development, Paris.

_____. (1981c), *New technologies in the 1990s: a socio-economic strategy*, Organisation for Economic Co-operation and Development, Paris.

_____. (1984), *OECD Science and Technology Indicators: No. 1 – Resources Devoted to R&D*, Organisation for Economic Co-operation and Development, Paris.

_____. (1986), *OECD Science and Technology Indicators: No. 2 – R&D, Invention and Competitiveness*, Organisation for Economic Co-operation and Development, Paris.

_____. (1988), *Industrial revival through technology*, Organisation for Economic Co-operation and Development, Paris.

_____. (1989a), *OECD Science and Technology Indicators, No. 3 – R&D, Production and Diffusion of Technology*, Organisation for Economic Co-operation and Development, Paris.

_____. (1989b), *R&D Statistics and Output Measurement in the Higher Education Sector: "Frascati Manual" Supplement*, The Measurement of Scientific and Technological Activities Series, Organisation for Economic Co-operation and Development, Paris.

_____. (1990), "Proposed Standard Method of Compiling and Interpreting Technology Balance of Payments Data: TBP Manual 1990", *The Measurement of Scientific and Technological Activities Series*, Organisation for Economic Co-operation and Development, Paris.

_____. (1991a), *Industrial policy in OECD countries: annual review 1990*, Organisation for Economic Co-operation and Development, Paris.

_____. (1991b), *Technology and productivity-the challenge for economic growth*, Organisation for Economic Co-operation and Development, Paris.

_____. (1991c), *Economic-Outlook: Historical Statistics, 1960-1990*, Organisation for Economic Co-operation and Development, Paris.

_____. (1991d), *Basic Science and Technology Statistics*, Organisation for Economic Co-operation and Development, Paris.

_____. (1991e), *Choosing priorities in science and technology*, Organisation for Economic Co-operation and Development, Paris.

_____. (1992a), *OECD Proposed Guidelines for Collecting and Interpreting Technological Innovation Data– Oslo Manual*, Organisation for Economic Co-operation and Development, Paris.

_____. (1992b), *TEP-technology in a changing world*, Organisation for Economic Co-operation and Development, Paris.

_____. (1992c), *TEP-technology and economy: the key relationships*, Organisation for Economic Co-operation and Development, Paris.

_____. (1992d), *Science and technology policy: review and outlook 1991*, Organisation for Economic Co-operation and Development, Paris.

_____. (1992e), *The OECD STAN Database for Structural Analysis*, Organisation for Economic Co-operation and Development, Paris.

_____. (1992f), *Oslo Manual: Proposed Guidelines for Collecting and Interpreting Technological Innovation Data*, Organisation for Economic Cooperation and Development.

_____. (1993), *Frascati Manual*, Fifth edition, Organisation for Economic Cooperation and Development.

_____. (1994a), *Proposed Standard Practice for Surveys of Research and Experimental Development*, "Frascati Manual 1993", The Measurement of Scientific and Technological Activities Series, Organisation for Economic Co-operation and Development, Paris.

_____. (1994b), *Using Patent Data as Science and Technology Indicators – Patent Manual 1994: The Measurement of Scientific and Technological Activities*, OCDE/GD(94)114,1994, Organisation for Economic Co-operation and Development, Paris.

_____. (1994c), *National Systems of Innovation: General Conceptual Framework*, DSTI/STP/TIP 94(4). Organisation for Economic Co-operation and Development, Paris.

_____. (1994d), *Canberra Manual. Manual on the Measurement of Human Resources Devoted to S&T*. Organisation for Economic Co-operation and Development, Paris.

_____. (1996a), *The Knowledge Economy*, Organisation for Economic Co-operation and Development Paris.

_____. (1996b), *ISDB 96: International Sectoral Database, 1960-1995*, Organisation for Economic Co-operation and Development Paris.

_____. (1996c), *Oslo Manual*, Second Edition, December Organisation for Economic Co-operation and Development Paris.

_____. (1996c), *Productivity Manual: A Guide to the Measurement of Industry-Level and Aggregate Productivity Growth*, OECD, Paris.

_____. (1997a), *The OECD Report on Regulatory Reform: Synthesis*, Organisation for Economic Co-operation and Development, Paris France.

_____. (1997b), *The Oslo Manual: Proposed Guidelines for Collecting and Interpreting Technological Innovation Data*, Paris OECD, Organisation for Economic Co-operation and Development, France.

_____. (1997c), *Technology and Industry: Scoreboard of Indicators*, Organisation for Economic Co-operation and Development, Paris: OECD.

_____. (1997d), *Manual for Better Training Statistics – Conceptual, Measurement and Survey Issues*. Organisation for Economic Co-operation and Development, Paris.

_____. (1997e), *Revision of the High-technology Sector and Product Classification. STI Working Papers 2/1997*. Organisation for Economic Co-operation and Development, Paris.

_____. (1997f), *Regional Competitiveness and Skills*. Organisation for Economic Co-operation and Development, Paris.

_____. (1997g), *National Innovation Systems*, Organisation for Economic Cooperation and Development, Paris.

_____. (1998), *Technology, Productivity and Job Creation*, Organisation for Economic Cooperation and Development, Paris.

_____. (1999a), *The Response of Higher Education Institutions to Regional Needs*, Organisation for Economic Co-operation and Development, Paris.

_____. (1999b), *Defining And Measuring E-Commerce: A Status Report*, DSTI/ICCP/IIS (99)4/FINAL, Organisation for Economic Co-operation and Development, Paris.

_____. (2000a), *Economic Outlook,* Organisation for Economic Co-operation and Development, Paris.

_____. (2000b), *A New Economy? The Changing Role of Innovation and Information Technology in Growth,* Organisation for Economic Co-operation and Development, Paris.

_____. (2000c), *Basic Science and Technology Statistics*, Organisation for Economic Co-operation and Development, Paris.

_____. (2000d), *Measuring the ICT Sector: Information Society*, Organisation for Economic Co-operation and Development, Paris.

_____. (2000e) "Innovation and the Environment", OECD, Paris (particularly Fukasaku Y. "Innovation and Environmental Sustainability: a background", chapter 2; and Kemp R. "Technology and Environmental Policy: innovation effects on past policies and suggestions for improvements", chapter 3), Organisation for Economic Co-operation and Development, Paris.

_____. (2000f), "Economic Growth: the Role of Policies and Institutions. Panel Data Evidence from OECD Countries" by Andrea Bassanini, Stefano Scarpetta and Philip Hemmings, Economics Department, Working paper, No: 283, Organisation for Economic Co-operation and Development, Paris.

_____. (2001a), *Economics Department Working Paper*, No. 248, (Scarpetta et al). Organisation for Economic Co-operation and Development, Paris.

_____. (2001b), *Towards a knowledge-based economy OECD Science, Technology and Industry Scoreboard 2001-* http://www1.oecd.org/publications/e-book/92-2001-04-1-2987/, Organisation for Economic Co-operation and Development, Paris.

_____. (2001c), *Basic research: statistical issues*. OECD/NESTI Document DSTI/EAS/STP/NESTI(2001)38. Organisation for Economic Co-operation and Development, Paris.

_____. (2001d), *The new economy: beyond the hype.* Final report on the OECD growth project. Meeting of the OECD Council at ministerial level, 2001. Organisation for Economic Co-operation and Development, Paris.

_____. (2001e), *Innovative Networks. Co-operation in National Innovation Systems*, Organisation for Economic Co-operation and Development, Paris.

_____. (2001f), *Science, Technology and Industry Scoreboard. Towards a knowledge-based Economy*, Organisation for Economic Co-operation and Development, Paris.

_____. (2001g), "Special Issue on Fostering High-tech Spin-offs: A Public Strategy for Innovation. STI Science Technology Industry", *Review No. 26*, Organisation for Economic Co-operation and Development, Paris.

_____. (2001h), *Innovative clusters: drivers of national innovation systems*, Organisation for Economic Co-operation and Development, Paris.

_____. (2001i), *Measurement of Aggregate and Industry Level Productivity Growth*, Organisation for Economic Co-operation and Development, Paris.

_____. (2002a), *Frascati Manual. Proposed standards practice for surveys on research and experimental development*. Organisation for Economic Co-operation and Development, Paris.

_____. (2002b), "Special Issue on New Science and Technology Indicators. STI Science Technology Industry. Review No. 27. Organisation for Economic Co-operation and Development, Paris.

_____. (2002c), *Public funding of R&D - trends and changes*. OECD Document DSTI/STP(2002)3/REV1 prepared by the ad hoc working group on «Steering and Funding of Research Institutions», Organisation for Economic Co-operation and Development, Paris.

_____. (2002d), *Research and Development Expenditure in Industry 1987-2000*, Organisation for Economic Co-operation and Development, Paris.

_____. (2002e), *Bibliometric Indicators and Analysis of Research Systems, Methods and Examples*, working paper by Yoshika Okibo, Organisation for Economic Co-operation and Development, Paris.

_____. (2002f), *Manual of Economic Clobalisation Indicators*, Organisation for Economic Co-operation and Development, Paris.

_____. (2002g), *Manual for Better Training Statistics: Conceptual Measurement and Survey Issues*, Organisation for Economic Co-operation and Development, Paris.

_____. (2002h), *Manual: Measuring Productivity*, Organisation for Economic Co-operation and Development, Paris.

_____. (2002i), *Education at a Glance*, Glossary, Organisation for Economic Co-operation and Development, Paris.

_____. (2002j), Frascati Manual, Sixth edition, Organisation for Economic Co-operation and Development, Paris.

_____. (2002k), *Intra-Industry and Intra-Firm and the InterECD Information Technology Outlook*, Organisation for Economic Co-operation and Development, Paris.

_____. (2021),. Intra-industry and Intra-Firm Trade and the Internationalisation of Production. *Economic Outlook,* Organisation for Economic Co-operation and Development, Paris.

_____. (2003a), *Main Science and Technology Indicators*–2003/1, OECD publications, ISSN 1011-792X- no 53122 2003. Organisation for Economic Co-operation and Development, Paris.

_____. (2003b), *Communications Outlook 2003*, Organisation for Economic Co-operation and Development, Paris.

_____. (2004), *OECD Information Technology Outlook,* Organisation for Economic Co-operation and Development, Paris.

OECD/Eurostat (1995), *The Measurement of Human Resources Devoted to Science and Technology – Canberra Manual: The Measurement of Scientific and Technological Activities.* Organisation for Economic Co-operation and Development, Paris.

OECD, & Office, E. C. S. (1997), *Oslo Manual: Proposed Guidelines for Collecting and Interpreting Technological Innovation Data*: OECD/Eurostat.

OECD, & Office, E. C. S. (2005), *Oslo Manual*: OECD/Eurostat.

OECD/Eurostat (1997a), *Proposed Guidelines for Collecting and Interpreting Technological Innovation Data – Oslo Manual*, The Measurement of Scientific and Technical Activities Series. Organisation for Economic Co-operation and Development, Paris.

_____. (1999), *Classifying Educational Programmes, Manual for ISCED-97 Implementation in OECD Countries,* Organisation for Economic Co-operation and Development, Paris.

_____. (2001), *Measuring Expenditure on Health-related R&D*, Organisation for Economic Co-operation and Development, Paris.

_____. (2002), "Measuring the Information Economy", Organisation for Economic Co-operation and Development, Paris.

_____. (Biannual), *Main Science and Technology Indicators*, Organisation for Economic Co-operation and Development, Paris.

_____. (every second year), *Basic Science and Technology Statistics,* Organisation for Economic Co-operation and Development, Paris.

_____. (every second year), *OECD Science, Technology and Industry Scoreboard*, Organisation for Economic Co-operation and Development, Paris.

_____. (every second year), *OECD Science, Technology and Industry Outlook*, Paris.

_____. (every second year), *OECD Information Technology Outlook*, Organisation for Economic Co-operation and Development, Paris.

OECD, STAN and National Accounts databases, Organisation for Economic Co-operation and Development, May 2001.

Ohta, Makoto (1974), "A Note on the Duality Between Production and Cost Functions: Rate of Returns to Scale and Rate of Technical Progress," Economic Studies Quarterly, 25 (1974), 63-65.

Oinas, P., & Malecki, E. J. (2002), The evolution of technologies in time and space: From national and regional to spatial innovation systems. *International Regional Science Review, 25*(1), 102-131.

Oliner, Stephen, and Daniel E. Sichel (2000), *The Resurgence of Growth in the Late 1990s: Is Information Technology the Story?*, Federal Reserve Board, March 2000, mimeo.

Olson, M. (1982), *The Rise and Decline of Nations: Economic Growth*, Stagflation, and Social Rigidities. New Haven: Yale University Press.

Ohmae, K. (1995), *The End of the Nation State*, Free Press, New York.

Otto, V., Löschel, A., Reilly, J. (2006), *Directed Technical Change and Climate Policy.* MIT Joint Program on the Science and Policy of Global Change, Report No. 134.

Paci R. and Pigliaru F. (1999), "Technological catch-up and regional convergence in Europe", *Contributi di Ricerca Crenos*, vol. 9.

Padoa-Schioppa, T. et. al. (1987), *Efficiency, stability and equity: A strategy for the evolution of the economic system of the EC*, report of a study group appointed by the Commission, Brussels, also published by Oxford University Press.

Page, S. and Davenport, M. (1994), *World Trade Reform: Do Developing Countries Gain or Lose?* London: Overseas Development Institute.

Pakes, Ariel and Zvi Griliches, (1984), "Patents and R&D at the *Firm Level: A First Look"*, in Z. Griliches (ed.), R&D, Patents, and Productivity, Chicago, IL: University of Chicago, 55-72.

Panas E.E.(1986), "Biased technological progress and theories of induced innovation: the case of Greek manufacturing, 1958-1975", *Greek Economic Review*, vol.8,No:1, November, p.p.: 95-119.

Park, W.G. (1995), "International R&D spillovers and OECD economic growth", *Economic Inquiry*, Vol. XXXIII, October.

Paraskevopoulos C.C. (1992), "Competitiveness and productivity between Canadian and US manufacturing industries", *Department of Economics, York University,* Toronto, (mimeo).

Paci R. and Pigliaru F. (1999), Technological catch-up and regional convergence in Europe, *Contributi di Ricerca Crenos*, 99/9.

Parente S.L. and Prescott E.C. (1994), "Barriers to technology adoption and development", *Journal of Political Economy*, vol. 102, p.p.: 298-321.

Pavitt, K. (1998), "Technologies, products and organisation in the innovating firm: What Adam Smith tells us and Joseph Schumpeter doesn't", paper presented at the DRUID 1998 Summer conference, Bornhom, June 9-11.

Pavitt K. and Walker W. (1976), "Government policies towards industrial innovations a review", *Research Policy*.

Pavitt, K., Robson, M., & Townsend, J. (1987), The Size Distribution of Innovating Firms in the UK - 1945-1983. *Journal of Industrial Economics, 35*(3), 297-316.

Pedler, R.H. (1994), "The Fruit Companies and the Banana Trade Regime (BTR)", in R.H. Pedler, M. van Schendelen (Ed.), *Lobbying the European Union*, p.p.: 67-92. Hants: Dartmouth.

Pelkmans, J. (2001), *European integration, methods and economic analysis*, second revised edition, Harlow, Pearson Education.

Pelkmans, J. and E. de Souza (2004), *Economic coordination in EMU: The quest for more analysis*, unpublished manuscript, College of Europe, Bruges.

Pelkmans, J. and J. P. Casey (2003), "EU enlargement: external economic implications", *Intereconomics*, July/August, Vol. 38, 4.

Perez, C. (1985), "Microelectronics, Long Waves and World Structural Change", *World Development, vol.* 13 No: (3).

Perez C. and Soete L. (1988), "*Catching-up in technology: entry barriers and windows of opportunity*", in Dosi et al.(eds.) "*Technical change and economic theory*".

Peterson J. (1991), "Technology policy in Europe: explaining the framework programme and Eureka in theory & in practice", *Journal of Common Market Studies*, vol. XXIX, No 3.

_____ . (1993), *High Technology and the Competition State. An analysis of the Eureka initiative*, Routledge, London, New York.

Petit P. and Tahar G. (1989), "Dynamics of technological change and schemes of diffusion", *The Manchester School*, December.

Petrocholis, G. (1989), *Foreign direct investments and implications to Greece*, Avebury, London.

Phelps E.S. (1966), "Models of Technical Progress and the Golden Rule of Research", *Review of Economic Studies*, 33, pp. 133-146.

Pindyck R. (1978), "Interfuel substitution and the industrial demand for energy: an international comparison", *the Review of Economics and Statistics*.

Pindyck R. and Rotemberg J.R. (1983), "Dynamic factor demands and the effects of energy price shocks", *American Economic Review*, vol.75, No:5, December, pp:1066-1079.

Pindyck R. and Rudinfeld D. (1991), *Econometric models & economic forecasting*, McGraw-Hill publishers.

Pizer, W. A., Popp, D. (2007), *Endogenizing Technological Change: Matching Empirical Evidence to Modeling Needs*. RFF Discussion Paper 07-11, Resources for the Future, Washington.

Polanyi, M. (1966), *The Tacit Dimension*, Routledge & Kegan Paul, London.

Poncet, Sandra, (2006), "The Long Term Growth Prospects of the World Economy: Horizon 2050." Working Paper 2006–16. Centre d'Etudes Prospectives et d'Informations Internationales.

Popp, D. (2001), *The effect of new technology on energy consumption*. Resource and Energy Economics 23, 215–239.

_____ . (2002), *Induced innovation and energy prices*. American Economic Review 92, 160–180.

_____ . (2004), *ENTICE: endogenous technological change in the DICE model of global warming*. Journal of Environmental Economics and Management 48, 742–768.

_____ . (2006), *ENTICE-BR: The effects of backstop technology R&D on climate policy models*. Energy Economics 28, 188–222.

Porter, M.E. (1990), *The Competitive Advantage of Nations*. New York: The Free Press.

Porter, M. E., Fuller M. B. (1986), Coalitions and Global Strategy. In: Porter, M. E. (Ed.): *Competition in Global Industries*, Harvard Business School Press, Boston, p.p.: 315-343.

Porter, M., & Stern, S. (1999), *The New Challenge to America's Prosperity: Findings from the Innovation Index* (No. 1-889866-21-0). Washington, D.C.: Council on Competitiveness.

Porter, M., and S. Stern (2003), "Ranking National Innovative Capacity: Findings from the National Innovative Capacity Index." In *Global Competitiveness Report*, World Economic Forum, Geneva.

Powell, W. W. (1990), Neither Market nor Hierarchy: Network Forms of Organization. In: Staw, B. M., Cummings, L. L. (Eds.) *Research in Organizational Behavior*, JAI Press, Greenwich, CT, p.p.: 295-335.

Prasad H.(1981), *Research in international business and finance: technology transfer and economic development*, vol.2.

Price, A., Morgan, K., and Cooke, P. (1994), *The Welsh Renaissance: Inward Investment and Industrial Innovation*. Cardiff: CASS.

Psacharopoulos, G. (2004), The Social Cost of an Outdated Law: Article 16 of the Greek Constitution. *European Journal of Law and Economics*, 16(2), Springer Netherlands.

Psacharopoulos, G. and H. A. Patrinos. (2004), Returns to Investment in Education: A Further Update. *Education Economics*, 12(2), pp. 111–34.

Quinn, A. (1990), *Trends in scientific R&TD in the EEC* (Brussels: CEC).

Rantisi, N.M. (2002), The Local Innovation System as a Source of 'Variety': Openness and Adaptability in New York City's Garment District, in *Regional Studies*, 36, 6, 587-602.

Rao, M. (1997), "Development in the Time of Globalization." Paper for the Workshop on Globalization, Uneven Development and Poverty, October 25–25, UNDP, New York.

Rasmussen P.N. (1956), *Intersectoral relations*, North Holland, Amsterdam.

Ray G. F. (1969), "The diffusion of new technology: a study of ten processes in nine industries", *National Institute Economic Review*, vol.48, p.p.: 40-83.

Regional policy - http://europa.eu.int/comm/regional_policy/index_en.htm

Reifschneider, D. and Stevenson, R. (1991), Systematic Departures from the Frontier: A framework for the Analysis of Firm inefficiency *International Economic Review*, 32: 3: 715-723.

Rennings Klaus and Sebastian Voigt (2008), *Data Sources for Measuring Endogenous Technological Change in E3 Models*, Centre for European Economic Research (ZEW) Mannheim, January 2008.

Reynolds, Paul D., Michael Hay, Wikliam D. Bygrave, S. Michael Camp and Erkko Autio (2000), *Global Entrepreneurship Monitor*, Kaufman Center for Entrepreneurial Leadership, Kansas City.

Richonnier M. (1984), "Europe's decline is not irreversible", *Journal of Common Market Studies,* vol. 22, No 3.

Ridker, R. (1994), *The World Bank's Role in Human Resource Development: Education, Training and Technical Assistance*. Washington, D.C.: World Bank Operations Evaluation Study.

River-Batiz Luis A. and Roomer P. (1991), Economic Integration and Endogenous Growth, *Quarterly Journal of Economics*, vol. 106, p.p.: 531-556.

Robertson T. and Gatignon H. (1987), "*The diffusion of high technology innovations: a marketing perspective*", chapter 8 in Pennings J.M. and Buitendam A. (eds.),"*New technology as organizational innovation: the development and diffusion of microelectronics*", Ballinger publishing company.

Robson M., Townsend J., Pavitt K. (1988), "Sectoral Patterns of Production and Use of Innovations in the UK: 1945-1983", *Research Policy*, 17, 1-14.

Rodriguez, Francisco and Wilson, Ernest J. (2000), *Are Poor Countries Losing the Information Revolution?* [www.infodev.org/library/working.htm].

Rogers, Everett (2003), *Diffusion of Innovations*, 5th edition, Free Press.

Romer D. (1986), "Increasing Returns and Long Term Growth", *Journal of Political Economy*, vol. 94, No: 5, p.p.: 1002-1037.

_____ . (1987b), "Growth based on increasing returns due to specialization", *American Economic Review*, May, vol.77, No:2, p.p.: 56-62.

_____ . (1989), "What determines the rate of growth of technological change?", *PPR Working Paper, The World Bank*, No: 279, Washington, DC.

_____ . (1990a), Endogenous Technological Change, *Journal of Political Economy*, vol. 98, p.p.: 71-102.

_____ . (1990b), Capital, Labor and Productivity, *Brookings Papers on Economic Activity, Macroeconomics*, p.p.: 337-420.

_____ . (1990c), "Human capital and growth: theory and evidence", *NBER Working Paper*.

_____ . (1994), "The Origins of Endogenous Growth", *Journal of Economic Perspectives*, vol. 8, No: 1, p.p.: 3-22.

_____ . (1996), *Advanced Macroeconomics*, McGraw-Hill.

_____ . (1963), "Technological change in the machine tool industry: 1840-1910", *Journal of Economic History*, December, vol. 23, No:4, p.p.: 414-446.

_____ . (1971), *The economics of technological change*. Harmondsworth: Penguin Books.

_____. (1976), *Perspectives on technology*, Cambridge, Cambridge.

_____. (1982), *Inside the Black Box*, Cambridge, Cambridge University.

Rosenberg, N. and L. E. Birdzell (1986), *How the West Grew Rich: The Economic Transformation of the Industrial World*, New York: Basic Books.

Rosenberg N., Landau R., and Mowery D.C. (1992), *Technology and the wealth of nations*, Stanford University Press, Stanford, California.

Ross, G. (1993), "Sidling Into Industrial Policy: Inside the European Commission", *French Politics and Society*, Vol. 11, No. 1, p.p.: 20-43.

Rothwell, R., and Dodgson, M. (1992), "European technology policy evolution: convergence towards SMEs and regional technology transfer", *Technovation*, Vol. 12, No. 4, p.p.: 223-38.

Sabel, C. F. (1994), "Flexible specialisation and the re-emergence of regional economies" in Ash Amin (ed.) *Post Fordism: a reader*, Oxford, UK, and Cambridge, USA.

Sagasti, Fransisco (2000), *The Knowledge Explosion: 50 Years of Emerging Divide*, Human Development Report 2001 background paper.

_____. (2003), *Knowledge and Innovation for Development: The Sisyphus Challenge for the 21st Century*. Cheltenham, U.K.: Edward Elgar.

Sah, R. and Stiglitz, J.E. (1986), "The Architecture of Economic Systems: Hierarchies and Polyarchies", *The American Economic Review*, Vol. 76, No: 4, September, p.p.: 716-727.

Sahal D. (1975), "Evolving parameter models of technology assessment", *Journal of the International Society for technology assessment*, vol.1, pp:11-20.

_____. (1977a), "Substitution of mechanical corn pickers by field shelling technology-an econometric analysis", *Technological forecasting & social change*, vol.10, p.p.:53-60.

_____. (1977b), "The multidimensional diffusion of technology", *Technological Forecasting and Social Change,* vol.10, p.p.: 277-298.

_____. (1980), *Research, Development and technological Innovation: Recent Perspectives on Management*, Lexington, Massachussetts.

Sahal D. and Nelson R.R. (1981), *Patterns of technological innovation*, chapter 5,-Addison-Wesley pub., Massachusetts.

Sajeva, M., & Gatelli, D. (2005), *Methodology Report on European Innovation Scoreboard 2005*: European Commission, Enterprise Directorate-General.

Sakurai, N., Papaconstantinou, G., Ioannidis, E. (1997), "Impact of R&D and Technology Diffusion on Productivity Growth: Empirical Evidence of 10 OECD Countries", *Economic Systems Research*, vol. 9, p.p.: 81-109.

Sala-i-Martin X. (1996), "The Classical Approach to Convergence Analysis", *The Economic Journal*, 106, pp. 1019-1069.

Sala-i-Martin, Xavier, Gernot Doppelhofer, and Ronald I. Miller. (2004), Determinants of Long-Term Growth: A Bayesian Averaging of Classical Estimates (BACE) Approach. *American Economic Review*, 94(4), pp. 813–35.

Salinas-Jimenez, M.M. (2003), Technological change, efficiency gains and capital accumulation in labour productivity growth and convergence: an application to the Spanish regions, *Applied Economics*, 35, 1839-1851.

Santangelo, G. D. (2002), The Regional Geography of Corporate Patenting in Information and Communications Technology (ICT): Domestic and Foreign Dimensions, *Regional Studies*, 36 (5), 495-514.

Sapir André (2003), A*n Agenda for a Growing Europe: Making the EU Economic System*, Deliver Report of an Independent High-Level Study Group established on the initiative of the President of the European Commission.

Sargan J.D. (1971), "Production functions", part V of Layard R.G., Jenis Denis Sargan, Margaret E. Ager, and Deborah J. Jones, eds *Qualified Manpower and Economic Performance*, London: The Penguin Press, pp: 145-204.

Sato R. (1970), "The estimation of biased technical progress and the production function", *International Economic Review*, vol.11, No:2, June, pp.179-208.

_____. (1975), *Production functions and aggregation*, North Holland, Amsterdam.

Sato R. and Suzawa G. (1983), *Research and Productivity*, Auburn House publishing company, Boston, Massachusetts.

Saviotti, P.P. (1988), Information, Entropy and Variety in Technoeconomic Development, *Research Policy*, vol. 17, p.p.: 89-103.

_____. (1998), On the Dynamics of Appropriability of Tacit and of Codified Knowledge, *Research Policy*, vol. 26, p.p.: 843-856.

Scherer Frederic M. (1982a), "Inter-industry technology flows and productivity growth", *Review of Economic and Statistics*, vol.64, No4, November, pp. 627-34.

_____. (1982b), "Inter-industry technology flows in the United States", in *Research Policy*, vol.6, pp. 227-45.

_____. (1984), *Innovation and Growth: Schumpeterian Perspectives*, Cambridge, MA: MIT Press.

_____. (1991), "Changing Perspectives on the Firm Size Problem ," in Z.J. Acs and D.B. Audretsch, (eds.), *Innovation and Technological Change: An International Comparison*, Ann Arbor: University of Michigan Press, 24-38.

Schmidt, P. and R.C. Sickles (1984), "Production Frontiers and Panel Data", Journal of Business and Economic Statistics 2, p.p..: 367-374.

Schmitz, H., and Misyck, B. (1993), *Industrial Districts in Europe: Policy Lessons for Developing Countries?*. Brighton: Institute of Development Studies.

Schmookler, J. (1966), *Invention and economic growth* (Cambridge, Mass.: Harvard University Press).

Schumpeter Joseph A. (1912), *The theory of economic development*, Leipzing, Duncker and Humblot.

_____. (1927), *Sombarts Dritter Band"*, *in: idem, Dogmenhistorische und biographische Aufsätze*, Tübingen: J.C.B. Mohr.

_____. (1934), *The theory of economic development*, Cambridge, MA, Harvard Economic Studies.

_____. (1939), *Business Cycles: A Theoretical, Historical and Statistical Analysis of the Capitalist Process,* 2 Volumes., New York, McGraw Hill.

_____. (1942), *Capitalism, socialism and democracy*, New York, Harper.

Sen, Amartya (1999), *Development as Freedom*, Oxford: Oxford University Press.

Senn A., & Peter R. (1996), "Sombart's Reception in the English-Speaking World: 'Je ne propose rien, je n'impose rien: j'expose'", in *Backhaus* 1996, Vol. 3.

Shapiro, C. and H. Varian (1999), *Information Rules*, Boston: Harvard Business School Press.

Sharp M. (1985), *Europe and the new technologies*, Pinter publishers.

_____. (1991), *Technology and the future of Europe*, (eds.), edited by Freeman, Marie Jahoda, Keith Pavitt, Margaret Sharp and William Walker, Pinter publishers.

_____. (1993), "The Community and the new technologies", in the Lodge, J:, *The European Community and the challenge of the future*, Pinter publishers, p.p.: 202-220.

Sharp, M, and Pavitt. K. (1993), "Technology Policy in the 1990s: Old Trends and New Realities", *Journal of Common Market Studies*, Vol. 31, No. 2, p.p.: 129-51.

Shell Karl (1966), "Towards a Theory of Incentive Activity and Capital Accumulation" *American Economic Review*, vol. 56(2), May, pp. 62-68.

_____. (1967), "A Model of Inventive Activity and Capital Accumulation" in K. Shell (ed.) *Essays on the Theory of Optimal Economic Growth*, Cambridge, MIT Press.

_____. (1973), "Incentive Activity, Industrial Organisation and Economic Growth" in J. A. Mirrlees and N. Stern, (eds.) *Models of Economic Growth*, London: Macmillan pp. 77-100.

_____. (2000), "The production recipes approach to modelling technological innovation: An application to learning by doing" *Journal of Economics Dynamics and Control*, vol. 24, pp. 389-450.

Shephard R.W. (1953), *Cost and Production Functions*, Princeton University Press.

Silberglitt, Richard, Philip S. Anton, David R. Howell, and Anny Wong (2006), *The Global Technology Revolution 2020*. Santa Monica, CA: RAND Corporation, National Security Research Division.

Simmie, J. (2003), Innovation and urban regions as national and international nodes for the transfer and sharing of knowledge. *Regional Studies, 37*(6-7), 607-620.

Simputer Trust (2000), *The Simputer Project* [http://www.simputer.org], March 2001.

Silverberg G. (1987),"Technical progress, capital accumulation and effective demand, a self organisation model" in Batten D., Casti J. and Johanson B. (eds.) *Economic evolution and structural adjustment*, Springer Verlag.

Sinn, H.W. (1993), H*ow Much Europe? Subsidiarity, Centralization and Fiscal Competition*, CEPR, London.

Skountzos T and Mathaios (1995), *Statistical Data for Capital Stock: Greek economy*, C. E. P. R. (Center of Planning and Research), Athens, Greece.

Smith, K. (1997), "Economic Infrastructures and Innovation Systems" in Edquist, C. (ed.) (1997) *Systems of Innovation: Technologies, Institutions and Organizations*. Pinter Publishers/Cassell Academic.

_____. (2005), Measuring Innovation. In J. Fagerberg, D. C. Mowery & R. R. Nelson (Eds.), *The Oxford handbook of innovation* (pp. 148-177). Oxford and New York: Oxford University Press.

Smith, M.Y. (2004), A model of linked adoption of complementary technologies, *Economics of Innovation and New Technology* 13, 91-99.

Snowdown B. and Vane H. (eds) (1999), *Conversations with economists. Interpreting macroeconomics*, Cheltenham: Edward Elgar.

Soete L. (1985), "*International diffusion of technology, industrial development and technological leapfrogging*", World Development, volume 13, No: 3, p: 409-422.

_____. (2006), Knowledge, policy and innovation. In L. Earl & F. Gault (Eds.), *National Innovation, Indicators and Policy* (pp. 198-218). Cheltenham: Edward Elgar.

Soete L. and Turner R. (1984), "*Technology diffusion and the rate of technical change*", The Economic Journal, volume 94, p:612-623.

Solow R. (1956), "A contribution to the theory of economic growth", *Quarterly Journal of Economics*, vol.70, February, p.p.: 65-94.

_____. (1957a), "Technical change and the aggregate production function" *Review of Economics and Statistics,* vol.39, pp.312-320.

_____. (1957b). "Technical change and the aggregate production function", in: Rosenberg (ed.) 1971, pp. 344-362.

_____. (1962), "Technical progress, capital formation and economic growth", *American Economic Review*, vol.52, No:2, May, p.p.:72-86.

_____. (1963), *Capital theory and the rate of return*, North Holland, Amsterdam.

_____. (1964), "Capital, labour and income in manufacturing", in *The behaviour of income shares, Studies in Income and Wealth*, Princeton University Press, N.J.

_____. (1967), "Some recent developments in the theory of production", in *The theory and empirical analysis of production*, (ed.) Murray Brown, Columbia University Press, New York.

_____. (1970), *Growth theory*, Oxford University press, Oxford.

_____. (1988), "Growth theory and after", *American Economic Review*, vol.78, No:3, June.

_____. (1994), "Perspectives on Growth Theory", *Journal of Economic Perspectives*, vol. 8, No: 1, p.p.: 45-54.

Sombart, Werner (1896), *Sozialismus und soziale Bewegung im neunzehnten Jahrhundert*, Jena, Gustav Fischer, English translation 1898, Socialism and the Social Movement in the 19th Century, New York: G.P.Putnam's Sons.

_____. (1911), *Die Juden und das Wirtschaftsleben, Leipzig* : Duncker & Humblot; English translation (1913): The jews and modern capitalism, London : T.F Unwin.

_____. (1916), Der moderne Kapitalismus, Vol. I: Einleitung - Die vorkapitalistische Wirtschaft - *Die historischen Grundlagen des modernen Kapitalismus*; Vol. II: Das europäische Wirtschaftsleben im Zeitalter des Frühkapitalismus; München und Leipzig : Duncker und Humblot.

_____. (1924), *Der proletarische Sozialismus*, 2 Vols., Jena : Gustav Fischer-Verlag.

_____. (1925), "Prinzipielle Eigenart des modernen Kapitalismus", in *Grundriß der Sozialökonomik*, IV.Abteilung/1.Teil. Tübingen : J.C.B.Mohr-Verlag.

_____. (1927), Das Wirtschaftsleben im Zeitalter des Hochkapitalismus. Vol III/1,2 of *Der moderne Kapitalismus*, München and Leipzig: Duncker und Humblot.

Sombart, Werner. 1929. "Die Wandlungen des Kapitalismus". In Verhandlungen des Vereins für Socialpolitik in Zürich 1928, ed. F. Boese, München and Leipzig : Duncker und Humblot.

_____. (1932), *Die Zukunft des Kapitalismus*, Berlin/Charlottenburg, reprinted in: Sombart 2002, pp. 439-464.

_____. , (2002), *Nationalökonomie als Kapitalismustheorie*, Ausgewählte Schriften, ed. Alexander Ebner and Helge Peukert, Marburg: Metropolis-Verlag.

Sombart, Werner, Die Ordnung des Wirtschaftslebens (1927), reprinted in: Sombart 2002, pp. 265-376

Soubattina, Tatanya (2006), "Generic Models of Technological Learning by Developing Countries." Draft. World Bank, Washington, DC.

Stamer Jörg Meyer (1995), "Industrial Policy in Europe—New Options", *Paper for Eurokolleg Series, Friedrich-Ebert-Foundation*, Bonn

Stelling, Petra, and Arne Jensen (2001), "Train Operators' Economies of Scale and Business Strategies."Working paper. Handelshogskolan, Gotteborg, Sweden.

Sternberg, Rolf (1996), Technology Policies and the Growth of Regions: Evidence from Four Countries, *Small Business Economics*, 8(2), 75-86.

Stewart, Frances (1977), *Technology and Underdevelopment*, London: Macmillan.

_____ . (2000), Innovation networks and regional development – evidence from the European Regional Innovation Survey (ERIS). *European Planning Studies*, 8 (4): 389-407.

Stiglitz, J.E. (1969), "The Effects of Income, Wealth and Capital Gains Taxation on Risk-Taking", *Quarterly Journal of Economics*, vol. 83, May, p.p.: 263-283.

_____ . (1987), "Learning to Learn, Localized Learning and Technological Progress," in *Economic Policy and Technological Performance*, P. Dasgupta and Stoneman (eds.), Cambridge University Press. p.p.: 125-153.

_____ . (1988), "Technological Change, Sunk Costs, and Competition", *Brookings Papers on Economic Activity*, volume 3.

_____ . (1995), "The Theory of International Public Goods and the Architecture of International Organizations", *United Nations Background Paper 7, Department for Economic and Social Information and Policy Analysis*, July.

_____ . (1998a), "Knowledge as a Global Public Good", *paper written as chapter in a UNDP book Global Public Goods*.

_____ . (1998b), *Towards a New Paradigm for Development: Strategies, Policies, and Processes*. Given as Raul Prebisch Lecture at United Nations Conference on Trade and Development (UNCTAD). Geneva. October 19.

_____ . (1999), *On Liberty, The Right to Know, and Public Discourse: The Role of Transparency in Public Life*. Given as 1999 Oxford University Amnesty International Lecture.

Stokes, D. E. (1997), *Pasteur's quadrant: Basic science and technological innovation*. Washington, D.C.: Brookings Institution Press.

Stokey N.L. (1979), Intertemporal Price Discrimination, Quarterly Journal of Economics, 93, 355-371.

_____ . (1988), "Learning by Doing and the Introduction of New Goods", *Journal of Political Economy*, 96, pp. 701-717.

_____ . (1995), "R&D and Economic Growth", *Review of Economic Studies*, 62, pp. 469-489.

Stoneman, P. (1976), *Technological diffusion and the computer revolution*, Cambridge, Cambridge University Press.

_____ . (1983), *The economic analysis of technological change*, Oxford University Press.

_____ . (1986), "Technological diffusion: the viewpoint of economic theory", *Richerche Economiche*, XL, 4, p:585-606.

_____ . (1987), *The economic analysis of technology policy*, Oxford University Press.

_____ . (1995), *Handbook of the Economics of Innovations and technological change*, Blackwell, Oxford.

_____ . (2002), *The economics of technological diffusion*, Blackwell, Oxford.

Stoneman P. and Ireland N.J. (1983), "The role of supply factors in the diffusion of new process technology", *the Economic Journal*, supplement, March, p.p.: :65-77.

Stoneman, P. and Toivanen, O (1997), The diffusion of multiple technologies: An empirical study, *Economics of Innovation and New Technology* 5, 1-17.

Storper, M. (1997), *The Regional World: Territorial Development in a Global World* The Guilford Press, New York London.

Sue Wing, I., Popp, D. (2006), *Representing Endogenous Technological Change in Models for Climate Policy Analysis: Theoretical and Empirical Considerations.* Managing Greenhouse Gas Emissions in California. The California Climate Change Center at UC Berkeley.

Sullivan, Nicholas P. (2007), *You Can Hear Me Now: How Microloans and Cell Phones Are Connecting the World's Poor to the Global Economy.* San Francisco: Jossey-Bass.

Summers, Lawrence H. (2000), *The New Wealth of Nations*, Treasury News, Washington D. V., the Department of Treasury.

Syrquin M. (1989), "Productivity growth and factor reallocation" chapter 8, in Kubo Y. Robinson S.Syrquin M.(eds.) *Industrialization and growth: a comparative study*, London.

Swan P. (1973), "*The international diffusion of an innovation*", the Journal of Industrial Economics, volume 22, September, p.p.:61-70.

Sweeney G.P. (1987), *Innovation, entrepreneurs and regional development*, Frances Pinter, London.

Teece, D. J. (1986), "Profiting from Technological Innovation: Implications for Integration, Collaboration, Licensing and Public Policy", *Research Policy* vol. 15, p.p.: 285-305.

Terleckyj N. (1974), "Effects of R&D on the productivity growth industries and exploratory study", National Planning Association, Report No. 140, Washington.

───. (1980), "What Do R&D Numbers Tell Us About Technical Change?" American Economic Review Papers and Proceedings, 70 (1980), p.p.: 55-61.

───. (1983), "R&D as a Source of Growth of Productivity and of Income," in Franke, R.H. and Associates, editor, The Science of Productivity, San Francisco: Jossey-Bass.

───. (1984), "R&D and Productivity Growth at the Industry Level: Is There Still a Relationship: Comment," in Zvi Griliches, editor, R7D, Patents and Productivity (Chicago: The University of Chicago Press for the National Bureau of Economic Research, 1984), 496-502.

Tijssen, R. J. W. (1998), "Quantitative Assessment of Large Heterogeneous R&D Networks: The Case of Process Engineering in the Netherlands", *Research Policy*, vol. 26, p.p.: 791-809.

───. (2003), *Scoreboards of research excellence*.

Thomas, K.P. (1993), *EU Regulation of State Aid to Industry: Lessons for North America*. St. Louis, mimeo.

Thomas R.L. (1993), *Introductory Econometrics: theory and applications*, second edition, Longman press.

Toda Y. (1974), "Capital-labour substitution in a production function:the case of Soviet manufacturing for 1950-1971", in the Altmann and others (ed.) *On the measurement of factor productivity: theoretical problems and empirical results*, Vandenhoeck and Ruprecht publishers.

Tödtling, F., Kaufmann, A. (2001), The role of the region for innovation activities of SMEs. *European Urban and Regional Studies*, 8 (3): 203-215.

Törnqvist, G. (1990), *Towards a geography of creativity*, in Shachar A, Öberg S (eds) p.p. 103-127.

Tovainen, O., P. Niininen (2000), Investment, R&D, subsidies, and credit constraints, Department *of Economics MIT and Helsinki School of Economics,* Working Papers no 244.

Trefler, D. (1993), "International Factor Price Differences: Leontief was Right", *Journal of Political Economy*, vol. 101, p.p.: 961-987.

_____. (1995), "The Case of the Missing Trade and Other Mysteries", *American Economic Review*, vol. 85, p.p.: 1029-1046.

Trimble, John (1999), *A Redesigning the Service Statistics Sector Program*, Presentation to the Census Advisory Committee of Professional Associations Meeting, October 21-22.

Triplett, Jack (1999), "The Solow productivity paradox: what do computers do to productivity?" *Canadian Journal of Economics, vol.* 32, No: 2, p.p.: 309 - 334.

Triplett, Jack E. and Barry Bosworth (2000), "Productivity in the Services Sector," presented at the *American Economic Association meetings,* January.

Tsipouri L. (1989), *Accession to the EC and the Greek technological policy: the experience 1981-1986*, Institute of Mediterranean Studies, Athens, Greece.

UNCTAD (United Nations Conference on Trade and Development), (2000), *World Investment Report*, United Nations, New York and Geneva, United Nations.

_____. (2005), *World Investment Report: Transnational Corporations and the Industrialization of R&D*. New York and Geneva: UNCTAD United Nations, New York and Geneva, United Nations.

_____. (2007), *The Least Developed Countries Report 2007: Knowledge, Technological Learning and Innovation for Development.* New York and Geneva, UNCTAD, United Nations, New York and Geneva, United Nations.

UNDP (United Nations Development Programme) (2001), *Human Development Report 2001:Making New Technologies Work for Human Development*. New York: Oxford University Press.

UNESCO Statistical Yearbook, UNESCO, Paris.

UNESCO (1969), *The measurement of scientific and technological activities*, Paris.

_____. (1983), *Manual for Statistics on Scientific and Technological Activities,* New York and Geneva, United Nations.

_____. (1984), *Transnational corporations in world development*, third survey, New York and Geneva, United Nations.

_____. (1992), *Scientific and technology in developing countries: strategies for the 1990s*, Paris.

UNIDO (United Nations Industrial Development Organization) (2002), *Industrial Development Report 2002/2003: Competing through Innovation and Learning.* Vienna: UNIDO.

_____. (2005), *Industrial Development Report 2005— Capability Building for Catching-Up: Historical, Empirical and Policy Dimensions.* Vienna: UNIDO.

United Nations (1983), "*Transnational corporations in world development*", third survey, New York and Geneva, United Nations.

_____. (2001), *Correspondence on Technology Exports*, Statistics Division, 25 January, New York.

United Nations Conference on Trade and Development (UNCTAD) (1994), *World Investment Report*, New York and Geneva, United Nations.

_____. (1996), *World Investment Report*, New York and Geneva, United Nations.

_____. (1997a), *Trade and Development Report, 1997: Globalization, Distribution and Growth*. New York/Geneva: United Nations.

_____. (1997b), *World Investment Report, Transnational Corporations, Market Structure and Competition Policy*, New York and Geneva, United Nations.

_____. (1998), *World Investment Report*, New York and Geneva, United Nations.

_____. (1998), *Globalisation, Underdevelopment and Poverty: Recent Trends and Policy*, David Woodward, Working Paper Series, United Nations, UNDP, February, New York and Geneva, United Nations.

_____. (1999), *World Investment Report*, New York and Geneva, United Nations.

_____. (2003), *Human Development Report*, United Nations, UNDP, June, New York and Geneva, United Nations.

Urata S. (1992), "Economic growth and structural change in the Soviet economy 1959-1972", in Maurizio Ciaschini, (ed.): *Input-Output analysis*.

U. S. Department of Commerce (1998), *The Emerging Digital Economy*, US Department of Commerce.

_____. (1999), *The Emerging Digital Economy II*, US Department of Commerce.

_____. (2000), *Falling through the Net: Toward Digital Inclusion*, US Department of Commerce, October.

US Standard Occupational Classification (SOC): http://stats.bls.gov/soc

Utterback, J.M. (1994), *Mastering the dynamics of innovation*, Harvard Business School Press, Boston.

Uzawa H. (1962), "Production functions with constant elasticities of substitution", *Review of Economic Studies*, vol.29, p.p.: 291-9.

_____. (1964), "Duality principles in the theory of cost and production", *International Economic Review,* vol.5, p.p.:216-220.

_____. (1965), "Optimal Technical Change in as Aggregative Model of Economic Growth", *International Economic Review*, 6, pp. 12-31.

_____. (1969), "Time preference and the penrose effect in a two-class model of economic growth", *Journal of Political Economy*, vol.77, No:4,July/August,pp:628-652.

Uzawa H. and Watanabe H. (1961), "A note on the classification of technical inventions", *Economic Studies Quarterly*, September, pp:68-72.

Van Schendelen, M.P.C.M. (1994), "Studying EU Public Affairs Cases: Does it Matter?" in R. H. Pedler & M. van Schendelen (Eds.), *Lobbying the European Union*, Hants: Dartmouth, p.p.: 3-20.

Varian R. Hall, Theodore C. Bergstrom, and R. Hal (1993), *Workouts in Intermediate Microeconomics* 3rd ed., New York: W. W. Norton.

Vasudeva Murthy, N.R and I.S. Chien (1997), "The empirics of economic growth for OECD countries: Some new findings", *Economics Letters*, 55, pp. 425-429.

Vaucleroy Guy (2000), *European Business Summit*, June, Brussels, Belgium.

Vernardakis N. (1992), "Structural and technological imperatives in the light of development prospects for the Greek economy", Chapter 14 in (eds.)"Issues in contemporary economics: the Greek economy, economic policy for the 1990s", by Thanos Skouras, (proceedings of the ninth world congress of the international economic association: volume 5).

Vernon, R. (1966), 'International investment and international trade in the product cycle', *Quarterly Journal of Economics* vol. 80, no. 2, pp. 190~207.

Verspagen B. (1992), "Endogenous Innovation in Neo-Classical Growth Models: A Survey", *Journal of Macroeconomics*, 14(4), pp. 613-662.

_____. (1992), Uneven growth between interdependent economies, Faculty of economics and business administration, Maastricht.

_____. (1994), "Technology and growth: the complex dynamics of convergence and divergence, in Silverberg G. and Soete L.(eds.), *The Economics of growth and technical change: technologies, nations, agents*, Aldershot, Edward Elgar.

Vickery, G. and Northcott, J. (1995), Diffusion of microelectronics and advanced manufacturing technology: A review of national surveys, *Economics of Innovation and New Technology* 3, 253-76.

Vincenti, W.G. (1990), *What engineers know and how they know it: Analytical studies form the Aeronautical Industry*, Baltimore, John Hopkins University Press.

Viotti, Eduardo (1997), *Passive and Active National Learning Systems – A Framework to Understand Technical Change in Late Industrializing Economies and Some Evidences from a Comparative Study of Brazil and South Korea*, Ph.D. Dissertation, The New School University, New York, 1997.

_____. (2001), *National Learning Systems A new approach on technical change in late industrializing economies and evidences from the cases of Brazil and South Korea*, Working Paper.

Von Bertalanffy, L. (1973), *General Systems Theory*, New York, Braziller.

Vyas, Seema, and Lilani Kumaranayake (2006), "Constructing Socio-economic Status Indices: How to Use Principal Components Analysis." *Health Policy and Planning* 21 (6): 459–68.

Wallsten, Scott (1998), "Rethinking the Small Business Innovation Research Program", in *Investing in Innovation: Creating A Research and Innovation Policy That Works*, Lewis Branscomb and James Keller, Eds. Cambridge, MA: MIT Press.

Wallsten S.J. (2000), The effects of government industry R&D programs on private R&D: The case of small business innovation research program, *RAND Journal of Economics*, 31(1), pp. 82-100.

Warda J. (2001), "Measuring the Value of R&D Tax Treatment in OECD Countries", *STI Review* No. 27, OECD, Paris.

Watanabe H. (1961), "A note on the classification of technical inventions", *Economic Studies Quarterly*, September, pp:68-72.

Watkins, Alfred and Anubha Verma (2007), "Government of Rwanda-World Bank, Science, Technology and Innovation Capacity Building Assistance Program: Developing Practical Solutions to Practical Problems." Internal report. World Bank, Washington, DC.

Werker Claudia (2004), *An Assessment of the Regional Innovation Policy by the European Union based on Bibliometrical Analysism*, the *Papers on Economics and Evolution* are edited by the Evolutionary Economics Group, Max Planck Institute of Economics Evolutionary Economics Group, Jena, German.

WIIW-WIFO (2000), *Database on FDI in Central and Eastern Europe and FSU countries*, February 2000.

Williams R (1973), *European technology*, Groom Helm publishers.

Williamson, J. (1996), "Globalization, Convergence and History." *Journal of Economic History vol.* 56(2).

Willoughby K. (1990), "Technology choice: a critique of the appropriate technology movement".

Wolf, E.N. and M. Gittleman (1993), "The Role of Education in Productivity Convergence: Does Higher Education Matter?", in *Explaining Economic Growth,* A Szimai, B. van Ark and D. Pilat (eds), Elsevier Science Publishers.

Wolfe, D. (2003), *Clusters Old and New: The Transition to a Knowledge Economy in Canada's Regions.* Kingston: Queen's School of Policy Studies.

Wolfe, D. (2002), Knowledge, Learning and Social Capital in Ontario's ICT Clusters, Paper prepared for the Annual Meeting of the Canadian Political Science Association University of Toronto, Toronto, Ontario May 29-31, 2002.

Wolfensohn. J. (1996), *Annual Meetings Address*, Washington: World Bank. www.worldbank.org/html/extdr/extme/jdwams96.htm

_____ . (1997), *Annual Meetings Address: The Challenge of Inclusion.* Hong Kong: World Bank. www.worldbank.org/html/extdr/am97/jdw_sp/jwsp97e.htm

Woodward D. (1992), *Debt, Adjustment and Poverty in Developing Countries.* London: Pinter Publishers/Save the Children (UK).

_____ . (1993a), "Regional Trade Arrangements in Latin America and the Caribbean." Mimeo, Oxfam (UK/I), Oxford.

_____ . (1993b), "Regional Trade Arrangements in Sub-Saharan Africa." Mimeo, Oxfam (UK/I), Oxford.

_____ . (1996a), "Effects of Globalization and Liberalization on Poverty: Concepts and Issues." In UNCTAD: *Globalization and Liberalization: Effects of International Economic Relations on Poverty.* New York/Geneva: United Nations.

_____ . (1996b), "Debt Sustainability and the Debt Overhang in Heavily Indebted Poor Countries: Some Comments on the IMF's View." In *Eurodad*: *World Credit Tables, 1996: Creditors' Claims on Debtors Exposed.* Brussels: European Network on Debt and Development.

_____ . (1997a), "The Next Crisis? Direct and Portfolio Investment in Developing Countries." Mimeo, European Network on Debt and Development, Brussels.

_____ . (1997b), "The HIPC Initiative: Presentation to the EURODAD Annual Conference, November 1997." Mimeo, European Network on Debt and Development, Brussels.

_____ . (1997c), "Submission to the House of Commons Select Committee on International Development: The Highly Indebted Poor Countries (HIPC) Initiative." Mimeo.

_____ . (1997d), "The HIPC Initiative: Effects of Changes to the Rules Governing the Fiscal Criterion." Mimeo, Jubilee 2000 Coalition, London.

_____ . (1998), "Fiscal Criteria for Debt Reduction: a Human Development-Based Approach." Mimeo, Catholic Fund for Overseas Development.

Woolcock S (1984), "Information technology: the challenge to Europe", *Journal of Common Market Studies,* vol. 22, No 4.

Woolcock, Michael (1998), 'Social Capital and Economic Development: Toward a Theoretical Synthesis and Policy Framework', *Theory and Society*, No. 2, Vol. 27: 151-207.

World Bank (1990), *Adjustment Lending Policies for Sustainable Growth.* Washington, D.C.:

_____ . (1996), *Poverty Reduction and the World Bank: Progress and Challenges in the 1990s.* Washington, D.C.: World Bank.

_____ . (1998), *World Development Report: Knowledge for Development.* New York: Oxford University Press.

_____. (2000), *World Development Report: Cross-Border Mergers and Acquisitions and Development: An Overview*, United Nations, New York and Geneva.

_____. (2001), *World Development Indicators 2001*, CD-ROM, World Bank, Washington, DC.

_____. (2002), *World Development Report 2002*, Building Institutions for Markets, New York: Oxford University Press.

_____. (2003), *Sustainable Development in a Dynamic World: Transferring Institutions, Growth, and Quality of Life*, New York: Oxford.

_____. (2005), *Sri Lanka—Offshoring Professional Services: A Development Opportunity*. Washington, DC: World Bank.

_____. (2006), *Transport for Development*. Washington, DC: World Bank.

_____. (2007a), *World Development Indicators 2007*. Washington, DC: World Bank.

_____. (2007b), *World Development Report 2008: Agriculture for Development*. New York: Oxford University Press.

_____. (2007c), *Making Finance Work for Africa*. Washington, DC: World Bank.

_____. (2008), *Global Economic Prospects Technology Diffusion in the Developing World*, Washington, DC: World Bank.

World Economic Forum (2000), *The Global Competitiveness Report 2000*, Oxford University Press, New York.

World Intellectual Property Organization (2000), *Industrial Property Statistics,* Publication A, World Intellectual Property Organization, Geneva.

Xochellis, P. and Kesidou, A. (2007), "Greece", in *The Education Systems of Europe*, W. Hörner, H. Döbert, B.V. Kopp and W. Mitter (eds.), Springer, pp. 326-370.

Young A. (1993), "Invention and Bounded Learning by Doing", *Journal of Political Economy*, 101(3), pp. 443-472.

_____. (1998), "Growth without Scale Effects", *Journal of Political Economy*, pp. 41-63.

Yuill D. and Allen K. (1989), *European regional incentives: a review to member states*, published by Bower-Saur in association with the European Policies Research Centre, University of Strathclyde.

Zander U. (1991), *Exploiting a technological edge-voluntary and involuntary dissemination of technology*, Institute of International Business (IIB), Stockholm School of Economics.

Zellner Arnold, Jan Kmenta and Jacques Dreze (1966), "Specification and estimation of Cobb-Douglas production function models" *Econometrica*, vol. 34:3, October, pp: 784-795.

Zhu, Susan Chun, and Daniel Trefler (2005), "Trade and Inequality in Developing Countries: A General Equilibrium Analysis." *Journal of International Economics*. 65: 21–48.

INDEX

A

Adopt, 128
Allen©Uzava, 84
Antonelli, 127
Average curve, 135

B

Basic material balance, 63
Benvignati, 127
Boskin, 83

C

Capabilities strength, 39
Carter, 63
Catching-up, 126
Cauchy, 132
Chenery, 63
Commodity©augmentation form, 83
Common link, 83
Competitiveness, 193
Complementarity, 84
Concavity principle, 83
Cross©partial elasticities of substitution, 84
Cumulative distribution function, 133
Cumulative lognormal, 134
Cumulative normal, 135
Cumulative probability function, 132
Current and constant prices, 63

D

Davies, 130
Deviation model, 65

Diffusion of technology, 117
Diffusion, 129
Direct investment, 144
Direct investments, 145
Dissemination of technology, 117
Domestic reaction lag, 127

E

Economic industrial characteristics, 125
Economic performance, 163
Efficiency equivalent, 82
Efficiency of the research, 38
Efficiency©equivalent, 82
Elements, 65
Engineers, 39
Epidemic, 130
Epidemic diffusion curve, 129
External patent applications, 12

F

Fast, 135
FDIs, 163
Final demand, 64
Foreign direct investment, 145
Foreign reaction lag, 127
Full-time equivalent, 40
Full-time equivalents, 39

G

GDPCP, 66
GERD, 66
Gradual adjustment, 135
Griliches, 125, 130

Growth decomposition, 63

H

High technology products, 193
Homogeneous, 83
Homoskedastic, 134

I

I-A matrix, 64
IMF, 144
Imitate, 126
Imitation lag rate, 128
Imitation., 117
Imitator's knowledge, 126
Innovation, 129
Innovation lag, 127
Input quantities, 83
Input-output coefficients, 64
Input-Output framework, 63
Inter-firm model, 125
Interindustry analysis, 63
Interindustry transactions, 65
International approach, 126
International communications, 127
International diffusion, 126
International technology transfer, 126, 163
Invention, 129
Investment share, 66

J

Joint-ventures, 144
Jorgenson, 83

K

Knowledge, 6, 144
Kondratieff cycle, 126
Kubo, 63

L

Lau, 83
Law of logistic growth, 132
Learning period, 127
Leontief, 63
Licensing, 126
Logistic curve, 132
Logistic law, 132

Logistic., 133
Long term Kondratieff cycle, 128

M

Malecki, 129
Mansfield, 125, 135
Material balance condition, 64
Maximum likelihood, 134
Measure of the speed, 136
Meta©production function, 82
Meta©production function, 83
Metcalfe, 127
Minimum normit x2 method, 134
MNEs, 163
Multinational, 127
Multinational corporations, 144
Multinational firms, 127
Multinationals, 126, 164

N

National technological level, 66
Nelson, 136
New state of technical knowledge, 129
Normal, 133
Normal equivalent deviate, 133
Normit, 133

O

OECD, 117, 144, 195
Origin of the technology, 127
Own©partial, 84
Own©partial elasticities of substitution, 84

P

Patent index, 15
Patenting activity, 67
Patterns of structural change, 64
Population, 132
Posner, 127
Probit analysis, 132, 134
Productivity, 128
Productivity growth, 84
Productivity, 66
Profitability, 126
Profitability of innovation, 125

Q

Quality advantage, 164
Quantities of outputs and inputs, 82

R

R&D, 127
Rasmussen index, 65
Research activities, 39
Research and development personnel, 40
Revealed comparative advantage, 195

S

Sahal, 135, 136
Sato, 84
Schumpeterian approach, 126
Schumpeterian hypothesis, 126
Scientific and capabilities strength, 40
Scientific structure, 38
Scientists, 39
Semilog function, 138
Sigmoid curve, 131
Size of the country, 127
Slow curves, 135
Speed, 128
Spreads, 128
S-shaped curve, 131
Stock of knowledge, 6, 144
Stoneman, 130
Subsidiaries, 145
Suzawa, 84
Swan, 127
Syrquin, 63

T

Technical change, 63
Technological and institutional differences, 125
Technological capabilities, 38
Technological capability, 127
Technological capacity, 38
Technological efficiency, 39
Technological inpu, 66
Technological inputs and outputs, 66
Technological intensity, 193
Technological knowledge, 129
Technological output, 66
Technological substitution, 117
Technology capacity, 6, 144
Technology of innovation, 6, 144
Technology transfer, 6, 117, 144, 163
Transfer cost, 126
Translog cost function, 84
Typical curve, 135

U

UNCTAD, 6, 144, 146
UNESCO, 39
United Nations, 6, 144, 146

V

Vintage approach, 126